Y0-DDP-147

Maritime Error Management

Discussing and Remediating Factors Contributory to Casualties

Geoffrey W. Gill

Disclaimer: This publication is designed to provide accurate and authoritative information in regard to the subject matter covered. It is sold with the understanding that neither the author nor the publisher is engaged in rendering by this publication legal, accounting, securities trading, or other professional services. If legal advice or other expert assistance is required, the services of a competent professional person should separately be sought.

Copyright © 2011 by Geoffrey W. Gill
Library of Congress Control Number: 2011930498

All rights reserved. No part of this work may be reproduced or used in any form or by any means—graphic, electronic, or mechanical, including photocopying or information storage and retrieval systems—without written permission from the publisher.

The scanning, uploading and distribution of this book or any part thereof via the Internet or via any other means without the permission of the publisher is illegal and punishable by law. Please purchase only authorized editions and do not participate in or encourage the electronic piracy of copyrighted materials.

"Schiffer," "Schiffer Publishing Ltd. & Design," and the "Design of pen and inkwell" are registered trademarks of Schiffer Publishing Ltd.

Designed by "Sue"
Type set in New Baskerville BT
ISBN: 978-0-87033-626-3
Printed in China

Schiffer Books are available at special discounts for bulk purchases for sales promotions or premiums. Special editions, including personalized covers, corporate imprints, and excerpts can be created in large quantities for special needs. For more information contact the publisher:

Published by Cornell Maritime Press. an imprint of Schiffer Publishing Ltd.
4880 Lower Valley Road, Atglen, PA 19310, Phone: (610) 593-1777;
Fax: (610) 593-2002, E-mail: Info@schifferbooks.com

For the largest selection of fine reference books on this and related subjects, please visit our website at **www.schifferbooks.com** . We are always looking for people to write books on new and related subjects. If you have an idea for a book please contact us at the above address.

This book may be purchased from the publisher. Include $5.00 for shipping. Please try your bookstore first. You may write for a free catalog.

In Europe, Schiffer books are distributed by
Bushwood Books
6 Marksbury Ave.
Kew Gardens
Surrey TW9 4JF England
Phone: 44 (0) 20 8392 8585; Fax: 44 (0) 20 8392 9876
E-mail: info@bushwoodbooks.co.uk
Website: www.bushwoodbooks.co.uk

Contents

Foreword

When I first began reading the draft manuscript of *Maritime Error Management*, I said to myself "just another maritime casualty book written by an attorney." However, by the end of the first chapter, I realized this is not "just another book" but rather is a well developed and researched treatise addressing the human role and error in marine transportation, especially in the area of marine casualties. Marine accidents have been part of this industry since its beginning. Early attempts to eliminate accidents were engineering in nature, i.e., build a better ship. However, since the early 1990s the focus increasingly has been on the role of human behavior and how that behavior factors into the casualty. But, casualties still occur at an alarming rate in spite of all the laws, regulations, best practices, training and audits that have been in place for more than a decade.

The 1995 amendments to the Standards for Training, Certification and Watchkeeping (STCW 95) have come into force. While STCW 95 amends STCW 78, STCW 95 was the amendment that signaled to the world that the maritime industry is going to begin to address the human factors element. STCW 95 set new standards for training and certification seafaring personnel and standardized levels of watchkeeping across maritime fleets. While this has been an important step forward, it has not resolved the issue of interaction among seafaring personnel.

In 1998 the International Safety Management Code (ISM) entered the picture. ISM was developed to open communication between ship and shore, and establishes a chain of command and responsibility for management as well as for shipboard personnel. While the intent of ISM is laudable, ISM's implementation has increased the work load upon shipboard personnel, and its overall effectiveness is not clear.

Within the same 1990s time frame, the maritime industry embraced the airline concept of "cockpit resource management." The maritime industry has renamed this concept "bridge resource management" (BRM) and the race is on for seafaring personnel to be "checked off" on BRM. BRM is an important step forward toward reducing accidents but there is scant empirical evidence of its contribution, if any, to actual reduction of casualties. Other applied concepts, such as risk and error assessment and management, decision making and multi-culturism, are surfacing as means to finding a path to accident and pollution reduction. But despite all these concepts and their application, a major corresponding reduction in maritime accidents has not occurred. Why? Because there is insufficient focus upon core human and organizational error issues.

In this book, Geoffrey Gill addresses human and organizational error in its whole. He has examined major aspects of error and logically walks the reader, one step at a time, through an understanding of error. He then applies this understanding to many of the established processes applied to avoid error, but clearly points out shortcomings attending these processes and suggests remedial measures. As an example, he addresses Bridge Resource Management as an excellent means to avoid "one person error," but also points out that a critical part of the operating team, the engine room, often is excluded. This quality of analysis makes this book unique.

This book is a must read for those in all aspects of the maritime industry. The industry continues to change, with larger and faster vessels, the application information technology to all parts of the industry, rapid communication opportunities, and the employment of people all over the world, each carrying his or her national culture. Human error will always be with us and we must apply logical and informed safeguards to prevent casualties. Reading and studying this book can provide a sound basis for real safety progress.

Captain Jerry Aspland,
past President ARCO Marine
and President Emeritus,
California Maritime Academy

Acknowledgments

Informally, research for this book began when I first set foot aboard a commercial vessel many years ago and has continued as I progressed as a deck officer and, more recently, a maritime attorney. Over this period there have occurred many personally experienced exposures to issues of maritime risk and error, all heightening a fascination with the subject and acceptance of a challenge to, insofar as reasonably possible, plumb error management strategies compatible with best watchkeeping practices as well as with shore side concerns and priorities. Enhanced safety at sea cannot be viewed as a utopian goal without due appreciation for the commercial realities of the maritime industry.

A major impetus to undertaking formal research potentially suitable for publication came as the result of a wintery evening lecture I gave several years ago at Maine Maritime Academy, a lecture facilitated by Captain G. Andy Chase. While both venue and opportunity were welcome, what particularly impressed was the active interest taken by the audience – watchkeepers of the future. The hour lecture was followed by almost two hours of insightful and expansive questions asked and probing issues raised by the student audience. This level of proactive concern and involvement expressed by Maine Maritime students, and others at the wheelhouse "sharp end of the spear," contrasts interestingly with a perceptible disengagement – perhaps more accurately an acceptance of the *status quo* – shown by certain segments of shoreside management, apparently content to rely upon rules, regulation, policies and procedures, as well as the convenience of too frequently misplaced reliance upon officially issued certifications.

As valuable as have been the printed resources listed in the Bibliography, those resources pale in comparison to the direct human assistance received – the many master mariners and others within and outside the maritime industry whose experiences, judgments, insights and confidences have greatly benefitted the following discussion. Out of respect for their candor and professional positions, I have chosen to keep the confidences of many interviewees.

Appreciation is expressed to Captains John Betz, David Boatner, Paul Foran, Derek McCann, Robert Moore (U.S.C.G., ret.), Carol Peckham, Steve Peckham, George Sandberg, Richard Smith, Prentice "Skip" Strong and Robert Wiley. Captain C.M.C. Stewart, an Elder Brother of the Corporation of Trinity House, gave an afternoon to discuss safety from the perspective of a venerable institution committed to maritime safety and the source of neutral nautical assessors providing nautical expertise to British admiralty courts. Philip Wake, Chief Executive, graciously has made available the resources of the justifiably prestigious Nautical Institute. R. Key Dismukes, a senior human factors scientist with NASA and author, provided great insight into advances within the aviation domain that may be transferrable to the maritime industry. Bosun John Pitts reacquainted me with safety concerns from the deck plates, and former shipmate, chief engineer and present maritime attorney Peter Clark has opened the engine room for me. Permission to use protected information was given by Professor Gerald J.S. Wilde, Emeritus Professor,

Queen's University (risk homeostasis theory); Peter Philips, President of Philips Publishing Group, provider of annual electronic navigation –eNav – conferences; and Gary Davies, Maritime Photographic (*Herald of Free Enterprise* photograph). Also greatly appreciated is the assistance from scholars from many countries, who made available studies and reports not available through the internet or otherwise, including: John Habberley, Warsash Maritime Academy; Hannu Hanninen, Helsinki School of Economics; Captain Margareta Lutzhoft, Chalmers University of Technology; and, W.L.G. Verschurr, Leiden University, as well as Craig B. Smith, an ocean wave authority. And, certainly, thanks to Captain Jerry Aspland, who read and critiqued (to the advantage of the final product) the draft manuscript and also graciously provided the Foreword.

Particular appreciation is extended to the United States Navy and its at-sea logistics force, Military Sea Command (MSC), for facilitating my embarkation on board the fleet oiler USS *Guadalupe* (T-AO 200) to observe the use of modern electronic navigation components underway and where I further observed how MSC professionalism over the years has successfully accomplished tens of thousands of underway replenishments of United States and allied naval vessels and, more recently, has undertaken international humanitarian relief missions. My sincere thanks are extended as well to MSC's Eastern Pacific staff at MSC Pacific and to the civil service master, officers and crew, and U.S. Navy military department personnel, on board USNS *Guadalupe*.

And, especial thanks and appreciate are extended to Christoph M. Wahner, Esq., a valued professional colleague who early on enthusiastically encouraged the writing of this book and extensively researched and drafted the Chapter discussing *Herald of Free Enterprise*.

He has provided further assistance, without which this book would not have seen the light of day. Also, especial thanks are due to my wife, Lynn, who steadfastly has encouraged the writing of this book.

1

Past and Present in Maritime Safety: Laying the Foundation

... in all my experience, I have never been in any accident of any sort worth speaking about. ... I never saw a wreck and have never been wrecked, nor was I ever in any predicament that threatened to end in disaster of any sort. — Edward John Smith, May 16, 1907, subsequently Master, RMS *Titanic*[1]

Ship safety, and the consequences of the lack of it, is a topic which is as fascinating as it is complex. — Lord Donaldson[2]

Recently, a respected maritime safety authority stated: "A ship is twice as likely to be involved in a serious grounding, collision or contact accident today compared to only five years ago."[3]

Granted, statistics exist suggesting that since introduction of the International Safety Management (ISM) and eventual accompanying Code there has been a lessening in the numbers of maritime casualties, but there has been shocking loss of life in some of these allegedly "fewer" casualties – *Doña Paz*, 1987, 4,341 fatalities; *Estonia*, 1994, 852 fatalities of 989 on board; *Princess of the Stars*, 2008, capsized in a typhoon with the loss of 802 of the approximately 860 persons on board; *Al Salam Boccaccio* 98, 2006, 1031 fatalities. And the potential for catastrophic property loss from a maritime casualty is huge. The 1917 explosion resulting from the collision between two vessels leveled a significant part of Halifax, Nova Scotia[4] as did for Bombay a World War II shipboard explosion, and for Texas City a 1947 explosion on board the French Liberty ship *Grandcamp*, with the latter bringing about 581 confirmed deaths, many missing, and the injured numbering about 5,000.[5] In 1976 the tanker *Sansinena* exploded at her berth in Los Angeles Harbor, killing 9 and injuring about 50. The vessel's midship structure, about 500 feet in length and 90 feet in width, was lifted bodily and deposited upside down some 230 feet away. Buildings 40 miles away reportedly were shaken by the blast.[6] And, the 2010 explosion and sinking of the Mobile Offshore Drilling Unit *Deepwater Horizon*, a maritime vessel, caused the "greatest oil spill in U.S. history and significant environment damage to the Gulf of Mexico[,]" as well as 11 fatalities and 16 persons seriously injured.[7]

But, even *if* there may be fewer casualties, the maritime casualties that are occurring are increasingly expensive.[8] Further, "the number of detentions [due to various kinds of safety lapses] has been fast increasing since 2005[,]"[9] suggesting that at least a number of vessel interests are willing to operate close to, if not below, acceptable standards. And, the evidence is clear that "[a] low reported accident rate, even over a period of years, is no guarantee that risks are being effectively controlled, nor will it ensure the absence of injuries or accidents in the future."[10]

One impediment to comprehensive analysis of maritime safety is the absence of readily available, objectively complete and reliable information concerning the extent and nature of maritime casualties. Therefore, "robust generalized statements about the type of accidents and incidents that are occurring worldwide cannot confidently be made … ."[11] Ship casualty data is heavily censored, highly subjective, and, due to proprietary restrictions, almost always incapable of being audited.

Problems with the data are compounded by the design of just about all maritime casualty databases that attempt to divide casualties into what really are overlapping categories, confuse cause and effect, and usually fail to record any real causal information. This makes easy the generation of often meaningless correlations which can be manipulated to produce just about any result desired by any special interest group. Also, recorded deficiencies worldwide (especially ones of ISM relevance) may be attributed to the Port State Control inspector's personal opinion, and so easily may be influenced by a host of subjective factors, such as crew attitude, ease of inspection, inspector's mood, and so on. Further, there is the apparent practice of under-reporting the magnitude of an incident (or breaking it into a series of smaller ones) in order to bring it under the P&I deductible. This suggests strongly that industry [occupational health and safety] performance is worse than the available data indicate.

Certain caveats are necessary when attributing specific causes to maritime casualties. First, there needs to be common coding or categorizing of causes and contributing factors. For example, if some category includes specific acts, omissions or conditions (e.g. "insufficient training for the task") but others do not, the end apportionment of contributing factors will be skewed and analysis correspondingly affected. This is a level of detail issue. The more detail, the deeper the analysis can be. Further, different analysts may ascribe the coding inconsistently – was the factor "insufficient training" or "insufficient application of the training" through a crew member's negligence or, a different matter entirely, was the cause incompetence? Maritime experienced analysts likely will see and apply the codes differently than non-maritime analysts. The result also may be influenced by the complexity of the incident and the equipment of the vessels.[12]

Lack of a common reliable data base has led to inconsistency and misunderstanding as to where the causes and, therefore arguably, the cure(s) lie. Or, as one researcher concluded, "it is not always easy to find those who took the risks; too often they are confused with those who ran the risks."[13] Also, without understanding *why* the mariner actors acted as they acted, any "cures" put into effect must fail to address all relevant "causes." Indeed, for this reason, the conventional term "root cause(s)" better would be changed to "explanatory factors."

Often lost in academic debate is the reality experienced at the "sharp end" of the spear, on the ship's bridge. The harsh effect upon the point man was summed up uncompromisingly:

> ... now everything was about to go wrong, one after the other, to make [the captain of *Amoco Cadiz*] the hapless protagonist of what was to become a textbook demonstration of the implacable mathematics of complacency, presumptuousness, stupidity, and cupidity. They added up to a terrible bill, and he was the one who got it, although plenty of others had contributed to its making.[14]

Not surprisingly a tendency has developed for mariners, fairly or not, to "look to ship operators and to regulators [as] perhaps more dangerous to the ships they operate than a hurricane or coral reef."[15]

A perception undergoing change is the historic knee-jerk attribution of error to the "sharp end" operator, pithily paraphrased by Joseph Conrad as: " 'ships are all right; it's the men in 'em ... '."[16]

There is general agreement among researchers that "human error continues to be a dominant factor in approximately 80 to 85% of maritime accidents[,]"[17] "[with] about 50% of maritime accidents ... *initiated* by human error, and another 30% ... *associated* with human error."[18]

As accident causation theory has matured, four theoretical "eras" have evolved. The first "era" looked to mechanical hardware failure as the primary cause of accidents. As mechanical reliability increased, the human operator began to be seen as the primary "human error" cause. With increased technology, the human-technical interface became the culprit, reminiscent of the "radar-assisted" collision days of the 1950s. Currently, the focus has moved upstream toward the organizational system that in large part creates the environment within which the operator functions. Of course, when "organizations" are discussed, the core issue inescapably remains the human component because organizations are comprised of humans, though frequently acting differently in an organizational body than individually.

Also, for understanding of error there must be recognition that error irrevocably is part of human nature. Despite this being so, "... the idea that we can eradicate error ... has a timeless hold on the human imagination."[19] But, the idea that error can be eliminated from human activity is as specious as the medieval alchemist's belief that gold could be made from materials of lesser value.[20] Because the maritime industry is a "people" system, the sailing, operation and management of vessels always will be subject to error.[21] While the substance of his comment easily and correctly can be expanded to embrace sea casualties of all descriptions, Admiral Sir Royston Wright wrote:

> Collisions at sea can seldom be completely explained; with all the care and attention that we give to the training of our officers, they usually seem to be 'impossible.' Yet with relentless regularity they crop up in the best trained Fleets.[22]

This being said, there is agreement that organizational, as well as operator human, error factors substantially contribute to maritime casualties – certainly enough to make their study and better understanding worthwhile. Recent authority suggests that only 4.5% of causal factors warrant being "ascribed to organizational influences," such as crew manning levels or business management.[23] Respectful exception must be taken to organizational factors being so marginalized. Why? Because hardly any "analysis has been attempted to assess the significance or frequency of organizational factors such as the incidence of commercial pressure or the effects of organizational culture upon accident causation[,]" or any of the many other contributory organizational factors.[24] But, as suggested, authorities of various persuasions are moving from a linear to a holistic systems view, one that "sees human error as a symptom, not a cause. Human error is an effect of trouble deeper inside the system ... [,] including such aspects as equipment design and integration (automation), usefulness of procedures and productive pressures."[25] Indeed,

> ...immediate causes are typically symptoms and seldom represent the ultimate cause. ... Experience from loss control principles has shown that the most substandard actions are caused by factors over which only the [shipboard and shore based] management has control. Most loss control experts place this number at 80%. Maritime accidents correspond very well to these results. ... Therefore, every decision and action that effects [sic] safety or the prevention of pollution must be based on sound organizational practices, regardless of the level within the company.[26]

Twenty five years ago, foreseeing the extent to which industrial mishaps are viewed as "organizational accidents" would have been unlikely and difficult.

Because "disasters are very rarely the product of a single monumental blunder,"[27] no single "cure" can be expected to improve maritime safety. There is no magic bullet. Consequently, addressing maritime safety on a systemic basis at all levels — regulatory, organizational, managerial, and individual — becomes necessary.

Where safety measures are relatively rudimentary and where the operative system is "simple," as in commercial shipping, relatively few unsafe acts are necessary for there to be an accident. Contrarily, where the defenses are robust, more unsafe acts or omissions, or acts together with omissions, must combine to create an accident. For example, one recent study demonstrated that in maritime shipping, an average of as few as 2 or 3 unsafe acts/omissions may lead to a major accident whereas in the (generally) more safety conscious oil and gas exploration and production industry, 50% or more of the accidents have required more than 7 combined unsafe omissions and acts.[28] This suggests that barriers to and defenses against error are especially critical within maritime domain shipping. A couple of studies, in the aviation industry, reveal that while pilots commit an average of between 4.9 and 7.49 errors per hour, effective cockpit resource management and other error traps result in there being an cumulative average of 7 inter-related acts and omissions required for an accident to occur.[29] Yet, aviation safety has shown impressive improvement. Surely this is compelling evidence that a safety conscious industry can handle error without error progressing into accident. Granted, the concepts making up a safe environment are specific to the involved environment and shipping is a very "context-specific" industry.[30] Yet, while there is much knowledge the shipping industry can and should draw from other domains, shipping "continues to lag behind" other safety-critical industries and the military.[31] Indeed, commercial shipping tends to take an almost ostrich-like willingness to hide its head in the sand to avoid grappling with safety issues.[32]

Yet, the value of truly quality operations has been demonstrated in the commercial shipping industry. A 2006 study determined that of oil tankers in excess of 10,000 gross registered tons, the 25% vessels operated to highest quality standards were involved in 10% of the random accidents analyzed, whereas the 25% vessels operated to lowest quality standards were involved in about 44% of the accidents. Therefore, the 25% safest tankers can be said to be about four times safer than the 25% least safe.[33] A more broadly focused doctoral thesis argues that 25% of the safest operated world fleet was involved in 7% of the total accidents but the lowest quality 25% had a 50% share of the accidents.[34]

However, informed restraint must be exercised. Maritime safety provides a fertile field for demonstrating the Law of Unintended Consequences. This "law," arising from the field of economics and validated by many examples from practical experience, states that the actions of people – especially of governments – often have effects either unanticipated or unintended. Examples from the maritime safety realm include:

- reverse homeostasis, whereby enhanced safety precautions stimulate more risky behavior, such as a vessel with radar failing to proceed at a moderate speed in conditions of restricted visibility;
- more regulation creates more paperwork demands that detract from task performance[35];
- skirting the edge of rules, regulations, policies and procedures (RRPP), leads to normalization of deviance from accepted RRPP, such as where on a tanker laden with hazardous cargo smoking was not permitted on the bridge wings but was permitted in the wheelhouse, leading to a

custom of the lookout being allowed to stand his watch in the wheelhouse with a subsequent collision being attributed to the improper lookout;[36]

• in RMS *Titanic*, when the iceberg was sighted close to, the ship was turned to port so, though the vessel did not strike the iceberg head-on, water-tight integrity nonetheless was breached as a result of several compartments having been sheared open by an underwater berg protrusion; and,

• in order to give the normal duty watch officer additional rest, *Exxon Valdez'* off-duty third mate took the duty officer's watch but was unfamiliar with the limited competence of the helmsman of that watch and so failed to timely notice that his helm orders to clear Bligh Reef were not receiving prompt and proper compliance.

Another example of unintended consequences is the substitution by the Royal Dutch/Shell group of its well run tankers by tankers of less prestigious repute to deliver Shell product to the United States. This introduction of arguably less well maintained, crewed and operated tankers enhanced the likelihood of oil spills in United States waters and was a consequence of the imposition of heavy financial exposure upon tanker operators by many coastal states and the Oil Pollution Act of 90 (OPA 90) as well as criminalization of negligence flowing from the 1989 *Exxon Valdez* oil spill.[37]

To guard against this experience-driven and proven "law," regulators and management are well advised to heed these words (the reader substituting for "economist" as fitting) of the French economic journalist Frederic Bastiat:

There is only one difference between a bad economist and a good one: the bad economist confines himself to the visible effect; the good economist takes into account both the effect that can be seen and those effects that must be foreseen.[38]

An overarching negative influence upon effective management of maritime safety is the often great distance – geographic, cultural, experiential, and different prioritization of goals to be achieved – between shore-side management and the assets – personnel and physical – to be managed. Also contributing is the uniqueness of the assets' social environment, that is to say the safety climate within which a management's safety culture is to be implemented. As to that safety climate, consideration should be given to the reality that:

> A ship on the ocean is a world of its own – cramped, self-contained, and prone to a unique remoteness that modern forms of communication have by no means eliminated. Emotions born of collective discontent, which in a larger social context may become diffused, channeled, or otherwise rendered harmless, may within the close confines of a ship fester and turn explosive, especially during a long voyage. Charles Vidil, a French writer who made a study of naval mutiny, regarded shipboard life as the ideal environment 'favoring the disturbance of minds, the spreading of false rumors, the growth of group suggestion.'[39]

While the above quotation comes from a study of shipboard mutiny, and mutiny is not suggested as a likely shipboard response to management's efforts to curb error, dispositions harbored by a ship's personnel will greatly influence whether and to what extent the organizational safety culture will be accepted. The sea is a dangerous place, and management needs no additional factors complicating on board acceptance of safe operating practices.[40]

The objective of this book is to bring forward a significant body of diverse research in the hope of expanding the safety consciousness of an inherently conservative industry, one largely bound up in rules, regulations, policies and procedures (RRPP). Again borrowing, John Masefield in his poem "Dauber" condensed the issue:

> Ships and the sea; there's nothing finer made.
> But there's so much to learn … .

Here, research based information is submitted for consideration by senior shipboard staff and shore-side management alike, in the belief that the more each group understands error and related issues from the perspective of the other, the greater will be the ability and likelihood of staff and management cooperating in a cost efficient manner to enhance safety within a fleet. Each group has the ability to frustrate, if not completely stymie, the efforts of the other, and too often that frustration, largely unintended and even unknowing, results in property loss and worse. In keeping with the philosophy of the International Safety Management Code, this is not a management "What to do" or "How to do" book. Instead, management may draw from the discussion whatever is compatible with the company culture and "way of doing business."

Also, many volumes already discuss how to stand a watch at sea. This book does not attempt replication of those books, but instead introduces cognitive aspects that, though rarely considered on the bridge, directly affect the development of situational awareness and decision making. The aim here is to assist in the development of a more capable, competent and confident watch keeping officer, better prepared for handling situations under way at sea.

The underlying premise of all that follows is that while error is inevitable, through better understanding of error much can be done to minimize the probability of error occurring and to trap such error as does occur. There has been extensive relevant research within a variety of safety-critical domains – including aviation, military, petro-chemical, nuclear, medical and disaster response. However, the maritime industry has been slow to draw upon lessons learned from these similarly safety-critical domains. R. Key Dismukes, Chief Scientist, Human Systems Integration Division of NASA, offered the following words after an interview with the author in which were discussed contrasting aviation and maritime human factor safety perspectives:

> ... much of what has been learned from studies of aviation human factors could be applied beneficially to maritime operations.[41]

In fact, broad consensus exists that the maritime industry in safety critical issues lags other safety critical industries by about 25 years.

An aviation study, citing the commonality of its conclusions to other safety-critical domains including the maritime domain, identifies four criteria relevant to assessing human factor issues:

> *Safety Culture*: the extent to which the individual agrees that the organization fosters a genuine and proactive commitment to safety.
> *Job Attitude*: morale and job satisfaction.
> *Teamwork*: level of satisfaction with the quality of colleague cooperation and participation in the concepts of crew resource management.
> *Stress Recognition*: extent to which the individual recognizes personal vulnerability to stressors – fatigue, personal issues, and crisis/emergency situations.

In addition to being slow to learn from other safety-critical domains, the suggestion has been made that the maritime industry has failed to learn the lessons taught, at great expense in dollars and lives, by past casualties "within its own house." This criticism misses the point. Maritime people are neither stupid nor foolish; the lessons have been learned. Rather, the failure comes with the final exam — whether the lessons learned are incorporated by management within the industry and into on board operation of vessels. And, on the management end, this failure may result from an emphasis perhaps too narrowly focused upon rules, regulations, policies and procedures, and, on the shipboard end, because a "halo effect" convinces the mariner actors that "accidents happen only to foolish people, and I'm not that foolish."

While foolish people do commit errors, so also do very competent professionals, and a serious loss can follow from the seemingly most inconsequential omission. An improperly secured barrel resulted in the loss overboard of an American large tanker's captain and chief officer. Another improperly secured barrel was in the error chain that resulted in the stranding and loss of the tanker *Braer*. At sea, no error or omission is too small for concern.

> Accidents do not occur because people gamble and lose; they occur because people do not believe that the accident about to occur is at all possible. Many accidents are outrageous and bizarre, not because people take outrageous risks, but because people assume that the bizarre will not occur.[42]

Does this require absolute clairvoyance to avoid accidents? No, but persons engaged in maritime risk assessment and management, and persons doing business upon the great waters, are well advised to heed seriously the long-ago words of Admiral Lord Horatio Nelson:

> In Sea affairs, nothing is impossible, and nothing improbable.[43]

2

Maritime Business Afloat as Uniquely Error-Inducing

Following a "doom and gloom" overview, Yale University Professor of Sociology Charles Perrow, who has long studied high-risk industries, concluded that the maritime industry is "error-inducing" in that "the configuration of its many components induces errors and defeats attempts at error reduction" and suggests "only a wholesale reconfiguration could make the parts fit together in an error-neutral or error-avoiding manner."[44] But, "wholesale reconfiguration" of the globe-straddling maritime industry is not likely and, in any event, neither could nor would eliminate error. There is a unique combination of "demands characteristic of the maritime industry," in which "there are a number of workplace dangers in combination, something rare in other industries."[45]

The industry and its practitioners simply must fist on and proceed as mariners traditionally have done for centuries – "do your best to make do with what you have."[46]

Informed study[47] and many years in the industry lead to the inevitable conclusion that the maritime industry not only is "error-inducing" but more accurately is *uniquely* error-inducing.[48] Many bases support this conclusion, and deserve acknowledgment for more complete understanding of the human – individual and organizational (as organizations are merely groupings of individuals, albeit that individuals in groups may be influenced differently than if acting individually) – factors contributing to maritime casualties and how these factors may be managed and their consequences mitigated. Consideration of these factors will be interwoven in the following chapters. But, early acknowledgement of at least some of the factors confronting the watch keeper at the "sharp end of the spear," and creating the environment within which the ship owning/managing/ operating organization must address risk and safety, lays the foundation for what follows:

Uninformed regulators: Recognition is increasing that latent organizational acts and omissions set the stage for accidents afloat. However, these organizations do not operate in a vacuum. They operate within a framework of rules and regulations promulgated and/or enforced by bureaucrats who too frequently have little or no understanding of, or respect for, the maritime industry. Examples abound, and range from: license prosecution without understanding Automated Radar Plotting Aid (ARPA) limitations;[49] inability or unwillingness to explain regulations but instead parroting the verbiage of the regulation; reacting to public outcry rather than to analysis and empirical data; failing to come to terms with core industry issues; and, demeaning the merchant marine officer's license to a wallet sized certificate. These issues, merely illustrative, can be expanded exponentially and may be perceived as ranging from petty to serious, but all may be said to be serious when a productive working relationship with the regulator is considered. Response of shore-side management to the pervasive, albeit not always constructive, regulatory regime may descend to abdication of its safety management responsibility in favor of mere enforcement of rules, regulations, policies and procedures, and insistence upon voluminous documentary presumed evidence of compliance. Too often, the cumulative effect in the ships at sea is excessive investment of limited time and effort to functions secondary to safety " … because of the demands upon their time [a number of seafarers reported] they felt that the only way they could cope was to complete paperwork without having undertaken associated tasks."[50]

COLREGS: The 1972 International Regulations for Preventing Collisions at Sea (COLREGS) are a risk management means intended and designed to manage the risk of collision and collision itself.[51] But the COLREGS are riddled with ambiguity. Consider what is meant by: "ordinary practice of seamen," Rule 2(a); "special circumstances," Rule 2(b); "risk of collision," Rule 7; and, "passing at a safe distance," Rule 8(d). And, of course, the interpretation of "proper lookout" required by Rule 5. Apocryphally in at least one ship a proper lookout was considered to be a large black dog that barked loudly upon the approach of other vessels and certainly on more than a few ships, a proper lookout is deemed an officer's wife, so the watch standing husband can attend to other tasks – usually on deck. One United States Court of Appeals was caused to comment "We are sensitive to the concern that the 'rules of the road' on the high seas must be clear, lest we create too much uncertainty in an area that requires a high degree of clarity."[52] The COLREGS recognize that the variety of rules promulgated to govern safe behavior will always be fewer than the possible variety of unsafe conditions, and so provide that an umbrella "ordinary practice of seamen" is to prevail[53] but, this language also creates a dangerous ambiguity.

Management divorced from ownership: Relatively few legacy owners and companies with a long tradition of vessel ownership and operation remain. The English master mariner and author Richard Woodman most poignantly commented upon this demise, writing about his return to England as cadet in the 1960s : "We slipped home unnoticed. Britain turned no hair at our arrival, just as she has turned no hair at our extinction."[54] The shipping industry has "abnormally low barriers to entry."[55] The ease with which ship owning and managing companies, and the identity by which ships are known, can come into and go out of existence recently has been commented upon in the media.[56] Interestingly, however, from a safety perspective one major recent study argues that more important than the corporate structure or nature of the business (whether owner or operator or manager) is the presence or absence of internal positive safety enablers.[57]

Multiculturism: Increasingly, the maritime industry is becoming a third-world industry. The issue is less whether particular nationalities are more risk-prone than others, but instead is how the interaction with other respective cultural aspects and language skills affect safe operations. I have encountered various manifestations of different cultures interfacing, most interestingly perhaps in connection with a discussion on the subject I had with a senior port captain with one of the major Far Eastern vessel owners. He was sufficiently impressed with the importance of the subject to recommend to his management that arrangements be made for me to speak overseas with senior management and in one or more seminars for senior officers. The recommendation was commended but declined by the home office, the explanation being that the recommendation had not originated within the company's training department. Protocol had been irretrievably violated and some aspect of "face" had been lost, so the merit of the recommendation had been subordinated to the national and corporate culture of the company. Several months later *Cosco Busan* allided with the San Francisco Bay

Bridge, illustrating, among other issues, a variety of multicultural issues.

Proficiency not tested: Merely holding a license or certificate falls short of establishing the holder's actual competence,[58] competence intended to be a much wider set of skills than are associated with the basic qualifications recognized as necessary to be awarded the paper document. Management has little opportunity to assure itself that personnel serving in the fleet truly are competent in skills, responsibility and judgment. But, as Joseph Conrad presciently wrote more than 100 years ago: "The hurry of the times, the loading and discharging organization of the docks, the use of hoisting machinery which works quickly and will not wait, the cry for prompt dispatch, the very size of his ship, stand nowadays between the modern seaman and the thorough knowledge of his craft."[59] The observation has been made that the "presence of company or external audits on board a vessel will often ensure that ship's staff are careful to simply be seen to comply with laid-down procedures and working routines."[60] Competence extends as well to proper use of the various equipment on board, which may vary from ship to ship. A collateral problem is that "put starkly, there are insufficient competent seafarers today to allow for every ship to be adequately manned 24 hours a day."[61] Related to the shortage problem is that people will be advanced faster than otherwise would be accepted, resulting in less experienced persons often moving into positions of command and responsibility in contradiction of the warning of famed mariner Captain Joshua Slocum that " … to insure a reasonable measure of success, experience should sail with the ship."[62] Similarly, there is unfortunately less passage through mentoring of traditional values and professional pride.[63] The current situation can be compared to the advancement practice

of the Cunard Steamship Company as described by Mark
Twain more than a century ago:

> The Cunard people would not take Noah as first mate till
> they had worked him through all the lower grades and tried
> him ten years or such matter. They make every officer serve
> an apprenticeship under their eyes in their own ships before
> they advance him or trust him. It takes them about ten or
> fifteen years to manufacture a captain; but when they have
> got him manufactured to suit at last they have full confidence
> in him. The only order, they give a captain is this, brief and
> to the point: 'Your ship is loaded, take her, speed is nothing;
> follow your own road, deliver her safe, bring her back safe
> – safety is all that is required'.[64]

*Introduction of a stranger into the vessel's operating
team in situations of increased risk and stress:* A pilot
steps into the bridge team and undertakes direction
of the vessel's navigation when the risk for collision,
allision and grounding is greatest. While not necessarily
attributable to the pilot, vessels suffer a greater
proportion of such damages in pilotage waters.

Fatigue: The subject of fatigue is beyond the
intended scope of this book, largely because fatigue
inducing circumstances on board and their consequences
are so obvious as to need no further comment, and
because there is already an abundance of relevant
literature.[65] However, an interesting aspect of fatigue
is the tremendous degree of maritime human factors
concern focused upon fatigue, often to the exclusion of
more broadly important issues. For example, in a human
factors discussion with a senior P&I club risk executive,
the comment was made, "Well, really isn't it all a matter
of fatigue?"

Oppressive working environment: About 15 years
ago a survey determined that 34% of the responding

merchant marine officers stated that occupational stress levels had worsened over the preceding 3 to 10 years.[66] Discussions and interviews with serving and recently retired merchant marine officers confirm no improvement in more recently experienced stress levels. The findings of a 2007 survey[67] are instructive as to what are the least appealing aspects of modern day seafaring:

Separation of family and friends	7.6%
Paperwork excesses	34.1%
Absence from children	29.7%
Fatigue	22.3%
Concern over criminalization	19.7%
Shipboard living conditions	18.3%
Maintaining home contact	17.5%
Absence of time ashore	5.7%
Under manning	14.8%

This negative aspect is a frequent refrain in contemporary maritime literature, summed up in the comment of mariner Michael Rawlins: "There is one reason above all else for what I do for a living. It's the time off. What does that say about a profession in which its best attribute is the time it allows a person to spend away from it?"[68]

Diminished professionalism: Commenting upon the practices of the watch officer on the container ship *Bunga Teratai Satu* that stranded in 2000 on the Great Barrier Reef, the Australian Transportation Safety Bureau report stated "The mate, though appropriately qualified, ... lacked the proper level of motivation to operate in a professional manner."[69] This is becoming an all too common refrain, expressed in different ways. There is the retort of the deck cadet, who says "I don't need to take any more star sights. That part of my sea project is finished." There is the concern of one major deck officer union, so great that new entrants are required to attend a class on professionalism.[70] That the union sees the need and responds is commendable; that the union sees the need so strong among maritime academy graduates and officers coming "through the hawse pipe" with years of inculcated values is worrisome.

Criminalization of simple negligence: This is a disturbing international trend. In the United States, there is an increasingly aggressive resort by prosecutors to the Seaman's Manslaughter Act,[71] as evidenced by the prosecution and conviction of the master of *Zim Mexico*, whose vessel while docking contacted a shore-side gantry crane with the resulting death of an electrician servicing the crane. Despite often serious consequences, the underlying act or omission generally has been no more than historical simple negligence, wholly lacking the "evil mind" commonly a requisite for a criminal act. And the trend toward criminalization is moving upstream, into management suites.[72]

Autocratic command structure: The historical "Master under God" command structure when exercised in an autocratic manner is the antithesis of error trapping Bridge Resource Management.

High level of risk acceptance: The high level of risk acceptance within the maritime industry "has arisen through the rich heritage and history of mariners."[73] Even today, " ... the marine world still tends to be characterized by 'macho' can-do attitudes, and the belief that accidents are inevitable and simply part of getting the job done; act now – risk assess later."[74] This approach is personalized by the testimony of the master of *Santa Clara I*, a cargo vessel which departed Port Elizabeth, NJ on January 3, 1992 with a deck load of containers in the face of "dangerous storm warnings." Less than a day out of port she encountered heavy weather, and lost hazardous material overboard and on deck. At the Coast Guard inquiry,

> ... the Master was asked if he considered not leaving port – waiting in Port Elizabeth for better weather. His reply: 'We are sailors – we go to sea.' Significantly, this disposition was echoed by other respected, professional mariners. Once at sea, a reasonable, explainable delay would be acceptable to protect the ship and cargo. But the prevailing expectation is that a commercial ship will get under way.[75]

An historical conservatism within the maritime industry runs hand in hand with the high level of risk accepted by mariners. Fortunately, however, matters are considerably improved from the days when the tendency among shore-bound owners was to scorn life-saving equipment upon the rationale that "safety devices made sailors cowardly" and expectation that if the crew could leave an imperiled vessel, there would be no incentive to work to save the vessel.[76] The British Merchant Shipping Act of 1876, sponsored by "the sailors' friend" Samuel Plimsoll,[77] decreed that a load line, for the allowance of freeboard, was to be painted on merchant vessels. Not until 1890 was the positioning of the mark established, so during the intervening period many owners were creative in the placement of the mark – one owner going so far as to paint the mark on the ship's funnel.[78]

Not least among the factors contributing to the maritime industry being uniquely "error-inducing" is the nature of the stage upon which the business is conducted – the sea: As Joseph Conrad has written:

> ... the sea never has been friendly to man. ... the ocean has no compassion, no faith, no law, no memory. Its fickleness is to be held true to men's purposes only by an undaunted resolution and by a sleepless, armed, jealous vigilance... .[79]

But, there is little reason for this negative side of the safety equation to prevail. Much knowledge is available to be gained from other safety-critical domains. And the maritime industry can apply in practice the safety culture espoused by the International Safety Management Code. Though a complex subject, maritime safety features circularity in the sense that many of the approaches to enhanced safety are mutually supportive. An informed view reveals that productivity and protection need not be trade-offs. The inherent nature of human beings is that the more they are informed and the more they understand safety issues, the more safe will be their performance. The closing thought of this discussion should be, in the words of Captain Slocum:

> To face the elements is, to be sure, no light matter when the sea is in its grandest mood. You must then know the sea, and know that you know it, and not forget that it was made to be sailed over."[80]

3

Evolution of Current
Maritime Safety Philosophy

Two major ship casualties — one American and one British — in the late 1980s jump-started reconsideration of how maritime casualties best can be avoided. Following the adage that these two nations are divided by a common language, both shared a common objective but responded in two very different ways. The two casualties were the 1989 grounding of the American Very Large Crude Carrier (tanker) *Exxon Valdez* on Bligh Reef in Prince William Sound, Alaska, and the 1987 foundering of the British ro-ro ferry *Herald of Free Enterprise* shortly after departing Zeebrügge, Belgium. The circumstances of each casualty are well known to professional readers, so only will be encapsulated here.[81]

The loaded *Exxon Valdez* departed Valdez, Alaska[82] in darkness March 24, 1989 en route in the Traffic Separation Scheme (TSS) to sea. Passage in the outbound lane was impeded by ice so, as had two other earlier departing loaded tankers, the Exxon tanker's captain Joseph Hazelwood decided that his vessel also would travel "outside the TSS in the vicinity of Bligh Reef to avoid ice."[83] Shortly after his vessel departed the TSS, Captain Hazelwood left the bridge "to send some messages that had to be sent before the vessel left Prince William Sound."[84] The duty third officer "decided not to call his relief, the second mate,"[85] who had put in a long day in port, and stayed over to take the second mate's watch.[86]

The relieving helmsman had begun his sea career in the Steward's department and, though holding a able bodied seaman's certificate, was regarded as a tentative helmsman. Unfamiliar with the helmsman's limitations, the third officer only belatedly realized that his helm orders were being carried out too slowly for the vessel to avoid Bligh Reef. Likely fueled by the media having highlighted that Captain Hazelwood, "one of Exxon's most highly regarded masters," had downed a few drinks ashore the afternoon of the ship's departure, in response to the grounding and resulting oil spill in pristine Prince William Sound "the public outrage generated in the United States was enormous."[87]

The United States took a largely regulatory response to the *Exxon Valdez* casualty by legislatively passing the Oil Pollution Act of 1990, informally referred to as OPA90.[88] One section of OPA90 bars from the waters of Prince William Sound any vessel that spills more than one million gallons of oil into that marine environment after March 22, 1989, two days preceding *Exxon Valdez'* mishap. That section effectively prevented the repaired and renamed *Exxon Valdez* from returning to Prince William Sound, her intended operating area. The vessel's interests understandably took exception to such singling out of their vessel and went to court, arguing that so barring *Exxon Valdez* from Prince William Sound was unconstitutional. Despite Exxon's legal arguments, the preclusive section was held constitutionally acceptable and the bar remained.[89]

While there is danger in expanding a principle beyond its intended perimeter, the barring from a specific area of an inanimate ship,[90] presumably never again to be crewed with the same personnel as were directly involved in the Bligh Reef grounding, does show that "[politicians] as always quick to react to perceived populist causes, have also sailed into maritime safety waters with enthusiasm[,]"[91] despite the fact that the "regulatory process has not reduced the likelihood of an otherwise competent individual to make an error in judgment at a critical point in time."[92]

The United States' legislative response to the *Exxon Valdez* grounding was largely reactive through OPA90, which increased the financial penalty for oil pollution and instituted a regulatory regime aimed at improving oil tanker safety, as was the United States maritime industry response which also was generally reactive by generating additional rules, regulations, policies and procedures and paperwork. And, in restricting Exxon's future use of its tanker asset by "punishing" *Exxon Valdez* with ostracism, Congress exercised its wisdom to revive *deodand*, a discredited legal concept rarely applied since medieval days and in England formally abolished in the reign of Queen Victoria. Deodand is the ancient disposition to sacrifice inanimate things and animals in consequence of the harm they cause: "If a man, in driving a cart, tumble to the ground and lose his life by the wheel passing over him, if a tree fall on a man and cause his death, or if a horse kick his keeper and kill him, then the wheel, the tree, and the horse are deodands."[93]

There was a rush among some tanker owners and operators to divest themselves from any public admission of oil tanker involvement: *Exxon* ships became *Seariver* ships and *Texaco* ships became *Star* ships. Such new identities may have had public relations appeal, and possibly an intent to avoid or minimize legal liability, but from a management/employee perspective can be seen to send the negative message to their employees manning their ships that "we don't trust you with our name." An admirable exception to such camouflaging

was Chevron Shipping Company naming, soon after the
Exxon Valdez casualty, one of its tankers *Chevron Employee
Pride*.[94]

A regulatory regime carries the danger of advancing
rigid and unthinking adherence to rule based safety
and risk management, a graphic example being the
circumstances surrounding *Titanic's* lifeboats.

Titanic at the time of her 1912 striking the iceberg
and sinking was in compliance with the then applicable
regulations, which required that vessels in excess of
10,000 tons with approved watertight subdivisions
carry sixteen lifeboats.[95] Alexander Carlisle, in charge
of specifying the vessel's equipment, and Thomas
Andrews, managing director of the builder's design
department, had recommended that *Titanic* carry a total
of 48 lifeboats, but that number gradually was reduced in
discussions with the builder's chairman and Joseph Bruce
Ismay, chairman of the vessel's owning company. *Titanic*
sailed with fourteen standard 30-foot lifeboats, two 25-
foot cutters, and four collapsibles, sufficient in capacity
for 1,176 persons of the 3,300 passengers and crew to
be carried with the liner fully booked.[96] The rationale
for reducing the number of lifeboats to basically the
minimum number required by the prevailing regulation
was that with passengers being assured that *Titanic* was
the safest vessel afloat, why "undermine their confidence
by crowding the upper decks with lifeboats?"[97] While
perhaps an extreme example, the story of *Titanic's*
lifeboats illustrates how easily proactive common sense
safety management can be abdicated to adherence to
the letter of a regulation.

European maritime safety management took a
different tack, though eventually memorialized in
international regulation. On March 6, 1987, the ro-ro
passenger and freight ferry *Herald of Free Enterprise
(Herald)* departed Zeebrügge without her bow doors

being properly secured. As a result, as the vessel gained speed after passing through the outer mole, sea water entered the car deck in such volume that *Herald* quickly capsized, with the loss of 188 lives.[98] There were noteworthy negligent omissions in *Herald* directly resulting in the loss but upon "full investigation," there were found to have been "cardinal faults" in a "failure of management ... infected with the disease of sloppiness[.]" and exhibiting "a staggering complacency ... [and] 'a vacuum at the centre'."[99]

The British, and eventually international, response to the *Herald* sinking was less regulatory, as would be the United States response to *Exxon Valdez* some two years later.[100] Instead, a more holistic approach would be taken toward reducing human and organization error, and mitigating the effect of error when error defenses and traps are breached, through the 1SM Code. The *Herald* casualty was not the sole trigger behind a renewed look at maritime safety issues, but the strong criticism of management "sloppiness" certainly provided a strong impetus.

Emphasis in the *Herald* Report upon management error is noteworthy because human error had long been recognized in the maritime domain, though its significance varied over time. The large number of shipping losses in the early 1800s prompted the British Parliament to appoint in 1836 a Select Committee to investigate the causes of these losses. A significant factor was found to be the poor standard of training of merchant officers and crews.[101] From this, "human factor" initially was defined as a lack of proper training and human based errors were attributed to faulty training and insufficient professional education.

Into the 1960s, the impact of human error within the maritime industry was accepted as being significant. Thereafter, on the one hand there was increased technological advance and on the other hand growing awareness of cognitive issues and of how humans inter-relate with technology. But contrary to expectations growing out of the better accident avoiding technologies increasingly being provided to vessels, groundings, collisions and other maritime accidents did not abate. The impact of human factors – viewed as a combination of error and the willful violation of rules, regulations, policies and procedures – was recognized as a center piece of causality. And this recognition was accompanied by growing realization that human factors are broad in scope and not limited to on board watch keepers – actual operators of the vessels – but extend as well upstream into and through the organizations owning, operating and managing these maritime vessel assets.

The approximate period 1985-1995 saw what seemed to be an eruption of significant maritime casualties, some well publicized such as *Herald, Exxon Valdez* and the mysterious heavy weather loss with her 44 person complement of the British registered bulk carrier *Derbyshire* in the Pacific.[102] But many losses, especially within the foreign registered bulk carrier fleet, were not so publicized.[103] Though perhaps not widely noticed by the public, the aggregate financial consequence of these casualties certainly was noticed within the marine insurance sectors – protection & indemnity, hull & machinery, and cargo. Also noticed, albeit more broadly, was the prevalence of "human element" reference in event-following investigation reports. The significant common denominator of maritime casualties, without quibbling over exact percentage points, was seen to be "human" failings of one sort or another.

In late 1993, the International Maritime Organization (IMO) Assembly, as an agency within the United Nations, adopted resolution A.741(18), the International Safety Management Code for the Safe Operation of Ships and for Pollution Prevention (the International Safety Management (ISM) Code).[104] Six months later, the ISM Code was incorporated into the Saving of Life at Sea (SOLAS) Convention of 1974 as Chapter IX, rendering the ISM Code mandatory on a vessel-type based time line, which concluded July 1, 2002.

The ISM Code put into play a major shift in the philosophy of maritime safety – from a rules, regulations, policies and procedures bounded mentality of "enforce the rules and all should be good" to a more holistic "safety culture," within which company and ship compatible safe operating practices are to be determined and complied with. The ISM Code Preamble at paragraph 1 states the purpose of the Code: "to provide an international standard for the safe management and operation of ships and for pollution prevention[,]" and continues in subsequent paragraphs to recognize that because "no two shipping companies or shipowners are the same, and that ships operate under a wide range of different conditions, the Code is based on general principles." Interestingly, an ISM authority, Lord Donaldson of Lymington, has used "a safety record more akin to that of the aviation industry" as the future benchmark for the commercial maritime industry,[105] validating at least in part drawing from aviation that which may prove successful and compatible with maritime operations.[106]

The ISM Code does not displace formally adopted regulations but does advance awareness that adherence alone does not assure a safe operation.

Perhaps one of the unanticipated and unintended results from introduction of the ISM Code is a shift in emphasis from "safety underpinned by [on board] professionalism and expertise to one inscribed within formal managerial systems and procedures."[107] Management ashore is charged with leading safety through a managerially constructed safety culture introduced to, if not actually imposed upon, the shipboard staff. To the extent that the on board shipboard safety *climate* (discussed ahead) is misunderstood on shore, the safety culture and attendant safety management system cannot help but be undermined, and likely defeated. Safety issues and new initiatives are likely to be misconstrued or disregarded on board if not introduced in a manner sympathetic to the mariner recipients' way of doing business. Such intrusions will be judged on board by source, content and style by, in the maritime domain, a group of mariners already geographically distant from and generally suspicious of management.

While the ISM Code may be likened to a skeleton that gives general form, the Safety Management System (SMS), encouraged – "every company should develop" – by the Code, can be likened to the flesh that fleshes out the particular form of the company. The SMS is intended to, and is essential to, put into operational practice the objectives of the Code. The fundamental, albeit not exclusive, requirements of an SMS are:

> 1.4.2 "instructions and procedures to ensure the safe operation of ships";
> 1.4.3 "defined levels of authority and lines of communication between, and amongst, shore and shipboard personnel"; and,
> 1.4.6 "procedures for internal audits and management reviews."

The ISM Code can be visualized as a three-legged stool:

> 1. *Say* what you do as set out in the SMS, manuals, procedures, instructions, circulars, house organs and expressions of the safety culture;

2. *Do* what you say you do by bringing to life what you say you do through the shipboard safety climate; and,

3. *Prove* that you do what you say you do through documentation so the company can measure and assess what works and what does not work as the company safety program is implemented as an evolving system of increasing awareness and learning.

This should not encourage proliferation of voluminous dust gathering Safety Management Systems designed more to protect the company in litigation from charges of gaps in the SMS than to protect the welfare of crews and ships. Indeed, the result of such volume is likely to be quite the opposite. Shipboard personnel may well lose respect for an imposed system if it appears not designed to enhance safety, and such documentation runs the risk of being "gundecked." Once the falsity of the documents is established, the efficacy of management is suspect and the end result is likely to be as embarrassing as the reality behind a Potemkin village type façade, as demonstrated in the loss of *Bow Mariner,* discussed ahead.

While all ISM Code sections are important, from a managerial perspective section 1.4.3, requiring "defined … communication between … shore and shipboard personnel; … " is of particular importance. The required communicative linkage is provided through a "designated person," whose role is set out in ISM Code section 4: " … a person ashore having direct access to the highest level of management [and whose] responsibility and authority … should include monitoring the safety and pollution-prevention aspects of the operation of each ship and ensuring that adequate resources and shore-based support are applied, as required."[108]

The significance is that the company more likely than not will be charged with liability, in situations where "due diligence" or "privity or knowledge" is at issue, from what the designated person (DP) knew or should have known of relevant facts. Guidance can be drawn from a 2008 United States District Court case.

The case involved a cruise ship grounding in the Columbia River as a result of a tug and tow failing to communicate a safe passing agreement. The same tug master similarly had failed to communicate a safe passage four months previously, also resulting in the other vessel grounding. The tug company had no procedure in place describing what sort of accident investigation should be undertaken and the company's marine superintendent had failed to fully investigate and respond to the faulty procedure revealed by the first incident. No training was in place covering how to communicate passing agreements, and so the second grounding occurred. The court determined the tug company, through the marine superintendent, had privity and knowledge, and limitation of liability was denied. The decision of the trial court is problematic in some respects, but is recent explication that a marine superintendent, functioning as presumably would a DP, can bind the company by what he knows or should know, and does or should do.[109]

Lord Donaldson has neatly summarized the situation of the DP vis-à-vis the company:

The 'bind eye' shipowner is faced with a 'catch 22' situation. If he hears nothing from the Designated Person, he will be bound to call for reports, for it is inconceivable there will be nothing to report. If the report is to the effect all is well in a perfect world, the shipowner would be bound to enquire how that could be, as the safety management system is clearly intended to be a dynamic system which is subject to continuous change in the light, not only of the experience of the individual ship, and of the Company as a whole, but also of the experience of others in the industry. So there will always be something to report.[110]

To what extent the ISM Code should be deemed to set an easily definable industry legal standard distinct from an aspirant goal is problematic because "the ISM Code envisages the development and improvement of a safety culture throughout the industry [and because] [s]ome variance is to be expected in the degree of application by shipping companies based on their own management strategies and operational policy."[111]

Beyond dispute, however, is that the Code anticipates a rising tide raising the standards of sub-standard ship owners and that all companies subject to the Code may be called upon in litigation to demonstrate adherence to the principles and objectives of the Code, and that those principles and objectives are likely to be viewed as an industry standard to which even companies not formally subject to the Code will be bound. So, ironically, though the Code is intended to be neither a legal standard nor punitive, the Code inevitably will be implicated as both.

Strong expression exists that as a result of so many collateral duties arising from the Code and SMSs, there is diminished opportunity to fulfill the primary watch officer's task of vigilance – "to look out the window." This may explain the shocking claim that in 43% of the merchant vessel collisions investigated by the United Kingdom Marine Accident Investigation Board (MAIB) over a ten year period, a watch officer either was made aware of the other vessel by the collision itself or too late to take effective avoiding action.[112] Whether attributable to fatigue, disengagement through competing tasks, or "single person error," reduced manning strongly appears to be implicated, a conclusion seemingly at odds with a contemporaneous informal IMO study.

Of the shore-based shipping company personnel responding to an IMO survey (89 responders out of an unascertained number of questionnaires sent out), 75% responded that their companies did not have to increase shipboard manning levels in response to the respective SMSs introduced under the Code. The implication is that current shipboard personnel took on added SMS responsibilities. Manning was increased by 1 to 3 persons in 23% of the companies and by more than 3 persons in but 2% of the companies.[113]

The preceding discussion highlights two philosophically different responses to the opportunity for avoiding organizational casualties – promulgation of and adherence to rules, regulations, policies and procedures or development of a safety culture. But from a management perspective, greater particularization is necessary for development of a strategy to interdict error before a casualty occurs. This can come from developing an understanding of the "error chain," as well as drawing upon and applying lessons from past casualties within a context of recognizing and accepting three premises:

1. a systemic view of causation, that casualties result from the linkage of a number of conditions and events, each of which is necessary but none [except in the rare situation of sole operator error] of which standing alone is exclusively sufficient,[114] and

2. accidents do not happen because people gamble and lose - they happen because people do not believe that the accident about to happen is at all possible, and

3. though casualties are negative events, they need not be the result of exclusively negative conditions, acts or omissions but may flow from normal behaviors and the normal variability of established work practices.

These several premises provide a framework, but for remediation of error, greater understanding is required of *why* the confluence of conditions and events occurs and *why* people function in ways that invite error. The following discussions provide that understanding.

Two accident types relevant to this discussion exist – individual accidents and organizational accidents. Individuals by act or omission commit errors or violations, or a combination of errors and violations, at the "sharp end of the spear" as on site actors or operators. On the other hand, organizational accidents may be relatively rare but often catastrophic, and occur within systems of varying complexity. Individual and organizational accidents are interrelated in that organizations and their systems are created and operated by individuals, and individuals as well as organizations are subject to error reduction and remediation dependent upon a system of error traps and defenses.

Individual errors and violations often may be anticipated through awareness of a variety of easily identified precursors, as will be discussed. But organizational accidents can be difficult to understand and therefore difficult to anticipate and prevent because they are relatively infrequent within their respective domains and because they tend to be facially surprising and unexpected, at least to people distant from the bridge or engine room event site. However, organizational issues do influence the environment and behavior of individuals on the bridge or in the engine room.

The basic error trap and defense system particularly oriented toward organizational accidents is styled the "Swiss Cheese" Model (SCM), because it allows visualization of how factors, acts and omissions can align, or form a trajectory, so as to result in a casualty. Since the late 1980s, the SCM as originated by James Reason[115] has been widely accepted as a means, compatible with the maritime domain, to conceptualize and illustrate this interaction and trajectory.[116]

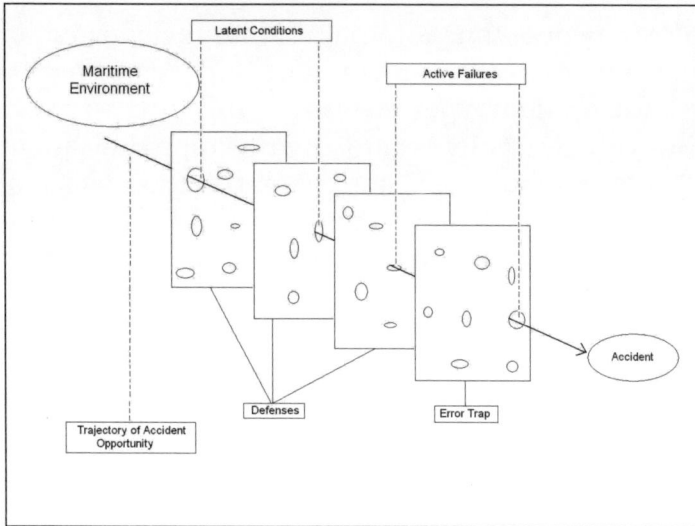

Figure 1. Traditional Swiss Cheese Model, showing trajectory of accident opportunity. *From J. Reason.*

A distinction is drawn between two major types of "pathogens" that can combine to cause accidents.

Latent errors, or conditions, are akin to resident pathogens in the body. They and their adverse potential may lie dormant in a system for years until, combining with other factors or alone, they breach the safe operation defenses of the system.[117] These latent conditions, because of their dormancy and because they are not obvious, pose particularly great danger to and within the system. Not only are they hidden, but latent conditions are common to organizations, and may include "poor design, gaps in supervision, undetected manufacturing defects or maintenance failures, unworkable procedures, clumsy automation, shortfalls in training, [and] less than adequate tools and equipment [and] arise from strategic and other top-level decisions made by governments, regulators, manufacturers, designers and organizational managers [while being] spawned in the upper echelons of the organization and within related manufacturing, contracting, regulatory and governmental agencies."[118] The presence of dangerous latent conditions is inevitable because they stem from such basic organizational activities as "designing, constructing, operating, maintaining, communicating, selecting, training, supervising and managing."[119]

Active errors are the acts, omissions and violations perpetrated by front line actors or operators. Unlike the often dormant latent conditions, active errors "usually have immediate and relatively short lived effects."[120]

The trajectory concept is shown in figure 1. Casualties rarely are the result of only one "blunder" or error. Rather, several errors must combine in an "error chain" that penetrates in the manner of an arrow the various "barriers," "defenses" and "error traps" interposed and intended to prevent or break such linkage and the resulting casualty. These barriers etc. can parallel and be the reciprocal of latent conditions — good design, integrated supervision, absence of defects in the manufactured product, sound maintenance practices, practical and accepted rules, regulations, policies and procedures, ergonomically sound automation, appropriate and updated training, and adequate tools and equipment. These defenses are represented by the vertical plates or "shields" in figure 1, and can be of any of several types: *physical,* so as to physically prevent either the event happening or the consequence(s) of the event from spreading; *functional,* interposes one or more preconditions to an event happening; *symbolic,* such as signs, alarms, or written warnings; and, *incorporeal,* remote from the site, such as training, education and RRPP. Error inducing conditions and errors are represented as "holes" in the defensive "shields." The combination of errors sufficient to bring about a casualty is depicted by the arrow – representing the trajectory of the combined errors — the "error chain." When the latent conditions and errors themselves combine in such a way as to bring about a casualty — when the defenses are inadequate to prevent or break up that combination — the error "holes" align such that the trajectory arrow figuratively passes cleanly through the aligned holes. The result, at the point of the arrow, is the casualty.

The "Swiss Cheese" Model has evolved over the past twenty plus years. The original term latent *failures* now is referred to as "conditions," a term more consistent with understanding that a condition is not a cause, but is necessary for a causal factor to have an effect, just as oxygen is a necessary condition for a fire but oxygen alone does not start a fire.

As helpful as the SCM is for understanding contributory factors to casualties, the SCM has been criticized. The criticism has been constructive and incorporates limitations upon application of the SCM which, when understood, enhance overall relevancy of the SCM.

The first major criticism is that the SCM is too generic and insufficiently specific in identifying what the "holes" – the breaches in the defenses – are and how, or even whether, there is any inter-relation between or among ways in which the defenses/error traps are breached. If operator error no longer is acceptable as the knee-jerk sole explanation of a casualty and if analysis of the contributing factors is to move upstream into organizational territory, more specific information is necessary regarding the nature of those "holes." As human factor terms - such as complacency, situational awareness, work-load, fatigue, bridge resource management deficiency, shared mental models, stress, and intentional violation of rules, regulations, policies and procedures - have become recognized, too often they are deemed to be self-explanatory. For these, and similar, terms to take on substance and meaning, and thereby become subject to managerial influence, there must be objective assurance that the underlying data or information equates with the given verbal shorthand – was there really, for example, "fatigue;" there must be assurance that the "fatigue" actually did play a contributory role in the casualty *and* understanding of how or why the "fatigue" came into the situation; but, the SCM fails to explain how or why the "holes," including fatigue, aligned to bring about the casualty.

In short, the visualization model falls short of explaining how it can be utilized proactively.

Additionally, the SCM runs the risk of creating an assumption that grows into a belief that *all* casualties are the result of upstream failures or conditions. Reason himself has come to be concerned that "the pendulum may have swung too far in our present attempt to track down possible errors and accident contributions that are widely separated in both time and place from the events themselves."[121]

Reason's concern was realized in the Australian Transportation Safety Bureau investigation report of a runway over run by a 747 in Bangkok, discussed ahead. A framework such as the SCM detracts from finding possible primacy of an operator's active errors. Also, discovery of existence of upstream latent conditions does not equate with an ability to control or eliminate those conditions. Nor does the SCM move causality analysis away from a "blame" culture mentality; the blame merely moves upstream.

However, none of these valid criticisms negate the SCM as a valuable conceptual and analytic tool. Also, the SCM is an asset in the re-direction of maritime safety management, which accurately has been characterized as "over-reliance on last-line-of-defense risk-control measures."[122]

Together with the SCM, formal casualty investigation reports and judicial decisions are viewed as containing information from which safer operating practices can be drawn. These are legitimate sources but, as with the SCM, reports and court opinions should be used appreciating their limitations. Reports and court decisions can be tainted by conclusions that are:

> *retrospective*, as they are formed after obtaining most if not all the relevant facts, many of which the operator did not have or appreciate the significance of at the time of the casualty;
> *proximal*, as cause and blame often are attached to the operator without searching upstream;
> *counterfactual*, as the operator is charged with exercising choices – what he "could" have done - that he may not have been aware of or thought were available;
> *judgmental*, as an expert or judge remote from the event decrees what the operator "should" have done.

Such reports and decisions run the risk of being read with the belief that the chafe has been peeled away and what remains is the nugget of causation. Yet, the "chafe" may be the situation as personally and directly perceived by the operator at the time and in the place of the event. From a perspective of managing error, that knowledge can be crucial to the promulgation of appropriate responses.[123]

As maritime casualties increasingly are recognized as resulting from ever more complex sets of factors, formal accident reports and analysis are receiving more attention and scrutiny. They may be given a disproportionately important role in safety management because accident investigators may be "the interpreters of reality and thus policy setters."[124]

The Columbia space shuttle report comments[125] that "[m]any accident investigations do not go far enough. They identify the technical cause of the accident, and then connect it to a variant of 'operator error'... . But this is seldom the entire issue. When the determinations of the causal chain are limited to the technical flaw and individual failure, typically the *actions taken to prevent a similar event in the future are also limited:* fix the technical problem and replace or retrain the individual responsible. Putting these corrections in place *leads to another mistake – the belief that the problem is solved."*

While the extent to which individual causes are involved in or contribute to a casualty may be impossible to determine, the important point is to establish basic principles for the study of casualties. The two principles either respectively accentuate the human component for the purpose of responsibility and disciplinary punishment or ask whether if any of the factors were absent or different, would the event have occurred in the light of cause and effect. From the standpoint of preventive measures the second principle clearly is preferable.

Not surprisingly, a 2005 questionnaire to shipping companies returned a finding that fewer than 20% of the respondents believed that accident analysis beneficially determined casualty root causes and appropriate preventative measures.[126]

To be meaningful from a cumulative perspective of managing risk attributable to organizational latent shortcomings as well as active operator error, the over-arching inquiry must go beyond "what" and "how" the event occurred and must address in detail the "why" of every "what" and "how."[127] Other than generally describing "what" happened, there tends to be no common denominator running through official investigation reports of various countries. The reports have varied in content and depth, as well as in the direction of analysis and emphasis.[128]

With increased awareness of potential managerial and organizational factors, the breadth of casualty

investigations and their resulting reports is expanding
without necessarily there being commensurate
expansion of the investigators' areas of expertise[129]
and comprehension. There may be fixation upon new
theories, such as acceptance of the Swiss Cheese Model
as an investigative tool, with a corresponding tendency
to force, gently perhaps but nonetheless force, an
event into the popular theory or model, or otherwise
misapply a theory or model to the situation.

This appears to have been so in the Australian
Transport Safety Bureau investigation into the 1999
runway over run of a 747 aircraft landing at Bangkok,
Thailand. There had been a troubled final approach
with the First Officer flying the plane, resulting in
the Captain communicating to the First Officer the
Captain's decision, just as the aircraft was about to
touch down, that the First Officer abort the landing and
"go around." This procedure as initiated was proper.
What followed was neither proper nor normal. About
four seconds later, without asserting verbally that he was
taking control and without informing the First Officer
of his intention, the Captain retarded the thrust levers
— because he decided in the last seconds to continue
the landing rather than "go around." Standard practice
decreed that the "go around" decision, once made, is
not reversed. Breach of that standard was contrary to
the Captain's training and experience, and occurred
exclusively at the "sharp end," in the cockpit. While
there were latent issues, they were wholly subordinate
to the Captain's seemingly irrational act. The operative
question should have been "why" did the Captain act
as he did? Yet, the SCM was applied despite the reality
that the event did not fit within the model. While
some minor organizational "lessons" were learned,
the most relevant issues and inquiries were missed.[130]
The overwhelmingly dominant event in the accident

sequence, or error chain, was "pilot error." As Sigmund Freud purportedly said, "Sometimes a cigar is just a cigar."

Investigations also may be tainted by "political" considerations interposed by organizations or regulators (or combinations thereof) reflecting their concerns or fears. An extreme example of such politicalization is that following the 1956 *Andrea Doria – Stockholm* collision, the Italian Minister of Maritime Affairs appointed a commission of inquiry which purportedly was unable to agree upon a statement because any relevant statement had the potential to "stain the glory of Italian shipping."[131]

Despite possible inherent limitations in the way in which casualties are investigated and reported, much operational benefit can be derived from well investigated and objectively reported casualties. However, notwithstanding this opportunity, two basic sociological phenomena interfere with fully and correctly "learning" from past casualties:

> *fundamental attribution error*: the pervasive tendency to blame bad outcomes upon an actor's personal failings (individual blame) rather than attribute the outcome to situational factors beyond the actor's control; and, *fundamental surprise*: a profound discrepancy between one's perception of the world and the way the world really is.[132]

Yet, lessons have been learned, with the price paid being lives and property losses. The failure lies less in the learning than in the failure to implement the lessons learned.

Safety management direction also can be gained from court decisions but here, as with investigation reports, caution is necessary. American and English litigation is deliberately adversarial, with the contending plaintiff(s) and defendant(s) being responsible for investigating the facts, amassing evidence supportive of their respective positions, selectively presenting to a neutral judge their evidence in the most persuasive way possible, and, through their attorneys, advocating the strength of their position and the weakness of the opponent's evidence and argument.[133] One side "wins" and one side "loses," and the written opinion strives to explain why, but in doing so often is a edited or synoptic rendering of the "case," leaving the casual reader uninformed of what "really happened" as well as what all the facts "really were." Only with a full understanding of all relevant facts can the most accurate and comprehensive conclusions be drawn for safety lessons to be learned.

Supporting and inherent in the adversarial nature of litigation is the role of the "expert," intended to offer case specific expertise otherwise unavailable to the judge deciding the case. Too often, however, the expert, intended to inform objectively, becomes an advocate. Also, the expert comes with 20/20 hind-sight unavailable to the actors. This advantage of the expert was described in a novel[134] based upon the 1932 encounter of the Blue Funnel freighter *Phemius* with a hurricane:

> Captain Abraham [the salvage master] ... knew what a tendency there is for the experts, with all the facts before them, with wisdom after the event, to declare unjustly but in all honesty that a man has acted wrongly. Nothing is harder than to bear in mind, when conducting such an enquiry, only the knowledge that was available to the Master at each time his decisions had to be made: to rule out completely from the reckoning indications which came to light even, it may be, only a few minutes later.[135]

Another limitation of judicial decisions is that litigation seeks out legal causes, not "root" causes of casualties. A point is reached, usually not too far upstream in the error chain, at which the legal system says the link between acts and omissions involved in the casualty has become too tenuous to justify liability – "[t]here may have been other faults which led up to this simple fault, but none [of those other faults] were causative [as recognized by the legal system]."[136] And, anyway, causation "continues to confuse lawyers."[137]

Finally, most judges called upon to decide cases of maritime complexity lack meaningful maritime knowledge and so are dependent upon the experts and attorneys, the latter perhaps also lacking maritime knowledge. While this scenario is not intended to suggest that every trial of maritime issues is the judicial equivalent of Pieter Bruegel the Elder's "Blind Leading the Blind," doubtlessly there can be real potential for a decision that misses the reality of the situation. And certainly nautically experienced attorneys questioning self-serving witnesses have had occasion to interject either the pre-testimony admonition or deposition comment that "No, that cannot be; that's not how things are done at sea."

4

Safety Culture and Safety Climate, the Critical Distinction Between Them

The cornerstone of good safety management is commitment from the top. —International Safety Management (ISM) Code, Preamble, para. 6

A threshold issue in any discussion of maritime safety must be the interrelationship between an organization's safety *culture* and shipboard safety *climate*. Safety culture[138] is widely recognized as "the product of individual and group values, attitudes, perceptions, competencies and patterns of behavior that determine the commitment to, and the style and proficiency of, an organization's health and safety management[,]"[139] whereas safety climate refers to the unique shipboard environment, peculiar to each individual ship within a fleet, into which the safety culture is received and integrated. Simply stated, "safety culture" is organizationally "what we say we do" and "safety climate" is "what we actually do or not do." The core concept of a safety culture is in the statement of Ulf G. Ryder, President and Chief Executive Officer of Stena Bulk AB: "We go to work every morning with the intention of doing everything a little bit better than the day before."[140] Safety culture and safety climate are distinct,[141] with the maritime industry being especially vulnerable to variable safety climates arising because of the nature of ships and their remoteness from shore side management.

Experience has shown that a safety culture does not arise by decree, but rather can only be the outgrowth of certain initial high level managerial decisions. These decisions include the willingness to engender trust[142] between management and shipboard personnel through implementation of a non-punitive policy addressing inadvertent error such as enables management to have clear knowledge of shipboard performance and to know the nature and types of threat and risk existing within the operational system. There must be management commitment to proactive reduction of error inducing conditions and effective assurance that the shipboard staff adheres to appropriate rules, regulations, policies and procedures. Also, safety rhetoric ought not be diluted by conflicting, stronger messages accentuating cost cutting, downsizing and productivity (such as "on time" performance) levels.

In the several years after Tony Hayward ascended to the position of BP CEO and preceding the *Deepwater Horizon* explosion, a serious effort was made to redirect BP's corporate culture toward safety. But, that effort was accompanied by a corrosive combination of mixed messages. On the one hand, operational processes were addressed, and patterned upon the EXXON Mobil model, known post-*Exxon Valdez* for the high quality of its operations. On the other hand, BP's new stress upon safety was paired with another round of "brutal cost-cutting," with Hayward saying "The mantra in BP today is 'Every dollar counts.'"[143] Such mixed messages inevitably will create cynicism and result in a corresponding degradation of safety performance. Though written in a novel, these words ring true: "The seamen come to expect almost as high a standard of conduct from the owners as from each other. Every act of the owners will be assessed by the whole fleet, and rigorously judged."[144]

The ISM Code sets the foundation for a safety culture by reorienting maritime operations away from a culture of 'unthinking' compliance with external rules toward a culture of 'thinking' self-regulation of safety – the development of a 'safety culture.' Formalistic rules are eschewed in favor of a company and ship compatible philosophy implemented through a Safety Management System.

There is recognition that "[c]oncepts which make up a safety culture are specific to an industry ... and measures adopted elsewhere may not simply be grafted on to the maritime industry [and because shipping is a very] context specific industry [there is need to develop] specific measures designed for the maritime environment ... to maximize the successes of attempts to build a safety culture across the sector."[145] A cultural phenomenon that challenges acceptance of anything new or different is the tendency of the people of a culture to adhere to their traditions, and the ISM Code has not been favorably received in all quarters.[146] In addition to perceived weaknesses of the Code, there is the fact that "[t]he seafaring community was and still is very conservative and not in favor of change. There are always some fears that changes may be negative for their profession."[147] Among weaknesses of the Code is that without requirements explicated by the Code, a shipping organization has latitude sufficient to formulate a self-serving safety management system in the belief, or upon the rationale, that merely through formulation of a system, safety has been attained, without recognizing that safety is an ever-ongoing process and not a port of call arrived at with the ringing down of "finished with engines."[148] So, the attitude to be adjusted is that most people so restrict their frame of reference, or context, for the problem they are facing that little change can occur. They get into such a routine with their work that they view virtually all problems in a similar way – back to all problems looking like nails when all you have is a hammer.[149]

Because there is no common metric for measuring the strength of a particular safety culture, there is no clear method by which an organization can assess its safety culture or diagnose its particular strengths and weaknesses. Unfortunately, "[t]he passing of time without a process accident is not necessarily an indication that all is well and may contribute to a dangerous and growing sense of complacency. ... People can forget to be afraid."[150] A healthy constraint upon such complacency in the maritime domain was aptly expressed by John Millington Synge in lines from his play *The Aran Islands*: "A man who is not afraid of the sea will soon be drowned ... for he will be going out on a day he shouldn't. But we do be afraid of the sea, and we do only be drowned now and again."[151]

A reflection of the company safety culture will be not only the ISM Code mandated safety management system but also, illustrating the shipboard safety climate, how effectively the system is implemented on board. The safety management system is of scant value if it is not accepted and practiced where it is intended to be practiced – in the ships of the company.

Among many other examples of the gap between ashore promulgation and shipboard adherence to a safety management system is the 2005 (post-ISM Code/ safety management system) grounding and subsequent loss, with pollution, of the 15,145 gross registered ton Bermudian registered containership *CP Valour* in a bay on the northwest coast the Azorean island of Fayal.[152]

While en route toward Spain from Canada, *CP Valour* entered the bay to effect engine repairs. The chart available on board was of a 1:175,000 scale, inappropriate for inshore navigation, and displaying only a single sounding (36 meters) within the bay. However, the United Kingdom Marine Accident Investigation Branch (MAIB) determined that given the totality of information available to (but not utilized by) the master, his decision to enter the bay and there anchor was "fully justified under the circumstances." The loss resulted from mutually reinforcing deficiencies in the exercise of bridge resource management by the master, who "liked to do things himself."

The master had failed to communicate to his chief and second officers where he planned to anchor. As a result, the former entered one position into the vessel's global positioning system (GPS) while the latter entered a different position into the electronic chart system. The master, however, intended to approach as close as two cables from shore despite the fact that the Admiralty Sailing Directions described the anchorage to be elsewhere in the bay. Relying upon the single 36 meter charted depth, the master assumed a uniform depth of about 36 meters, though the chart was silent as to when and by what means the bay had been surveyed and sounded. He failed to call out the third officer to monitor the fathometer, located behind and out of sight of anyone in the forward area of the wheelhouse.

Once in the bay, in 70 meters of water and when about 12 cables from the head of the bay, the master put the engine telegraph to slow, then half ahead and altered course to proceed toward a shallower and more appropriate area for anchoring. The vessel arrived at the recommended area for anchoring but, unnoticed by anyone in the bridge team, had picked up speed to about seven knots from the half ahead bell. A minute or so later the master moved the telegraph from half to dead slow ahead. Concerned about the vessel's speed, he asked the second mate and heard in apparent reply "point six." He assumed this to have been the ship's speed as read from the GPS information on the radar, but did not confirm his assumption. Accepting an advance speed of "point six" knots, the master entered the chart room and read from the echo sounder (fathometer) an under keel depth of about 15 meters. Over the next several minutes he telegraphed various astern orders whereupon *CP Valour* ran aground, unnoticed by anyone, still making six knots ahead over the ground. Believing his vessel was still underway, the master ordered that the starboard anchor be walked out and also telegraphed for full astern to set the anchor. Expecting a strain to be taken upon the anchor chain, the master doubtlessly was surprised, both that the chain remained "up and down" and that his vessel was not moving. Eight minutes later he realized the vessel was aground.[153]

Here was a shipboard safety *climate* that failed to implement the company safety *culture* as embodied in the safety management system.

The MAIB determined that "the second officer and the master [were] fully qualified, and [had] received good quality bridge resource management training... [and] the ISM [safety management] system appeared good and in order... ." This sharply contrasted with the poor performance by the bridge team and led to the observation that " [t]here is no benefit to be gained from good training and qualifications unless they are used as the basis for good practice when the crew return to their ships[,]" thus raising the question "how employers and others can be sure that bridge teams are actually following instructions and guidance [from BRM training and safety management procedures], and performing well on board their vessels." This in turn resulted in the MAIB concluding that there is "thus a need for shipowners and managers to ensure that their orders and training are being put into practice by those operating their ships." Passing reference was made to onboard auditing by company managers, which was acknowledged as only partially effective because performance undoubtedly would improve while being monitored – that is to say, personnel would be exhibiting their best behaviors and proficiencies. The danger comes in the old saying, "When the cat is away, the mice will play." Further, monitoring and auditing catches only a "snap shot" of performance in an environment which, unlike aviation and other safety-critical domains, lacks specific observable maneuvers and reactions, such as flying on fewer than all engines, shutting down a system in a nuclear plant in reaction to a programmed failure, checklist proficiency, etc. Also referenced was voyage data recording, but a voyage cannot be dissected effectively as can a flight of an hour or so.

When assessing what happens when "the crew return to their ships[,]" consideration must be given to the fact that a ship is a "living, micro-culture, micro-political system in motion[,]"[154] reflected in and influencing the safety climate of the ship. Groups, such as a ship's crew, are recognized as viewing safety through their own subcultures, instead of sharing an overall organizational view of safety. The matter has been stated as: "The frame of reference for understanding people's behavior is their own normal, individual work context, the context they are embedded in and from whose point of view the decisions and assessments made are mostly normal, daily, unremarkable, perhaps even unnoticeable."[155]

Every ship's complement constitutes an individual and distinct "safety climate." Every such unit presents a unique environment, depending upon vessel type, trading area, ownership, management, senior officer nationality, subordinate complement nationality, etc. For the safety culture of an organization to penetrate the on board safety climate, the ship's personnel must have a sense of "ownership" in proper safety procedures.

An example of deck plate safety climate ownership occurred on board the tanker *Concho*. As she was getting off a pier, a vibration and bump were felt. Neither the pilot nor officers on the bridge did more than assume a tug coming alongside was the cause. However, two ABs on deck were concerned enough to investigate and determined that a ballast tank was flooding, indicating a breach in hull plate integrity. In fact, *Concho* had touched bottom sufficiently hard to rupture the hull.[156]

Too often, the prevailing on-board attitude is one of "company's procedures, not ours." A rationale for such an attitude may stem from conflicting orientations between management and front line actors. This type of "conflict" was illustrated in an airline survey that revealed: "[Mechanics] believed they were responsible for the safety of the aircraft and should be allowed to exercise their skill and experience to carry out this responsibility as opposed to management who believed the [mechanics] must follow task procedures exactly."[157]

Not surprisingly, surveys have been developed to assess safety culture and safety climate effectiveness in commercial and military aviation and civilian health care. The results consistently show a higher positive rating among supervisors than frontline workers. A reasonable conclusion to draw is that managers and workers have different and incompatible views regarding the organization's safety culture and safety climate.[158] This is disturbing because a safety climate is an important indicator of the strength or weakness of the safety culture umbrella and evidences a communication disconnect as well as primacy of the organizational safety climate.

Without every ship and its personnel accepting the organizational safety culture and vessel specific safety management system, either or both are likely doomed. Studies in a variety of industries confirm the "critical role" that managers play in the formation of attitudes and behavior toward safety, but in the maritime industry distance from shore side management heightens the importance and influence in this area of shipboard senior officers as managers.

The *Monarch of the Seas* 1998 grounding provides graphic proof of the influence a senior officer exerts over the manner in which a vessel will be operated and on board reception of safety procedures. In the early morning hours of December 15, the vessel, with 2,557 passengers on board, was departing the area of St. Maarten after landing a sick passenger when at 0130 hours she "raked" Proselyte Reef at a speed of 12 knots. About an hour later the vessel was intentionally grounded on a sandbar and the passengers evacuated. The vessel had suffered extensive damage, and the deliberate grounding was to prevent possible foundering. The initial "raking" resulted from "a myriad of human performance deficiencies" stemming from violations of the ship's ISM safety management system procedures, with

> the primary reason for the master and crew's decision not to adhere to SMS procedures centered on the master's disregard for and lack of "by[sic]-in" to the formalized requirements of the ISM Code SMS. He voiced his displeasure for the sort of company oversight, bureaucracy and micromanagement that the SMS procedures represented. *Without the master's expressed support of the ISM procedures* the crew unsurprisingly failed to embrace the newly established SMS and disregarded the established procedures, guidelines and job aids made easily accessible to them on the vessel's bridge.[159]

The *Monarch of the Seas* situation illustrates the general premise that "[a]t the ship level, the master can exacerbate or mitigate the adverse effects of high level decisions, but the master can also introduce other [failures] into the system [and, further] [a] conning officer's perception of importance will be directly influenced by the master and the prevailing attitudes of the experienced personnel on aboard."[160] Additionally, if the vessel's master believed that the ISM safety management system procedures truly represented "company oversight, bureaucracy and micro-management," in all likelihood the manner of presenting the SMS procedures to the master had been faulty. If presented as a fairly evaluated means developed and intended to enhance safety, the procedures likely would have been more favorably received. As with a gourmet meal, presentation counts.

Also, the operating, managing or owning organization will be charged with knowing the sort of safety climate that exists on board, as was made clear in the National transportation Safety Board (NTSB) report addressing the 2007 *Empress of the North* grounding in Alaskan waters:

> the master did not follow critical aspects of either [the company's safety management system or the requirement that Federal regulations be followed] and did not establish on his vessel an ethos of compliance with all policies, rules, and regulations. The company *should have been more aware before the accident of the actions of the master and the type of safety atmosphere that he had established.*[161]

Closely related to safety climate is the extent to which a culture of professionalism exists in a vessel. The International Maritime Organization states that "the safety of life at sea, the marine environment and over 80% of the world's trade depend on the professionalism and competence of seafarers."[162]

A "professional" in this sense is said to possess specialized knowledge, differing from commonly held knowledge, that is institutionally (in one form or another) provided and exercised on a full time basis. Practitioners are subject generally to an "ethical code" peculiar to the profession, stressing primacy of the "clients'" interests as well as a degree of accountability.[163] The profession, by its members, undertakes to transform the initiate into a member of that profession.[164] He or she identifies with a job sub-culture that is at least somewhat autonomous from the public. This sub-culture is work based, especially where the professional learning is largely based upon hands on practice and experience, and is a characteristic of many high risk industries, not least being seafaring where a strong tradition has developed over centuries. Mariners not only learn how to "do" mariners' work, they become mariners with mariners' unique concerns, objectives and behaviors.[165]

One characteristic of maritime professionalism is a "can do" attitude of accomplishing a task with what is available. While this may be a positive characteristic, albeit born of necessity, the "can do" attitude also can be carried to risky conclusions. For example, while en route to Tacoma, Washington the bulk cargo vessel *Dona V* was forced to shut down her main engine in the inbound Traffic Separation Scheme lane and drift with attendant risk of grounding or collision. Subsequent investigation established through the vessel's chief engineer that " main engine maintenance was difficult to schedule because of the vessel's short stays in port ... [and] the chief engineer indicated that he had to maintain the vessel's machinery within the scheduled port times to load cargo. He did not feel comfortable in requesting additional port time to perform routine maintenance of machinery. *This dilemma is an indication of maritime industry culture.*"[166]

Another professional characteristic, in common with aviation, is a denial of personal vulnerability –

aviators and mariners show through surveys a belief that their decision making is unaffected by stress and so is believed to be as "good" under stress as under "normal" circumstances. This belief can lead to dangerous over confidence in challenging circumstances, resulting in a safety climate acceptance of risk taking and disregarding constructive comment from others.[167]

Nonetheless, the many positive attributes of maritime professionalism led Joseph Conrad to comment through one of his novelistic protagonists that: "If we at sea went about our work as people ashore high and low go about theirs we should never make a living. No one would employ us. And moreover no ship navigated and sailed in the happy-go-lucky manner people conduct their business on shore would ever arrive into port."[168]

Pride in professionalism and respect for the "Code of the Sea" among the public and practitioners of the "fellowship of the craft"[169] heightens the disparagement shown those who are considered to have conspicuously violated the Code. Consider the opprobrium heaped upon Captain Yiannis Avranas, who by helicopter abandoned by his sinking passenger ship *Oceanos* while some 160 passengers were still on board. His purported rationale, to better direct evacuation of the vessel from ashore, was undermined by his comment: "When I order 'abandon ship,' it doesn't matter what time I leave. Abandon is for everybody. If some people like to stay, they can stay."[170]

5

Recognizing and Dealing with Maritime Risk

... the often misunderstood and complex concept of maritime risk ... — A. Elmer, President, SeaRiver Maritime, Inc.[171]

He that will not sail till all Dangers are over, must never put to Sea. — Dr. Thomas Fuller[172]

"Your act was unwise," I cried, "as you see by the outcome." He calmly eyed me: "When choosing the course of my action," said he, "I had not the outcome to guide me." — Ambrose Bierce

An example of risk assessed and appropriate action taken: The tendency of deck officers on American merchant ships to have their cabins on the starboard side of the vessel, the starboard being less vulnerable to being struck by a crossing "give-way" vessel that fails to adhere to her obligation to "keep out of the way" under COLREG Rule 15.

Some risk accompanies practically all activities, varying in degree depending upon the activity, situation, personality and motivation, with one aspect of the variance presented by risk clear from the observation of Captain Robert FitzRoy, master of Charles Darwin's acclaimed *HMS Beagle* and later inventor of the marine weather forecast:

Those who never run any risk; who sail only when the wind is fair; who heave to when approaching land, though perhaps a day's ail distant; and who even delay the performance of urgent duties until they can be done easily and quite safely; are, doubtless, extremely prudent persons: - but rather unlike those officers whose names will never be forgotten while England has a navy.[173]

"Risk" in the context of this discussion refers to the product of the probability of some adverse occurrence and the magnitude of harm resulting from an act or omission or, because a casualty only rarely results from but one act or omission, a combination of one or more acts or omissions, or both. And, because these acts and omissions are usually natural or customary to the task or operation or organization, the resulting casualty seems unnatural and unexpected. The casualty, being unexpected, was not "foreseen" and so the risk was not considered by the actor as a guide for or constraint upon his or her action. Nor is there a black or white distinction between risky behavior or conditions and the happening of an accident. Fleet Admiral Chester W. Nitmitz described the situation well:

... safety and fatal hazard are not separated by any sharp boundary line, but shade gradually from one into the other. There is no little red light which is going to flash on ... ."[174]

Many informed books address risk, a multi-faceted concept, generally and can be referred to for general principles but maritime risk, as is true of so many maritime issues, stands somewhat apart due to the uniqueness of the maritime environment. This uniqueness has repercussions upon the shipboard operational as well as the shore side managerial level.

Whatever the perspective, the underlying premise is that risk cannot be successfully managed without awareness of what risk "is." And, for risk to be managed, managers must understand how people perceive risk, Professor Wilde's risk homeostasis theory, discussed in Chapter Nine, being particularly adaptable to the shipboard application. Unfortunately, the "complexity of risk management is not widely appreciated, even within the marine community."[175] Nor can risk be considered in isolation as numerous factors influence risk, not least being economic.

Risk to the mariner is anything that tends to jeopardize the safety of ship, personnel and goods on board, and may come from within as well as without the vessel. Watch keeping mariners now have and historically have had two basic skill sets for managing risk: "the practice of good seamanship and the effective use of informed judgment derived from accumulated experience and expertise."[176] The first, "practice of good seamanship," is largely a result of the second, and is so pervasive as to justify, in appropriate circumstances, a violation of RRPP.[177] Both are intertwined with sound decision making.

Yet, "[c]ommand at sea entails risk that can never be reduced to zero." But, that inevitable risk can be reduced to an acceptable level by the captain's exercise of alert wariness, commitment, competence, and active concern for his "primary tool," his officers and crew.[178] A mariner's operational environment includes the planning and risk reduction policy of the vessel owning or operating company as reflected in large part by the company safety culture and the safety climate of the vessel.

While various means exist for assessing risk and human error, there is no exclusively accepted methodology for assessing maritime risk nor for assessing performance from a wholly safety oriented perspective. Similarly, there is no common denominator accepted for normalizing safety related data. However, accident free operation does not necessarily equate with safe operation — it may be only a lucky operation.

A 2010 *Journal of Navigation* article, applying statistical analysis of casualties experienced to cargo carrying vessels world-wide over the period 2005-2006, overturns much conventional wisdom and highlights the randomness of maritime ship casualties.[179] Among the findings were: 1) The rate of incidents is the same among the groups of ships registered in Paris Memorandum on Port State Control (Paris MOU) "black list" countries (whose vessels are presumed to have the lowest safety standards) as those registered in "grey" and "white" list countries (presumed to have higher and the highest safety standards); 2) There was no relation between levels of classification societies and the occurrence of casualties, notwithstanding that class societies are a principal means by which the maritime industry self regulates itself in as much as class societies are the major technological resource of the industry; 3) Older vessels are not more prone to structural failure than new ships; 4) Accidents happen randomly to ships despite their size, with most major claims involving ships between 10,000 and 30,000 gross registered tons; and, 5) Accidents happen randomly to cargo carrying vessels regardless of their safety standard level. The suggested risk homeostasis explanation is that operators of "safer" vessels, newer vessels equipped more modernly, are willing to press the operational envelop in order to obtain maximum financial return. These conclusions are based upon Paris MOU detention records, which present a bias, and conflict with previously cited figures that demonstrate high organization vessels are overall safer. The most appropriate conclusion is likely to be that there is a significant element of randomness in maritime accidents, emphasizing the complexity of maritime risk assessment.

One of the challenges to accurate maritime risk assessment is, ironically, the fact that statistics from which realistic conclusions can be drawn are too sparse to be meaningful, due to the fortunate fact that in the maritime domain low probability, high consequence events from which statistics would be drawn are rare. But statistics, even if available, would not be the complete answer to risk management. A 1996 Massachusetts Institute of Technology engineering study of tanker environmental risk commented: "Until there is better understanding of accident mechanics, any attempt to minimize accidents based on statistics alone is reactionary, with questionable effectiveness."[180] Because the desirable trend in maritime safety is to be proactive, any argument favoring as a guide reactionary statistics, notwithstanding a sense of certainty implied from empirical data albeit sometimes misleading, loses force. Nonetheless, reliable risk assessment does require legitimate research, rather than emotion or perception, though "[t]he pressures of public opinion rather than valid research have facilitated national and transnational efforts to improve the safety of passengers and crew."[181] In any event, the real risk, rather than a perceived risk, is what is relevant. This is not to say, however, that the psychological risk is without significance.

Considering risk from a ship handler's perspective, the psychological aspect of risk has been found more powerful than the intellectual aspect. When a bridge spanning the waters between Denmark and Sweden was being designed, consideration was given to how the bridge design, and distance between the supports, would influence the passage of vessels under the bridge. The bridge and its approaches were computerized for simulated passages. With alarming frequency, the supports were struck in simulation despite a 330 meter clearance. There was much fine maneuvering and many captains displayed considerable insecurity and stress. The eventual recommendation was that the channel between the supports be kept relatively narrow such that the consequence of error would be a gentle grounding rather than striking either of the bridge supports. This reflects the dual components of risk: 1) the potential for an undesired event, which is a statistical intellectual concept, and 2) the adverse consequence, which is emotional. The response to the risk was intellectual whereas emotion governed response to the consequence. When the intellect was caused to act in opposition to emotion, stress and diminished capability resulted. The intellectual likelihood of striking a support was small relative to the distance between the supports, but the potential seriousness of striking a support was large. Yet, with a narrower channel, the emotional consequence of a gentle grounding was significantly less. The risk presented by the narrower channel was found "lower" than the wider channel bounded by supports. Valid research yielded a counter-intuitive resolution.[182]

Effective July 1, 2010 clause 1.2.2.2. of the ISM Code was amended to make mandatory some form of risk assessment as the basis for Safety Management Systems, thereby making risk assessment explicit whereas previously risk assessment had been implicit, albeit a practical necessity in order to comply with many of the Code's provisions. A practical effect of this amendment is that additional documentation is required so a company is able to demonstrate examination of its operations for the purpose of risk assessment.

Various models do exist for assessing and managing risk in the maritime domain. Such risk management "... should answer whether evidence is sufficient to prove specific risks and benefits."[183] Most notable are the Probabilistic Risk Assessment (PRA) and the Formal Risk Assessment (FRA) models. Each has the advantage of introducing science and objectivity, whereas previously assessments tended to be adversarial, usually with one group of "experts" pitted against another group of "experts." These, and other models, present results and conclusions intended to influence significant investment decisions and management practices. However, the considerable degree of uncertainty in any such analysis should be noted, and a decision maker ought not be led to believe that the expressed results and conclusions are definitive; there is danger that without awareness of such uncertainty, the decision maker will act in total reliance upon the assessment and proceed rigidly despite a shaky premise.

Such uncertainty is of two types: aleatory uncertainty, describing the variability and randomness inherent in the system under study, and espistemic, arising from the lack of in depth knowledge about the system. Together, they undermine accuracy in predicting the type and frequency of system events.[184] Event probability in such assessments is a factor of three probabilities, that: 1) a particular combination of risk values occurs within the system; 2) within that combination, a particular triggering event occurs; and, 3) an accident occurs once the triggering event occurs.[185] Because of their inherent uncertainty, each of these "probabilities" can only be estimated. Expert judgment therefore is solicited to set a reasonable perimeter about these necessary estimates.[186]

PRA attempts to capture the dynamic nature of risk by combining various precursors to accident with accepted probabilistic determination of their likelihood from objective expert judgment. An example[187] is the 1996 post-*Exxon Valdez* assessment covering Prince

William Sound in the event of an oil tanker casualty such as collision, drift grounding, powered grounding, foundering, fire or explosion, or structural failure. The "consequence" was oil spilling into the Sound.[188] Among the questions raised and answers sought are how are risks targeted, how effective is the targeting and how much is known about the types and causes of human error that contribute to maritime casualties. These questions are partially answered through objective and reasonable quantitative estimates of the linkages in the error chains leading to accidents in which human error is a factor. The wrinkle is that such estimates require specific data that allow description of the relevant types of human error and their inter-relations. For there to be meaningful analysis, given the high rate human error contributes to maritime casualties, types of human error need to be categorized meaningfully and the linkage between human error and accidents understood as fully as possible.[189] There is an inevitable circularity: the objective of the analysis is better understanding of how human error functions as a precursor to accident but for the analysis to be of value, there must be knowledge of human error as a causal factor of accidents. As a foundation for PRA, a modeling system is necessary that decomposes generic human error into logical, mutually exclusive categories. Attempts in this direction fall short because classifying human error using a theoretical framework requires knowledge of the actor's intent and personality. To this human error categorization must be added performance shaping factors sufficient to describe organizational factors that contribute to human error.[190] Categorization of human error probabilities, performance shaping factors as well as management and organizational factors are enumerated and discussed in the Nature of Error chapter, Chapter Seven. Specific mention of the organization's safety culture, important as it is, is absent from the management and organization factors category because an organization's safety culture (or absence thereof) by its nature influences all such factors and so is considered inherent in each of the included factors.[191]

Initially the accident most expected was a drift or powered grounding but the Prince William Sound PRA demonstrated that of greater frequency would be collisions in the subject area. Ironically, a significant contributor to oil spillage was collision between outbound laden tankers with inbound escort tugs, whose function is to assist tankers in cases of steering or propulsion failure. From this finding, the escort procedures would be modified to reduce risk. Also, some proposed risk interventions were found to increase risk, such as weather closure of the port increasing traffic and collision risk. For risk management purposes, the assessment found value in identifying "patterns, unusual circumstances, and trends in system risk and in changes in system risk made by the implementation of risk-intervention measures."[192] Unfortunately, absolute statistical validation of the assessment conclusions is not to be expected because fortunately risk assessment typically concerns itself with low probability, high consequence events. And, because the objective of any risk assessment process is reduction in the occurrence of significant accidents, nor should empirical dollar measurement of the benefit in increased profit or reduced operating expenses be expected. However, accident frequency was estimated in the assessment to have been reduced 75 percent since the *Exxon Valdez* grounding, while "further reduction in accident frequency from all measures taken as a result of the Prince William Sound risk assessment is 68 percent, with a 51 percent reduction in the expected oil outflow[,] [for an] accident frequency [estimated total reduction] of 92 percent."[193]

Another methodology addressing risk assessment is the Formal Risk Assessment (FRA), commonly used to evaluate regulatory procedures and policies, but which can be applied to specific ship types (i.e. high speed ferries) and particular risks (i.e. fire or explosion). FRA has been accepted by the International Maritime Organization for maritime rule making and, properly applied, has proved a powerful analytic tool. Several successive determinations form the FRA structure:

1. Accurate determination and definition of the situation to be assessed, with "brainstorming" to ensure that historical data does not create an unreasonable or unrealistic boundary upon the defined risk;

2. Determine the "risk" through a probability of occurrence and severity of consequence (human life and injury and property loss) analysis – assigning, if feasible, a dollar value to life and injury;

3. Determine risk control options and what may be required to prevent the losses or minimize their severity;

4. Perform a cost versus benefit analysis; and,

5. Based upon the results of 1 through 4, recommendation(s) is made with respect to what actions are to be taken.[194]

A third means whereby risk can be assessed is a three-region scheme into which risk may fall under a United Kingdom Health and Executive framework for the tolerance of risk. There is an Unacceptable Risk region, determined to exist where the event or situation would occur with high probability and result in many fatalities or much property loss, or both. This event or situation would not be permitted to exist. At the other end of the spectrum is the Acceptable Risk area, where the probability of occurrence and severity of consequence are so negligible that no action need be taken as the resources most appropriate to reduce the risk are likely to be greatly disproportionate to the reduction achieved.

Between these two regions is the ALARP region – As Low As Reasonable Practicable. Risk within this region is to be reduced to the point beyond which further reduction is no longer financially feasible. A question is, to what extent is the still risky activity or circumstance still desired by society for whatever benefit is bestowed by the activity or circumstance.

Another assessment looks to the potential for legal liability if an accident occurs. Referred to, at least in United States legal circles, as the "Hand" formula named for Learned Hand, the federal judge who "devised" it, the "formula" states that liability may exist where the cost of prevention is less than the probability of the event multiplied by the gravity [economic cost] of the event.[195] This formula was cited in a 2007 case arising out of a sole pilot navigator "blacking out," with the result that a large ferry struck its pier with substantial property damage, eleven fatalities and many personal injuries. There was no cost to enforcing an internal rule that two pilots already on salary be in the wheelhouse at all times when the ferry was underway.[196] The Hand formula has been described as a "tolerable, although not perfect, approximation of an economically efficient concept of care and negligence."[197]

And, there is the operational aspect of risk assessment, which looks retrogressively to what has been put into practice: "The funding and adoption of specific risk reduction measures and the rejection of others as 'too expensive' or 'not cost effective' provides an operational definition of an acceptable level of risk."[198]

However, risk analysis involves more than mathematical calculation, as has been commented upon by the New Orleans Independent Levee Investigation Team following Hurricane Katrina: "… the acceptability of risk cannot be extracted from science or mathematics; it is a social judgment."[199] Disregard of the human cost will appear callous, as illustrated by the Navy's handling of an F-14 problem. In the F-14A "Tomcat" there was an "engine/flight control problem" that the Navy knew about but determined was too expensive to immediately fix. The Navy secretly calculated how many F-14s the Navy could financially afford to lose before engine replacement would be necessary and the control surfaces replaced, all at a cost of $2.5 billion. Eventually, and consistent with the financially oriented risk management decision, almost 40 Tomcats were lost. Omitted from the calculation was the human toll borne by the two- man crews.[200] Little imagination is required to anticipate the appealing emotional argument that could be made to a jury in a personal injury or wrongful death case where such calculations are at issue.

One of the factors to be included in a risk assessment is changed circumstances. But detecting, interpreting, and adapting to changing or changed circumstances, whether environmental, or technological or societal, is difficult for organizations, as well as individuals. In the former situation – organizations – an entire cultural shift may be necessary. Often standing in the way of advancement are those who may politely be styled "traditionalists," representative of bureaucratic resistance to change. This principle applies to situations that may implicate risk in some manner. Several examples from the United States Navy, an historically conservative organization, illustrate the point (though the examples are not immediately current, the principle evidenced is indisputably valid today, as well as being relevant to other issues here discussed, such as implementation of a safety culture as well as a "just" culture encouraging incident reporting).

In 1868 the 4,200 displacement ton vessel *Wampanoag* was commissioned into United States naval service.[201] Her primary propulsion was steam and she was heavily armed for her time. Her performance was praised by her commanding officer and a board of engineers. A year later, *Wampanoag* came under the scrutiny of a board of naval officers appointed by the Secretary of the Navy to report. The philosophical predisposition of the board against steam and in favor of sail was not understated, quoting from their report:

> Lounging through the watches of a steamer, or acting as firemen and coal heavers, will not produce in a seaman that combination of boldness, strength and skill which characterized the American sailor in an elder day; and the habitual exercise by an officer, of a command, the execution of which is not under his own eye, is a poor substitute for the school of observation, promptness and command found only on the deck of a sailing vessel.[202]

But, interpretation of the board's philosophy suggests a realistic concern, one that continues to be manifest more than one hundred years later:

> What these officers were saying was that the *Wampanoag* was a destructive energy in their society. Setting the extraordinary force of her engines against the weight of their way of life, they had a sudden insight into the nature of machinery. They perceived that a machine, any machine, if left to itself, tends to establish its own conditions, to create its own environment and draw men into it. Since a machine, any machine, is designed to do only a part of what a whole man can do, it tends to wear down those parts of a man that are not included in the design.[203]

As a result of the board's report, the otherwise successful *Wampanoag* and fore-runner of the modern warship[204] was laid up in ordinary for a year, then became a receiving ship in New London for some years and eventually was sold out of the Navy. While in this instance, the risk was to a way of life and inculcated beliefs rather than to property or life and limb, the point is that change to the potential benefit of the Navy was not factored in to the decision. Years later, such "risk" successfully was ameliorated by changes introduced into the system after altered circumstances revealed a risk arguably tolerable in the original situation.

Another example: For a period after America's entry into World War II, success of American submarines in the Pacific was frustrated in many instances by the effects of the conservative peacetime training of their commanding officers.[205] That training of officers, superb technicians formally trained as engineers, emphasized conservative tactics and rewarded the ability to remain undetected, even at the expense of operational success. Approved tactics included remaining deeply submerged and torpedo firing on sound bearings alone, whereas surface night attacks were avoided and innovative tactics, such as racing to get ahead of a target, were unknown or frowned upon. With recognition of the problem came "house cleaning." One third of the early war submarine commanding officers were replaced for lack of aggression or failure to sink enemy ships. A "new breed of risk-taking leadership ... made the American submarine a major instrument of victory."[206]

Change as a necessary component of risk assessment is reflected as well in adapting risk management to advances in knowledge and applying that knowledge to operational circumstances. For instance, in 1875 the early iron battleship HMS *Vanguard* was rammed and began to sink. "Abandon ship" was ordered. The order was carried out, with all hands saved. The vessel's captain was found wanting by court martial comprised of wooden ship captains, who believed that measures historically effective in saving wooden vessels would have succeeded to save an iron ship.[207]

Recent satellite measurements by scientists at the Southampton Oceanography Centre, and elsewhere, show that average winter wave heights in the north-east and central Atlantic Ocean and the north Pacific have increased from 2.5 - 3.0 meters to 4.0 – 4.5 meters over the past 30 years, with large waves almost doubling in height. Also, a greater prevalence of "rogue" waves has been found. The significance is that the energy carried by a wave is proportional to the square of its height. Class societies and insurers may rely upon written authority to promulgate rules and set rates, " … but in practice nature hasn't read the text books."[208] This "new awareness" should be of particular concern to passenger ship and container ship operators whose vessels are especially vulnerable to sea conditions, and this concern should be amplified because of container ships' vulnerability to the newly "discovered" phenomenon, parametric rolling. Vessel owners and operators have an obligation toward self-regulation because formal action by regulatory bodies and classification societies has a habit of lagging significantly behind newly available or acquired knowledge. For example, design criteria may have failed to address the dynamic effect of waves of a height that reasonably can be expected to be encountered in a 25 year service life.[209] And the threat posed by waves breaching the wheelhouse by breaking bridge front windows is worthy of consideration. Console components may be vulnerable to failure if soaked by salt water. The tragic consequence of analogous cockpit equipment failure through coffee immersion was depicted in the movie *Fate is the Hunter.*

In the maritime domain there are two primary levels of management – management of vessels and crews from ashore and the management of the on board operations by the master, chief engineer and senior officers. These two managements are distinctively different, as has been judicially noted: "There is a management which is of the shore, and a management which is of the sea."[210] Not surprisingly, there often exists a difference in risk perception between the two.[211] And, between the two, the view (incompatible with the belief in the primacy of the safety climate aboard the vessel) has been expressed that the safety management of a vessel depends upon the perception of risk held by shore side management.[212]

An in-depth study[213] has shown a number of areas in which a difference in risk perception has been found. For instance, managers considered contact with a fixed structure, collision or grounding to be higher risks than the fire or explosion danger emphasized by ship board personnel. This suggests shore side concern over the periods when the vessel's navigation is being directed by a pilot.[214] Managers perceived risk of experiencing an adverse incident twice as likely as did shipboard personnel. Managers with less than two years shore side experience were more inclined to see ship casualty risk considerably higher than managers with more than two years shore side experience. Shore side experience and experience away from ships significantly alters risk perception. Those managers lacking sea experience rated low the likelihood of all types of adverse shipboard incident while those with sea experience rated the likelihood higher. This difference was elsewhere pithily expressed by Terence Coghlin, a former chairman of Thomas Miller & Co., manager of the United Kingdom Protection & Indemnity Club: "Those of us who came to shipping carrying a pen rather than a sextant sometimes forget what a ferocious and unpredictable environment the sea can be."[215]

The study also showed a trend toward more managers with less than five years experience having no sea experience, and illustrates the observation that: "It is extremely difficult if not impossible for someone without command experience to understand and appreciate the problems and concerns of the [ship] master."[216] This suggests an impact upon future shore side perception of shipboard risk, and perhaps highlights a further distinction that management "run risks, but they do not take them."[217]

The willingness to take risk is based in large part upon one's perception of one's ability and historical experience and "information."

One study of mariners (European fishing vessel masters) demonstrates the preeminence of professional situational expertise and self analysis upon addressing risk:

> This willingness to take risks is actually based on genuine craft-style knowledge of resilience, centered on a familiarity with the environment and the ability to anticipate the changes both of this environment and of one's own skill, thus achieving permanent and favorable adequacy [to prevail in the face of the risk]. [218]

This is true even when the perception is incorrect. Therefore, decision making as relates to risk management must focus on perceptions balanced, where possible, by evidence of reality.[219] As a result of the IMO's introduction of safety culture into the maritime domain and requirement that there be appointed one or more "designated persons" to serve as a communicative "bridge" between ships and senior shore side management, a new dimension has been placed upon risk assessment. Owners and operators are denied resort to a Nelson-like "blind eye" defense.[220]

Of course, risk assessment and management requires some understanding of legal responsibility. Frequently, managers lack this knowledge. Two operative concepts here are *due diligence* and *seaworthiness*.

Due diligence refers to a broad requirement that reasonable care be exercised in an undertaking. Surprising to some is the fact that the duty to exercise due diligence is not satisfied fully by obtaining vessel required certificates. Seaworthiness is a vessel's reasonable fitness in all respects for her intended service. Illustrating how these two concepts merge is the experience of the bulk carrier *Great Century* in ice.

The vessel was American Bureau of Shipping classed for "unrestricted" service, but was not ice classed nor built for navigation in ice. Nonetheless, she was routed to a port in Quebec, Canada for February arrival and so would be navigating in ice infested waters and extremely cold weather. The engine personnel were unfamiliar with cold weather and ice related effects upon the ship's engineering systems. Ice clogged the sea suction strainers, reducing inflow of cooling sea water to the point when the generators' overheat protection kicked in and eventually engine power was lost. Neither anchor could let go as each was frozen in by ice, and the drifting vessel shortly thereafter grounded. Reasonable care had not been taken to provide an engineering staff familiar with ice imposed limitations upon the engine and its related systems and the vessel was not reasonably fit for navigation in ice.[221]

More may be required than what currently is customary within the maritime industry. Only if what is customary is "practical and reasonable" may current practice succeed as a defense.[222] However, the defense of "everyone else does it this way" is not likely to prevail where "everyone" is lagging behind what is reasonable: "… a whole calling may have unduly lagged in the adoption of new and available devices ... . [T]here are precautions so imperative that even their universal disregard will not excuse their omission."[223] This principle is not restricted to mechanical devices but rather applies to all aspects where proactive innovation reasonably may be expected. Moreover, the standard of seaworthiness "does not remain the same with advancing knowledge, experience, and the changed appliances of navigation."[224]

Another aspect of managerial responsibility is an ability to foresee certain risks and plan appropriate response for their eventuality. Following the 1994 sinking of the Baltic ferry *Estonia* with 852 fatalities among the 989 persons on board in stormy seas, there was wide spread industry recognition of the difficulty by high sided vessel rescue of people in the water. However, Stena Line, an operator of high sided ferries, " ... despite what was well known about the near impossibility of rescuing a man overboard to a high sided vessel ... Stena had not carried out any appropriate risk assessment of such an emergency."[225]

6

Bridge Resource Management

No officer, whatever his rank and experience, should flatter himself that he is immune to the inexplicable lapses in judgment, calculation, and memory, or to the slips of the tongue in giving orders, which throughout seagoing history have so often brought disaster to men of the highest reputation and ability. Where a mistake in maneuvering or navigating can spell calamity, an officer shows rashness and conceit, rather than admirable self confidence, in not checking his plan with someone else before starting it, if time permits. This is not yielding to another's judgment, it is merely making sure that one's own has not 'blown a fuse' .... — Admiral Chester W. Nimitz, Fleet letter

The mysteriously born tradition of sea-craft commands unity in a body of workers engaged in an occupation in which men have to depend upon each other. — Joseph Conrad[226]

Bridge Resource Management (BRM) may be defined as: the effective use by a vessel's bridge team (officers, crew and pilots) of all available resources – information, equipment and personnel – to safely operate the vessel. ... One of the principles of bridge resource management is that everyone on the bridge should understand his or her responsibilities and be able to freely and professionally communicate observations about the vessel's progress to others on the bridge.[227]

Additionally, BRM was "developed to help mariners recognize and correct operational and human errors before they lead to an accident. ... [and is] a model for effective communications among bridge watchstanders, a means to trap errors, and an aid to decision-making in an operational environment."[228]

In short, BRM is intended to eliminate "one person error." Among the factors that influence the effectiveness of BRM are – the cultural distance between team members, the level of challenge and stress present, differences in "first" languages, and the power distance resulting from the hierarchical distance between or among team members.

Unfortunately, common reference to "Bridge" resource management tends to exclude the engine room. This is a mistake. There are many instances in which engine room personnel necessarily and appropriately are involved, as demonstrated by the 2002 grounding of *Hanjin Dampier.* As the vessel was being piloted to sea, numbers one and two main generators shut down, leaving only number three generator on line. The chief engineer did no more than inform the master in effect that "we need to check the generators and make repairs after we clear the channel ... ." Though the chief knew the vessel was in a narrow channel and so was restricted in her ability to maneuver, and had not yet reached open water, he did not tell the master that two of three generators had shut down nor the consequences and limitations thereby imposed. The pilot was not told of this exchange, so believed all was well in the engine room and ordered "full ahead," though doing so increased the risk of a plant shut down (unknown to him). Shortly thereafter, number three generator's circuit breaker tripped and the main engine shut down, with the ship making about eight knots. The ship's momentum and limited under keel clearance precluded letting go either anchor and, making about six knots, she grounded in mud.

Given his uncertainty regarding what caused the initial loss of two generators and his awareness of the ship's critical navigational situation, the chief engineer should have been more forthcoming with the master and explained the gravity of the engineering situation. Doing so would have allowed the master an opportunity to discuss the situation with the pilot and form a contingency plan, and also would have restrained the pilot from increasing the load upon the ship's electrical system by ordering "full ahead."[229] BRM training cannot be said to be complete without including engine room personnel.[230]

Though BRM generally is referred to as a relatively new concept originating within the aviation industry,[231] reference to principles of BRM appears in the *Treatise on Seamanship and the Duty of a Good Seaman*, written in 1632 by the acclaimed French explorer and mariner Samuel de Champlain:

> The wise and cautious mariner ought not trust too fully to his own judgment, when the pressing need is to take some important step or to deviate from a dangerous course. Let him take counsel with those whom he recognizes as the most sagacious, and particularly with old navigators who have had most experience of disasters at sea and have escaped from dangers and perils, and let him weigh well the reasons they may advance; for it is not often that one head holds everything, ...[232]

BRM focuses less on technical knowledge and skills than upon "non-technical skills of operation,"[233] the cognitive and interpersonal skills necessary to manage an operation. Cognitive skills are mental processes used for gaining, maintaining and assessing situational awareness, problem solving and decision making. Interpersonal skills include communication, cultural sensitivity and a range of behavioral attitudes and activities associated with effective team work.

Over the period 2002-2008, of 126 accidents to which MAIB investigators were deployed, contributing factors in 94 were linked to bridge team management issues.[234] A particularly acute area of BRM concern is the interaction between pilots and the bridge team of master and watch officer.[235]

A 1995 study by the Canadian Transportation and Safety Board reviewed by interview and questionnaire 273 maritime incidents occurring between 1987 and 1992

> [t]o measure teamwork, communication, and to evaluate the master, pilot, and OOW [officer of the watch] relationship. Of the questionnaires distributed, [the return rate was]: 40% pilots, 43% masters, and 16% bridge officers. Approximately 80% of each group responded that communications are 'often' or 'always' effective. When asked if a pilot makes sure his/her orders are understood and acknowledged by the OOW, 84% of pilots responded that this was the case, while only 50% of masters and 50% of OOW agreed with this statement. When asked whether OOW asks for clarification if he/she is unsure of the pilot's intentions, 90% of the OOW, 76% of masters, and only 39% of pilots respond that the OOW 'always' or 'often' asks for clarification. There appears to be a discrepancy here between an individual's self perception of effective communication and other's interpretations of these interactions. When asked whether bridge officers were reluctant to question a pilot's decision: 92% of masters and 81% of bridge officers said 'sometimes,' and 12% of bridge officers said they were 'always' reluctant to question the pilot. These communication issues can often result in errors or accidents.[236]

Informative as are the figures from this study, notice should be taken that it reflects data from more than 15 years ago, prior to implementation of the ISM safety management system and, likely, when there was a lesser presence of Third World masters and bridge officers. This being said, the data illustrate a prevailing tendency to misjudge others' assessment of the effectiveness of pilot – bridge personnel communication.

An overwhelming number of maritime collisions and allisions have occurred when one or both vessels were under the direction of a pilot, some authorities suggesting a factor of 70%.[237]

An issue may arise over just what information should be communicated during the master-pilot exchange. A guide may be recognition that the pilot's "box," relating to specific knowledge of the waters to be transited, is different from the master's "box," which encompasses specific knowledge of his vessel, her handling characteristics and anomalies, and the personalities and qualities of the watch officers and helmsmen with whom the pilot will be interacting. These "boxes" successfully can be merged by an effective master-pilot exchange.[238] Similarly, an effective exchange allows for each to get the "measure" of the other, and some sense of the other's professionalism and perhaps even competence. In one situation, the master stated after an allision that his vessel's tendency to sheer at slow speeds was no more than a "behavior aspect of the ship," so (in his mind) not a safety issue that required disclosure, and "that if the problem arose, one just needed to be focused and react in time."[239] Surely, the master's evaluation expected too much of the pilot and denied the pilot critical information. In another situation, the vessel's "bridge team management was weakened by the whole team accepting, in good faith, the pilot's superior knowledge of not only the estuary, but also his general navigational skills. The master's general navigational skills and knowledge of collision avoidance should be as good as any pilot's, and [the master] should have voiced his concerns at their speed, if not early on in the river passage, most certainly when the other ship was apparent on radar."[240]

The better and more comprehensive the exchange, the better will be the co-ordination and co-operation between the pilot and the bridge team. Among the items that should be discussed is generally the evolution the pilot anticipates. The better the bridge team understands the pilot's intentions in advance, the better will the bridge team be able to monitor and, if necessary, challenge the pilot's direction of the vessel. Ambiguity in this area compromises the bridge team's ability to properly perform its function – the bridge team is responsible for more than merely observing what is going on and has an affirmative duty to participate actively in the navigation of the vessel. That duty was abdicated in the circumstances of the unsuspected touching of the bottom as the laden Indian registered oil tanker *Desh Rakshak* was being piloted from sea toward the Melbourne outer anchorage:

> ... [the pilot] did not set limits at which he should [have been] challenged. The master had allocated some tasks to the bridge team prior to the pilot boarding the ship. The master was to visually monitor the passage, the third mate was to check the ship's position and plot it on the chart, and the cadet was to record the echo sounder readings. However, no one knew when, or if, they should bring information to the attention of the pilot, or challenge his decisions. In effect, the ship's crew observed the pilotage, but they did not actively participate in it.
>
> The evidence does not suggest that any member of the ship's bridge team was aware that the ship was to the west of where

the pilot intended it to be. However, had they been more fully briefed, and fully understood the pilot's plan for the passage, they would have been better placed to assist him.[241]

The problem, as stated in the MAIB investigation report concerning the collision between *Sea Express I* and *Alaska Rainbow*, is that "[i]n a situation where no member of the team is entirely sure which roles other members of the team are carrying out, some of the duties are likely to be either duplicated or missed altogether. In this case, duplication of effort in identifying the landing stage and discussing the 'blind approach' led to *Alaska Rainbow's* presence in the river being missed."[242]

Certainly, BRM issues are not limited to the pilot-bridge team relation, but can proliferate within the vessel's own bridge team, often exacerbated by internal cultural and personality factors. A personality issue among navigating officers in *Quint Star* was a factor in her collision in fog with *Aleksandr Marinesko*. Likely also relevant was "power distance," discussed in Chapter Twelve. *Quint Star's* Japanese master "appears to have been something of a 'stickler.' " The subordinate officers were Vietnamese. In practice, "the master had in the past been angry when called to the bridge," though his standing orders instructed that he be called for any change in weather or if needed. Only the master was permitted to reduce speed. Given the authoritarian personality of many ship masters, this scenario is not likely atypical. Rare would be the nautical reader who has not experienced something similar. The court called upon to resolve liability issues arising out of the collision concluded "the second officer was inhibited from calling the master in fog because of the master's previous attitude." The Trinity House Elder Brother advising the court as an expert unsurprisingly commented that this "was certainly not ... a satisfactory state of affairs."[243]

A breakdown in team performance can result when the "gradient of authority" degenerates, meaning that the superior member of a team has less experience and knowledge than a subordinate member of the team and the superior surrenders control to the subordinate, as happened in 2007 on *Empress of the North*. *Empress* was a passenger vessel cruising in Alaska waters. A third mate newly graduated from a respected maritime academy joined the vessel and, as a result of a sudden illness of a watch officer, was assigned to take over that officer's watch upon joining the vessel. The new officer was unfamiliar with the waters to be transited though his assigned helmsman was "superior to the officer on watch in knowledge, experience, and skill [and] probably in response to the junior third mate's failure to exercise authority over the vessel's navigation, exceeded his own authority by maneuvering the vessel in the absence of commands and, worse, failed to inform the officer of his intentions."[244] The original intention had been that the new officer would observe for seven days before taking a watch. However, when unexpectedly assigned a watch, his understanding was the "[helmsman] would be in control of the boat, and I would be there because I have a license."[245] Without receiving an order to do so, the helmsman commenced a turn that resulted in the vessel taking to the ground.

Numerous maritime casualty investigation reports comment upon one or more failures in areas addressed in conventional BRM courses, strongly suggesting that contemporary BRM instruction falls short in convincing bridge team members to interact among themselves in ways conducive to pulling together effective BRM teams. This discouraging trend is echoed to some extent in the aviation domain, where the Crew Resource Management (CRM) equivalent of BRM has a longer formal history and, arguably, is more widely accepted.[246]

There can be several explanations. A significant number of mariners and pilots, maritime and aviation, simply refuse to "buy in" to BRM or CRM.[247] Also, BRM and CRM have been found to not export well. Despite the many advantages of BRM, because BRM teaches "Western" cultural views and "Western" understanding of human interactions, there must be recognition that, as in aviation's CRM counterpart, there is a "marked difference" from the "Western" culture in how BRM training is perceived by non-Western cultures and is implemented in practice.[248] The way in which the people of one culture "think, feel and act" cannot be changed merely by "importing foreign institutions."[249]

Additionally, initial acceptance of basic BRM principles may diminish over time. People, despite training, tend to revert to past familiar practices and attitudes, especially within the context of a traditional hierarchical command structure and where there may be a perceived lack of managerial support for core BRM principles. Training, intended to enhance overall performance, stretched to include unlicensed personnel may dilute the specificity necessary to alter behavior. And, proceduralization of BRM may be seen as marginalizing BRM to being just one more rule, regulation, policy or procedure imposed from without and the training seen as merely "checking off a box." There remains uncertainty, even disagreement, over all factors that influence group based behavior and there may be a false sense that redundancy in humans replicates redundancy in systems. In fact, "[r]edundancy in people is not the same as mechanical redundancy where true redundancy can be achieved with independent parallel systems."[250]

Not least, underlying a policy of team based interaction support often is a form of skepticism about the ability of co-workers individually to perform appropriately and adequately, which team members may perceive as management mistrust.

Numerous steps can be taken to maximize positive reception and retention of BRM principles. The training should be audience specific, and reflect the national and organizational culture as well as the operational issues of the involved personnel. BRM should be advertised by senior management as more than merely a procedural necessity, and its core principle of enhancing safety by reducing the potential for disastrous one person error emphasized. Senior management should know and address the personality of senior shipboard officers as those officers have the power to exacerbate or mitigate an adverse onboard safety climate and to introduce positive or negative behavior and practices. There is no exaggeration in recognizing that "[a]t the ship level, the master can exacerbate or mitigate the adverse effects of high level decisions, but the master can introduce other pathogens into the system"[251]And, certainly the degree to which effective BRM practices are followed or not is a reflection of on board professionalism.

A worthwhile study of numerous BRM breakdown issues is provided from the February 7, 2009 grounding of the 29,266 gross ton Hong Kong registered products tanker *Atlantic Blue* on Kirkcaldie Reef, Torres Strait, Australia.[252]The waters of the Torres Strait are shallow and strewn with small islets, reefs, shoals and island clusters. Also, the area is fraught with potentially strong tidal currents. Navigation there is especially challenging.

The vessel was equipped in conformity with SOLAS,[253] with paper charts in use as ECDIS was not required. Because the vessel's destination unexpectedly was changed, two charts necessary for the Torres Strait transit were brought by the compulsory coastal pilot, who boarded at 2200 the day before the grounding.

The second officer immediately began marking the planned courses on the large scale chart. The pilot also provided voyage notes for the master and mates. The 123 mile eastbound transit was expected to require 9.5 hours, and was discussed between the pilot and master. The pilot used visual cues and glanced in the starboard radar instead of using his ECS and GPS-equipped laptop computer. The watch officer plotted the vessel's position on the large scale chart every five minutes.

At 0130 the vessel was put on a heading and course line of 066 degrees True, within the charted two-way traffic lane, but without any allowance being made either for the prevailing 25 knot northwesterly wind abaft the port beam or for an approximately east by south flowing 0.8 knot tidal current. The wind drift and tidal set resulted in a course being made good of 070 degrees True. The pilot then marked on the chart a long line, with an outward pointing arrow at each end, roughly perpendicular to the charted 066 degree course line and marked it "PCP" (please call pilot) "in case [the pilot] inadvertently dozed off."[254]

At about 0230 the master left the bridge, advising the second officer that he would return within about 20 minutes, after checking emails. He did not return as he said he would, however.

By 0235 the vessel was one nautical mile south of the course line and outside the traffic lane. The second officer informed the pilot of this fact. Kirkcaldie Reef, marked with a flashing light and RACON, was then about 8.5 miles ahead, fine on the port bow. At that time, the course to steer, allowing for set and drift, toward the charted way point was 053 degrees True. Instead, at 0237, 0246 and 0256 the pilot directed small course adjustments to port, resulting in a heading of 059 degrees True. These small adjustments put the reef fine on the starboard bow but were insufficient to return the vessel to her track line. So, *Atlantic Blue* continued to close with the reef. When at 0307 a charted outcropping of the reef was one mile ahead, the pilot initiated further heading alterations to port but they were "too little too late," and at 0312 the bow struck a sandy shoal, nearly one mile south of the charted 066 degree course line. The vessel refloated several hours later on the rising tide, without having suffered damage.

The PCP line was about 2.8 miles west of the critical area represented by Kirkcaldie Reef and "is intended to allow the pilot enough time to assess the situation and take [all] action necessary for the ship's continued safe progress."[255] Given the ship's position south of her course line and her then position relative to Kirkcaldie Reef, emergency action was required to clear the danger presented by the reef. No such action was taken, however.

Effective management and utilization of all available resources – human as well as technical – are required to maximize the likelihood of safe completion of the passage and to minimize the chance for one-person error. This need is magnified in pilotage areas because of smaller safety margins due to factors generally including an abundance of navigational hazards, reduced depths and widths of navigable waters, increased traffic, tidal height and current effect, and cultural difference (*Atlantic Blue*'s officer complement was Indian and the pilot Australian). Also, in pilotage waters most decisions are made by one person – the pilot. Here, an accurately shared mental model takes on added importance.

Atlantic Blue's progress along the 066 degree course line should have been more closely monitored. Track monitoring was limited to visual, radar/RACON on the reef despite those aids being fine on the bow and so of diminished accuracy when used to obtain a plotted position, GPS and the pilot's occasional radar glances.

The pilot failed to use his ECS and GPS-equipped laptop, from which he would have gained improved situational awareness. The second officer could have programmed the ship's GPS by setting course alteration positions (way points) allowing for bearing and distance display to successive waypoints as well as highlighting off-track error. However, the master had instructed the second officer to not do so because track and limit lines on the radar display "might confuse the pilot." A result was disablement of automated alerts of deviation from planned tracks.[256] Nor was any other notification provided addressing any maximum acceptable off-track distance. The PCP line fell short of declaring what the pilot may have considered an allowable off-track distance. The pilot expected the ship's bridge team (which, after the master's 0230 departure, lacked the master) to inform him if the ship were "sufficiently off course so as to run into danger."[257] Depending upon the involved officers' experience, training and knowledge, as well as upon cultural and authoritarian issues, such optimistic dependence on the part of a pilot may well be unrealistic or otherwise expect too much. *Atlantic Blue*'s pilot believed that "irrespective of the fact that specific off-track limits were not specified, it was readily ascertainable for the second mate and master to determine whether the ship was off track." Quite true, but the ship's bridge team could reasonably believe that the pilot was piloting upon the strength of his local knowledge and normal practices.[258] A fatal disconnect resulted between the mental models held, respectively, by the pilot and by the second officer.

After 0130, the pilot intermittently checked the radar and saw the second officer plotting positions "but did not look at the chart to check what these positions were indicating" and the second officer "on watch thought that the pilot was aware of the ship's progress but the bridge team had not discussed or defined off-track

limits[,] but did not bring this [off-track information to
the pilot's] attention [and] he thought that the pilot was
aware [from the radar] that the ship was moving south
of and away from the charted track."[259] This disconnect
illustrates the danger of *presuming* that another member
of the bridge team is in fact pro-actively evaluating,
participating and communicating toward the shared
objective of effecting a safe passage and illustrates as
well the phenomenon characteristic of groups, that
there may be "social loafing" by one or more members.
Task related dialogue can minimize degrading team
performance from social loafing.

The second officer did inform the pilot at 0235 that
the ship was one mile south of the course line. However,
he appears to have failed to mention the effect of set
and drift, as well as the presence of the reef ahead. He
may have been seduced into silence by the fact that the
pilot, in response, did order course alterations to port,
albeit insignificant, and showed no evidence of concern
or alarm and, further, the fact that the pilot had given
a ready explanation when the second and third officers
had challenged the pilot's course selection earlier in the
transit.[260] This suggests the presence of confirmation
bias. Still, the second officer should have appreciated
that the pilot's small course changes at and shortly after
0237 were inadequate for the situation presented by
the reef ahead. He also should have realized that a call
to the absent master (whose return to the bridge had
been expected some ten minutes earlier) was warranted.
He would have been more comfortable communicating
with the pilot through the master, with whose style and
personality he was familiar. With a new bridge team
member – the pilot – present, the watch officer likely
would have difficulty taking the initiative in the absence
of the master.[261] Authoritative communication with the
pilot in an impending dangerous situation would have

been easier through the master.

Of particular concern is the extent to which the "state of the bridge" had degraded. "No [bridge] team member had comprehended the increasingly serious situation while [degradation] was developing or had suspected what was about to happen. The state of the bridge could be described as being inattentive at a critical phase."[262]

Several factors contributed to this gradually degraded attentiveness. By 0130 early critical areas of the transit, with small safety margins, had been cleared. For the 1.5 hour period until closing with Kirkcaldie Reef, the way was clear of navigational hazards. This brought about a sense of relaxation and relief following a period of relatively tense concentration.

> At this stage, navigation did not require as high a level of the pilot's attention than it had in the preceding [3.5] hours. Now with less stimulation after the long period of nearly continuous concentration, [the pilot's] level of arousal probably reduced. A moderate arousal level is associated with optimal performance and too high or too low arousal levels with a decline in performance. The relationship between performance and arousal, known as the Yerkes-Dodson law, probably contributed to a decline in the pilot's performance after the ship entered the more open waters ... .[263]

A lessening of one's guard can be expected under such circumstances. The second officer easily could have been lulled toward complacency when he realized that after 0130 the pilot had reduced his own workload to occasional glances at the radar and could have interpreted the master's departure from the bridge as indicating that the ship was in safe waters. He also assumed the pilot accepted as safe the ship's position relative to the course line, though he did state that "had the pilot not been on the bridge, [the second officer] would have kept the ship within 2 cables [0.2 nautical mile] of the planned track."[264] This statement by the second officer reflects the common but erroneous belief that the pilot is responsible for the ship's safety and is aware of every aspect of the ship's situation.

The pilot failed to give proper deference to the second officer's warning because the pilot's situational awareness was inadequate, in part because he expected the local Vessel Traffic Service to advise him if the vessel strayed from the two-way traffic lane. The master, off the bridge, was unaware of the deteriorating situation and had given email traffic priority over ensuring the safety of his vessel. The second officer by 0312, when the ship struck, had been awake for more than 16 hours, for more than 10 of which he was working on the bridge or busy with drills. Fatigue was for him a likely issue, resulting in a decline in his task performance. A false sense of security prevailed over all.

7

Nature of Error

Over the past several decades substantial improvement has occurred in marine technology and engineering, resulting in significant decrease in casualties attributable to these factors. This, in turn, has resulted in an increase in the relative proportion of human and organizational errors determined to have been factors, with the latter category escalating as the realm[265] of human error has become more closely analyzed. Currently a combination of human and organizational error is deemed to be a factor in about 80% of maritime casualties. Studies have broken down this contribution by casualty type: 89-96% of collisions; 75% of fires and explosions; 79% of towing vessel groundings; 84-88% of tanker casualties; and, 75% of allisions. In a study of 268 casualties to Greek flagged vessels over 500 gross tons from 1993 to 2006 investigated by the Hellenic Coast Guard, the human element was found responsible for 57.1% of those casualties. Of that percentage, 78.7% was on board error, 12.6% ashore error, and 8.9% a combination of the two.[266]

The concept of human error over the past decade or so has undergone a quantum shift.

In the "old" view, human error was seen as a consequence of the inherent unreliability of individuals operating within basically safe systems or safe environments. Human error in this context has been defined as:

... there were mistakes. Mistakes of the kind that all men are liable to make on occasions. Seeing what they expect to see, not seeing what they should see, failing to recognize a mistake in a colleague, reacting too late, or not at all, in the face of the unexpected. ... in every case, the consequences of the mistake were eminently avoidable. They were not avoided because those in charge remained quite unaware .. until too late ... .[267]

An all too common but illustrative example is the verbal "slip," resulting in the tanker *Julia N* colliding with a raised drawbridge span. The ship handled well and was piloted as usual with various rudder commands being given. Approaching the draw, the pilot thought back to an earlier incident when one of the bridge leaves was contacted by another tanker, with substantial damage. The pilot commented,

[I] picked the middle of the channel, and when I felt I was in the shape that I wanted to be, I wanted to come hard to *starboard*, half ahead. It came out hard to port. When the captain repeated hard to port, it took me I don't know how long, I said to myself, 'I don't want that.' Then I realized ... calling for 'port, port, port, port,' I said 'hard to port' instead of 'hard to starboard'.[268]

One may wonder at such a slip, but need look no farther for explanation than Fleet Admiral Chester Nimitz, who observed, "No officer, regardless of rank, should flatter himself that he is immune to the inexplicable lapses in judgment and slips of the tongue which had led many fine officers to disaster."[269]

Under the old view, safety would be enhanced by dealing with the human component through reprimand, retraining or replacement. A striking example of such human element analysis being misapplied was showcased after the watch officer on a large passenger vessel, in an effort to counter a turn not ordered, disengaged the automatic steering mode of the vessel's sophisticated integrated navigation system and took manual control. The ultimate result was the vessel heeling about 24 degrees to starboard, causing people to be tossed about or struck by unsecured objects. There were 14 serious and 284 minor personal injuries. The president of the cruise line publicly stated that "personnel changes have been made."[270] In fact, the major contributing factor was found to have been improper training of the senior bridge personnel.[271]

Relying upon broadly accepted conventional wisdom that 75% or more of maritime casualties are "due" to the human element, an analysis by three human factor experts concluded that "any *attempts* to reduce accidents at sea should concentrate on eliminating errors *on board ships*, since this is where the problem is greatest and where the biggest improvements should be made."[272] Not surprisingly, this "old" view of error caters to our cultural and psychological norms that include a blame mentality and belief that individuals can, should and will be made to control their behavior.

The "new" more enlightened view sees human error as a symptom of one or more shortcomings within the system within which the individual functions, and human error not itself usually a cause of failure. The error arises from the nature, design or constraints of the system, such as inherent conflicts or contradictions between or among multiple goals the operator must simultaneously pursue.[273]

This view has grown from a 1947 study of how the layout in World War II aircraft cockpits influenced the way in which pilot error occurred; for example, wing flap and landing gear handles were situated close to each other, and looked and felt similar. The study initiated and played into understanding *why* individuals perform as they do.

Human error in the context of this study looks to the functioning of humans in their professional capacity as mariners, and how and why they act as they do to accomplish their respective responsibilities, whether as licensed senior officers, watch keepers or unlicensed personnel performing more mundane but safety critical tasks. In the course of their activities, mariners: resolve conflicts, anticipate hazards, accommodate unexpected variation and change, work around obstacles, close gaps between plans and reality, and detect and compensate for faulty assessment and miscommunication, all within a less than optimal environment imposed by man and nature. Also considered are factors influencing the interplay between shore side management and the shipboard personnel as management strives to mitigate error and its consequences.

In the main, these, and similar, impediments to task accomplishment are successfully surmounted. But sometimes not, as a result of some species of error, a term not used here judgmentally. And lest "error" be considered too harshly, several threshold facts are worth noting.

First, practitioners, whether mariners or in other fields, overwhelmingly intend to do well the job they are charged with performing, and they intend to do so successfully, efficiently, professionally and within their employer's operating perimeter. They do so by drawing upon and applying their individual personalities as well as their experience, training and education. But there are limits upon their experience, training and education, as well as limits upon the information available to them and perhaps limits upon their assimilation of that information, and they may be confronting multiple simultaneous conflicting goals, with time often being tight. Also,

There are certain psychological factors which have fully as much to do with safety at sea as any of the more strictly technical ones. A large proportion of the disasters in tactics and maneuvers comes from concentrating too much on one objective or urgency, at the cost of not being sufficiently alert for others. … preoccupation with navigation, with carrying out the particular job in hand, or with avoiding some particular vessel or hazard has resulted in collision with ships to whose presence we were temporarily oblivious. There is no rule that can cover this except the ancient one that eternal vigilance is the price of safety, no matter what the immediate distraction.[274]

What may appear inexplicable after the fact may have been quite rational in the mind of the actor given the then existing circumstances. Errors do not always look like errors when committed, and the casualties that follow may look impossible beforehand.

Awareness of this "local rationality" should be maintained when judging behavior as well as when managing future activity. Such objective awareness of local rationality – the actor's knowledge in context, mindset and attempt to honor interacting goals – goes a long way toward explaining the "how" and "why" of an event.

"Knowledge in context" refers to what knowledge is possessed and is relevant to the system or situation – is the knowledge complete, correct, easy to process or is it "buggy?" Is the knowledge, or information, adaptable to the specific situation or is it not associative? Does relevant knowledge readily come to mind and can the actor apply it to the situation? For example, lack of ship specific knowledge was cited as a problem by 78% of mariners surveyed in one Coast Guard study.[275] But, mere possession at one time of domain knowledge does not alone make one competent in that domain. One may be reminded of Joseph Conrad's Captain MacWhirr in the short story "Typhoon":

> The wisdom of his country had pronounced by means of an Act of Parliament that before he could be considered as fit to take charge of a ship he should be able to answer certain simple questions on the subject of circular storms such as hurricanes, cyclones, typhoons; and apparently he had answered them, since he was now in command of the *Nan-Shan* in the China seas during the season of typhoons. But if he had answered he remembered nothing of it.

"Mindset" refers to "attention," recognized as a limited resource necessarily allocated on a priority basis between information input and demands of varying importance. The attention demands escalate as the task becomes more difficult or as the level of demanded performance increases.[276] At the same time, the actor must remain sensitive to new stimuli from the unfolding event(s). This tracking goes forward, but because attention and information absorption is limited, a basic challenge exists: where to focus attention and what is the proper balance between the task at hand and stimuli from outside the current focused mindset. These latter stimuli may be irrelevant to the task at hand – a distraction, triggered by inattentiveness or ignored because the source is a nuisance alarm or a false alarm. Particularly relevant to discussion of the watch keeper's mindset is "situational awareness."

"Goal conflicts" addresses multiple goals simultaneously competing around the task at hand. The challenge is to prioritize and balance between or among these conflicting goals with the limited resources available by effective planning. And, to be sure, though difficult to establish documentarily, economic pressure is omni-present, as ships make money while underway but not while lying idle in port.[277] For example, in 1967 the tanker *Torrey Canyon*, rushing to catch high water, stranded on the Scilly Isles, a casualty that was forebearer of maritime pollution concern. In her loaded condition, a five day delay would have resulted if she failed to catch high water.[278] Where conflicting goals are anticipated, guidance in unequivocal language from management as to proper priorities may be necessary and appropriate.

An illustrative analysis of an erroneous thinking process is provided by a Dutch social scientist. Some years ago, four seamen were cleaning No. 6 cargo hold of a Dutch freighter at sea. Suddenly the bulkhead between holds 5 and 6 collapsed. The four men were hit by a 6,000 ton wall of seawater, and three drowned. Investigation showed that, unknown to the crew, No. 5 hold had flooded and the weight and pressure of the seawater had overwhelmed the bulkhead.

The ship had sailed with No. 4 hold intentionally ballasted with seawater. In heavy weather, an undetected leak had sprung in the bulkhead between holds 4 and 5, allowing the ballast water to enter hold No. 5. The mate realized that hold No. 4 was losing seawater but also recognized that the ballast pump in No. 4 inadvertently had been left open so instead of pumping into No. 6 as part of the intended cleaning process the mate believed No. 4 was being pumped. As a result, he pumped into No. 4 despite the physical improbability that the low power ballast pump could have emptied No. 4 to the extent the mate was filling No. 4. But the open valve in No. 4 provided a hypothesis for the mate's conviction and the missing water confirmed the hypothesis and conviction, though each would have been dispelled if the mate had calculated the respective volumes of water into and out from No. 4. But, doing so would have required "work" or thinking, or both, and studies show that individuals tend not to think a problem through if a simpler hypothesis (especially if correct in past and an arguably similar situation) presents and, further, that individuals prefer to accept hypotheses when confirming information is present, without critically testing the hypothesis or confirming information. In fact, the 3,300 tons of water lost from No. 4 were replaced by almost 6,600 tons, almost the total capacity of No. 4, with that water migrating into No. 5 through the undetected bulkhead breach. The same article describing the ballasting accident pointed out that in a study of 100 accidents at sea between 1982 and 1985, false hypotheses were present in 51 of the accidents.[279] The concept of false hypotheses, in one form or another, runs through the subject of this book.

A widely accepted breakdown of how individuals approach task performance comes from the work of James Reason and Jens Rasmussen. Their analysis, while not the exclusive study of why or how humans commit errors, has the virtue of simplicity and directness, and combines cognitive and practically oriented non-cognitive considerations. Though other more intricate models suggest greater empirical accuracy, the breadth and depth of human behavior variability diminish the latters' advantage over the simpler Reason-Rasmussen analysis accepted for this discussion.

The Reason-Rasmussen analysis views human tasks as falling within one of three performance levels: Skill-based; Rule-based; and, Knowledge- based, named in ascending order of cognitive demand.[280] Of course, the work environment influences performance in a much more complex manner than through the information domain alone including, as it does, performance conditioning factors related to affective and motivating aspects of the work as well as physiological factors.

Least cognitively demanding is *skill-based* performance. Here, activity is accomplished at an almost subconscious level and performance is governed by stored patterns of reaction to the triggering situation, which the actor has experienced so frequently in type that relevant familiarity and reaction virtually are simultaneous and automatic through stored patterns of behavior. An example could be driving on the right (at least in certain countries, including the United States). An error at this level may be a "slip," where one or more incorrect actions are performed as the result of inattention, such as "daydreaming," or distraction, or a "lapse," the omission of one or more steps in a sequence as the result of forgetting some piece of information or how to perform the activity. "Mistakes," those errors where the human did what was intended but the intended action was incorrect, are reserved for other performance levels.

Rule-based performance, the intermediate level of performance, reacts to familiar situations in which resolution is governed by stored rules that function in the alternative: *if* [as the situation is defined] = *then* [the correct resolution is drawn upon and effected from the stored "rules"]. The more often the situation is repeated, the more ingrained becomes the accepted response, so increasingly less active attention is paid to the situation and its evolution. Depending upon the situation and its evolution, response increasingly may approach skill-based performance. An example would be a vessel crossing from one's own starboard side [the *if*] and the actor recognizing that he is obligated under the COLREGS to keep clear if risk of collision is present [the *then*]. This basic situation becomes more complicated and demanding, and hence approaches more demanding levels of performance, if instead of clear visibility there is restricted visibility. Errors at this level typically are mis-classifying the situation, resulting in applying the wrong rule, or incorrectly recalling the appropriate rule-based response. The border between skill and rule-based performances is not distinct other than that rule-based performance can be verbalized through explicit "know-how."

Knowledge-based performance, most cognitively demanding, is called upon in novel, unfamiliar situations, where successful resolution requires "thinking" out and implementing some original situation specific plan. There must be analysis and decision based upon knowledge and understanding of all factors relevant to the situation as well as prioritization of various goals necessary for successful resolution. That resolution, successful or not, depends upon the actor's "mental model" of the situation. Successful examples include United Airlines DC-10 landing at Sioux City after losing hydraulic power and the salvage by *Cherry Valley* of a valuable barge on a lee shore. At this level, errors arise from incomplete or incorrect knowledge reflected in the mental model, with time usually an inhibiting factor.[281] The border between rule and knowledge-based performance is where training no longer is sufficient and success depends upon education. This distinction is clarified by the expression: "you train for certainty and educate for uncertainty."

From a managerial as well as operational perspective, the point to be aware of is that usually the mind will attempt to think as little as possible. This is not necessarily a mark of laziness but rather of the mind's attempt to conserve its limited attention resources. For this reason, increasing emphasis is being placed on checklists as aids to performance.

With the above groundwork laid for understanding human error, consideration can be given to influences upon human error. Expressed somewhat differently and emphasizing the effect that managerial decisions have upon human error, the issue can be addressed as the prediction of human error through "human error probabilities" (HEP) that have been studied in the psychology and cognitive sciences communities. These HEPs have been found to be readily influenced by Performance Shaping Factors (PSFs) and by Management and Organizational Factors (MOFs).[282] These PSFs and MOFs also serve to give definition to the "holes" that represent breaches in the defenses conceptualized in the previously discussed Swiss Cheese Model.

The influence of PSFs and MOFs upon human error in the context of maritime casualty analysis can be projected through a hierarchical process, a methodology developed for solving multi-attribute decision problems using a combination of informed judgment and expert opinion to measure the relative value or contribution of these factors and then to synthesize a solution.[283]

While this list is not intended to be exclusive, Performance Shaping Factors determined to be significant contributors maritime casualty human error include:

> **Inattention:** failure to exercise full vigilance or the vigilance exercised is lost through distraction.
>
> **Lack of Motivation:** there is insufficient desire to perform tasks appropriately.
>
> **Poor Physical Condition:** fatigue, lack of physical fitness, adverse health issues.
>
> **Poor Performance Ability:** insufficient training, education, aptitude and experience.
>
> **Inadequate knowledge of rules, regulations, policies and procedures.**
>
> **Conflicting Performance Motives:** confusion over conflicting priorities to be applied in task performance – protection versus profitability, schedule or safety – to give a

couple of examples, generally attributable top management "doublespeak."

Poor Ergonomics: poor vessel design features and awkward interface between humans and integrated systems – personified by the cliché that those who design the ships rarely sail them.

Inadequate Situational Awareness: discussed in the following Chapter.

Faulty Exchange of Information: relative to issues important ashore or on board, or both.

Blurred Areas of Responsibility: failure to know what tasks must be performed or lines of responsibility/authority are unclear or not defined.

Hazardous Natural Environment: Joseph Conrad's accurate description of the sea as "never ... friendly to man" together with the transition from open waters to congested and challenging port areas.[284]

The above PSFs are directly or indirectly influenced by Management and Organizational Factors, with the MOFs being influenced by the company's safety culture, so much so that the safety culture is not treated as an independent variable but merges into the MOFs. MOFs that significantly affect PSFs and less directly influence Human Error Probabilities include:

Workload: hours on duty relative to the tasks to be accomplished and relative to personnel physical and mental well being.

Formalization: well articulated rules, regulations, policies and procedures for handling or responding to routine and emergency situations.

Work Coordination: for efficient accomplishment of tasks.

Organizational Culture: the safety culture of the organization.

Benefits: salary, insurance and other employee enhancements as a component of the company's overall allocation of financial resources.

Physical Resources: completeness and ready availability of physical assets necessary or helpful to accomplishing tasks.

Quality of life: the living quarters and work area compatibility with human needs.

Performance Evaluation: people want to know by way of fair communicated assessment how well they are "fitting in" and performing their work related responsibilities.

Company Programs; a corollary to "quality of life," in the nature of company supported alcohol and drug interdiction programs, and fitness, health and related programs. These could be expanded to include programs to facilitate communication by phone or otherwise with distant family members.

Personnel Selection: hiring for training, education, experience and compatibility to perform the necessary tasks.

Personnel Turnover: does the company assign personnel with a view to their familiarity with a ship and its equipment.

Training Programs: quality and extent of training undertaken by the company.

Supervision: is the level of oversight commensurate with what is necessary or desirable – is there absentee oversight suggesting indifference or micro-managing.

Time Urgency: extent to which maintaining a schedule is stressed over safety.

Organizational Learning: extent to which the company endeavors to learn from past incidents to improve safety.

Communication: whether the important communicative link is maintained between ship and shore.

The Human Error Probabilities that are manifest in the job performance of the watch officer include:

Failure to Initiate and Carry Out Plans Properly: including updating and referring to publications without error, faulty chart work, failing to determine safe waypoints, and failing to lay down safe course lines.

Failure of Master to Detect and Correct Navigational Errors.

Failure Correctly to Read Radar Ranges.

Faulty Chart Plotting: of bearings/distances.

Failure to Order Proper and Timely Course Change.

Failure to Drop Anchor as Necessary: there is the apocryphal story that no navigator should ever run around with an anchor still in its hawsepipe.

Failure to Request Assistance in an Emergency.

The preceding Brown and Haugene assessment demonstrates the safety resulting from adherence to proper MOFs by stating that a maritime organization with its MOFs "adequate" has a 93.1% reduced probability of a tanker grounding compared to an organization with its MOFs "inadequate." An organization with "excellent" MOFs shows a 99.55% reduction.[285] Of course, these data are readily extrapolated into other maritime vessel operations.

The objective of maritime safety management is to determine and implement the most effective defenses to, and traps of, those types of error that most significantly contribute to maritime casualties, as well as initiating strategies oriented toward finding and mitigating latent hazardous conditions. For this objective to be attained, as much as possible needs to be known about error and understood about precursors and predictors of error. This is complicated by the complexity of the interrelated components of the shipboard environment and challenges to effective management from afar. This endeavor is assisted by recourse to human error analysis models proven most relevant to the maritime domain.[286]

The Reason Swiss Cheese Model efficiently depicts the error chain in a descriptive, but non-analytical, manner. For the model to be practical and useful in practice, some definition needs to be given to the latent and active failure "holes" in the "cheese." Such definition has been developed in the aviation domain as a means for analyzing human causes of aviation accidents through a Human Factors Analysis and Classification System (HFACS). HFACS is the result of analysis of "hundreds of [aviation] accident reports containing thousands of human causal factors."[287] Specifically, HFACS, first fielded in 1997 by the aviation branches of the United States Navy and Marine Corps, gives definition at each of the four levels of failure (working backward from the accident) corresponding to Reason's unsafe acts, preconditions for unsafe acts, unsafe supervision and organizational influences.

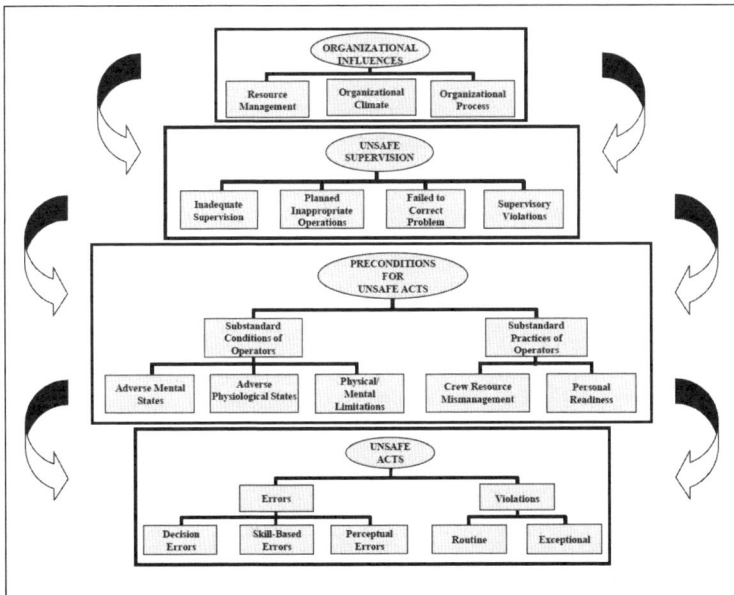

Figure 2. Overview of the Human Factors Analysis and Classification System. *From Department of Defense.*

Closest to the casualty is the category "unsafe acts" of the operator/watch officer. These are singular or a combination of acts, omissions or decisions that contribute to the casualty or magnify its consequences, or both. These "unsafe acts" may be among four types, three relating to Reason's three performance levels. Skill based errors are those occurring during the least cognitively challenging skill-based performance. Decision errors occur during rule-based performance, where the chosen "rule" is inadequate or inappropriate to the situation. "Perceptual errors" refers not specifically to knowledge-based performance but rather to when the action is based upon imperfect or incomplete information. The forth "unsafe act" category is "violations," reserved for separate discussion in Chapter Ten.

The next ascending level is "preconditions for unsafe acts," with three categories. One category, "condition of operators," mentions "adverse mental states," such as mental fatigue and pernicious mental states such as over-confidence, complacency and misdirected motivation. "Adverse psychological states" includes illness, intoxication and, increasingly noteworthy, a variety of pharmacological issues.[288] "Physical and/or mental limitations" includes the objective lack of necessary sensory information or the subjective inability to process information correctly. The second category is "personal factors" and refers to bridge resource management skills and personal readiness to handle the tasks to be undertaken. The third category is "environmental factors," consisting of the physical and technological environment within which the tasks are to be performed. The physical environment refers to the external operational environment, such as prevailing weather and visibility conditions, and the internal ambient environment, such as vibration, ship's motion, noise, and heat or cold. The technological environment also is separately discussed in Chapter Eleven.

The third level, "unsafe supervision," refers to latent failures attributable to four issues, including "inadequate supervision," meaning that subordinates are denied appropriate training, mentoring, oversight and operational leadership. "Planned inappropriate operations" refers to an excessive pace of operations that puts the venture at risk. An example of such a situation is a pace of container handling so fast and with details planned ashore that the cargo officer has little control or influence (and sometimes even knowledge, until after the vessel has sailed) over the placement of containers on board in relation to the containers' respective weights and contents. This frequent situation has been elaborated upon:

> In this environment, where speed of operations is the imperative, the chief [cargo] officer is unlikely to have the necessary influence to be able to stop or slow the operation while he makes a detailed check of all aspects of the stowage plan or of individual containers. Without such a check, it is inevitable that errors made during the planning/loading process will be undetected.[289]

"Failure to correct recognized problems" is self-explanatory. The danger lies not only in the uncorrected problems but in also the "if they don't care, why should I care" mentality that follows. And, "supervisory violations" is reserved for situations where supervisors willfully disregard established rules, regulations, policies and procedures. Here also there is collateral effect in that such disregard encourages subordinates to similarly violate rules, regulations, policies and procedures.

Atop the HFACS frame is "organizational influences." "Resource management," represents the imbalance between demands front line actors face and the resources available to meet those demands.

The "organizational climate" equates well with the safety culture and safety climate relation previously discussed. And "operational processes" is a catch-all reference to essentially those practices by which the organization conducts its business. These are significant categories as there tends to be lack of management awareness over the implications of organizational policies.[290]

For a feel for the type of information HFACS is capable of providing, United States data were culled from the commercial air industry for the period 1992-2002, with 1020 "accidents" emerging. Of these 1020 accidents, the majority were categorized within the "unsafe acts" level. Just over one half were associated with at least one skill-based error, followed by decision errors (36.7%), rule/regulation/policy/procedure violation (23.1%) and perceptual errors (7%).[291] This demonstrates the usefulness of HFACS in deconstructing human error and differentiating among skill-based, rule-based and knowledge-based error. From this, though the timing and aggregate number of errors cannot be predicted, familiarity with the practices of a particular operation (LNG, oil tanker, break bulk or container vessel, for example) and the trading pattern followed, allows general prediction of the type of error most likely in a particular situation. This approach to risk management is validated through the fact that "[i]n the aftermath of catastrophes, it is common to find prior indicators, missed signals, and dismissed alerts, that, had they been recognized and appropriately managed before the event, might [well] have averted the undesired event."[292] Risk management then can be directed toward that eventuality. Informed analysis of HFACS data opens the door to developing and answering the crucial "why" question that underlies "what" happened. If the "what" is a bad decision, accident prevention needs to know why and how that bad decision came to be made – was it due to fatigue, insufficient knowledge, too little time, other explanations or some combination?

However, while HFACS provides an analytical framework, HFACS of itself does not answer underlying questions. HFACS sees the casualty through hindsight and also through a classification that is judgmental in the sense that two people, especially if coming from different disciplinary backgrounds, are unlikely to see a particular error in exactly the same light. But these reservations should not diminish the fact that HFACS serves the valuable function of giving definition to the error chain and to the "holes" in the "Swiss Cheese" defenses against error and its consequences.

Having discussed conceptualization of error, we are ready to discuss the watch officer's task of conducting the watch under way. Past the point of vigilance, the watch officer's task is to decide courses of action necessary to accomplish watch related objectives and to implement those decisions through his or her handling of the vessel. This handling of the vessel can be broken into three discrete stages: plan, advance[293] and execute. Of course, throughout this process any one or several of the skill, rule and knowledge-based performance levels will be engaged, and the performance potentially be influenced by one or more of the human factors discussed previously.

In the "plan" stage, there is initial perception of a situation that may develop into something requiring more than simple monitoring. Absent anything out of the regular, the performance level will be skill-based and identifying the objective to be attained may be done at no more than the semi-subconscious level. As the situation develops, relevant information is gathered and preliminary evaluation of that information begins. The performance level begins to press toward or into the rule-based level. Situational awareness commences, as does a growing assessment of which objectives, among possibly several, are consistent with the situation. The question becomes: is the incoming information (whether obtained personally or second hand through technology) accurate, is it likely to be sufficiently complete, and is the interpretation accurate? At this stage, the watch officer is most likely to be checking for error, even if only sub-consciously, with the warning perhaps being no more than a "gut" feeling that something may be amiss.[294]

At the "advance" stage, there is further and more refined augmentation, sifting and analysis of information deemed relevant to the situation and objective. The objective ripens into decision as to how the chosen objective is to be achieved. At this stage, likely at the rule-based or knowledge-based level, any error is most likely knowable to only the watch officer as the decision maker.[295]

The final stage is "execute," at which the decision is put into effect.

Further meaningful insight into the magnitude of error occurring in the three above described stages can be derived through another HFACS study[296] undertaken in the commercial aviation domain. There, "error" was defined as "action or inaction that leads to deviation from crew or organizational intentions or expectations," and is broken into five categories showing the percentage of occurrence and, of that percentage, the degree to which that class of error had consequences, meaning that an additional error had resulted or the aircraft entered an undesired state:

intentional non-compliance with rules, etc. 54%	consequential 2%
correct intentional but flawed execution 29%	consequential 23%
information incorrectly transmitted/interpreted 6%	consequential 11%
proficiency error 5%	consequential 69%
decision faulty 6%	consequential 51%

While these findings involve air carriers, several illustrative points are noteworthy and arguably to some extent can be extrapolated into the maritime domain. First, of the errors observed (an average of 2 per flight), 18% were trapped, 5% were exacerbated and 77% went without response. Though not shown in these figures, there was a very large difference in threat, error and percentage of errors becoming consequential between fleets within an airline and between airlines, highlighting the danger of loose enforcement of standards and rules, regulations, policies and procedures. The magnitude shown by the study of intentional non-compliance with rules is alarming and suggests that such misbehavior is widespread and so likely to be expected in the maritime domain. The study acknowledged that the three airlines (two U.S. and one foreign) involved in the study were from countries that scored low in the Hofstede classification of power groups (discussed on Chapter Twelve). Other studies have shown that persons who commit intentional non-compliance errors commit 25% more errors of other types, and so may be said to be error prone. The low adverse consequential rate supports evidence that such violations often are committed for a "proper" purpose of increasing task efficiency.

8

Situational Awareness

To see, to hear, means nothing. To recognize (or not to recognize) means everything.— Andre Breton

We see the world, not as it is, but as we are – or as we are conditioned to see it. — Steven Covey, *The 7 Habits of Highly Effective People*

[It] ... often happens that the correction of one premise, and the knowledge of chance events which have arisen, are not sufficient to overthrow our plans completely, but only suffice to produce hesitation. Our knowledge of circumstances has increased, but our uncertainty, instead of having diminished, has only increased. The reason of this is, that we do not gain all our experience at once, but by degrees; thus our determinations continue to be assailed incessantly by fresh experience; and the mind, if we may use the expression, must always be "under arms." — von Clausewitz[297]

As discussed in the preceding chapter, the initial shipboard operational performance stage is *plan*, at which a situation is first perceived and development of *situational awareness* begins. Situational awareness (SA) may be defined as "the perception of the elements in the environment within a volume of time and space, the comprehension of their meaning, and the projection of their status in the near future."[298] More immediately,

SA may be recognized as the sufficient ascertainment and comprehension of all facts relevant to the current situation and the analysis of those facts so as to be able to exercise sound judgment in formulating a strategy and decision appropriate to favorable resolution of the developing situation. SA is the ability to see the "big picture," involving multiple cues, and to think ahead. More than mere perception of information is involved and, as suggested in the von Clausewitz quotation above, the process is an evolving process. Though in common usage, the term "situational awareness" may be faulted if used too broadly, thereby "masking" the important distinction between the cognitive and operational aspects of SA.

SA became a distinct subject of study in the mid-1970s within the military aviation domain, but without gaining significant public recognition until about ten years later.[299]

Because SA requires multiple abilities, investigators have determined that categorizing SA would enhance understanding and facilitate improved SA. From interviews with 231 aviation pilots and instructors, variables were rated to assess their respective importance to maintaining effective SA. Clustered, these variables are:

1. Knowledge;
2. Ability to anticipate and understand future events;
3. Ability to manage stress, and maintain effort and commitment;
4. Ability to acquire and process information obtained directly as well as from instrumentation; and,
5. Ability generally to maintain awareness.[300]

"Stress" as a factor incorporating available time is likely to be a lesser issue in the maritime domain and instrumentation at sea would relate to e-navigation components, including ECDIS, AIS, RADAR, ARPA, etc. rather than aircraft cockpit dials and gauges. But, certainly there is congruency of the five variable clusters between aviation and maritime operations.

Maintaining complete SA necessarily requires attention shifts among cues competing for attention, the more complex the situation the more numerous and competitive the cues are likely to be. An accurate and updated mental model must be maintained and every effort made to not "fall behind the situation." Casualties only rarely spring full blown upon the mariner: events evolve into incidents and incidents evolve into casualties, with numerous opportunities to correct or trap error.

Failure to progressively assess the situation and to take these opportunities to correct or trap error is referred to as a *fixation*. The basic defining characteristic of fixation is that an immediate "problem" or cue has biased the mariner's mindset in some inappropriate direction. Perhaps an earlier situation seems to be reoccurring but with one or more subtle but critical differences, setting the mariner upon a "garden path." Or one cue seems dominant in relation to the others.

A compelling warning against fixation is the crash of an Eastern Airlines L-1011 passenger flight into the Everglades in darkness just after Christmas in 1972. While approaching Miami to land, only two of the three landing gear "down" lights showed green, suggesting that the nose wheel had not deployed and locked. The aircraft was cleared to circle west of Miami, over the Everglades, so the status of the nose gear could be investigated. While over the Everglades, the autopilot was engaged to hold 2,000 feet altitude. The flight engineer entered the electronics bay under the cockpit while the two pilots and a deadheading Eastern employee addressed their entire attention (became fixated) upon removing the undercarriage indicator light assembly from the panel. As this was going on, the autopilot somehow became disengaged and the aircraft began an undetected descent, crashing with 176 fatalities after a few minutes.[301]

The generally accepted theoretical framework representing SA is provided by Dr. Mica Endsley,[302] who has written extensively on the subject. This framework highlights three numbered progressive levels of SA formation: perception, comprehension and projection.

LEVEL I SA – *Perception*: This initial and most basic level involves perceiving the status, attributes, and dynamics of the relevant elements within the operational environment. This picking up, monitoring and recognizing informational cues leads to awareness of multiple situational elements (objects and environmental conditions) and their current status (location and movement). A "snap-shot" of the situation results.

At this level, some relevant information may not be available or perceived because it is inadequately developed and displayed or otherwise poorly communicated, perhaps between individuals through faulty bridge resource management. There may be information overload, masking what really is important. Or, the opportunity to gain first hand hard information is ignored – the all too common situation of the watch officer's head being buried in the gadgets or console instead of looking out the wheelhouse window.[303] Also, information may be forgotten, perhaps due to high workload, multi-tasking, distraction or disruption of normal routine. For example, prior to her grounding on Lymington Banks in the west Solent, numerous cues were missed by the bridge personnel of the chemical tanker *Attilio Ievoli*. From 1624 to 1632 the vessel's head altered slowly, from 249 degrees to 240 degrees, as bank effect was experienced. Yet the falling off was not detected despite audible "clicking" of the gyro or tracking on the course recorder as the autopilot attempted to counter by applying 10 degrees starboard helm, or by vibration and a change in the engine noise indicative of reduced water depth. Also, use of the bridge mobile phone by the master was a distraction, as he failed to hear or respond to the watch officer's position reports.[304]

Infamous for other reasons as well, the grounding of the passenger vessel *Royal Majesty* on Nantucket Shoals demonstrated how numerous visual cues can be mishandled or disregarded. The GPS antenna inadvertently had become disconnected at the commencement of an otherwise routine voyage from Bermuda to Boston. As a result, the autopilot steered the vessel on a pre-determined course line toward Boston but failed to compensate for set, drift or sea conditions, resulting in the vessel eventually being about 16 miles west of her intended course line and heading toward the Shoals. A buoy west of the vessel was detected by radar and visually, and was assumed to be whistle buoy "BA" (see Figure 3) but was in fact bell buoy "AR". This visual cue was mishandled because the buoy was silhouetted against the setting sun, which prevented reading of its identifying lettering, and because buoy "BA" was expected in that place at that time. The next expected buoy was "BB". Shortly before the grounding, responding to the master's inquiry the second officer falsely told the master that buoy "BB" had been sighted. The second officer had not seen the buoy but assumed the radar had simply failed to pick the buoy up as a contact. The lookout's report of blue and white water shortly before grounding was disregarded as were radio calls from commercial fishermen commenting about a large passenger vessel being in the wrong place.[305]

Contributing to the officers' failures likely was a complacency engendered by the routine of a transit successfully accomplished many times previously. The second officer was not concerned wnen he did not see buoy "BB" because the

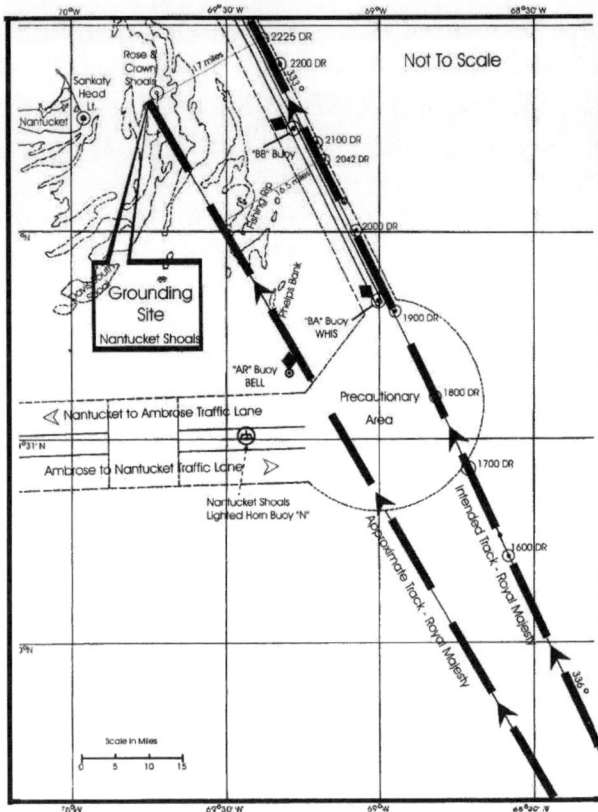

Figure 3. Intended track and approximated actual track of *Royal Majesty. From National Transportation Safety Board.*

buoy always had been there in the past: "Why wouldn't it be there, so I must have just missed seeing it."

Such complacency, or such willingness to be convinced, is referred to as "routinisation," and is further illustrated by a "close call" grounding situation involving the vessel *Aratere*.[306]

In late afternoon September 29, 2004 the large New Zealand ferry *Aratere* was entering Tory Channel toward Picton on her regular route between Wellington and Picton. The vessel had a following spring flood tide. On the bridge were the well experienced master and chief

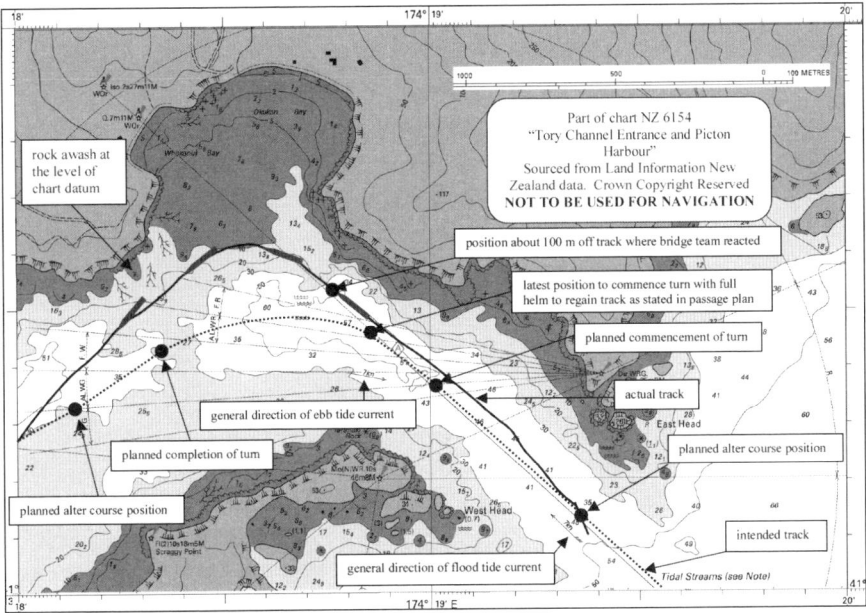

Figure 4. Plan showing the actual versus intended track of *Aratere*. *From Transport Accident Investigation Commission.*

officer. *Aratere* was operating in automatic track keeping mode ("ANTS Track"). As the vessel approached a way point where course would be altered, the chief officer noticed and commented that the vessel was tracking to starboard of the programmed course line by some 40 meters. The master replied that he had seen the off track error up to 85 meters with a flood tide. The vessel continued to widen the off track lateral distance, was picking up speed, and had arrived at a position 320 meters beyond the programmed wheel over point, where course was to have been altered to port. Finally the master and chief officer realized that on her then course and speed, *Aratere* soon would run aground. The master then overrode the ANTS Track by taking manual control from ANTS and an accident was averted. The investigating body commented:

> Routine tasks are frequently underestimated by mariners
> in terms of the risk they can pose to the safety of a vessel, its
> passengers and crew. Navigation Officers can often manage
> complex operations effectively, but at times fail to exercise
> adequate control over risks arising from routine operations.
> ... Routine tasks need to be adequately supervised and
> the appropriate documented procedures developed and
> implemented to make them as tolerant as possible to human
> error and variations in human behavior.[307]

Aligned with routinisation is the bias influence of prior
expectations.

Also, several human limitations adversely impact
Level 1 perception. Cognitively, most humans are
limited to handling concurrently only about 12 pieces
of information. And, the period of attentiveness is
normally only about 25 minutes. This human limitation
places strain upon one's ability to develop an accurate
"picture" of the situation. The actor may not "pick up"
every detail of the situation but those factors outside
the actor's immediate focus may be those that have the
potential to be the most dangerous. With these critical
elements unnoticed or improperly evaluated for the
degree of risk each presents, the Level 2 "mental model"
will be incomplete and "wrong."

Though counter-intuitive, in reality, team
participation, such as a bridge team, may adversely
affect effective SA. The collective SA of the team, as
well as of the individuals, is at issue, triggering aspects
of group psychology. Each team member needs only
that part of SA necessary and relevant to his particular
responsibility. The team will fail if one team member
possesses critical information but that information is
not communicated to or known by a member needing
that information. Studies have shown that in a group
setting, some individuals become non-contributors for
a variety of reasons. On the other hand, citation has

been made to a finding that effective team participation can decrease the potential for single person error by a factor of ten.[308]

LEVEL 2 SA – *Comprehension*: Because Level 1 input is disjointed - perceived in bits and pieces of the overall scene - Level 1 input must be synthesized through a process of pattern recognition, interpretation and evaluation sufficient for Level 1 input to meaningfully impact the objective. But, the significance or meaning of Level 1 data may not be comprehended. At Level 2, information may be correctly perceived but its importance, meaning and relevancy to the situation or objective may be misunderstood – often this occurs when the situation is encountered for the first time. The result is that correct comprehension is not attained. The actor at this level is constructing a "mental model" of the situation, and this mental model "becomes" the situation. The concept of a mental model is further explained by the concept of bounded reality. Bounded reality is the notion that in decision making, individuals' rationality is limited by the information they possess, the cognitive restrictions of their minds and the limited period of time available within which the decision must be made. These factors may limit the decision to something less than an optimal decision. Bounded rationality explains that the human capacity for problem solving is relatively small contrasted to the variety of situations that may require decision and resolution. The decision maker is better equipped to make as sound a decision as the circumstances permit if he or she understands these limitations upon optimal decision making.

The mental model may be pre-determined and information rejected that is inconsistent with the mental model. Such a "wrong" mental model, or "bias," is demonstrated by the 2000 striking, in clear visibility darkness, of the Canadian Coast Guard ship *Griffon* by the bulk carrier *Atlantic Huron* on Lake Eire.

Griffon was anchored four cables to the right (relative to Huron) of the chart printed recommended course line. *Huron* was coming to starboard to give more room to an approaching vessel and in so doing struck the well lighted *Griffon*. *Griffon* was lying near a light tower, which may have masked her radar return. *Huron*'s watch officer was navigating by ECS with an ARPA overlay that did not display *Griffon*, whose lights failed to register in *Huron*'s watch officer's mental model of the situation. *Huron*'s watch officer navigated by ECS instead of by his eyes. The report of the Transportation Safety Board of Canada commented:

> Once an individual has developed a working model of a situation, information is incorporated selectively and will favour that which confirms the individual's mental model. Information which does not match the mental model may be rationalized into the model or discounted altogether. In essence, an individual will use information that he or she expects to see and may not incorporate information which is present but does not fit the model. [footnote omitted] In such situations, barring strong intervention, be it by way of a strong cue or by outside intervention, the individual may experience difficulty in realigning the model to correspond with the situation.[309]

Information perceived through technology, as was the situation onboard *Atlantic Huron*, tends to be given greater respect than information received directly:

> Pre-interpreted, indirect information, presented with apparent exactness by a technological aid, tends to make us disregard normal and direct human observation. Technologically aided information particularly, takes precedence in cases when direct human observation needs

to be interpreted, is ambiguous, vague or contradictory.[310]

Selective use of apparently precise information while de-emphasizing real world cues, such as visual cues, is a manifestation of the confirmation bias that may arise at Level 1 SA or Level 2 SA.[311]

LEVEL 3 SA – *Projection*: Here future actions of the elements within the operational environment are anticipated, or "projected." This projection embraces knowledge of the status and dynamics of the elements and comprehension of their interrelatedness, and advances this integration forward in time to determine their effect upon the operational environment. Here, one "thinks ahead," such as navigating 15 minutes ahead of the ship. This is the most challenging level, given that mental projection is difficult. At the knowledge-based performance stage, the tendency of individuals is to avoid complex thinking if an alternative is thought possible. This Level is also challenging to designers of automated equipment, who, instead of creating information overload, must design a unit that supports decision making and goal attainment.[312] Proper integration of information, derivative of accurate meaning and projection allowing for timely appropriate decision making is an attribute of a skilled expert. Generally, a novice will be more attentive to "new" information but experienced professionals have heightened sensitivity to the possibility for error and to the quality of the information present.[313]

A comprehensive example of the progressive failure properly to attend to SA is presented by the striking of the anchored Spanish bulk carrier *Urduliz* by the nuclear powered aircraft carrier USS *Dwight D. Eisenhower*. On the morning of August 29, 1988, *Eisenhower* was in the channel inbound toward Norfolk. At least twenty officers and crew members were engaged one way or another in navigating *Eisenhower*. To bring her back from about 380 yards right of track, left rudder was given and, to arrive on schedule at buoy 3 for tugs and the pilot, speed was reduced from five to three knots. Shortly thereafter, at 0818 the bearing of *Urduliz* was determined no longer to be changing, and collision was imminent. Corrective action was attempted but was unsuccessful, and collision resulted.[314]

Eisenhower's conning personnel had failed to compensate for current set and wind drift effect upon *Eisenhower* as she transited close to *Urduliz*, and her navigator relied more upon the plot than upon recognizing from visual cues the effect set and drift had at the reduced speed and as exacerbated by more exposed *Eisenhower* "sail" and underwater surface area as she turned to port. He was more concerned that he arrive at buoy 3 "on time" for professional reasons than he was with closing the intended track line and avoiding the anchored *Urduliz*, and focused his attention accordingly. "The slower speed would have two effects: the amount of movement to the right caused by the current and the wind per unit of time would be increased and the rudder would be less effective."[315] The Safety Board recognized that *Eisenhower*'s captain apparently had been distracted and so failed to hear the order for speed to be reduced from five to three knots. If heard, the speed reduction order likely would have triggered his intervention. The Safety Board also made the pointed observation that: "The *Urduliz*, a similar sized civilian vessel, had been piloted to its anchorage with only four persons (pilot, master, mate, and helmsman) on its much larger sized bridge (about 13 feet by 54 feet, plus port and starboard bridge wings measuring about 10 feet by 37 feet), in contrast with more than 20 persons on the much smaller bridge (about 10 feet by 40 feet) of the *Eisenhower*."[316]

The significance of SA is highlighted by a 2002 study that analyzed, from the perspective of deficient SA, 177 maritime navigational casualties occurring between 1987 and 2001. The basis of the study was reports issued by eight nations.[317] Of the human errors contributing to these 177 casualties, 71% involved SA issues. Of those SA issues, 58.8% involved *plan* stage/Level 1 SA, failure correctly to perceive relevant information, such as failing to obtain information or misperceiving the information obtained; 32.7% involved *advance* stage/Level 2 SA, failing correctly to integrate or comprehend the information; and, 8.8% involved *execute* stage/Level 3 SA, failing correctly to project future actions.[318] Interestingly, a study of aviation accidents during a generally similar period (January 1986 to May 1992) produced roughly similar results as to SA error: 80.2% Level 1 SA – perception errors; 16.9% Level 2 SA – comprehension errors; and, 2.9% Level 3 SA – projection errors.[319] And, a similar pattern was forthcoming from a 2004 study of a multinational oil and gas company's offshore drilling incidents – 66.7% of the incidents were due to perception errors (sense) and 20% triggered by comprehension issues (know).[320]

These figures are important from a managerial perspective, showing as they do that the overwhelming majority of accidents appear to be rooted in errors in the perception and comprehension levels, or the sense and know stages. From this, the conclusion can be drawn that management should consider the "why" of these error types and provide relevant information to shipboard personnel in an effort to heighten operational awareness and sensitivity to this risk area.

Level 2 SA is a major factor during the advance stage, as the situation does not remain static but instead develops in ways that generally increase or decrease risk. If assessment is not continuously maintained, there is no true SA. In 1998 NASA studied 107 aviation incident reports, from which were identified 21 routine task types neglected while the operator was attending to some other situation related task. Of the neglected tasks, 69% involved either failure to monitor the present situation or failure to monitor the actions of the active operator.[321] This finding provides further evidence substantiating the irony that often efforts conceived to enhance safety may have the opposite effect. Making safety a team effort may simply add to the team members' cognitive workload without commensurate SA benefit, as illustrated in the striking of the anchored *Urduliz* by the heavily manned carrier *Eisenhower*.

SA is the forward looking basis for decision making. Without itself guaranteeing a successful decision,[322] SA structures the cue recognition, assessment and projection upon which decisions appropriate to the situation may be based. There is a distinction, however, in that the watch officer actor makes a decision correct for his or her mental picture of the situation and that mental picture as constructed by the watch officer may not correctly depict the reality of the situation. The SA error is fundamentally different from a decision error. SA errors result in a decision correct within the mental model and bounded rationality, but the mental model was wrong. On the other hand, with a decision error the situation is understood correctly but the action chosen is wrong for the situation. The decision is a wrong choice in relation to a correct mental model.

9

Decision Making

… the hardest part to learn in standing a bridge watch is the complexity of decision making; the prioritization of conflicting problems and the resolution of competing (and sometimes contradictory) information.— Anonymous

The ideal seaman is he who says and does the proper thing in just the proper way and at the proper time, a man who has developed sea sense and nautical sagacity. But ideal conditions and the ideal man seldom, if ever, confront each other in an emergency at sea.
No man can hope to acquire a full and complete knowledge of all nautical subjects either from the personal experiences of a lifetime or from a prolonged reading of textbooks, but the prudent seaman reads every shipping publication that comes his way, takes reasonable precautions and studies the ways of ships and men, visualizes possible contingencies and mentally decides what action he would take in the event of sudden emergency.
— Nicholls. *Seamanship and Nautical Knowledge* [323]

[The] quality of [a decision maker's decision is] as good as the quality of the information he [is] provided as well as his ability to exercise sound judgment, which is a function of training and experience.— K. Dotterway, "Systemic Analysis of Complex Dynamic Systems: The Case of the USS Vincennes" [324]

Because ... the job of decision makers [is] to decide, they cannot react to ambiguity by deferring judgment. When the problem is [within] an environment that lacks clarity, an overload of conflicting data, and lack of time for rigorous assessment of sources and validity, ambiguity abets instinct and allows intuition to drive analysis. — Richard K. Betts[325]

From the watch officer's perspective, his or her primary duty and objective is "don't hit anything" — the bottom, another ship, an object, "anything."[326] This worthy objective is attained through two phases: vigilance, involving situational awareness, and decision making, both merging through determination of the objective to be attained that is unique to the specific situation. For example, a meeting between two vessels gives rise to an analysis characterized as situational awareness, leading to recognition that some action must be taken to avoid risk of collision.[327] Avoidance of such risk is achieved through the making, and then execution, of a decision patterned to meet the need to avoid risk of collision. The situation may be simple, requiring no more than skill-based performance, perhaps then merging into some rule-based performance. Or, the situation may be more complex, requiring knowledge-based performance. And, anywhere along the plan-advance-execute path, human error can intervene, as well as the personality of the actors. The risk may be summarized as follows:

Uncertainty, and the need for individual judgements [sic], are the necessary precursors of poor judgements [sic] ('human error') and resulting accidents. There are particular encounter geometries for which uncertainties of interpretation are more severe (e.g. overtaking or converging course). There are also likely to be particular individual watchkeepers whose behavioural characteristics place them at the extremes of the general population of watchkeepers, and who are more likely to make 'erroneous' and risky judgements [sic]. The chance combination of one such peculiar encounter geometry and one such particular individual could clearly lead to a very dangerous situation.[328]

In the latter situation, an individual's cognitive abilities[329] alone are generally insufficiently robust to surmount high-level complexity, and so require coping strategies such as pattern matching through experience or decision making contexts. These decision making contexts may be rule oriented, such as the COLREGS,[330] or a cognitive scheme.

The context particularly relevant to the maritime environment is Naturalist Decision Making (NDM), also referred to by its military anachronism TADMUS – Tactical Decision Making Under Stress. NDM/TADMUS is characterized by:

1. a limited period of time within which to assess an evolving situation and come to a decision where there is,
2. a dynamically changing situation, and
3. information of varying reliability.

And, to these elements there may be added "an element of risk."

The TADMUS variant of NDM results from studies undertaken by the U.S. Navy addressing decision making in the wake of the shoot-down of an Iranian civilian passenger airliner in 1989 by USS *Vincennes* (CG 49).[331]

NDM pre-dated the *Vincennes* incident and, like TADMUS, concerns itself with how individuals and teams in dynamic, uncertain and often fast- paced risk potential environments identify and assess the situation, make decisions and take actions that may have major consequences.[332]

Significantly, situation assessment and plan formation are not discrete sequential stages but rather are closely interwoven processes, evolving as the situation develops. All relevant information must be integrated into and retained in the mental model the actor begins constructing as the situation initially is perceived. That information must be projected forward in time to determine the future situation of the vessel within the evolving environment. External error inducing factors may intrude as this process progresses. To take into account the projection aspect, the watch officer should apply a practical plan ahead "rule of thumb" that the vessel should always be "seen" (this is to say that the vessel is navigated within the mental model) some 10 to 15 minutes ahead of her present situation. The failure to retain information and update the mental model – to navigate 10 to 15 minutes ahead of the vessel – is illustrated by the near collision scenario inadvertently allowed to develop between the vessels *Ormiston* and *Searoad Mersey*.

At about 0512 on May 16, 2007 the 16,602 dwt. bulk carrier *Ormiston*, outbound from Melbourne and making 15 knots, entered "The Cut," the narrowest part of the channel. At the same time, the inbound ro-ro *Searoad Mersey* entered The Cut. *Mersey*'s captain had pilotage for the area and had transited the area some 1,300 times previously. He had received but had forgotten VTS notification of *Ormiston*'s departure and also had failed to sight *Ormiston* visually. The vessels passed within 60 feet of each other in The Cut at a combined speed of about 30 knots.[333]

When *Mersey*'s master arrived on his vessel's bridge, he arrived with an already determined mental model of his entrance into the port, based upon his familiarity with the task. He displaced the *Ormiston* information to the back of his mind because she would not be an issue for some time and his concern was with a more immediate overtaking situation. Once the overtaking was accomplished successfully, he failed to adjust his mental model to account for *Ormiston* and proceeded close to the center of the channel, as was his normal practice absent traffic.

The Australian Transport Safety Bureau also commented upon *complacency* as the flip side of technical skills enhanced through experience:

> Some repetitive experience can also be detrimental, as it induces a sense of routine, safety and normality in an otherwise risky environment. Over time, an officer's respect for what he or she is doing might decrease while the skills and quantity of experience increase.[343]

An example of inaccurate information leading to faulty decision making is the May 2008 close quarters situation between the passenger vessel *Costa Atlantica* and car carrier *Grand Neptune*. *Atlantica* was transiting the northeast Traffic Separation lane in Dover Strait, intending to turn to port and cross the southwest lane. With several vessels ahead in the southwest lane, *Atlantica*'s master directed that an ARPA trial maneuver be conducted. Such a trial maneuver allows the ARPA operator to evaluate navigational consequences upon all tracked targets that would result from an own-ship action. *Atlantica*'s watch officer complied, but without entering any time delay and while his vessel gradually was altering course to port. These factors, together with the system limitation that for ARPA to display accurate information a steady tracking state of 3 minutes is necessary, degraded the accuracy of the ARPA response upon which *Atlantica*'s master was basing his decision. *Atlantica*'s bridge team did not understand how ARPA was to be used nor ARPA's limitations. The actual closest point of approach would have been 120 yards, the "give way" *Atlantica* passing ahead of *Grand Neptune*.[335]

Cognitively, the Recognition-Primed Decision (RPD) model has been developed to reduce decision error.[336] This model results from research recognition that human strengths and limitations affect how individuals function under adverse decision making circumstances. Two factors influence the model: first, how the situation is "sized up" and then, how the out-come is projected. These are, essentially, Levels 1 and 2 SA and then Level 3 SA, respectively, discussed in the previous Chapter.

In the RPD model, if the situation is familiar, the decision maker proceeds without much ado. He or she draws upon skill-based or rule-based performance stages. If, however, the situation is unfamiliar or not analogous to a situation previously experienced, or perhaps is similar to a situation where there had been an adverse outcome, more thought is necessary. Knowledge-based performance must be activated.

The decision maker acquires more information relevant to the challenge presented. Objectives proper to a desired outcome must be determined and prioritized. Irrelevant information is filtered out,[337] a sequence of likely stages or events is determined and responses decided. A preferred course of action is set and analyzed through a process of *mental simulation.*

This process looks ahead and anticipates the likely progression of the selected course of action – potential impediments to success – and mentally adjusts or fine tunes, as the situation may require. If the simulation suggests, an alternative course of action may be substituted. After the mental simulation has run its course, the final decided action will be executed.

The greatest danger in mental simulation is the tendency to "imagine away" cues or evidence.[338] For example, there have been many head to head collisions, occasioned when one vessel meeting another vessel head to head turns to starboard and the other turns to port. Accepted practice is that each, when in sight of the other, shall turn to starboard, to effect a safe port to port passing.[339] Yet, if one vessel turns to port, the other will likely presume (absent an agreed upon radio or whistle signal exchange) this to be an error (a "slip" in giving the order or a misapplied helm order) and further presume that corrective action promptly will be taken by the other vessel, and so will herself turn to starboard. The mental simulation creates a reality that is acted upon, even though that "reality" may be false because an important evidentiary piece of the situation is excused away – that the other vessel has turned to port and one's own vessel turning to starboard creates risk of collision.[340] But, operating in the assumed "reality" that the other vessel knows the rules (Rule 14(a) at least), has erred, and will correct her error, is "safer" and more reasonable than figuring that the other vessel deliberately has violated a rule or otherwise is acting irresponsibly, and so that assumed "reality" is most easily accepted.

Within this Klein theory of decision making, there are, as his title suggests, "sources of power" possessed by the decision maker. In addition to mental simulation, these include intuition, the power to see the invisible, the power of stories, and the power of metaphors and analogies.

"Intuition" is the use of past experience "to recognize key patterns that indicate the dynamics of the situation."[341] This sometimes is referred to as a "sixth sense," or, as the captain of *Cherry Valley* described the sensation, "the hairs on the back of my neck going up."[342] Admiral Henry G. Chiles USN (ret.) elaborated: "If it doesn't feel right, a seaman of any rank or rate better find out why."[343] Though not infallible, deposits in the bank of experience deserve respect in decision making.

The "power to see the invisible" refers to an experienced person's ability to "have an overall sense of what is happening in a situation ... ."[344] This is "seeing the big picture," without necessarily having all components or elements particularized.

The "power of stories" is mentally organizing the actor's cognitive world in such a way as to make sense of events. This is a strategy for explaining past events and, like the "power of metaphors and analogies," is not immediately relevant to the present discussion.

What is clear is the value of experience. Insufficient experience may result in the inability to recognize and gather necessary information, as well as inability to recognize or acknowledge weaknesses in chosen courses of action. Little wonder that Captain Slocum wrote: "[i]t is only right to say, ... , that to insure a reasonable measure of success, experience should sail with the ship."[345]

However, as previously discussed, the decision maker must be mindful that experience can cut both ways: experience can be a foundation for proper timely analysis but also can lead to thinking that becomes "automated" by past successes. The distinction is illustrated by the thought processes of the captain and co-pilot, respectively, in the cockpit of US Airways flight 1549 immediately before the plane successfully ditched in the Hudson River after losing both engines to bird ingestion:

First Officer: "I was thinking that somehow we're going to get some power back on these engines and we're going to be arriving back at the gate. That's what's always happened, that's what always been, you know, and so I was always expecting to do that."
Captain: "The only option, the only place in the whole metropolitan area long enough, wide enough, smooth enough to land a jet airliner, is the river. There's just no

other place to go. We're out of time. We're out of airspeed. We're out of ideas. This is it."[346]

From the time of the bird strike until ditching, only 3 minutes and 32.3 seconds elapsed.[347]

Successful decision making is heavily reliant upon - in addition to experience - training and education. Studies indicate that elements contributory to sound decision making can be learned.[348] That senior officers and watch officers will be exposed by formal teaching of these issues is unlikely but they are worthy of being addressed in senior officer seminars, and personnel should be encouraged to incorporate realization of their importance as decisions are considered.

The preceding may give the impression that decision making is an orderly progression of logic, largely tempered by experience. Unfortunately, even with experience and an abundance of relevant information, decision making can go awry as a result of any of a multitude of *biases* that interfere with objective assessment of information and adversely affect the decision making process.[349] Awareness of biases and how they may affect the decision making process allows for taking them into account and mitigating their consequences.

First among biases may be the "de minimus" error, in which warning cues are recognized but rationalized away. One or more reasons are found to not take seriously each piece of evidence that is a cue indicating existence or imminence of an anomaly. The result is that warnings go without response and eventually the forewarned problem materializes.[350]

Seemingly similar but distinguishable is "confirmation" bias, where reliance selectively is placed in information that tends to validate the course of action most comfortable to the actor or that the decision maker wishes to follow, and is strongest when supporting a belief or desire that has a strong foundation in experi-ence, faith or prejudice, instead of empirical evidence. Confirmation bias was particularly present in the 2007 grounding of the Panamanian bulk carrier *Pasha Bulker* off Newcastle, New South Wales, Australia.

Pasha Bulker had anchored May 23, 2.4 miles off the coast in a recognized anchorage, anticipating an approximate three week delay before entering port to load. She was sufficiently ballasted for the good weather then prevailing. In the anchorage area there were 55 other vessels anchored. June 7 at midday, *Pasha's* master veered additional anchor chain in response to gale warnings. By 0500 on June 8, the weather was severe, with strong gale force winds. By 0625 the vessel was dragging anchor toward shore. Decision was made to put to sea and at 0748 the anchor was aweigh, but the vessel was then 1.2 miles off the shore. Various maneuvers to stem the dragging and to advance against the on shore wind and sea conditions failed to gain sea room or to keep the vessel off the shore. At 0951 *Pasha Bulker* grounded on Nobbys Beach.

While the master, despite his seven years' experience as master, made numerous decisions contrary to good seamanship, there was strong evidence that confirmation bias adversely influenced his thinking.

Though the vessel's anchored position was appropriate for the initial good weather, the master failed properly to take into account the propensity for sudden adverse weather that was described in relevant navigational publications. His underlying belief well could have been that absent explicit external information to the contrary, the normally used anchorage outside the port would be sufficient for the several week wait. The passage plan omitted reference to local weather, suggesting a belief that local weather was a non-issue. With this belief, the limited ballasting appropriate for good weather conditions could confirm the master's expectation that ballasting contingences need not be considered. Despite the knowledge of *Pasha's* master that with the onset of gale conditions other vessels had begun dragging anchor, the fact that *Pasha* was equipped with a newly designed anchor and with additional scope payed out could have justified a belief that *Pasha's* anchor would not drag. The fact that some, but not all, of the many other vessels departed the anchorage for sea, together with the local VTS not ordering vessels to leave the anchorage, could have supported the master's decision to stay. The vessel's limited engine power could have rationalized the "stay" decision, though that same fact could have been interpreted as a warning that the vessel was too under powered to be able by engine power to take sufficient strain off the anchor chain or to be controllable if compelled to get underway in the face of heavy weather. So pre-disposed was the master to remain at anchor that he failed to make any plan to implement if wind, sea and other conditions reached pre-determined tolerance limits. With the weather strengthening, the "situation was becoming significantly worse and the master appears to have ignored these warning signs[,] further suggesting a confirmation bias."[351]

A major factor to be weighed in the decision making process is *risk*. Unfortunately, risk, or fatal hazard, does not always carry its own warning. In 1944, a typhoon savaged fast carrier Task Force 38 in the Western Pacific, sinking several destroyers, damaging other vessels, and taking nearly 1,000 lives. In response, Admiral Chester Nimitz signed a confidential letter to the fleet addressing the subject of risk at sea, commenting that " ... safety and fatal hazard are not separated by any sharp boundary line, but shade gradually from one into the other. There is no little red light which is going to flash on ... ."[352]

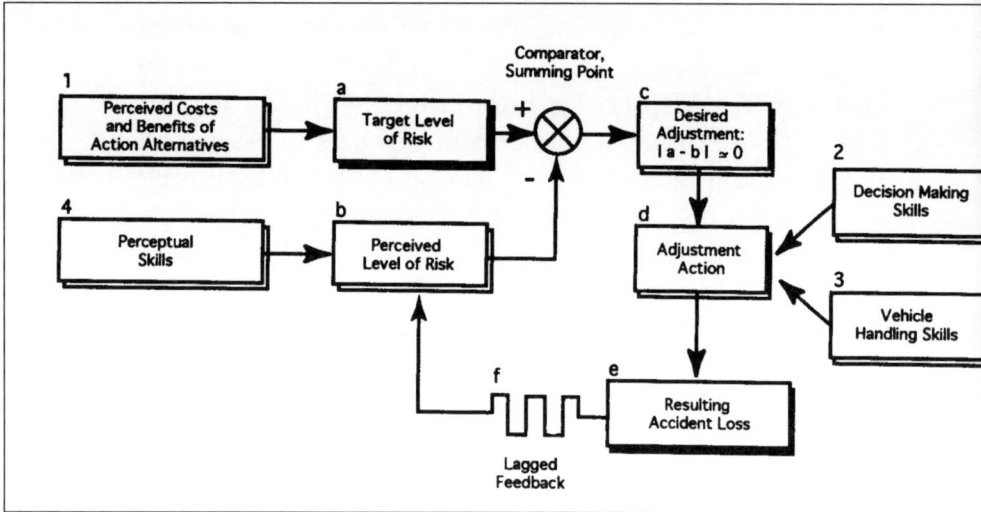

Figure 5. Risk Homeostasis Model. *Courtesy of Gerald J.S. Wilde, Target Risk 2.*

Analysis, readily adaptable to the maritime domain, of an actor's risk perception is provided by Canadian psychology professor Gerald J.S. Wilde, who has made a study of transportation safety and developed a theory of "risk homeostasis," referring to a balance between risk taking and actual risk.[347] Professor Wilde's theory maintains that in any activity, the actor accepts a certain variable level of subjectively estimated risk in exchange for the benefit(s) to be gained from accepting and taking that level of risk.

Box 1 represents the variety of factors — the perceived costs and benefits of alternative actions — affecting the degree of risk, box *a*, that an actor is willing to accept. The greater the perceived benefit of risky behavior and the lower the expected cost of such behavior, the greater will be the actor's acceptable or tolerable level of risk — box *a*. The degree of risk is determined by the actor's evaluation of four variables: the expected advantages and costs of comparatively risky behavior weighed against the advantages and costs of comparatively safe behavior. These variables may be a combination of economic, cultural, personality, and social, as well as psychological, concerns personal to the actor. Other than economic and personality issues, these concerns are internalized so much so that generally the actor is not judgmentally aware of them. Consequently, the actor's acceptable or tolerable degree of risk is the result of the actor's motivation and "explicitly calculating probabilities of various possible outcomes ... ."[354]

The degree of acceptable or tolerable risk is that "level of subjective accident risk at which the difference between benefits and costs (including the perceived danger of accident) is believed to maximize."[355] Absent risk analysis with a concurrently evaluated decision to undertake a perceived level of risk, most risk is passively accepted as an inevitable consequence of one's deliberate choice of action. There always is some degree of risk because zero risk is equivalent to a totally static situation.

Many reasons may explain, if not justify, why a person will choose a particular level of risk greater than zero risk. Foremost is likely to be economic – the urge or incentive to accomplish a task quickly, such as completing the voyage expeditiously. Reduced transit time has an advantage, but includes the "costs" of enhanced risk of accident (such as greater speed in conditions of restricted visibility[356] or in heavy sea conditions), greater fuel consumption and expenses, and more wear and tear on the vessel asset.

Returning to Figure 5, box *b* indicates the degree of danger experienced or anticipated by the actor, generally not as an empirical calculation but instead as an awareness in the back of the actor's mind. This level of awareness derives from: 1) the actor's knowledge of relevant information (including knowledge gleaned from past relevant accident/incident reports) represented by jagged line f "lagged feedback")[357] and the actor's past experience, general as well as specific to the situation; 2) situational awareness of the immediate situation; and, 3) the actor's confidence level in his or her ability to make the proper decision, and ship handling skills relative to the situation. This latter "confidence level" is represented by box 4. The actor compares the box b degree of danger against his or her target level of risk, box a, and attempts to reduce any difference. The actor wants box a to be slightly greater than box b. This comparison in normal circumstances is usually at an intuitive or modestly conscious level, and may be followed by a wide array of possible decisions.

A situation altering decision is not necessary if the perceived risk is less than the target level of risk, but is necessary when the perceived risk exceeds the acceptable-tolerable risk level, the difference represented by box c "desired adjustment."

The decided upon adjustment action to be taken is represented by box d "adjustment action," whereas the overall casualty experience, including past relevant incident/accident reports, is represented by box e "resulting accident loss." Because the actor's knowledge or ignorance of past similarities influences the box b "perceived level of risk," past incident/accident reports and dissemination of information derived from such reports takes on great significance.

Three skill types affect the level of risk perception and compensating action taken: 1) perceptual; 2) decision making; and, 3) ship handling. Perceptual skills, box 4, include the actor's ability and willingness objectively and honestly to assess his or her decision making and ship handling skills, so box 4 contributes to determination of the extent to which the actor's subjective perceived risk, box b, accurately corresponds to the actual risk.

Incorporation of one's awareness of one's limitations is important – as Leonardo da Vinci said: "He who fears dangers will not perish by them."[358] Of course, the more the actor overestimates his or her skills, the greater will be the likelihood of undertaking excessive risk and the likelihood of an accident happening.

Decision making skill, box *2*, refers to the actor's ability correctly to decide what to do – box *d* - to produce the desired adjustment, box *c*. Here the objective is to minimize toward zero the difference between the acceptable or tolerable level of risk and the perceived level of risk. The actor's ship handling skill, box *3*, in the present nautically oriented discussion (in a different context, the skill could be flying an aircraft or driving a car) may determine how successfully the decision will be put into effect, also box *d*. Research shows that individuals routinely underestimate box *2* decision making skills and overestimate their box *3* shiphandling skills; "an accurate evaluation of one's own abilities in context" of a particular hazard is "most difficult to achieve and assist" in its development.[359]

From the foregoing are readily demonstrated the benefits of training and education directed toward increasing knowledge, acquiring actual experience (positive as well as negative) and management's dissemination of information derived from incident and accident reports. Particularly, education should emphasize aspects of risk perception; the incontestable benefit of better risk perception education is that shiphandlers will become more sophisticated "risk managers." The better are the actor's three skill types, the greater will be the latitude within which to choose actions commensurate with one's acceptable or tolerable level of risk.

The Wilde theory hypothesizes that in practice an actor performs not to avoid an accident as such but rather to perform commensurate with the actor's acceptable or tolerable level of risk and thereby maximize the benefits afforded by the available resources. Therefore, one may say skills serve less to minimize risk than to optimize risk.

This theory must be considered with the realization that individuals vary considerably in the level of risk deemed acceptable or tolerable, box *a*.

An interesting aspect of the Wilde theory is that as safety devices increase - such as radar, integrated and automated navigation and command centers, and rules, regulations, policies and procedures to name but a few - the actor absorbs these devices into his or her thinking processes and likely is willing to act in a more risky manner, from the assumption that these enhanced safety devices balance out, and justify, the more risky behavior.

Subtle and not so subtle organizational pressures, as well as the implicit social pressures of one's peers, can exert a powerful force impelling shipboard personnel to undertake or accept greater risk in their decision making than is wise. The reader may recall the negative attitude expressed by many in the naval community about taking a pilot, as was set forth in the *Eisenhower* incident discussion. Also, frequently management sends a mixed message: "sail safely but keep to the schedule." The effect of such a mixed message has been aptly summarized: "Safety and schedule keeping were [the master's] two obsessions, and the ship's bridge the powerbase from which he struggled to reconcile one with the other."[360] Under such circumstances, the effect senior management may assert, explicitly or by implication, over a ship's master is illustrated in dialogue from the short story "Winter, North Atlantic," in which a Captain Browning, master of a tramp steamer preparing for a winter North Atlantic crossing, realizes his need for 300 tons extra of ballast to keep the propeller submerged and to reduce excessive rolling. He spoke first with the company stores manager and "in a proper seamanlike way declared that he was damned if *he* was going to make a winter passage to the westward without the ballast … ." That entreaty being unsuccessful, Captain Browning went "upstairs," where he was questioned over the need and expense by the company's new chairman and responded: "Refuse to go to sea, sir! *Me*, refuse to go to sea! Never! … Object! Well – er – yes, sir, but I'm quite prepared to do my best to make the passage even if I don't get the ballast."[361] At times, a strong personality, buttressed with strong empirical argument demonstrating the risk to the company's personnel, asset and insurance, must prevail in the interest of safety.

Many other influences can adversely affect coming to well advised decisions.

Time can be the enemy of sound decision making.[362] The situation was summarized by Captain Will Rogers of the USS *Vincennes*, speaking about the shoot down by his vessel of an Iranian civilian aircraft, mistaken for an aggressive Iranian F-14: "If I [sic] have a long time to sort things out, you are going to take more time to look at this, and more time to look at that. But when you don't have time, you basically take what you have and … at some point in time you have to make the decision."[363] If possible, the best response to time pressure is to expand the time available for making the decision.[364]

When the cues are not clear cut or present multiple interpretations, *ambiguity* is present and decision making uncertainty results. Absent strong contradictory cues, a person is unlikely to reassess an apparently reasonable interpretation. An example is the 1974 stranding of the VLCC *Metula* in the Magellan Strait. The two Chilean pilots brought with them a new Chilean chart compiled from a recent survey, so presumably the Chilean chart was more up to date than the British Admiralty chart used on board. Comparing the two charts, the master noticed a 14-15 meter shallow patch on the Chilean chart. That patch was not on the Admiralty chart. Transferring the patch to the Admiralty chart, the master saw that the patch was squarely on the recommended track line shown on the Admiralty chart. He also found that the latitude and longitude of a reference point common to the two charts did not coincide. The master understandably was unsettled by the chart grid discrepancy. He felt he could not rely upon the Admiralty chart, despite other vessels of his company having successfully done so, but was unable to view more closely the Chilean chart because that chart was frequently in use and taken over by the pilots. Nor could he check either of the two radar displays because both radars were hooded and being used by the pilots. So neither he nor the watch officer checked the pilots' navigation. Because a course change was made too soon, the vessel stranded. The master could have resolved the ambiguity by taking time to more carefully study the Chilean chart and ascertain its reliability through the pilots and any other accessible resources, by reserving one radar for his and his watch officer's use, and by determining reference points to insure he knew where and when the course should be altered.[365]

A recent dissertation authored by an experienced mooring master, Captain Derek McCann, advances a suggestion that nautical decision makers tend to give relatively little thought to the process of decision making and so are unlikely to be aware of and sensitive to factors that contribute to either sound or unsound decisions. In common with many professionals, such as airline pilots and medical personnel,[366] many professional mariners are unaware that they are vulnerable to stress as a contributor to unsound decisions. Interestingly, a focus group of master mariners acknowledging generally that "experienced personnel could make an irrational decision," the group answered "No" to the question: "Are you aware that *you* could make an irrational decision while doing *your* job."[367] Captain McCann's finding supports the result of a study of 100 accidents at sea in which the combination of erroneous processing of information and high situational stress occurred more frequently than would be expected by chance.[368]

And, decision making authority occasionally is abdicated by the person responsible for making the decision to another person, as happened in the case of *Cosco Busan*. The master held ultimate responsibility and authority whether the vessel would sail under the prevailing conditions. Instead of evaluating the conditions in active consultation with the pilot, the master appears to have abdicated the decision to the pilot, who initially commented: " … I think we'll be able to go as soon as [the tug and barge go] past us." The master responded: "Yeah, yeah, yeah." Subsequently, the pilot said to the master: "You can single up, if you want." The master replied, "OK, single up." Later, the master stated "I have to follow [the pilot's] direction" as to deciding whether to get underway.[369]

The elements of sound professional decision making are displayed in the 1994 successful rescue of a tug crew and barge by the master, officers and crew of the tanker *Cherry Valley*.[370]

The 3,500 h.p. ocean-going tug *J.A. Orgeron*, with a crew of five, departed southern Louisiana for Port Canaveral, FL with the unmanned barge *Poseidon* in tow. The barge was laden with a large aluminum external fuel tank used in NASA's space shuttle missions. The large volume comparatively light weight fuel tank was covered by a Quonset hut-like canopy, resulting in the barge and its cargo having significant sail area. Shortly after the tug and barge sailed, *Cherry Valley*, Captain Prentice "Skip" Strong commanding, departed the lower Mississippi River toward Jacksonville. The single hull *Cherry Valley* was laden "to her marks," to a maximum draft of 35 feet, with 235,000 barrels of No. 6 oil. She was powered by one high pressure steam turbine and one low pressure steam turbine geared to a single propeller. A significant advantage with *Cherry Valley*'s steam plant was that an exact number of propeller revolutions per minute – between 0 and 78 – could be ordered to give a desired ship speed between "stop" and "full" speed.[371]

When the tug and tow were just north of Miami, mechanical troubles were developing on the tug. Eventually, in 18 to 22 foot seas and against a 40 knot wind, both engines of the tug had to be shut down, leaving the tug powerless and with her tow drifting at 1.5 knots downwind toward Bethel Shoal, six miles distant. The holes in Reason's "Swiss Cheese" model had aligned. A call for help was sent by the tug.

Cherry Valley received the tug's distress call via the Coast Guard shortly after 0100 on November 15, when the tug was close to Bethel Shoal and approximately 40 miles and about 3 hours steaming time distant from *Cherry Valley*. The Coast Guard requested that *Cherry Valley* "render any assistance" she could.[372] While *Cherry Valley* certainly would proceed toward the distressed tug, Captain Strong was confronted with having to decide what action, if any, he would take once he arrived on site. *Cherry Valley*'s owner had no promulgated written restrictions at that time as to what the ship's captain could do with the vessel in regards to safety, allowing Captain Strong broad discretion.[373] His initial awareness was that he "need to know [his] limits, especially" given the recent trend toward maritime negligence being criminalized.[374] Captain Strong was confronted with many challenges, including: his tanker was single hull,

fully loaded and drawing 35 feet while the downwind
Bethel Shoal was charted as shallow as 28 feet in parts,
resulting in the potential for an ecologically disastrous
major oil spill on Florida's touristy East Coast; in the
prevailing 15 - to - 20 foot seas, *Cherry Valley*'s keel could
drop as much as 55 feet below the mean surface of
the sea; any rescue would be undertaken in darkness;
the tug was powerless, so would not be capable of
maneuvering to assist; and, *Cherry Valley*'s new mooring
lines were inaccessible, stowed below deck,[375] leaving as
towlines only two old 9-inch polydacron high stretch
coefficient mooring lines, at the end of their service life.
Compounding the pressure was that *Cherry Valley* was the
only vessel in a position to render assistance. Attempting
to get some rest in the several hours before arriving on
site, Captain Strong's thinking process included:

> I think again about the fine line between foolishness and
> skill, how so often luck is more of a deciding factor than
> you might like to think. I think about some of the captains
> I have known and wonder what they would be considering
> were they in my position now, what they would be deciding.
> I think that whatever happens in the coming hours that I will
> always keep a margin of safety between myself, meaning my
> crew and my ship, and danger. After many years' experience,
> I know that if we are called on to help this tug we will need
> more than a simple Plan A; in fact, I suspect we may get
> quite far down the alphabet when it comes to plans [, and]
> I don't want to go back up to the bridge and pace and show
> the nervousness that I feel.[376]

Beginning to formulate a plan, Captain Strong
took into consideration "the available equipment and
personnel and the conditions of the sea off Bethel
Shoal."[377] Fortunately, he had experience as a pilot and
was "comfortable maneuvering [*Cherry Valley*] in tight

quarters with another vessel close by."[378] He contacted
the Coast Guard and advised of his on-scene estimated
arrival time, established VHF voice contact with the
tug's captain to discuss several potential scenarios, and
reviewed engine room related issues, including replacing
boiler burner tips to maximize engine control, with his
engineering officers.

Captain Strong limited his cognitive resources to
assessing the possible and did not waste effort upon
the futile – such as calculating the potential load upon
his mooring-now-tow lines — he was compelled to
use what he had available, so "[t]here's no point" in
making calculations beyond recognizing that "they
should do the job."[379] Such a limitation is a necessary
compromise between the demands of the task and the
need to conserve one's limited cognitive resources. He
discussed the situation broadly with his chief officer, who
would be running the deck, and other mates, inviting
their thoughts and suggestions. Though he had made
only one prior voyage with his chief officer, he had taken
that opportunity to favorably assess the chief officer's
competence and attitude.

Radar indicated the barge, with its large sail area,
and tug were being blown toward Bethel Shoal at 2.5
knots. He inquired of the Coast Guard and tug captain
regarding what was expected of *Cherry Valley* – not to
have a "get out of jail free" card if something were to go
wrong but rather "to clarify how serious the situation is,
and that we are the only people around to help."[380] With
these preparations and evaluations in hand, as well as
an agreed upon plan to close with the tug and shoot a
line to the tug, Captain Strong "decide[s] to commit us
to trying to rescue the *Orgeron*."[381]

Prior to closing with the tug to pass a messenger
line for bending on to the mooring/tow lines, Captain
Strong determined that 80 degree 10 minutes west

longitude would be his "drop dead point," beyond
which he would not permit his vessel to pass. That line
of longitude coincided with the charted 10 fathom/60
foot water depth contour line. "With the seas we have
running tonight and our 35-foot draft, I feel we can
'safely' operate east of that line and not worry about
touching the bottom."[382] Among other tasks, the third
officer was directed to monitor the longitude on the GPS
and advise the captain of the ship's relation to that "drop
dead line." Subsequently, to avoid multi-tasking the third
officer, the radio officer was delegated to exclusively
monitor the GPS. This allowed for constant monitoring
and the third officer to exclusively operate the engine
order telegraph during the critical maneuvering period.
Similarly to permit focus upon maneuvering the ship,
Captain Strong limited his voice contact with the tug's
captain to a radio channel not available to the well-
meaning but powerless to assist Coast Guard, which was
barraging him with questions and commentary.

His original "Plan A" was to close the tug to port
but with her engine on "stop" in the rough seas and 50-
knot wind conditions prevailing, *Cherry Valley* was "still
moving an estimated four knots and approaching the
shoal with effortless inertia."[383] Captain Strong, through
instinct honed by experience, reassessed the risk and
decided to revert to Plan B, by which the tug would
be closed to starboard. Three tries were made before
the messenger line successfully was passed, with each
attempt requiring skillful shiphandling, accompanied
by the "one hand for yourself, one hand for the ship"
admonishment to *Cherry Valley*'s deck crew. Before the
third attempt, Captain Strong determined that only one
more attempt would be made because of the vessels'
continued closure toward the shoal.

In the tempestuous seas, on the third try *Cherry Valley*
was maneuvered so close to the tug that the heaving line

was simply handed over to a tug crew member. *Cherry Valley*'s "towing" lines were made fast on the tug – words inadequate to communicate the drama and risk of the overall operation – and in a "fine balancing act to get [the *Cherry Valley*, tug and barge flotilla] away from the shoal, where the difference of a degree or two in heading, or a change of one or two rpm will determine success or failure[,]"[384] the tow began, the result of "exemplary[,]" "daring and successful seamanship under very difficult conditions."[385]

Captain Strong's performance illustrates that decision making broadly involves characteristics of analysis as well as intuition. The analysis looks to process "rules" as a result of the decision maker being generally unfamiliar or inexperienced in the particulars of the situation. Intuitive decisions, to the contrary, are based upon the decision maker's familiarity with those particulars, but risks vulnerability to biases that introduce a potential for error. In such circumstances, the benefits of supportive shoreside assistance from management cannot be over emphasized. As Captain Strong has commented: "Having someone on the end of [a phone] line who knows the situation you are in, has had lots of experience at sea, and is removed from the scene is a captain's dream."[386] Throughout, the decision maker must reject convenient "hazardous" thoughts but rather crystallize "safe" thoughts:

Hazardous Thought	**Safe Thought**
"It won't happen to me."	"It might happen to me."
"I can do it."	"Why take that chance?"
"Do something quickly."	"Not so fast–think it out."[387]

The faulty decision process employed in sailing the bulk log carrier *Jody F. Millennium* from Gisborne, NZ to escape excessive surging alongside her berth in 2002 illustrates incorporation of hazardous thoughts – where presumed efficiency trumped thoroughness.[388]

The ship's master as well as the harbor pilot agreed that some action needed to be taken to protect the vessel, her crew and port facilities from the vessel's excessive surge, and parting mooring lines, alongside her berth. A heavy swell was running, generated by an off-shore depression whose local effects were difficult to predict, so specific measures to minimize the effect were not determined. Each potential in-port remedy suffered from a countervailing risk; the master and pilot agreed the ship should leave the port and ride out the swell at sea until the condition abated. The accompanying decision was that the vessel immediately depart: "Do something quickly." This decision closed the pilot's mind to other possibilities, other conditions and consequences: "We must get this done." He also disregarded his own criteria for sailing so large a vessel deeply laden as she was: "It's close enough." Because the discussions were through the ship's agent rather than directly between master and pilot, there was confusion over whether the decision was an "order" of the Port or mutually agreed: "I'm not an expert, so I'll let you decide." Attention exclusively was upon what could happen if the vessel remained in port, and disregarded the potential, vulnerability and consequences of grounding while departing: "It won't happen to me." Grounding warranted consideration because the hasty departure had the vessel underway at less than high water and the swell caused there to be insufficient underwater clearance: "It's good enough for now." The pilot – the only pilot for the port – feared being stranded aboard the vessel, so opted to disembark inside the breakwater: "It's more efficient this way." This required the vessel to slow – resulting in diminished control and steerage. As the vessel emerged from behind the breakwater in her more vulnerable condition, her bow was caught by a large wave and by wind and sea was set down on a shoal, where she remained for eighteen days. Urgency and hazardous thoughts had prevailed over caution and safe thoughts.

10

Violation of Rules, Regulations, Policies and Procedures: the Shore-Ship Disconnect

Clearly, rule-making by itself is of little value in achieving safe operation. What is required is compliance.— Andrew Hopkins[389]

Distinct from "error," and definable as an intentional act or omission committed within a regulatory and procedural framework, a "violation" is the willful disregard or rejection of one or more operational norms. Important to understand at the onset is that, contrary to the negative stigma associated with the term "violation," in the majority of situations the violator is acting from a perceived necessity compelled by the actor's then "bounded rationality" and with some degree of good intention motivated by a desire to accomplish a particular task. Errors and violations are alike in that both generally can be detected before taking effect, so avoidance of adverse consequences generally is possible but cannot be presumed. Constructive consideration of violation reduction requires recognition and analysis of the nature and causes of violations, as well as what underlying conditions propagate violations.

Violations can be classified generally as: routine, situational, optimizing or exceptional,[390] and in each case the danger is that the violator compromises the otherwise existing margin of safety because there

172   **Maritime Error Management**

follows from the violation greater vulnerability to the adverse effects of unintentional error.

Routine violations usually are some sort of "short cut," giving the violator some advantage in effort, time or in some other valued outcome, such as convenience, reputation or prestige. Common to routine violations is the tendency of people to take the easiest course allowing for accomplishing a task in what seems to be a neutral environment – the violation is not punished nor is adherence to the rules, regulations, policies or procedures (RRPP) rewarded. [391] Routine violations are relatively common and generally share the characteristic that no one in a position of authority seems to care that they are occurring. If not "punished" in some manner, such as by the occurrence of an accident or a "close call," or by disciplinary action or peer disapproval, routine violations can infect a system through *normalization of deviance*, to be discussed later. Routine violations narrow the gap between real danger and the prescribed operational situation. Routine violations can be dangerously easy to drift into. A frequent example is excessive speed in restricted visibility.[392]

A tragic example of a company condoning routine violation of at least one of its regulations was the striking and knocking down, with numerous fatalities, of the Tampa Bay bridge by the vessel *Summit Venture*. In effect was a Company Regulation that provided:

> The employment of a pilot, voluntary or compulsory, does not absolve the master or his officers of their responsibility in the navigation of the vessel. Too often the common practice of seamen is waived as soon as the pilot embarks. This is wrong.

Despite the imperative of the Company Regulation, at trial evidence was admitted showing that the vessel's owner had an "actual practice" of permitting all navigational decisions to be made by the pilot, who could be relieved only if he were "acting in a drunken or crazy manner."[393] Further evidence of discrepancy between a company's established procedures and on board practices includes issued safety instructions not being found on board and such instructions that are found on board being "spotlessly clean, ...indicating that they are rarely or never looked at."[394]

Another routine violation that comes readily to mind, hopefully less prevalent today, is the failure of watch officers (myself included) to call the captain in accordance with the common standing order that the captain be called by the watch officer "when in doubt regarding any situation."[395] Under appropriate circumstances, including a junior officer who has proven his or her competence and trustworthiness, the standing order as understood internally might be: "Call me if you need me, but try not to need me." This gives the officer the invaluable opportunity to independently gain decision making experience – always provided the situation is not one that would "scare the pants off" the captain if he or she later were to learn of the situation.[396]

Situational violations relate to the working environment and occur where there appears no means other than to violate one or more RRPP "in order to get the job done." There may be time pressures, insufficient personnel, necessary gear is not available or absence of knowledgeable supervisory personnel. Such workplace deficiency may require improvisation on the part of the violator, who fails to think the matter through carefully enough or to consider the factors affecting safety. There is failure to bridge the gap between rule- and knowledge-based performances. An example could be the failure to wear a life jacket in a congested on-deck work area. Also, RRPP often are aimed at actions or omissions implicated in some prior accident or series of prior incidents and may so multiply as to constrain options to the point of the task being difficult without some degree of violation.

Optimizing violations often reflect an aspect of the violator's personality in relation to the task at hand – a need or desire to make the task more interesting, challenging or exciting. For example, a study previously cited supports the conclusion that extroverts may accept a comparatively closer "closest point of approach" than would introverts. Another example is the 2004 crash of a Bombardier jet, flown without passengers by a two-person crew re-positioning the jet from Little Rock to Minneapolis for commercial service.[397] That type aircraft had a 41,000 foot maximum operational ceiling, at which and above the aircraft's performance deteriorated. Despite this known hazard, there existed an informal "410 Club," "open" to Bombardier pilots who on their own initiative pushed the limits of the aircraft at that height. The two pilots agreed to depart the flight plan and, as one told Air Traffic Control upon reaching 41,000 foot altitude, "we decided to have a little fun and come on up here."[398] Both engines flamed out, control could not be regained, and the plane crashed. Interestingly, NTSB commented that repositioning flights "seemed to bring out the worst,"[399] suggesting that the relatively young and inexperienced pilots likely to be found flying smaller jets tended to be less responsible when not flying the line and without passengers on board.

Exceptional violations are likely where the situation is exceptional, perhaps of such novelty that only a unique application of education or training, together with experience, permits successful resolution, which may require violation of procedures established for conventional situations. An example might have been, in spirit anyway, taking the loaded tanker *Cherry Valley* into shallow waters in the face of a tropical storm to tow to safety a tug and barge at risk of being blown upon a lee shore.[400]

Akin to but distinct from exceptional violations are situations, sometimes exceptional and sometimes mundane, that are outside the realm of formalized RRPP. Not all situations are RRPP compatible. As James Reason as commented: "the requisite variety of the procedures necessary to govern safe behavior will always be less than the possible variety of unsafe conditions."[401] Often situations or conditions come into being before a rule or procedure can be formalized or perhaps a situation is so exceptional that no RRPP can be formalized, so not all decision making or all situational reaction is readily subject to formal RRPP. A major challenge created from subservience to RRPP is that RRPP often lag behind the depth and scope of activities that legitimately warrant regulation. For instance, the "size of ro-ro vessels grew and their designs altered so fast that regulatory agencies could not keep up with the new developments."[402]

The folly of relying exclusively or overwhelmingly upon formal RRPP to provide an appropriate level of safety is shown in the 2007 sinking in Antarctic waters of the Liberian flagged passenger vessel *Explorer*. The vessel was in compliance with class requirements for a vessel of her type and geographical area of operation.[403] The master, familiar with Baltic icing conditions but unfamiliar with Antarctic[404] ice, believed he was driving his vessel into "first year ice" but in fact was encountering ice thicker and harder than anticipated.[405] The vessel's side plating was holed by the ice and flooding eventually resulted in capsizing and sinking of the vessel. The fortuitous close proximity of another vessel and benign weather and sea conditions contributed significantly to there being neither fatalities nor serious injury. However, the event suggests noteworthy deficiencies in the then prevailing regulations. Notwithstanding inevitable contact with ice, this 1969 built ice-classed vessel as to shell plating thickness was "grandfathered" in on a thickness percentage basis rather than subjected to a more realistically advanced design load of ice pressure criteria.[406] Only one of her four lifeboats had a readily functioning engine, so 10 non-regulation Zodiacs were used to maneuver the "dumb" lifeboats to avoid their drifting into the ice or possibly broaching.[407] Though only a limited number (12) of immersion suits were carried, the Investigating Officer concluded that "vessels traveling to polar waters should carry immersion suits for all the passengers and crew on board ..."[408] Additionally, given that bulky clothing and life jackets would be worn by the occupants, a question arose whether the approved lifeboat capacity based upon number and size of persons was realistic, taking into account the need to access lifeboat gear compartments as well as freeboard considerations in any sort of less than calm sea.[409] And, the four lifeboats were open, with their occupants exposed to brutal and unforgiving Antarctic elements.[410] In sum, with the increased presence of commercial passenger vessels in polar waters, "[r]ather than just meet the current SOLAS regulations[,] should cruise companies not carry out a safety case analysis based on the reality of working in these harsh waters?"[411]

This is especially true in areas where regulation historically has been reactive. In such situations, on site individuals must draw upon their experience, education and training to assess the situation and themselves devise a resolution.

Without adequate preparation of some sort, whether through bridge resource management competence, training, education or experience, or some combination thereof, a favorable outcome should not be expected when the situation is exceptional. An impressive demonstration of one favorable outcome is the crew's performance on United Airlines July 19, 1989 DC-10 Flight UA232, en route from Denver to Philadelphia. With the plane at an altitude of 37,000 feet, the No. 2 engine fan disk disintegrated, with the debris disabling all three hydraulic systems. The plane's primary and secondary flight control systems were designed to be manipulated through these three independent hydraulic systems; failure of all three independent systems had not been envisioned, and was considered so unlikely that no backup system was provided. Nor had any procedure been written to address such a three system failure, nor training provided.

With no manual backup available, the flight crew had no means available to move any flight control surfaces, leaving control of the aircraft dependent upon proper manipulation of the thrust developed by the two remaining engines. A dead-heading company DC-10 check and training pilot joined the three man flight crew and at the captain's request took over handling engine Nos. 1 and 3 power levers, while the others by radio tried to sort out the problem and possible resolution with Flight Operations in San Francisco. Engine thrust control to establish some degree of stabilization and direction was proving ineffective and the crew realized an emergency landing was imperative. Fuel was dumped and emergency landing preparations initiated. With neither flap nor slat control, a much faster than normal landing speed was required, necessitating great care with the power settings to maintain a satisfactory descent profile. Unfortunately, the crew's extremely limited control was insufficient to prevent the right wing dropping and contacting the ground just before touch down. The plane skidded, rolled, caught fire and broke up. Of the 296 persons on board, 111 perished. But, 185 people survived.

Subsequent simulator re-enactment confirmed that control under such circumstances was so arbitrary that any sort of successful landing was purely a matter of chance.[412] Captain Al Hayes, pilot in command of the flight, subsequently attributed the degree of success to significantly, among other factors, the expertise represented by the cumulative flying experience in the cockpit and effective application of crew resource management:

> And we had 103 years of flying experience there in the cockpit, trying to get that airplane on the ground, not one minute of which we had actually practiced, any one of us. So why would I know more about getting that plane on the ground under those conditions than the other three. So if I hadn't used [CRM], if we had not let everybody put their input in, it's a cinch we wouldn't have made it.[413]

The three performance levels – skill-based, rule-based and knowledge-based performance - as relevant to RRPP violation factored into a 1986 study, undertaken by J. Habberley and others, of collision avoidance behavior practiced by qualified watch officers, using a simulator replication of approaching traffic at night. The premise was that:

> In bridge watch keeping, the detection and routine plotting of other ships is an example of skill-based performance, not requiring much conscious effort once well learned and forming a continual part of the task. The watch keeper uses rule-based behaviour to manage the large majority of encounters with other ships (not only with reference to the formal Rules, but in accordance with what is customary practice on his ship). It is only in rather exceptional circumstances, such as a close-

quarters situation, that he needs to switch to knowledge-based behavior, in order to find a safe situation to the problem which has developed.[414]

The study determined that the transition from skill-based to rule-based performance occurred at a range of between 6 and 8 miles, and from rule-based to knowledge-based performance at between 2 and 3 miles. If traffic density permits, standard operating procedure requires that a significant (in my experience, 2 miles) closest point of approach (CPA) be maintained. A surprising finding of the study was that the subject watch keepers allowed the on-coming vessel to close the range substantially before course was altered. The underlying rationale seemed to be that while a small CPA could be a precursor to collision, without more a small CPA would not necessarily result in collision. Despite the subjects' adherence to "close encounter" behavior, the eventual collision avoidance performance was adequate in 136 of 141 simulations, yielding a serious error rate of 3.5%. If a similar error rate were attributable to the other vessel, collision would result in 0.1% of such encounters.[415] The authors concluded:

> … if near-accidents usually involve an initial error followed by an error recovery (as marine near misses seem to do), more may be learned about the technique of successful error recovery than about how the initial error might have been avoided. Watch keepers who become expert ship handlers may see no reason to avoid close-quarter situations from which on the basis of their past experience they know they can extricate themselves. Confidence in one aspect of the task may engender a carefree attitude to another. Some may even believe the converse is true: a watch keeper who always avoids close-quarter situations (by over-zealous observance of the rules) will have difficulty acquiring the "knowledge" he would need to act safely in such situations [sic].

The best solution would be maximize the safety of both rule
and knowledge aspects: to have watch keepers who seldom
expose themselves to close-quarter situations, yet know
exactly how to act in any unpredictable "tight spots" that
arise. If it is not possible to have both, it is easy to see why
teaching and certification authorities would lean towards
the former as the more prudent alternative. The present
research strongly suggests that the professional leans towards
the latter, and prides himself or herself upon it.[416]

The confidence engendered by successful escape
from near miss situations can, unaddressed, encourage
future violations. As the study suggests, however, many
mariners will argue in favor of such otherwise inadvisable
behavior upon the rationale that a "deliberate courting
of a moderate degree of risk is ... a necessary way of
keeping [their ship handling] skills sharp."[417]

Adverse consequences of RRPP violation can be
multiple and rippling in their effect. The entire strategy
of the ISM safety management system, as well as of
the COLREGS, is put at risk, often to or beyond their
respective intended or calculated limits. For example,
risk of collision is compounded when one vessel
violates the COLREGS because the intended certainty
and predictability of the COLREGS thereby has been
compromised. Risk from RRPP violation is compounded
by the fact that management is hard pressed to defend
against this gap created by one or more RRPP violations
because management, more likely than not, is unaware of
the violation(s). Further, a person who willfully violates
one rule will more regularly than a non-violator also
violate other RRPP. And, without there being a bad
outcome of some sort, the violator is encouraged to
repeat and possibly expand the violation(s). Studies in
the aviation domain show that air crews that intentionally
deviate from RRPP are approximately *three times* more

likely than non-violators to commit additional errors with consequential results.[418] There is no reason to believe this multiplier effect is any different in the maritime domain.

Peers who see violators go unpunished, whether by the violator not suffering an accident or a "close call" or by not being disciplined, feel emboldened to themselves violate. Given that maritime systems are "simple" in that relatively few safety breaches are required for there to be an accident, violators are especially dangerous in the maritime domain.[419] Another aspect of RRPP violation may be some act or omission falling short of a violation but nonetheless one that undermines the defenses intended by the RRPP and so "trivializes the process." The bare letter of the RRPP may be followed while disregarding the spirit and purpose of the RRPP, thus reducing the process to its lowest level. Only the illusion, not the substance, of protection will be present.

However, occasionally RRPP violation is desirable and necessary to avoid an accident, and may even explicitly be allowed for. The General Prudential Rule, Rule 2(b) of the COLREGS, so provides:

> In construing and complying with these Rules due regard shall be had to all dangers of navigation and collision and to any special circumstances, ... , which may make a departure from these Rules necessary to avoid immediate danger.

Rule 2(b) allows latitude for legal departure from the COLREGS, so in such "special circumstances," an otherwise proscribed act is not a violation because sanctioned by the more encompassing Rule 2(b).[420]

The research stream reveals that relatively little is known as to "why" professionals violate RRPP. Conclusions drawn from simulator performance can deceive because on a simulator the performer is likely

to be on his or her best behavior. Casualty analyses can
be deficient in determining "why" because the actors
may be less than forthcoming or candid, for lack of
commonly agreed upon human factor benchmarks, or
an investigator's unfamiliarity with human factor issues.
But what is known is significant and offers some, albeit
incomplete, guidance toward managing a variety of
conditions conducive to violations. Not surprisingly,
both the why and potential means for remediation are
related to the type of violation under consideration.

Shedding some light upon human factor issues
are the *cognitive* and *behavioral* approaches to RRPP
violation.

The *cognitive approach* draws upon cognitive
psychology to construct a Human Information
Processing Model (HIP) of 23 interrelated categories of
non-adherence (notice should be taken that not every
category is intentional):

1. Lack of information
2. Misperception of information
3. Inaccessible procedure formats cause interpretation
problems
4. Relevant information missed due to competing
activities
5. Complacency
6. Error due to insufficient training/experience
7. Company culture stresses other elements as more
important
8. Inconsistent company philosophy/policies/
procedures
9. Shipboard personnel fail to buy into company
philosophy
10. Professional shipboard culture renders personnel
overconfident of their abilities
11. National culture influences adherence to RRPP

12. Shipboard safety climate

13. Personality influences adherence to RRPP

14. Psycho/sociological factors influence adherence to RRPP

15. Physiological factors influence availability of attention resources

16. Stress influences

17. Shipboard personnel determine certain RRPPs are ineffective/inappropriate

18. Shipboard personnel determine certain RRPP absorb too much of available resources

19. RRPP determined to contain one or more mistakes relative to implementation

20. Confusion between new and old RRPP

21. Confusion between current RRPP

22. Failure to provide shipboard personnel with direct feedback

23. Failure in decision making strategy[421]

The authors of the above 23 categories suggest the following groupings:

No perception of relevant information (input) [1, 5, 22]

Misperception of information (pattern matching) [2]

Procedural design (input, interpretation) [3, 8, 17, 18, 19, 20, 21]

Procedural experience/training (long term memory) [6]

Cultural aspects (influencing factors) [7, 10, 11]

Personality aspects/attitudes (influencing factors) [9, 12, 13, 14, 15]

Situational factors (influencing factors) [16]

Decision making heuristics [23]

Bridge resource management (attention resources) [4, 18]

Given the above breakdown, as well as the earlier discussed HFACS and the following behavioral approach, the inadequacy of the all too common investigatory conclusion "proper procedures were not followed" is self-evident.

The cognitive approach allows for no one single remedy capable of addressing cumulatively all 23 categories of non-adherence, but with grouping, remedies appropriate to individual groups can be devised. On the other hand, the *behavioral approach*, providing an objective evaluation of RRPPs and the nature of the violation, suggests that the remedy for their violation lies within the RRPP themselves.[422]

An illustration of the behavioral approach internal opportunity for correction can be found in the 2007 allision of the Bahamian-registered tanker *Axel Spirit* with the Ambrose Light Tower at the entrance to New York Harbor. In its investigation report of the casualty, the NTSB observed that:

> [d]espite [the vessel owner's] organization and thorough SMS policies, the master did not follow certain aspects of the SMS on the night of the allision, and he did not require the navigational crew to comply with critical risk-mitigation procedures. The master told investigators that to enforce the SMS was paperwork-intensive and difficult, and he felt that the system was "huge." Because the master felt that the SMS was overwhelming, he was disinclined to follow certain procedures in it.[423]

Not surprisingly, the company severed its relation with the master and watch officer, but one has to wonder what likely would have happened (or not) if only the ISM/SMS Designated Person had questioned the master thoroughly regarding his opinion of the SMS and his practice with respect to following or not following SMS procedures, and also had seriously questioned the watch officer regarding the ship's navigation practices and investigated the accuracy of his response. Objective appraisal of the

SMS could have resulted in constructive modification, if warranted, of the SMS such that the master could have found acceptable. And, generally if one master had found the SMS off-putting, other masters likely would have had a similarly negative opinion. What is hard to fathom is that despite these apparent omissions on the part of vessel interests to ask relevant questions *before* the allision, the NTSB in its report and just preceding the above quoted language concluded that the vessel interests' "operational oversight and commitment to safety were adequate."

Based upon and confirmed through intensive study undertaken on North Sea oil rigs, a *behavioral approach* model to intentional RRPP violations was refined in the 1990s.[424] This model works backward from the behavior comprising the violation, the premise being that in planning the violation a violator makes a conscious willful decision to violate, based upon one of four motivations:

1. Expectation that to accomplish the task— there must be some violation of RRPP;

2. External goals — such as rewards or requirements of the job;

3. Opportunism - the task can be done more quickly or there is no supervision; and,

4. Intention that things be done a certain way.

Results from the study included a finding that 62% of the violations could be predicted by looking at only four predicates:

Expectation, as above, and the largest single factor leading to violations;

Feelings of control, referring to powerfulness and the belief that one need not follow RRPPs because of experience or ability;

Opportunism, as above; and,

Planning, referring to the failure to plan things out in advance.

A second study[425] went on to find that even in the absence of violations, there is the potential for violations "coming like a bolt out of the blue," a conclusion derived from discussing with people their past history of adhering to RRPP or not. Looking into whether people *would* violate if conditions were appropriate led to two dimensions in which the researchers classed people as *sheep* - persons normally disinclined to violate RRPPs - or *wolves* - persons without such scruples. The first dimension was *Sheep v. Wolves* and the second was *Sheeps' Clothing v. Wolves' Clothing*. The point of this further inquiry was to determine an overall propensity for violating.

Sheep in Sheeps' Clothing (confirmed non-violators) – 22.5% of respondents, these are the guardians of the standards.

Wolves in Sheeps' Clothing – 33.8% of respondents (the largest group), these have not yet violated, but would not have a problem violating if conditions were appropriate.

Sheep in Wolves' Clothing – 14.1% of respondents, who were violators but not happy or comfortable doing so.

Wolves in Wolves' Clothing – 29.6% of respondents, who were unabashedly wolves and would not hesitate to violate. (Interestingly, a separate study in the aviation domain found 20% of the pilots studied to be admitted regular violators, whom those researchers styled *drongos*, a species of Australian bird that is said deliberately defecates upon the heads of passers-by.)

From these figures, 56% of the respondents did not report a significant history of violations, but 63.4% were Wolves, while only 43.7% reported having violated recently. Strikingly, 78% either reported violating or will have no qualms violating when the time comes.[426] Only 22.5% were likely to not violate.

Arguably, sheep *and* wolves provide respective benefits to an organization. The sheep uphold safe operating procedures and can be relied upon to exclusively work within the RRPP. Of course, while such behavior enhances safety, productivity may be sacrificed - the fact that gives "working to rule" such leverage to labor in pre-strike labor negotiations. The wolves are opportunists, and construe RRPP as merely guidelines. The study suggests that "[a]n organization composed totally of Sheep may go bankrupt, while an organization of Wolves is likely to go bang!"[427] The manager of such a mixed group, as is most likely to comprise the crews of naval and merchant ships, is tasked with balancing the two forces (though managers are likely to have more Wolf than Lamb personalities). He or she ideally will structure the operation such that the "need" for violations is minimized and that initiative is channeled into productive, not dangerous, directions. While there may not be overt violations, with so many wolves the potential for violations is high. That potential can be diagnosed and remedial steps taken before the "bang!" The prevalence of Wolves sends a clarion call for effective and proactive management.

An instructive PhD thesis addressing the motivating factors and risk associations with intentional RRPP violation was authored by David Lee Huntzinger in 1994. The actors studied were aviators, but the conclusions drawn are broad enough to be relevant to mariners. The underlying "proposal" was that "not every rule break ends in disaster but many disasters begin with rule breaks."[428] He interviewed thirty licensed North American male pilots, ten from each of three groups: commercial, general and airline, asking that each interviewee describe two events: one where a RRPP was broken and another where a violation was considered but rejected. The study confirmed the *situational control*

theory, which postulates that rule breaking has three
conditions: 1) a benefit gained by the violation; 2)
low probability of detection or, preferably, because
punishment does not always follow detection, high
probability of "success" meaning non-detection; and,
3) no adverse reaction from one's peers.

Expanding upon these three conditions, the first
observation is that there are many situations in which
any of several alternative ways exist to accomplish a
task, thereby presenting the actor with a dilemma. One
choice is RRPP oriented and conforming, whereas the
alternatives are not. The motive to violate defines the
non-conforming alternatives.

The actor need not personally reap the benefit of
the violation. The beneficiary may be the company,
whose schedule is maintained, or the passenger who is
not inconvenienced by delay. Though not commented
upon in the thesis, the high probability of success may
be an expectation founded upon past successful routine
or situational violations such as were discussed in the
previously cited Habberley study. This highlights the
danger of "normalization of deviance," to be discussed
ahead – "It turned out OK the last time, so I can get
away with doing it again."

Finally, the peers whose approbation is significant
are limited to fellow practitioners, and excludes
management, regulators and other outsiders. The
Huntzinger study highlights that the violator's "discovery
is not the end of the investigation."[429]

Further insight into thinking that may lead to
RRPP violations can be drawn from a recent study that
looked at collision avoidance strategies implemented by
"expert" professional watch officers on board ferries and
cargo vessels transiting Dover Strait.[430] The purpose of
the study was to determine what people *actually* do in an
evolving environment notwithstanding formal RRPP – in

the study, the COLREGS - being present. The finding was that experienced people tend to use their experience to generate a single, plausible and satisfying (though, not optimal) resolution, validating a "recognition-primed decision." The several scenarios involved ferries crossing the traffic separation lanes being transited by cargo vessels. The COLREGS implicated were Rule 15 (the "give-way" vessel) – vessels crossing so as to involve risk of collision, the vessel which has the other on her own starboard side shall keep out of the way and, if the circumstances of the case admit, avoid crossing ahead of the other vessel – and Rule 17 (the "stand-on" vessel) – shall keep her course and speed unless and until the "give-way" vessel clearly is failing to act.

The "give-way" ferries almost always altered course, 64.5% of the time to starboard and 23.5% of the time to port, with a "mean amplitude of 18 degrees, at an average distance of around 3.5 nautical miles to cross astern of the cargo ship at a distance of 0.7 nautical miles (nm) or ahead at a distance of 1 nm[,]" whereas the give-way cargo ship much less frequently (performance probability of 0.67, compared to ferry probability of 0.94) took action.[431] The greater the speed of the cargo ship within the 5 to 20 knot range, the more likely she was to take action. A significant number of "give-way" ferry course alternations were to port to cross ahead – contrary to Rule 15 – and most commonly occurred when, without a course change, the ferry would have crossed ahead. Thus, altering to port was for the ferry the most "economical" action to take, presumably in recognition that ferries were relatively fast and had schedules to keep.

Where the ferry was the "stand-on" vessel, 13 of the 29 stand-on ferries altered course, in 7 of those cases the action was taken at less than 2.6 nm, the average distance at which the cargo ships maneuvered. Of these 29 encounters, in 16 the cargo ship took action, altering to starboard in 14 at a mean distance of 2.68 nm. and to port in 2. The rationale of the stand-on ferry watch officers was to close the closest point of approach (CPA) and thereby "oblige the other to alter his course to starboard too and to cross astern[,]" or, relying upon stereotype, recognizing that a slow give-way cargo ship is unlikely to alter so the ferry will take preemptive active early enough to negate the likelihood that the cargo ship will take countering action.[432] Thus, the motivating factors in these situations included efficiency (where the faster give-way ferry would have crossed ahead anyway) and mastery of the situation by the stand-on ferry. The ferry officers "use predictions about future events to perform anticipatory actions [that] allow them to keep their cognitive resources to face other potential situations and to avoid the increase of workload [commonly accompanying] the situation of the 'stand-on' vessel."[433] This adheres to the fact that experienced professionals tend to perform in an effort to conserve limited cognitive resources and to avoid knowledge-based performance, if possible. So, analysis of the study data shows that performance that may violate the letter of the COLREGS is not necessarily haphazard, even though the performance is not predictable – predictability being one of the goals of the COLREGS. Of course, notice should be taken of the fact that the ferry watch officers may be presumed to be especially experienced and comfortable in navigating the crowded waters of Dover Strait.

The above cited study serves as further evidence of the fact that in reality, no matter how a rule is written, it is always "contingent in such a way that it is dependent upon or conditioned by something else and that its defeasible nature is due to its capability of being annulled or made void[.]"[434] So in practice people have been found not to follow, in knee-jerk fashion, prescriptive RRPP but instead to use their experience and expertise to "interpret" those RRPP to conform to their own perception of how the situation actually is. An example, as cited above, is that collision avoidance practices followed at sea are "elaborations," albeit widely followed in certain busy areas of the COLREGS, such as Dover Strait ferries generally tending to keep clear of vessels in the Traffic Separation Scheme.[435]

In sum, usually the violator acts with constructive motivation and the violation is usually not cut and dried but rather is a complex matter. Management is well served by being mindful of the dilemmas that underlie many RRPP violations. As will be reiterated, instead of creating ambiguity among options, management should provide a safety culture and specific direction that enhances clear understanding among the actors that safety is pre-eminent.

Dealing with RRPP violations

In the previous discussion of the *CP Valour* grounding, reference was made to MAIB's comment that "[t]here is no benefit to be gained from good training and qualifications unless they are used as the basis for good practice when the crew return to their ships[,]" thus raising the question how employers and others can be sure that bridge teams are actually following instructions and guidance [from BRM training and safety management procedures], and performing appropriately on board their vessels. This in turn resulted in MAIB concluding that there is "thus a need for shipowners and managers to ensure that their orders and training are being put into practice by those operating their ships."[436] With this language the issue is joined as to how the potential for and reality of RRPP violations can be minimized.

Shore side management understandably is frustrated when shipboard personnel violate RRPP – especially when the violation is held to have contributed to a casualty and the more so when management is convinced that all reasonable steps had been taken by management to ensure compliance. The question for management to ask *before* the casualty and, better yet, before the violation, is: have all reasonable steps been taken in fact?[437] And, the answer more often than not lies in objective and informed evaluation of whether the RRPP were adequately communicated and were appropriate to the shipboard environment within which the RRPP were to be put into effect.

However, before embarking upon such an inquiry, a look should be taken at what management practices are *least* likely to succeed. In a recap of his reading of violation related literature, researcher Ed Mitchell raised several "flawed assumptions" that "managers must address if they expect to make progress to reduce [intentional violation of RRPP] events."[438] The "primary" flawed assumption is an organizational expectation that "good managers create good RRPP."[439] In the maritime domain, many managers are "landlubbers," well intentioned perhaps but lacking real awareness or feel for what goes on in the fleet, or have been brought ashore from the fleet and loose connection with the concerns of their former peers or simply have become subverted to the economies of senior management.[440] Even if the RRPP are "good," there is the challenge of their being read and absorbed on board, as was recognized in the investigation report into the grounding of the vessel *Bunga Teratai Satu*: "Procedures are an important part of any operational safety system. They are however, also one of the least effective forms of safety assurance. Procedural documents do not usually make interesting reading."[441] Aside from "turning off" the reader, the

RRPP may be improperly read and understood, or simply forgotten or disregarded if not sensibly adapted to the needs and convenience of the intended user.

Managers should begin with the assumption that every procedure is flawed to some degree until it is reviewed, evaluated, and validated by key employees actually using the procedure. Studies have shown that individuals' abstract perceptions of the effectiveness of RRPP generally is a poor predictor of the RRPP's quality. Indeed, "[r]searchers do not, ... , agree on the extent to which regulations may improve safety in practice,"[442] Thus, the quality of the RRPP in relation to the likelihood of their being followed or not must not be presumed in isolation but rather be determined by the deck plate mariners. What happens is that "people do not bureaucratically follow prescriptive rules, but rather utilize their own experience and stock of knowledge to adapt the rules to their perception of the reality of the situation." [443] Similarly, absent an applicable RRPP, the actor must "fill the gap" by making one or more decisions where appropriate action(s) need be taken to resolve a situation never previously encountered. For managers to presume they are more qualified to understand a procedure than those currently doing the work is presumptuous and possibly hazardous.[444] So much so that "[a]ny lack of trust caused by inappropriate or clumsy procedures will increase the perceived benefit of violating."[445] Further evidence for the propensity of deck plate "experts" to adapt procedures commensurate with their reality comes from flight deck operations aboard United States aircraft carriers, where:

> a set of highly unusual formal and informal rules and relationships are taken for granted, implicitly and almost unconsciously incorporated into ... rules and regulations that make up those factors [most critical to maintaining

performance without sacrificing either operational reliability or safety] [that] are reasonably well known internally, but are written down only in part and generally not expressed in a form that can be readily conveyed outside the confines of the Navy.[446]

Another flawed assumption is that RRPP in place with a relatively clean track record are self-proven as "good." But, avoidance of accidents or, perhaps more accurately, the absence of accidents may be equally attributable to good fortune as to good RRPP.

A third flawed assumption is, as may be expected, the assumption that most personnel adhere or will adhere to the RRPP. This assumption has been disproved, absent constructive management intervention, in preceding pages.

In addition to these "flawed assumptions" may be added various approaches to remediation that were found in the previously cited *Bending the Rules* study to have a false appearance of effectiveness. Though perhaps counter-intuitive, these less than effective policies include:

> **Selection** – hiring people who adhere to RRPP from the beginning;
> **Training** – training people about real risks and their consequences;
> **Detection** – sharpen the outlook for violations;
> **Reporting** – encourage people to report their and others' violations; and
> **Incentives** – pay for compliance, "bonus for attaining 'zero accidents' goal and punish violations.[447]

In fact, subsequent studies have encouraged Training, Detection and Reporting, provided done correctly but upon this issue more will be discussed.

Also relevant to discussion of how management will be less effective in stimulating adherence to RRPP is management's own adherence, or non-adherence. Blatant management violation speaks for itself, and is unworthy of discussion. More subtle is *normalization of deviance*,[448] which can be a significant factor explaining how "good" people and organizations come to violate RRPP, and can be seen as a reflection of how strong the safety culture effect is upon the organization as well as the safety climate of a vessel.

Once a deviant organizational or shipboard practice becomes "normalized," that practice ceases to be viewed as aberrant and as such deserving any sort of corrective response. What had been idiosyncratic becomes shared, without suffering adverse peer criticism. The practice has become routine and commonly anticipated and regularly resorted to. Overall behavior adapts to a diminished standard. While an outsider would see the behavior as a violation and worthy of condemnation, the organization insiders see the behavior as an acceptable norm that violates nothing. Too often the existence and magnitude of normalization of deviance is not revealed until after a casualty. "It won't matter" before an accident has become after the accident "it does matter."[449]

While commonly analyzed from a limited organizational perspective, whether a company or the organization on board a vessel, normalization of deviance can be seen in an entire industry as well as in the performance of tasks by an individual. Important to recognize is that normalization of deviance, like most violations, generally arises out of a desire to achieve a proper objective by proper means. With this understanding, the "normalization" takes the characteristic of a "drift."[450]

Four mutually reinforcing stages have been described as necessary for normalization of deviance:

institutionalization, rationalization, socialization, and stakeholder acceptance.

Institutionalization refers to assimilation into the organization's procedures or practices of the initial deviant behavior. *Rationalization* refers to the process by which new thinking develops subtly or overtly to justify or perhaps even valorize the deviance, such as increasing the cost of opposition or increasing the benefits of conforming. *Socialization* refers to the process by which the traditions of the community encourage new entrants to accept the deviance as permissible, if not actually desirable. Finally, *stakeholder acceptance* is achieved when people within and without the organization no longer feel a need to challenge the deviance by "whistle-blowing" from within or criticizing from without, given that each such prior adverse response has been shown to have unsuccessfully countered or failed to reverse the deviance.

As previously shown through cumulative research, RRPP violation is the result of less than satisfactory RRPP as well as the motivation to satisfy conflicting goals and, to a lesser extent, the personality of the actor. The unfortunate fact is that there are more organizational factors conducive to violations than there are organizational factors conducive to compliance. If organizations more effectively manage the conditions conducive to violations, the rate of violations would be expected to decline.

Better RRPP will take into account the environment whose safety they are expected to influence. The shipboard environment often presents conflicting goals – frequently a conflict between RRPP adherence and time constraints inherent to meeting commercial pressures and schedules. Shipboard personnel must be provided realistically attainable procedures, without management creating impossible, impractical or otherwise difficult barriers inhibiting compliance. Such organizational obstructionism is too frequently common, obviously apparent after the event but not credited before. Put another way, management must "resource the procedure."

In January of 2006 a containership suffered a tier collapse and loss of containers in heavy weather. Though the exact cause of the collapse was not determined, the cargo loading manual was violated in that the maximum stack weight was exceeded. The MAIB investigation report commented that the stow plan showed improper weight distribution that went uncorrected by the shore staff and that due to time constraints "[o]nce cargo operations were underway, there was little realistic chance of the cargo officer imposing his own requirements." The report continued: "Instructions contained in safety management systems are often well considered and intentioned, but full compliance with such instructions can sometimes be difficult for staff to achieve in practice[,]" leading to the situation that though "the onboard paper audit trail was being completed, in reality, the cargo officer might have been unable to fulfill his duties to the standard required by the SMS." Then followed the cautionary note that management "should check not only that its instructions are understood, but also that they are achievable with the manpower available in the turnaround times allotted."[451] Here again, a situation of "resource the procedure." Where RRPP are incompatible with reality, job performance may be perceived, at least by the usually present Wolves, as more important than compliance.

Another example of conflicting goals is the situation confronting USS *Cole*, the destroyer attacked in 2000 by terrorists in Aden, Yemen. That port had been deemed a high threat zone and there was no reason for *Cole* to be there other than that she needed to top off fuel as a result of high fuel consumption during her 27-knot passage down the Red Sea. *Cole* was transiting from one battle group to another, each group wanting *Cole* to remain within its respective operational area as long as possible. Thus, she was compelled to run at maximum speed with maximum fuel consumption to transit the geographical gap between the two battle groups as quickly as possible. Procedural safety was sacrificed to achieve the battle groups' respective goals, goals in conflict with *Cole*'s best interest – running at a fuel efficient speed so as to avoid the need to call at a high threat port to top off fuel.[452]

A violation results from the selection made between or among options with varying risks and benefits attached. From the Wilde Risk Homeostasis Theory, a risk-benefit analysis emerges. In assessing the risk of any behavior, not least the violation of a RRPP, the actor is offered four categories of motivating factors, taking, as an example, laying out a voyage plan between two ports:

1. Expected benefit derived from comparatively risky behavior: save time and distance by taking a route not recommended;
2. Expected cost of comparatively risky behavior: vessel suffers a casualty from risks peculiar to the route not recommended;
3. Expected benefit from comparatively safe behavior: greater likelihood of safe arrival; and
4. Expected cost of comparatively safe behavior: being called a "wimp" by peers and owners' disappointment in less efficient use of their money making vessel asset.

The expected cost of comparatively risky behavior was exacted when, in April of 2008, the German containership *Pacific Challenger* ran up on an uncharted reef during her first charter voyage from Rabaul, New Britain to Oro Bay, Papua New Guinea. To save 70 nautical miles (the expected benefit), a direct course line was selected over the longer preferred route. The Admiralty Sailing Directions warned of "imperfect" surveys, potential shoal build up due to seismic activity, and coral pinnacles on the route chosen (the comparatively risky behavior).[453] Similarly, the "wimp" cost of comparatively safe behavior is demonstrated by the attitude of naval personnel toward commanding officers who took a pilot seaward of a particular buoy, mentioned in the discussion of the carrier *Eisenhower* striking an anchored vessel.

Of course, the above categorization only partially addresses the decision to be made by the decision maker – lurking behind are often economic considerations at least impliedly imposed by management. Also present may be national cultural issues, resource limitations, and the decision maker's self assessment and personality, to name but a few.

In the Wilde risk homeostasis model, management directly can intervene in the risk assessment at the point of box "e" ("resulting accident loss"), which refers to the opportunity to disseminate information describing various incidents and accidents. Taken objectively and seriously, the more a decision maker knows of industry particular incidents and accidents resulting from others' poorly made decisions, the better the decision maker will be able to evaluate the potential risk level and so avoid the common propensity to under-estimate risk at box "b" ("perceived level of risk" – a common condition conducive to RRPP violation) and moderate his decision and behavior accordingly.

Of Dr. Huntzinger's three violation criteria, adverse reaction from one's peers would seem to be the criterion most feasible for management to address, due to the variability of the other two criteria. The power of economic considerations prevailed among 28 of the 30 violations: "I ... think economic pressures will continue and the economic violations will also continue."[454] This indicates that notwithstanding any contrary suggestion, actors will decide economic benefit, i.e., perceived company satisfaction, over safety.

In sum, "it would appear that there is a better than even chance that people will break the rules more often than not, especially in the absence of a *clear* 'No Go!' determinant."[455] This should concern safety conscious management, and strongly evidences that a "safety first" message must be explicit and direct, and demonstrably supported, to get across to shipboard personnel.

Therefore, the wording of safety admonitions from management in the maritime domain deserves comment.

In 1978 the fully loaded VLCC *Amoco Cadiz* lost steering not far seaward off the rocky lee shore of Ushant and the French coast in onshore gale-force wind. Clearly tug assistance was needed, whether by towage or salvage, and a capable tug soon was on site. With the tug demanding salvage but the cost of a tow being substantially less, the tanker's master was at a loss "as to how much authority he had for making decisions that might cost his employers a lot of money."[456] His confusion stemmed largely from the ambiguity[457] of the relevant section in the company's Tanker Operation Manual. Following formalistic direction that when human life, the vessel or cargo is "in peril ... the Master shall immediately take all precautions ... and ... exercise his own best judgment without restraint[.]"

So far as is consistent with the foregoing, the Master should endeavor to notify the Marine Manager's office by the quickest possible means when outside assistance is required, and when the circumstances of the case permit, utilize the assistance of available Company vessels. Before accepting assistance from a non-Company vessel, the Master shall, if practicable, advise the Marine Manager of the terms of the agreement to assist, i.e., whether salvage or towage.

Awaiting instruction from management located in Chicago, the tanker's captain in his negotiations directly with the tug's master held out for a towage rate while his vessel drifted ever closer to shore and destruction. Direction came too late to save the vessel and prevent the ensuing massive pollution. The Liberian board inquiring into the casualty commented critically that the last two sentences from the Manual "are capable of being construed so as to limit the over-all authority and responsibility of the Master ... ."[458]

Also, in 1995 the Liberian tanker *Patriot* came close to grounding on the Yucatan Peninsula in hurricane-associated high winds and seas. Though without formal jurisdiction, the NTSB accepted the owner's invitation to investigate the circumstances of this close-call situation "to determine why a qualified and experienced seaman such as the master of *Patriot* would take such a course" as to place his vessel in the eye of a hurricane in an effort to satisfy the terms of the vessel's charter.[459] The Board criticized what it characterized as "general guidance" that the master "is to observe weather conditions closely at all times and he is not to hesitate to alter course, reduce speed, or put into port to avoid weather that may be hazardous to the vessel or endanger those on board." The generality of this language was deemed insufficient to overcome the master's concerns over failing to fulfill all charter terms and his perception of his employer's job performance criteria.[460]

The issue of shadowy real authority and company support to act in the interest of safety doubtlessly continues to exist in the maritime industry and enhances at least implicitly an attitude of tolerance (so long as nothing goes wrong) for at least approaching the border line of RRPP violation.

Of course, even with the most artfully worded RRPP, violations will occur for a variety of reasons, including the employment of Wolves, that situations are so varied that no set of RRPP can be expected to cover all situations and circumstances, and that sometimes the situation is such that an otherwise good RRPP must be violated to prevent greater harm.

Lest management throw up collective hands in frustration, helpful guidance is available. Dr. Patankar prepared in 2002 a *Root Cause Analysis of Rule Violations by Aircraft Maintenance Technicians*[461] in which his consideration of 13 primary organizational causal factors and 12 individual-type factors leads to the conclusion that none are beyond the ability of organizations and individuals to at least influence, if not control. While the survey was directed toward aviation maintenance workers, several of the conclusions correlate well with the maritime domain. These conclusions include organizational improvement in: 1. drafting RRPP and dissemination of information relevant to those RRPP; 2. encouragement of "training, planning and task supervision;" and 3. coordinating with equipment manufacturers to "Murphy-proof system and component design." On the individual level, the suggestions include: 1. improve situational awareness; 2. reduce complacency; and 3. expand training and experience.[462]

A challenge to RRPP adherence is the conflict between the rigidity of RRPP on the one hand and on the other hand mariners' recognition of and pride in their professional knowledge and competence. This conflict is common with professionals and lies deeply embedded in organizations, even where RRPP are acknowledged as being desirable, at least in principle. A study of health care professionals found that despite an overwhelming belief that protocols are a good thing and should be used widely, there was a 50% violation of the protocols in place. The protocols were seen as taking second place to professional judgment. This view is widely held – among, for example, nuclear operators as shown in another study. Similarly, there is general recognition that about 50% of mariners confirm that they regularly violate safety RRPP. [463]

While shipboard personnel may well have a sense of risk assessment through their training and experience, the unevenness of that training and experience can be strong argument in favor of comprehensive and appropriate RRPP to govern shipboard work practices. The various factors previously discussed as conducive to RRPP violation are as prevalent among mariners as with other groups, perhaps more so. Pride in performance as well as mariners' historical spirit of independence and acceptance of risk may result in their working ever closer to risk. Mariners are likely to be quick to recognize which RRPP are too general and those that are ill-suited to the realities of the task to be undertaken. [464] There will be foreseeable routine non-compliance with RRPP deemed inadequate or unnecessary. In any of these situations, management should provide a prompt, easy and non-punitive conduit whereby management can be informed that there is an issue. Whether management agrees or not, management should respond, with a thorough explanation for the position taken. Failure of management to respond appropriately is a fatal error. A shipboard sense of futility and frustration is likely to result, with the attitude – "If they don't care, why should I care?"

Mariners are likely to be particularly hostile to burdensome RRPP imported from other domains and that have no local benefit. An example could be a requirement that helmets be worn aboard tankers, a requirement perceived as having no local value but imposed by a shore side manager striving to "make points" without regard to what might be dropped on a tanker and from where, but because a similar requirement applies to oil refinery workers. Mariners will quickly see through such managerial abdication of respect for mariners' "professional knowledge, professional pride, and experience-based common sense." An understandable aversion will exist in mariners against "following a fixed procedure" in lieu of "acting according to the dictates of good seamanship by taking the situation into account."[465] The helmet on a tanker requirement could be compared against a similar requirement imposed on container vessels in port, reasonable due to the risk of being struck by lashing gear dropped by longshoremen from atop a container tier. Mariners generally share a quality of seeking practicality and shunning the unnecessary.

Without a shipboard safety climate that endorses risk awareness and some procedure for addressing inappropriate RRPP, a policy of relying upon RRPP to dictate worker behavior may encourage a belief that safety is merely a matter of complying with RRPP that take the place of personal attention to and responsibility toward the risks of the work undertaken.

In parallel is concern that excessive and overly restrictive and regimented RRPP frustrate development of that quality of judgment needed when a situation, emergency or crisis is outside the perimeter of the existing RRPP.[466] One master is quoted: " ... when you are at sea, you have to be able to think, and you can't [think] when you must slavishly look up [written procedures] in a book. ... No matter if your own thought is better or not, you have to do what is written."[467]

An excess of RRPP has been found to be detrimental to self-managed safety and renders the system artificially rigid.[468] A result is that discretionary behavior is restricted as well as is free thinking that is a basis for sound decision making. As one authority has stated: "Detailed rules and procedures, however well intentioned, are undermining the skill that wisdom requires."[469]

Management no doubt would argue that a competent ship's master always is expected to exercise sound judgment, and no-one would disagree. But, isn't judgment a factor of experience, and how much real "experience" is a senior officer able to acquire, given the current reliance upon simulator training, short staffing, taking pilots in congested waters, being overseen by VTS (Vessel Traffic Systems) and, with the exponentially increased paperwork, reduced opportunity for professional reading and self-education?

Ultimately, the question is not who has the authority to represent risk but is instead, who has the authority to bring the representation of risk to bear upon operational policy.

Destructive Obedience

The term "destructive obedience" is coined to emphasize the danger of deliberate or slavish acquiescence to orders or practices recognized as unsafe or contrary to standing orders or procedures. Destructive obedience may result from power distance arising from cultural differences, or command distance created by an intimidating senior officer, or the confidence of a junior in the senior's competence or experience, or lack of any comfortable method for addressing a breach of good practice, as well as other possibilities. Whatever the cause, the consequence is that one of the last and most important defenses against harm is penetrated. An air industry study found that destructive obedience was present in 75% of air accidents.[470] The most effective defense to destructive obedience is proactive encouraged appropriate monitoring and challenging.

Despite the frequency of situations calling for the challenging of violations and other unsafe practices, this aspect of watch keeping is one with which senior and subordinate officers are least familiar and comfortable. Instead, the subordinate all too often is concerned that: "I'm damned if I ignore what I am seeing or hearing and something bad happens, but I'm doubly damned if I say anything, especially if I'm wrong." There are many examples adverse consequences from the failure to speak up. At 0142 on June 23, 1995, the Liberian registered passenger vessel *Star Princess* struck a charted submerged rock in the deep water channel connecting Skagway, Alaska, with the Inside Passage. The ship's watch officers were convinced that the pilot had the situation under control, in part because they were used to relying on this pilot and his expertise. They chose not to interfere with his decisions or actions – even though they knew the vessel was approaching dangerously near to Poundstone Rock – because they had full confidence in the pilot's abilities. In their post-accident testimony, the watch officers, defending their silence, said of the pilot: " ... he was piloting the vessel, ... he is a professional, he knows where we should be, ... he has been here before, ... he is making the necessary course changes."[471]

The Liberian bulk carrier *Montrose* grounded 0600 February 28, 2007 in Chesapeake Bay with a bay pilot conning the vessel and the first time master absent from the bridge. On boarding, the docking pilot signed the proffered pilot exchange card but the bay pilot forcefully declined, asserting his 30 years of experience. The subsequently "sedentary" bay pilot failed to order and execute a course change at the "CR" buoy. The watch officer later admitted his suspicion that the pilot was not ordering a necessary course change, yet failed to speak up in any way. The Coast Guard investigation report concluded that the "pilot's demeanor and mannerism were such as to command authority and the mate failed to assert himself [and] became complacent in allowing the pilot to take full responsibility and control of the vessel."[472]

The United Kingdom registered container vessel *Maersk Kendel* ran onto a reef in Singapore Strait in 2009 after failing to resume her intended course following a course change to allow passage of three vessels, despite warnings received from Singapore Vessel Traffic Information System (VTIS). The bridge team of the British master and Indian chief officer, though aware the vessel was heading toward the reef, failed to monitor her speed or relative position and failed to appreciate the significance of the VTIS information. The MAIB determined that the chief officer failed to challenge the master's performance because:

His previous experience with the master gave him no reason to do so;
He did not appreciate the impending danger;
The master did not engage the chief officer in terms of the navigational support he required;
The master appeared to be in control and comfortable with the situation;
The chief officer was culturally reluctant to challenge the master;
The master had signaled an irritation to interventions in his response to VTIS; and,
The chief officer had received no crew resource management or bridge team management training.[473]

In February of 2001 the United States fast attack nuclear submarine USS *Greeneville* was having its capabilities demonstrated to distinguished visitors on board off Hawaii within a "fairly tight" schedule. Steep angled depth changes, frequently at high speeds ("angles and dangles"), were demonstrated. Eventually, the commanding officer ("CO") ordered the officer of the deck ("OOD") to prepare and bring the boat from a substantial depth to periscope depth within five minutes, this despite the CO's own standing orders that no less than eight minutes would be allocated for necessary preparations. This eight minute period was allocated, among other factors, to permit verification of the surface contact situation. The "unusual" five minute time constraint imposed by the CO inhibited proper ascertainment of the surface contact situation but the OOD nonetheless proceeded, later explaining "Here's a man [the CO] with much more experience than I have, much more schooling than I have, [who] can much more rapidly assess and evaluate information … ."

The CO explained his decision to shorten the time for preparation: "I chose not to follow specific things out of my standing orders because I deemed at that time them not to be necessary." A brief periscope search failed to disclose any close aboard surface contacts, so the CO proceeded to demonstrate an emergency deep dive followed by an emergency main ballast tank blow intended to surface the boat as quickly as possible. As *Greeneville* reached the surface, the Japanese fishing and training vessel *Ehime Maru* was struck and sank, with 9 fatalities.[474]

A study of United States and European male and female aircraft pilots and co-pilots evaluated the effectiveness of crew communication strategies in monitoring and challenging situations of varying complexity and stress.[475] The underlying premise was that error or omission intervention should be explicit and direct, but those criteria have been determined to underestimate the profound impact of social considerations arising out of the superior/subordinate relation, personalities and national culture. This impact is channeled through two components of verbal communication (beyond intelligibility): the "referential," which makes a statement about something, and the "relational," which signals something about the speaker's relation to the audience. In short, *what* is said and *how* it is said together determine how the message is received. Success of the communication, in the sense of it being acted upon as the speaker desires, depends critically upon this combination of *what* and *how.*

An added factor in challenging error or omission is often the desire or need of the speaker to "save face" of the erring recipient and avoid or minimize that person's embarrassment and loss of stature or reputation. And, to be sure, the norms that define social and acceptable behavior vary significantly across cultures and generate distinctive communicative styles. Interestingly, there was impressive commonality within the study findings, so suggestion is offered that these aviation domain findings warrant attention within the maritime community.

The most effective communicative strategy overall was neither too direct (commanding) nor too indirect (requests for permission) but was in the nature of a "crew obligation statement" ("I think we need to ----- right now."). A crew obligation statement has the attributes of specifying a joint crew responsibility to perform a definite action compelled by some external necessity as well as an implication of who is to act, without being authoritarian. Also effective were preference statements ("They want you to ----" or "I think it would be wise to ----" or "I would prefer to ---- .") and hints ("That contact at 4 miles is looking more threatening."). Not surprisingly, the more immediately threatening the situation, the greater is the directness that can be justified and accepted. When the challenge was for correction of a potentially embarrassing error or omission, "hints" were found especially effective; but hints were not the strategy usually chosen. Overall, outright commends were deemed of lesser effectiveness.[476] Most effective strategies addressed an issue without disrupting the team-working-as-a-team concept and appealed to the crew's shared responsibility that a problem should be confronted and resolved. Similar to commands, these strategies are explicit in declaring what needs to be done. They save face without being timid.

The less effective deficiencies suffered from several negations. Commands may lead to complacency, as in a subordinate failing to evaluate and verify the appropriateness of an ordered action, or feeling a challenge difficult.[477]

Hints, while a favored strategy if time permits, may leave the issue unresolved, and may be ignored or be too docile for the situation. For example, in 1893 two British battleships, HMS *Victoria* and HMS *Camperdown* and their respective divisions in two columns, were ordered by the admiral in command to turn toward each other so as to reverse direction by 180 degrees preparatory to entering port. The close proximity of the two columns and limited turning diameter of the battleships broadcast to the admiral's staff commander and flag lieutenant the danger inherent in the order – that the two battleships would turn into each other and collide. However, because the admiral "was not a person who was agreeable on being asked questions or cross-examined," these subordinate officers were reduced to "dropping clumsy hints and talking loudly about the distance" between the lead ships, and assumed the admiral "had chosen his distance for an express purpose which had eluded their pedestrian minds."[478] He hadn't. HMS *Camperdown* rammed HMS *Victoria*, the latter sinking with 358 fatalities.

Nor is casual conversation likely to be any more successful. In January of 1982 an Air Florida Boeing 737 impacted the Potomac River on take-off due to excessive snow and ice accumulation on the 737's flying surfaces and a frozen indicator that gave the crew a false reading of engine power. Awaiting takeoff clearance, the first officer was sufficiently concerned about the snow and ice build up to address the issue in his conversation with the captain, but was unsuccessful in securing the latter's attention and action:

First Officer: *Look how the ice is hanging on his, ah, back, back there, see?*

First Officer: *See all those icicles on the back there and everything?*

Captain: *Yeah.*

(After a long wait following de-icing.)

First Officer: *Boy, this is a, this is a losing battle here on trying to de-ice those things, it (gives) you a false feeling of security, that's all it does.*

(Shortly after being given clearance to takeoff, the first officer again expresses concern)

First Officer: *Let's check those tops again since we've been sitting here awhile.*

Captain: *I think we get to go here in a minute.*

(Finally, when the aircraft was rolling for takeoff, the first officer noticed something wrong with the engine readings.)First Officer: *That don't seem right, does it?* [three second pause] *Ah, that's not right ...*

Captain: *Yes, it is, there's 80.*

First Officer: *Naw, I don't think that's right.* [seven second pause] *Ah, maybe it is.*[459]

The aviation industry has developed a PACE procedure, which has proved effective for communicating concern:

P[robing for better understanding] -"I need to understand why --- ."

A[lert to anomalies]

"I am afraid if --- the result will be --- ."

C[hallenge appropriateness of strategy]

"This course places the ship in immediate danger from --- ."

E[mergency response to immediate danger]

"Captain, if you do not immediately ---, my duty and responsibility is to take the conn."[480]

In the extreme situation of the Emergency warning not having the desired effect, the final step is Intervention and Take-over, whereby the watch officer verbally takes the conn – "Captain, I am taking and now have the conn."[481] Doing so is a drastic step, and should be carefully considered.

11

Technology and eNavigation: Advantages and Challenges

Ships change more readily than men, ...— S.W. Ryder, *Blue Water Ventures*

The new ship here is fitted according to the reported increase of knowledge among mankind. Namely, she is cumbered end to end, with bells and trumpets and clock and wires, it has been told to me, can call voices out of the air of the waters to con the ship while her crew sleep. But sleep Thou lightly. It has not yet been told to me that the Sea has ceased to be the Sea.
— Rudyard Kipling

To ensure safety at sea, the best that science can devise ... must be regarded only as an aid, and never as a substitute for good seamanship, self-reliance, and a sense of ultimate responsibility which are the first requisites in a seaman ... . — Fleet Admiral Chester W. Nimitz, Fleet letter

The science of navigation can be taught, but the art must be developed from experience.— *The American Practical Navigator,* 1995

It is on men that safety at sea depends and they cannot make a greater mistake than to suppose that machines can do all their work for them. — *The Fogo* [1967] 2 Lloyd's Rep. 208, 211 (Adm.)

In September of 1923 a flotilla of United States destroyers was en route from San Francisco to San Diego, intending to pass Point Honda to port, and thereafter alter course easterly to enter the Santa Barbara Channel, notwithstanding heavy prevailing fog. The flotilla was running at high speed, rendering fathometers ineffective. A form of radio direction finding (RDF), whereby a radio compass station ashore received a radio signal from a vessel at sea and responded with the compass bearing from which the signal was received (reciprocal relative bearing), was in its infancy and so was mistrusted due to the numerous errors to which it could be subject. A bearing issued by the shore station was received by the flagship and when plotted placed the flotilla north of its deduced "dead" reckoned (DR) position. A choice between the DR position and the new northerly RDF system generated position had to be made. Trust in the DR position won out, and on the basis of the DR position course was altered from 150 degrees true to 095 degrees true to enter the Channel. Five minutes later, the lead destroyer USS *Delphy*, doing 20 knots, struck on Point Honda, followed in succession by nine of the trailing destroyers. All together, seven destroyers were total losses, with 23 fatalities. Four destroyers at the tail of the flotilla escaped unscathed.

The Point Honda tragedy was among the first and one of the worst maritime casualties in which some form of electronic navigation system was at issue. But the RDF system was not at fault and the mistrust was misplaced: "... it was not the compass bearings ... which were wrong, but the judgment of the men who interpreted these bearings and who used them wrongly."[482] The Naval Court continued:

> The price of good navigation is constant vigilance. The unusual is always to be guarded against and when the expected has not been eventualized [sic], a doubtful situation

always arises which must be guarded against by every precaution known to navigators. ... no ship is safe when close to the coast unless it actually knows where it is. Dead Reckoning alone can never be relied upon. It is always the Captain who is sure in his own mind without the tangible evidence of safety in his possession, who loses his ship.[463]

Today's extensive electronic navigation capabilities and integrated navigation systems, collectively to be referred to as eNavigation (eNav)[484] (electronic navigation, comprised variously of Global Positioning System (GPS) with integrated auto pilot and ship control elements, Automatic Radar Plotting Aid (ARPA), Automated Identification System (AIS), Electronic Chart Display and Information System (ECDIS), Vessel Data Recorder (VDR) and the like), with associated technologies[485] carry forward the lesson and admonition derived from Point Honda, as well as compel a reorientation of the mariners' two historic means of managing maritime navigation risk – the practices of good seamanship and the exercise of sound judgment honed through experience, training and education. Hand in hand with this technological evolution is a belief, shore side at least, that a solution to the human element component of maritime casualties is "to improve the degree to which decisions are automated and, through realizing automatic navigation, to avoid the mistakes caused by the subjective judgments of people."[486]

Today's mariners must confront and accommodate a quantum shift from personally processing and integrating information directly obtained through traditional means of *lead, log* and *lookout*[487] and celestial navigation[488] to accepting data mechanically obtained and presented through console displays. "Confrontation" is not too extreme a characterization because when there is a disconnect between the technologically advanced system and the mariner, the mariner, as the last line of defense against the risk and potential for casualty toward which technology has drawn the mariner, now must restore the failed integration in a way he or she best understands. This despite the tendency of eNav technology to withdraw the mariner from the reality of the physical environment within which the risk must be directly resolved.[489]

This integration of historic and modern means has not been seamless. Care must be taken that what has been gained comes not at too great an expense in traditional skills. Concern is justified that common sense, experience and basic seamanship and marine engineering skills are taking back seat to increased automation, inanimate decision support systems and the like. This reality has not complemented the objective of eNav to provide tools that are optimized to clearly delineate risk for improvement of decision making and prevent single person error. Ideally, the mariner's role will not be marginalized to merely monitoring the gadgetry.

Aside from the potential of eNav to deskill and convert the mariner into an observer, the risk homeostasis theory previously discussed postulates that as certain elements within a system increasingly offer greater potential for safety, that perceived increase in safety will induce greater risk taking because of the resulting belief that the greater safety will compensate for more risky behavior ~ the level of acceptable risk rises. So, paradoxically, the potential benefit in safety may be cancelled out.[490] In the maritime domain, recognition of the truth of risk homeostasis came at least as early as the 1950s, with reference to "radar assisted" collisions occurring when radar equipped vessels failed to reduce speed in conditions of restricted visibility. The concern was so great that at least one owner removed radar units from its vessels.

The trend is toward "increasingly complex shipboard systems," handling navigation, engineering and cargo operations, because the "possibility to develop systems with an increasing level of functionality encourages the design and construction of ever more complex systems."[491] This being so, exacerbation of present challenges is likely, providing greater incentive to come to grips with the human-automated systems interface. Analysis of the relevant literature as well as study of incidents and casualties involving automated systems confirms and reconfirms that automation "creates new human weaknesses and it amplifies existing ones. Human error does not vanish; automation changes its nature."[492] The manual workload is reduced but the mental workload increases.

Facially, eNav would be expected to ease the bridge watch officer's task because "[l]argely, the job of seafarers is to convert expectations to reality: to minimize surprises, to contain them, to relate the new to the old and to mediate the transition."[493] In this view, the navigating officer "becomes a system manager, choosing system presets, interpreting system output, and monitoring vessel response."[494] As the contribution of eNav to the watch officer's hold upon situational awareness is significant, a momentary return to the previous situational awareness discussion is warranted:

> A total of 177 maritime casualty reports, relating to events during the period 1987-2001 and originating from eight different countries, were analyzed, revealing that 71% of the errors were situational awareness related:
>
> 58.5% involved failure correctly to obtain or perceive information;
>
> 32.7% involved failure correctly to integrate or comprehend information; and,
>
> 8.8% involved failure appropriately to project future action.[495]

Expansion of this study determined that the newer the ship, the greater was the loss of situational awareness, indicating that situational awareness "is a problem with increasing levels of technology ... ."[496] Confirmation comes from the involvement of the watch officer increasingly in a passive role and the truth of the anonymous saying that the "greatest hazard to navigation is a bored navigator."[497]

Generally, eNav performs tasks and "decides" on bases radically different from human performance. While the system may more quickly sift through collected data than a human being, the data available to the system is limited to factual empirical data within the situation as selected by whomever engineered or programmed the system. Ideally, eNav would provide exactly the information necessary for accurate position determination or for arriving at the best solution for achieving a desired or necessary vessel maneuver. But what eNav provides may not include all that is truly relevant and helpful to the mariner's immediate task because either the designer possessed a limited awareness of all that is truly relevant at sea or because such data is not readily perceived by other than human senses. Humans are more adaptable in generating, overseeing and adjusting plans and action in response to changing circumstances. Systems are narrowly focused, predicated upon rule-based thinking (if event A, then response B, as previously discussed). As one experienced mariner noted: "The marine environment is an intrinsic set of variables that are part of an equation that can not[sic] be solved by the linearity of a traditional mechanized model."[478] On the other hand, humans see situations through a wide-angled lens (a holistic or gestalt approach), which allows humans to incorporate non-analytic, intuitive (hairs go up on the back of humans' necks) factors in converting data into information and assessing that information, and deciding a course of action.[499] These restrictions arise from eNav's limitations in system design, the nature of and need to integrate the data and information provided, the effect of eNav upon decision making, mixed signals as to how much trust should be given eNav generated information, and the mariner's inadequate familiarity with the system.

The view of the world that is programmed into eNav is what the shore side designer or engineer believes the mariner wants and needs to know about his or her world afloat, but this is not always what mariners find necessary. The new technologies result in a "shift in the site of risk assessment, both conceptually and physically, from those close to the work to those in different occupational groups."[500] eNav can be ruthless[501] in doing what it is programmed to do — eNav will do no more and no less than what its designers and engineers allow. A recent on board study undertaken by a Swedish licensed master mariner elicited the frequent user comment "When we need it the most, the technology cannot help us."[502] Generally, where there is a difference between the mariner's view and how the system presents its programmed perception of relevant information, the burden is upon the human to adapt and harmonize with the system,[503] something not always easy to do, especially in times of stress. Collaterally, designers and engineers can "inadvertently … make it easy to err and difficult or impossible to discover error or to recover from it."[504] Ironically, the "more autonomous the [eNav], the more the consequences of error get displaced into the future, further compromising opportunities to recover."[505] Additionally, eNav "is never 'ahead,' can never really anticipate, whereas anticipation and thinking ahead is fundamental to maritime safety."[506] Not surprisingly, many mariners consider eNav to be "scary" to them. Such attitude is not conducive to effective eNav usage.

Design limitation was demonstrated when in 2005 the Australian frigate *Ballarat* was driven astern and grounded on Christmas Island. To avoid overrunning a line in the water ahead, the bridge team attempted to tighten an ahead turn by the conventional maneuver of going ahead on one propeller and astern on the other. This was not possible while only one of the vessel's three engines was operating, however, so the manual mode "froze" and shut down. As designed and as intended, the automated system took over and ordered full astern, based upon the shore dwelling designer's assumption that in *any* maritime emergency the proper response would be a "full astern" bell, apparently overlooking the possibility that there could be land or some other hazard astern.[507]

Data becomes "information" only after being appropriately transformed or interpreted and then presented or communicated meaningfully to the person who, in the fulfillment of his or her tasks and responsibilities, needs or is assisted by that information. Too often there is data or information overload, which overwhelms and confuses the watch officer in his or her making a necessary decision.

There is reason to believe that the watch officer on *Norwegian Dream,* as a potential collision situation was evolving and a third vessel entered the situation, "simply became overwhelmed with information at the critical time before the collision [with *Ever Decent*]."[508] Sir Arthur Conan Doyle summarized the situation well in his Sherlock Holmes short story "The Naval Treaty:" "The principal difficulty lay in there being too much evidence [data]. What was vital was overlaid and hidden by what was irrelevant."

There is further risk that eNav data and information becomes the watch officer's whole environment, to the exclusion of the "real" environment outside the console.[509] The console, where the electronically derived data is consolidated and converted into forms of information, can wrongly be perceived as *the* place where all information necessary for safe navigation of the vessel is to be found. As to this, the NTSB commented in its report into the grounding of *Royal Majesty,* "all ... watchstanding officers were ..., for all intents and purposes, sailing the map display instead of using navigation aids or lookout information."[510]

Another manifestation of this shortcoming is the recurring practice of watch keepers assessing a situation solely by looking into console screens instead of looking out the wheelhouse windows. Typical is the ship master who tells of entering a Far Eastern port at night when the watch officer yells from the ECDIS station "come left, come left, you're out of the channel." The officer was invited by the master to get his head out of the console and to look out the forward facing windows; he then saw the vessel was squarely on the channel range.[511]

Joseph Conrad wrote of " ... the sense of insecurity which is so invaluable in a seaman."[512] Too often, what the watch officer user knows of the gap between what eNav discloses and reality is no more than catch-phrases, such as "Trust but verify" or "Use one electronic system and you always know where you are. Use more than one and you're always in doubt."[513] The unfortunate result can be a user uncertain of the extent to which eNav can be trusted or should not be trusted.

By equipping a vessel with the bells, whistles, readouts and displays of eNav, together with reduced manning, watch officers may understand the shipowner to be at least impliedly conveying a message that eNav is to have primacy in reliance and decision making. This, together with the volume of RRPP and extensive directives from management, can foster a sense of dissociation and abdication of responsibility in favor of eNav. This, of course, would be a serious mis-reading of the circumstances. To the contrary, " ... to extract the full risk-reducing potential, mariners must *not* fully trust their equipment [because the] *entire weight of the seafaring tradition is that nothing is to be trusted.*"[514] But, the equipment is deserving of some level of trust, otherwise its presence is superfluous. The challenge is that there is no bright line between deserved trust and deserved suspicion and results in a dilemma:

> The problem with reliance versus overreliance is ... that it is impossible for any officer to judge at any specific moment what is too much and what is an adequate level of reliance. Semantically speaking, in cases when technology works and an officer trusts it, then it must be labeled reliance. If, on the other hand, technology fails, and the officer still trusts it, then it must be labeled overreliance. The degree of reliance, too much or adequate, seems therefore in hindsight to be defined by accuracy of technology rather than by operator performance. The consistent advice to operators never to trust technology may, however, be hard to follow in an increasingly technological world. Furthermore, if mariners are expected to always distrust technology then we are creating a totally abnormal professional and psychological situation where no person is able to maintain his or her mental health for any lengthy period of time.[515]

Lack of ship-specific knowledge has been cited as a problem by 78% of the mariners surveyed.[516] This is perhaps not surprising, given the movement of personnel from ship to ship and without vessels having the standardization of equipment common in commercial aircraft. But, the consequences, operationally and legally, of an unfamiliar crew can be severe. The legal effect is explicit: "Management effectively denied the ship this valuable information when it failed to sufficiently train

the ship's master in the use of ARPA, ... it is really as
if the [ship] were not equipped with ARPA because she
was not equipped with a master or officers trained to
use it."[517]

The maritime industry has proven more conservative
in financing training than other safety-critical industries.
Training of personnel newly joining a ship generally is
left to be accomplished in a cascading flow by personnel
anxious to depart for home and with themselves having
perhaps questionable knowledge of the equipment. Over
time, such jury-rigged training leaves the information
exchanged far removed from what manufacturers
would consider thorough and appropriate. Even if new
personnel do read the instruction manuals (assuming
they are located and are complete), they may be poorly
written, in language unfamiliar to the reader, and difficult
to comprehend in substance.

The obligation of personnel utilizing shipboard
equipment to be knowledgeable in all aspects of its use
is real. This issue could be eased considerably if systems
were standardized. A prime example of the dangers
flowing from non-standardization of equipment, symbols
used and user ignorance, compounded by master-pilot
communication difficulties (together with other causative
factors) is the allision in heavy fog of the outbound
container ship *Cosco Busan* against the pier fendering
system of the Delta tower of the San Francisco-Oakland
Bay Bridge in November of 2007, with substantial fuel oil
pollution resulting. The pilot intended to pass through
the 2,200 foot passage between the Delta and Echo towers
of the bridge.

He initially was satisfied with the functionality of
the vessel's two radars and presumably satisfied as well
with the vessel's ECDIS. At about 0822, referring to the
electronic chart, the pilot asked the master, "What
are these ... ah ... red [unintelligible]?" The master

replied, "This is on bridge." The pilot then said, "I couldn't figure out what the red light ... red ... red triangle was."

Because of alleged deterioration in the radar display, the pilot had decided to use the electronic chart and "aim for" the location (identified on the chart by the red triangles) that the master "had pointed [out as] the center of the bridge[,]" when the vessel was about one mile from the bridge. At about 08:28:08 the pilot asked the master, "This [apparently referring to a point on the electronic chart] is the center of the bridge, right?" The master answered, "Yeah." At 0829 the bosun on lookout called in Mandarin by radio, "The bridge column. The bridge column." Evasive action ordered by the pilot was unsuccessful and at 0830 the forward port side of the vessel struck the corner on the Delta-Echo side of the Delta tower fendering system. The two "red triangles" inquired of by the pilot represented the two buoys on either side of the Delta tower pier.

The NTSB report quotes from the vessel's voyage data recorder the following exchange occurring after the allision:

> **Pilot:** [unintelligible] you said this was the center of the bridge.
> **Master:** Yes.
> **Pilot:** No, this is the center. That's the tower. This is the tower. That's why we hit it. I thought that was the center.
> **Master:** It's a buoy. [unintelligible] the chart.
> **Pilot:** Yeah, see. No, this is the tower. I asked you if that was [unintelligible] ....   Captain, you said it was the center.
> **Master:** Cen...cen...cen...center.
> **Pilot:** Yeah, that's the bridge pier [expletive]. I thought it was the center.

Shortly after this dialogue, the master is heard saying in Mandarin, "He should have known - this is the center of the bridge, not the center of the channel."

Subsequently, the pilot commented to the NTSB investigators that he looked at the electronic chart before getting underway and saw that "the symbols on the ... electronic chart didn't look similar to me to the symbols that are on paper charts." He continued, "I see probably 10 different ECDIS [electronic chart and display information] during a week" but "I have never seen a red triangle on any piece of navigation information, electronic, paper or otherwise... . That's why I asked him, I said 'What does this mean?' "[518]

In another case of a navigator directing a vessel while unfamiliar with the relevant equipment, the newly joined chief officer had the watch when the 6,170 TEU German containership *LT Cortesia* grounded in clear visibility at 0454 January 2, 2008 on Varne Bank in the English Channel. To avoid traffic, course was altered with the result that the vessel was heading directly between the east and west Varne Bank cardinal buoys. These buoys, not easily identified as such because of the Chartpilot setting, were misidentified by the watch officer's misinterpretation of the radar return as two fishing vessels. For about nine minutes, as the vessel closed ever closer to Varne Bank, about 15 to 20 different acoustic signals were heard by the watch officer but were misidentified by him as evidencing an engineering problem. The fact that the vessel eventually grounded was not initially recognized, despite the ship making zero speed over the ground. All eNav equipment was operating as it should.

Contributing factors included excessive work hours, improper evaluation of the traffic situation, inappropriate use of the chart display and faulty lookout. The chief officer navigated "according to the computer"[519] though he "must have been able to foresee that such action entails extreme risks." What is "incomprehensible" is grounding in good visibility between two buoys adjacent to a lightship. Obviously, no one conscientiously was "looking out the window."

Shore side management similarly can be infected by a misguided notion of what eNav can and cannot do.[520] While the expectations of management tend also to err toward presuming more than can be delivered, those expectations spring from a motivation different from the motivation held by the operator. Likely an outgrowth of the evolving view of error previously discussed, where technological advances are seen to "reveal" the human error factor, increasingly "[s]eafarers are now seen as both operational and risk objects …, costly and prone to failure, so the fewer aboard, the better."[521] There may be misplaced satisfaction in bolstering the economic argument for reduced manning by complementing it with the argument that safety is enhanced by minimizing the number of error prone humans. But this over estimates the capability of the technology. Error prone as humans may be, humans have the quality of adaptability that is lacking in a technological system and that quality is a prime justification for retaining human monitors in complex systems, such as eNav. In an emergency or crisis situation, the human monitor must rely upon his or her training and experience to adapt or integrate and first detect the system "glitch" or failure, or detect a change in the operational situation, that warrants adjustment to maintain safety, and then make decisions appropriate to the changed circumstances.[522] The balance to be struck from a managerial perspective is allocation of tasks and domains between human and technology. What do humans do better and what does (well designed) technology do better? And, in that former category, let technology complement the human performance. However, in that balance seeking equation, there must be understanding of the human-technology interface. The linchpin of that understanding is the reminder that "[a]utomation creates new human weaknesses and it amplifies existing ones. Human error does not vanish; automation changes its nature."[523] The situation is neatly summed up:

> Although in principle the more information that can be made available to the watchkeeper the better should be his understanding of the situation and the better informed his decision-making, this is not entirely the case in practice. It is probable that technology is having an adverse effect on the way in which watchkeepers do their business, not least the universal problem of a generation that is being brought up to rely on technology to solve problems without having to think for themselves.[524]

This, of course, tracks earlier discussion suggesting that wherever possible, individuals are inclined to avoid acting at the more challenging knowledge-based performance level.

Another issue worthy of concern is the extent to which automation may, or does, degrade traditional skills. This raises two questions: 1) to what extent, if at all, are the traditional skills of mariners required in the maritime world of today, and 2) if traditional skills no longer are required (or, are less required than previously), what new skills do today's mariners need?

The concern expressed in many quarters over the deterioration, if not loss, of traditional mariners' skills is strong evidence that those skills remain valued. The perception is that those skills are being replaced not necessarily by new skills but rather by selection of the easiest means to accomplish a task; again, avoidance of the more challenging knowledge-based performance level. Edmund Hadnett sums up this view:

> [Automation] has severely degraded the standards by facilitating a significant shift away from the professional skills of watch-keeping that were the hallmark of previous generations. ... The drive to improve safety at sea by the introduction of electronic navigation equipment to enhance situational awareness and assist the watch-keeper has unwittingly compromised safety standards by reducing the core competencies that were demanded of previous generations and engendering the undesirable human trait to select the easiest option.[525]

Overall, studies illustrate that when new technology meets an operational environment, repercussions generally include:

new capabilities that create increased demands of system and personnel, accompanied by new complexities in that interface;

compounded complexities when the new technology is used inappropriately or incorrectly;

users adapt their use of the technology to maximize the technologies' potential outside the system's design criteria;

the complexities and adaptations are "surprising" and unintended;

the adaptations are prone to failure because they are poor and may combine with other factors adverse to successful operation; [and,]

the adaptations conceal shortcomings from persons outside the operational environment, including designers, engineers and post-event investigators, who will thereby be unaware of the technology's limitation(s) and so attribute the event to human error.[526]

A recent study highlights the premise that risk of maritime casualties best can be reduced by attending to human factor issues rather than by pushing for technological solutions. Analysis was performed upon 75 serious casualties investigated through the Greek Ministry of Merchant Marine utilizing Det Norske Veritas' "DAMA" database comprised of seven groupings: A) "circumstances not related to the ship;" B) "ship construction and equipment location on board;" C) "technological conditions of available equipment;" D) "equipment use and design;" E) "cargo related aspects;" F)"procedures and routine degraded;" and, G) "on board personnel." Group dependency interrelations were found: A with B and G; B with A and G; C with F; F with C and G, and G with A, B and F.

Violation of procedures was a significant component within Group F, from which the conclusion was drawn that a "fix" within Group C would be insufficient without a corresponding "fix" in Group F and, by extension, in Group G as well, i.e. " emphasis in reducing the risk of marine accidents should be placed mostly on the human factor and less on technological solutions."[527]

Given wide, and often uncritical, acceptance of eNav, management must come to an informed understanding of what humans and technology, respectively, are together best as well as least capable of handling. The allocation of activities and drafting of RRPP compatible with the limitations of eNav should flow from that understanding. The greatest danger is that enthusiasm for technological solutions, an enthusiasm based upon the flawed assumption that technology can (should) replace human input, has the potential to psychologically, and in fact, reduce watch keeping to little more than monitoring displays. Watch keepers increasingly are seeing themselves as denied the need to remain vigilant and personally to be directly aware

of their surrounding environment. The suggestion has
been advanced that "it is impossible for any [watch
keeping] officer to judge at any specific moment what is
too much and what is an adequate level of reliance."[528]
Technology's proven advantages and reliability[529] can
be integrated into the watch officer's duty of vigilance
and desired level of skepticism by application of the
admonition: TRUST – BUT VERIFY.[530]

The 1995 grounding of the passenger liner
Royal Majesty (cited previously) on Nantucket Shoals
highlights many issues arising from the technological-
human interface. The error chain began with the
vessel's departure from Bermuda toward Boston, her
regular run, when, somehow, the GPS antenna cable,
routed across the deck of the flying bridge, became
disconnected. This resulted in loss of GPS input to the
integrated navigational system, which consequently
defaulted to DR ("dead" or deduced reckoning) mode.
The DR mode operated off the gyro compass for course
input and from a Doppler log for speed, but did not
compensate for the effects of current (set) or wind (drift)
upon the vessel. The brief aural alarm went unnoticed
as also went unnoticed the continuous visual DR mode
indication. The lighted notice that the system had
defaulted to DR mode was visually present between the
latitude and longitude readouts on the console and so
was within every viewing officer's line of sight but was
not of such a readily noticeable character as to make a
strong impression beyond what the officers expected
to see. The officers "saw" but failed to "observe" the
visible warning. "Observation" involves the additional
cognitive process of critical evaluation of what is seen.
But where, as in the case of *Royal Majesty*, an officer's
activity is relatively routine, the tendency, in terms of the
previously discussed performance levels, is to function at
the rule-based performance level rather than at the more

challenging and demanding knowledge-based level.[511] *Royal Majesty's* officers routinely were looking to see the digitized position readout – nothing more, though there was present the lighted warning to be observed.

Because they had been designed and, engineered to do so, the auto pilot and the NACOS navigation and command systems in "steering" *Royal Majesty* were "ruthless" in failing to distinguish between "real" GPS information and the DR information actually received:

> Automation is able only to do exactly what it is programmed to do, ... Human problem solvers are *creative* in their reasoning and their search for solutions to a problem. They can and will draw knowledge or evidence from any available source (either in memory or external to themselves: reference books, manuals, contact with others by radio, etc.) as long as that knowledge is relevant to the problem to be solved. Automation, on the other hand, is constrained by its instructions and as such is insensitive to unanticipated changes in goals and world states that may fall well within its usual operating range but were unanticipated by the designers of its software.[532]

The transition from GPS to DR input was automatic when the GPS satellite input was lost.

The officers' mental model, based upon their expectation, training and the prior proven reliability of the system's GPS mode performance, did not trigger suspicion or investigation beyond casual glances to read out the latitude and longitude numerals.[533]

During the voyage, there was no cross-check by plotting positions taken from available Loran C or celestial navigation means.[534] This situation is likely to be often replicated, given the lessened perceived importance of celestial navigation,[535] and follows normal human behavior of exerting oneself no more than is considered necessary, and particularly the tendency to casually monitor when relying upon technology and even more casually when that technology has a proven track record of reliability.[536] Without availing themselves of independent second source cues and references, nonetheless if the *Royal Majesty* officers had reviewed their performance, experience and peer response, such a review quite likely would have been a potent force validating their performance because normalization of deviance had been allowed to take over.

Their performance, however, became significantly more questionable as Nantucket Shoals loomed ahead. The first separation lane buoy was passed to port and in keeping with "local rationality" theory, was identified by the chief officer as "BA" buoy though in fact it was "AR" buoy, some 15 miles to the west-south-west of "BA." How could this erroneous identification have occurred? Easily: a buoy showed on radar where "BA" was expected; a buoy was "seen;" therefore, the "seen" buoy was "BA." Unfortunately, the identifying "AR" lettering on the buoy could not be read, as the buoy was silhouetted against the setting sun. This error is consistent with the fact that "[p]re-interpreted, indirect information, presented with apparent exactness by a technological aid, tends to make one disregard normal and direct human observation. Technologically aided information particularly, takes precedence in cases when direct human observation needs to be interpreted, is ambiguous, vague or contradictory."[537]

The second officer took the watch at 2000, presumably having been told by his senior, the chief officer, that *Royal Majesty* was following her track line. The lookout's report of lights conflicted with the second officer's mental model of the situation, so was disregarded. About an hour into the watch, two fishing vessels called *Royal*

Majesty to warn that she was standing into imminent danger, but the Portuguese accented language and vessel identification were too imprecise to warrant (in the second officer's mind) further investigation and the radar, set on the 6-mile range, failed to pick up for relative positioning the more distant fishing boats from which the warnings were coming.

The "BB" buoy should have been passed at about 2120 but was not sighted visually nor on radar. Because the several cues/anomalies indicating something was awry had not been perceived, recognized or understood, the second officer easily rationalized the buoy's non-appearance. More difficult to understand, however, is the fact that he *twice* upon specific inquiry falsely told the master that he *had seen* the "BB" buoy. He later explained these false statements as justified because "perhaps the radar did not reflect the buoy" and "GPS" showed the vessel "on track." Interestingly, of two technological devices available, he chose to rely upon one – the GPS - but not the other - the radar.

Royal Majesty touched ground at 2225, some 17 miles west of where she should have been, the place where her officers believed her to be.[538]

The *Royal Majesty* and *LT Cortesia* groundings, and many other maritime casualties, may stand for many propositions but foremost must be recognition that visual cues independent of eNav were present and, if heeded, the casualty thereby avoided. Saying that navigators must be more than "potted palm" console observers and "look out the window" presupposes that navigators possess traditional mariners' wariness and the skills enabling appreciation of the navigational significance of what is there to be seen "outside the window."

12

Multiculturalism

The deep sea commercial maritime industry is global and among the world's most multicultural businesses.[539] Beyond dispute is the fact that the overwhelming majority of vessels in international trade are multi-national in their crew complement, and crews are becoming increasingly of the Third World.

Though this need not be so, multiculturalism has been determined to be a factor creating significant issues in areas of vessel operational safety, including especially bridge resource management, through existence of "power distance," emergency responsiveness largely due to language differences, and, occasionally, outright racism[540] and prejudice.[541] A consequence, at least in part, of prejudice was the loss of the chemical tanker *Bow Mariner* in 2004 off Cape Hatteras, with 21 of the 27 crew members perishing.[542] The master, chief officer and chief engineer were Greeks, who wholly lacked trust and confidence in the Filipino junior officers and unlicensed crew. "Filipino officers did not take their meals in the officer's mess, were given almost no responsibility and were closely supervised in every task."[543] There being no evidence that distrust in the professional competence of the Filipinos was justified, a reasonable conclusion can be drawn that the senior officers' negative attitude was rooted in prejudice. During cargo operations, the chief officer would take only short naps in the cargo control room; there was neither delegation nor training in cargo related tasks given to the Filipino mates. As a result, unsafe actions and practices went unquestioned (presuming those actions and practices performed were recognized as unsafe) and on the day of the loss, the 22 cargo tanks recently discharged were opened at sea without question and in a manner allowing flammable vapors to accumulate on deck. The vapors somehow ignited, resulting in explosions, fire, the vessel sinking, and fatalities. This situation may be a reflection of the phenomenon that in nationally mixed crews, the "foreigners" may be more likely to be outside the social and ethical "universe of obligation" shared by the master and senior officers.[544]

When speaking of multiculturalism within the concept of cultural differences, there is the unfortunate risk of misinterpretation and misuse of the term as a basis for contending that one culture is "better" or "worse," "safer" or "less safe" than another culture. To do so would be a perversion of an acknowledgeable difference among national or communal cultures.[545]

A particularly enlightening study is one the Dutch sociologist Geert Hofstede derived out of interview data from an extensive International Business Management (IBM) international employee base in the 1960s and subsequently reaffirmed through further investigation. Comparable application has been validated in the maritime domain through experience and, though perhaps a little too "soft and fuzzy" for the hardened mariner to be comfortable with, this application has considerable significance in the realm of maritime safety.

Cultural differences address, from an organizational perspective, the phenomenon of peoples from different cultures collectively exposed to common challenges that demand cooperative response for successful resolution.

How do people from different cultures interact in their
assessment of the particular challenge and respond as
an effective unit? The response will be an interweaving
of the individuals' learned and experienced patterns of
thinking, feeling and potential response for action as
affected by training and education.[546] These patterns
may be referred to as "software of the mind," an
outgrowth of the individual's social environment within
which he or she grew up as well as life experiences
gathered along the way through family, friends,
neighborhood, school, professional training/education
and the workplace. This software of the mind equates
with culture, and may be understood as parallel with
such sayings as "we are what we eat" and "we are where
we have been."

Several cautionary comments are in order. When
cultural groups — such as Japanese, Western European,
Basque, etc. — are discussed, the common denominator
is generalities and no more than generalities. In any
such cultural group, there will be individuals —
many individuals — of the group but quite different
as individuals from the generality associated with the
group. Also, studies dealing with large groups tend to
create segments within the group. For example, while
the initial Hofstede study looked at IBM employees
and categorized them by nationality, across the board
those IBM employees may be presumed to have been
at least somewhat better educated and with a higher
standard of living than the national group as a whole.
And, particularly important for the purposes of this
discussion, those groups functioned within a "normal"
shore side work-home environment.

This discussion, on the other hand, considers the
significance of cultural differences within ships – small,
close quartered, isolated spaces inhabited for months
on end by a relatively small number of mostly males

operating in the hostile environment of the sea. This world afloat has been described as:

> a world of its own – cramped, self-contained, and prone to a unique remoteness that modern forms of communication have by no means eliminated. Emotions born of collective discontent, which in larger social context may become diffused, channeled, or otherwise rendered harmless, may within the close confines of a ship fester and turn explosive, especially during a long voyage.[547]

In short, a ship at sea is an artificial environment in which individual personality traits as well as the "software of the mind" will be dominant, with this environment being sufficiently peculiar that the observation was offered many years ago that "[w]hen men come to like a sea-life, they are not fit to live on land."[548]

Nonetheless, relevance can be gleaned from the Hofstede studies. A first principle is that "we cannot change the way people in a country [read "culture"] think, feel, and act by simply importing foreign institutions."[549] Also, there exists what Hofstede has called a "power distance index" (PDI), the "emotional distance" that separates subordinates from their bosses.[550]

The PDI derives from responses of non-managerial employees from different national backgrounds to three basic inquiries: 1) Frequency of the subordinate being fearful to express disagreement with hierarchical seniors; 2) Whether the hierarchical senior is perceived as having an autocratic or paternalistic decision making style; and, 3) What decision making style is preferred. Cultures having a low PDI prefer consultation in the course of making a decision and there exists an interdependence between senior and subordinate wherein the subordinate feels comfortable approaching and even contradicting the hierarchical senior. Countries whose culture conforms with a low PDI include generally Western European countries, New Zealand, Australia, the United States and Israel. Large PDI countries present the opposite characteristic – power is viewed as being distributed unequally and the subordinate is unlikely to approach the hierarchical senior to offer input or contradiction, but instead expects to be told what to do. Included among high PDI countries are the Philippines, China and Russia. At least in the aviation domain, " … low power distance cultures with a high degree of individualism seems [sic] to be superior to collective, high power distance cultures for promoting aviation safety, especially in terms of the processes and procedures at the higher organizational levels."[551]

Several PDI aspects are illustrated in the 2008 circumstances of the Hong Kong registered containership *APL Sydney*, whose starboard anchor fouled an underwater gas pipeline.[552] On the afternoon of December 13, the starboard anchor was let go in the Melbourne anchorage and soon thereafter the pilot disembarked. The 35 knot south-southwest wind was gusting to 48 knots. The pipeline was 1.1 km. downwind. Within less than 30 minutes, *APL Sydney* had dragged anchor and was outside the anchorage area. The master advised harbor control of his intention to weigh anchor but was instructed to hold and await a pilot. When, within about another 25 minutes the vessel was some 50 meters from the pipeline, harbor control authorized weighing anchor. Weighing commenced, but the vessel continued to drag her starboard anchor. The anchor soon snagged the pipeline. Soon thereafter the pilot returned to the vessel. Consultation with the master followed and harbor control decided to have the vessel dredge the anchor clear. About 20 minutes later, and one minute after the main engine was run ahead, the pipeline ruptured.

APL Sydney's master was Chinese, China having

an especially high PDI, and was interacting with an
Australian pilot and port control officer, Australia
having a particularly low PDI. The master would likely
have perceived both the pilot, with his expertise of local
knowledge, and port control officer, the representative of
the local authority, to have been in substantially higher
positions of power and authority than himself, even on
his vessel, in the context of his ship's situation within
the port area. Therefore, the master likely would have
expected to have been told by them what he should do
and to accept their advice or instructions with minimal
hesitation or challenge.

The port control officer and pilot would be expected
to rely upon a ship's master to act and take such initiative
as would be appropriate to safeguard his vessel, with
minimal outside prompting. The Chinese master, on the
other hand, given his high PDI, could be expected to
await guidance until possibly an *in extremis* situation had
been allowed to develop. The port control officer could
be mislead into believing the master's acquiescence to
guidance or instructions showed agreement, suggesting
a joint common evaluation whereas in reality the
master could have agreed merely because he expected
to be instructed and hesitated to issue an appropriate
challenge based upon his better understanding of his
vessel's capabilities and limitations. The pilot could have
understood the master's lack of providing input to have
resulted from a normal relaxation once the pilot asserted
himself. But, the master's quiescence could be attributed
to his high PDI culture. If the pilot expected challenge
and consultation as he probably would have received
from an Australian master, he should have considered
inviting more input from the master.

If the master understood PDI, he would recognize
the Australian low PDI pilot and port control officer
would expect challenge and consultation, and the

lack of either from the master would be interpreted as agreement, whereas the master in reality may have been experiencing ever greater anxiety as the situation was developing. *APL Sydney* demonstrates the safety risk arising from culturally uninformed senior persons working together. Granted, the preceding discussion is somewhat speculative, but such speculation is firmly grounded upon established PDI bases.[553]

Significantly, organizations as well as individuals exhibit the cultural traits of their national constituency and these national cultures are recognized as having a "profound effect" upon safety because "different underlying error mechanisms are prevalent in different cultures."[554]

Additional light was cast upon this issue by the results of a 2006 aviation study, Li's "Eastern Minds in Western Cockpits," that examined the relative frequency in aviation accidents of contributory factors drawn from Indian, Taiwanese and United States participant HFACS data.

HFACS organizational influences including "resource management," "organizational processes" and "organizational climate" were found significantly more prevalent in the Indian data and significantly less so in the United States data. HFACS unsafe supervision was notably under-represented in the United States data. At the HFACS Preconditions for Unsafe Operation level, "adverse mental states" were observed significantly more often in the Taiwanese data and considerably less so in the United States data. "Physical/mental limitations" was over-represented in the Indian data. In "unsafe acts of operators," "decision errors" were observed as significantly less likely causal factors in the Indian and United States data.

These findings using HFACS tend to validate Hofstede's classifications and to be relevant to safety assessment within the maritime domain – at least to the extent of showing that national culture is a factor to be taken into account.

Taiwan and India share a high PDI and show a greater frequency of "organizational influences" (HFACS level 4) categories underlying relatively recent aviation accidents compared to the United States. Under the Hofstede classifications of national culture, Taiwanese and Indian working environments prefer tall organizational pyramids, with centralized decision making and large layers of supervisory personnel. Subordinates expect to be told what to do. In contrast, The United States is low PDI, high on individualism. There is a thin layer of supervisory personnel. Subordinates expect to be consulted.

These national cultural differences may explain the better "organizational influences" and "unsafe supervision" record of the United States, with its low PDI and great individualism, which may provide greater facility in addressing issues within these two broad HFACS categories. Similarly, the United States culture allows greater autonomy of action than cultures that discourage autonomy at lower levels.

Despite the strength of the empirical data underlying the conclusions of the "Eastern Minds in Western Cockpits" study, caution should be exercised lest too much be read into it. The aviation business, and also the concept of bridge resource management, is permeated with "Western" influences. Cultural mores are not easily displaced, even with education. HFACS itself may be argued to carry within itself a cultural bias as might the factors attributed to each accident studied.

However, the safety advantages arguably inherent in a lower power distance culture such as the United States may be undergoing a dilution within the United States maritime industry. Numerous interviews with personnel serving in United States deep-sea vessels compel the impression that the increasingly fewer in number American maritime shipping companies are drifting toward an organizational high PDI philosophy, if not structure. The shipboard view expressed is that more "meddling" is "coming down from on top" for no better purpose than to justify shore management's existence and to change things for the sake of making an impression in order to enhance individual advancement prospects, analogous to the military's "punching one's ticket" to secure promotion. In short, there is a shipboard perception of increased responsibility and accountability charged against ships' personnel with decreased authority and little real meaningful consultation.

The *APL Sydney* situation, as well as the earlier discussed *Montrose* grounding, highlights the influence of PDI in the context of a shipboard – harbor authority/ pilot interface. A further example comes from the allision of the Chinese crewed *Cosco Busan* against the Bay Bridge in San Francisco harbor, where the PDI differential may have caused the master to be hesitant about questioning the pilot's authority in the navigation of the vessel, despite the master's overriding responsibility for the ultimate safety of the vessel. Such hesitation will be exacerbated when a pilot or other authority figure has a naturally domineering personality. The NTSB noted that the American pilot involved "had, in the past, demonstrated a an assertive presence with individuals who were nominally his superior in either authority or education, such as the examining physician and the naval officers on the *USS Tarawa*. The pilot's assertive demeanor may have made the *Cosco Busan*'s master even more reluctant to challenge him, even with regard to the conduct of a formal master/pilot exchange."[555] The master later commented:

> Normally as a captain I would welcome the pilot with my
> open arms, enthusiastic, and I would show my hospitality in
> offering him if he needed any food or coffee or tea, et cetera.
> And [this] pilot came on board with a very cold face. Some
> of them just don't want to pay any attention on us and some
> of them would not like to talk with us … . It seems the pilot
> coming on board was with cold face, doesn't want to talk. I
> don't know if he had a hard day before or because he was
> unhappy because I was a Chinese.[556]

However, PDI is an everyday occurrence in the shipboard environment. Across the board, there is a hierarchical structure. An example is the idiosyncratic or irascible (sometimes both) master, doubtlessly familiar to most maritime readers. His (or her[557]) effect, for better or worse, on a junior officer can be significant: "It is not too difficult to imagine the scene: after a few 'run ins' with the always intimidating personage of the master, over the interpretation the COLREGS, the junior officer will accept that he probably was taught complete rubbish and adopt the master's interpretation as the correct one."[558] While this quotation mentions COLREGS interpretation, the intimidation could equally affect a myriad of other watch standing issues.

Related to but distinct from the PDI is the "authority gradient," which refers to the balance of decision making power or the steepness of the command hierarchy in a given situation. Some authority gradient is necessary, otherwise roles within the bridge team will be blurred and decision making adversely affected. But if the authority gradient is unbalanced,

> members of a crew … with a domineering, overbearing or
> dictatorial team leader experience a steep authority gradient
> where expressing concerns, questioning, or even simply
> clarifying instructions requires considerable determination

on the part of the team members who perceive their input as devalued or unwelcome. Conversely, members of a crew … where the authority gradient is too low or 'flat' have an overly relaxed attitude toward cross-checking each other's actions or confirming other information. Effective team leaders consciously establish a command hierarchy appropriate to the training and experience of the team members [and to the PDI].[559]

The hierarchical effect of the authority gradient can be exacerbated where the officers and crew are multicultural, especially where there are low power distance senior officers and high power distance subordinate officers and unlicensed personnel.

A case in point is the early morning 1999 striking of the Nab Tower, a light tower marking the eastern end of the Spithead approaches in the English Channel, by the reefer ship *Dole America*. The ship departed Portsmouth for Antwerp. Before being dropped, the pilot pointed out the Tower visually and on radar to the ship's Norwegian master (low power distance country) and Filipino second officer (high power distance country) The second officer subsequently was called by the master to assist in ascertaining the source and nature of several lights ahead. Following a course change to clear the lights, course was altered to port and two minutes later, while swinging to port and as the second officer was returning to the chart table, the ship allided with the Nab Tower. Safe passage clearing the Tower had been "guesstimated" by the master, who had been unaware of the ship's position relative to the Tower and had failed to allow for his ship's advance and transfer, and also had failed to fully utilize the second officer. The MAIB report commented: "[i]n this instance the [61 year old] master was Norwegian and the [48 year old] second officer Filipino. It is probable that the differing nationalities and social backgrounds of the master and second officer were factors in their failure to work as an effective team."[560] The MAIB elaborated:

> The evidence suggests that an autocratic management style was in place, such that the [Filipino] second officer was reluctant to offer information to the [Norwegian] master, and the master was reluctant to request it. Although an autocratic management style may be a short-term solution to cultural barriers in attempting to operate the vessel efficiently, this accident has highlighted the need for a long-term solution in the form of good communications and teamwork, through education and training. The potential problem could be reduced by having a bridge team drawn from a single nationality.[561]

Though the MAIB did not reference explicitly Hofstede's study, among the Board's recommendations was: "Consider the potential effect on bridge teamwork when appointing multi-national groups of masters, deck officers and bridge watchkeeping ratings to a particular vessel."[562] This recommendation would have been based upon findings that teams comprised of different national cultures work together in noticeably different ways. There is a tendency particularly in three person teams – such as pilot of one culture and master and watch personnel of another – for the two person team to not consciously but in fact "isolate" the third person.

Hierarchical power distance was cited in the Australian Transport Safety Bureau report discussing the 2000 grounding of the Malaysian container vessel *Bunga Teratai Satu* on a reef in Torres Strait, 23 minutes after passing a programmed way-point. The course change indicated at the way-point had not been made. The Pakistani watch officer had "developed the practice" of having his Malaysian seaman watch stander plot the vessel's GPS position. This was done by the seaman at

0700, who affirmatively noticed that the position plotted coincided with a course change indicated at that way point. The seaman "kept expecting the mate to come back into the wheelhouse [from the bridge wing, where the mate was speaking with his wife] to alter course" but "did not feel that it was his place to suggest to the mate that he should alter course."[563]

The report mentions "power-distance" not based upon different nationalities but rather as reflecting "a strict hierarchy, between the senior officers and junior officers and crew. This is seen as quite normal and proper in some organizational systems, but such a working environment increases the likelihood of a one-person error."[564]

Hierarchical power distance was commented upon as well in the MAIB report addressing the 2004 stranding of the Italian chemical tanker *Attilio Ievoli* in the west Solent at 1632. While the Italian master was engrossed in a mobile telephone conversation, the vessel departed the course line but the Ukrainian second officer failed to advise the master of that fact. The report noted " … the contrast of cultures was significant. Different cultures have different attitudes to the importance of hierarchy in the workplace [and] research has shown that eastern European cultures (such as Ukrainian) expect a far greater deference to be shown to superiors than most western cultures, such as the Italians."[565] With this in mind, the second officer likely was reluctant to question the master's authority or competence, and also may have been uncertain what his responsibility was after 1600 when his watch ended, knowing that the master and cadet were taking the following watch. And aboard the previously discussed *Bow Mariner* the hierarchical structure was so rigid that the subordinate Filipino officers and crew "failed to question unsafe actions and procedures [because] the orders of the Greeks were 'like words from God'."[566]

Through the PDI, multiculturalism asserts itself pervasively as an active aspect of the master/watchkeeper – pilot relation and related pilot bridge team integration issue. This is obvious from the findings of a Canadian study addressing the operational relation between bridge personnel and marine pilots. Pilot interviewees expressed strong concern over the fact that "an increasing number of foreign masters consider the arrival of the pilot on board as a relief, a way to discharge some of their responsibilities, a chance to get some rest."[567] Though the study does not cite power distance index, the increased number of bridge personnel from countries with high PDI is strikingly compatible with the interviewees' "increasing number" choice of words.

The above examples strongly support the proposition that multicultural issues do affect maritime safety. Nonetheless, given the somewhat limited and selective group sampled in the late 1960s and early 1970s by Hofstede, a question might arise as to what extent, if at all, his findings should be considered relevant to today's maritime community of more technologically sophisticated and experienced, cross-culturally exposed mariners working in a highly regulated domain. Would there be influences more significant than the nationally based cultural influences Hofstede found dominant?

As a generality, team members coming from diverse social-personal and cognitive-perceptual backgrounds "may be more likely to commit errors than are those in culturally homogeneous teams," especially in the course of high stress operations, though there is evidence that over time "as the culturally heterogeneous teams continued to work together, performance differences between the teams disappeared."[568] Yet, a 2003 study taken of personnel on multi-nationally crewed Norwegian vessels supports the conclusion that "vessels with crews from a single country or from two countries had better attitudes toward safety and risk than did those with multi-national crews."[569] Care should be taken when considering this generality within the context of a commercial shipboard environment which, due to its unique characteristics, may tend to exacerbate conflicts as well as have the potential to stimulate greater cooperation upon the reality that "we're all in the same boat." Cultural adaptation, of course, can be hastened by "recognizing, acknowledging, and addressing cultural differences within the team."[570]

A study published in 2000 and taken among more than 9,000 commercial pilots from 26 airlines of 19 nationalities showed sufficient correlation with Hofstede's results to justify the conclusion that "even in a highly specialized, highly regulated profession …, national culture still exerts a meaningful influence on attitudes and behaviors over and above the occupational context."[571] The implications from this conclusion for BRM indoctrination and training are significant. In a high PDI culture, BRM training could most effectively be directed to captains first, whereas in low PDI cultures, captains and subordinate officers could be trained together.

Another aspect of multiculturalism is the variation of languages in play, especially dealing with pilots and in emergency situations. The master/pilot exchange on *Cosco Busan* was commented upon by the NTSB: " … although sufficiently competent with English to be deemed qualified for his position, the [Chinese] master was not a native English speaker. Therefore, to engage the pilot in a discussion of departure issues, although within the master's ability, would have been more difficult for him than for someone with native English-speaking ability."[572] The language issue certainly was significant and, together with cultural "power distance" and the pilot's authoritative knowledge of San Francisco Bay (to say nothing of his strong personality), the total deference of the vessel's master to the pilot "for all decisions regarding vessel navigation, from the decision to depart up to and including the time of the allision ... may explain why the master did not assert his authority [over the pilot] and why the bridge team proved ineffective in preventing the allision."[573] None of these factors, of course, relieved the master of his authority and responsibility to intervene when navigation of the vessel became questionable though, here again, culture and power distance likely came to the fore, as suggested by testimony at the NTSB *Cosco Busan* hearing: "An American or a U.S. captain would probably be a lot quicker to [relieve a pilot] than a foreign master, ..."[574] Similarly, the deference of *Cosco Busan's* master is suggested by the comment spoken in the wheelhouse, in Mandarin shortly before the allision, that " ... American ships under such conditions, they would not be under way."[575] This issue was highlighted in the MAIB report following the striking of a moored vessel by the inbound *Xuchanghai*, which lost steerage when slowed and was caught by the wind and strong tide. The language difference might have "influenced the master's decision not to intervene when it became apparent the vessel was standing into danger. ... unable to converse in English to pass on his intentions to the pilot or control the tugs, [the master] was not well placed to offer advice or take over from the pilot."[576] The Report also commented that " ... basic information [helpful to the master-pilot interchange] was not expanded upon by the master. A more comprehensive exchange of information might have been possible had there been no language difficulties, [to have allowed the pilot to have] been more probing and the master more forthcoming."[577]

Culture also affects the meaning behind seemingly straight forward words. For example, "no" is considered impolite in some cultures, including the Chinese culture. As a result, there may be a tendency with Chinese shipboard personnel to answer "yes" or in some other affirmative manner to authority figures, such as pilots or harbor control people, in a form of "concealing" communication. For example, in 1996 the bulk carrier *Bright Field* struck New Orleans' Riverwalk Marketplace after an engine failure. Before getting underway from an anchorage, the master of the Chinese crewed vessel answered "yes" to the pilot's inquiry whether the ship's navigation equipment and engine were in good working order. In fact, well before the allision there were problems, discussed only in Chinese, with starting the engine.[578]

Different languages pose an added level of difficulty in surmounting an emergency, perhaps best stated in the accident report issued after a 2005 Boeing 737 crash:

> In general, sufficient ease of use of English for the performance of duties in the course of a normal, routine flight does not necessarily imply that communication in the stress and time pressure of an abnormal situation is equally effective. The abnormal situation can potentially require words that are not part of the "normal" vocabulary (words and technical terms one used in a foreign tongue under normal circumstances), thus potentially leaving two pilots unable to express themselves clearly. Also, human performance, and particularly memory, is known to suffer from the effects of stress, thus implying that in a stressful situation the search and choice of words to express one's concern in a non-native language can be severely compromised.[579]

Abnormal situations are not necessary to illustrate safety degradation attributable to multiple languages. Following the 2004 collision between *Hyundai Dominion* and *Sky Hope,* reference was made by crew interviewees to the language situation on board *Hyundai Dominion,* crewed by nationals from six nations, none native English speakers:

> ... the extra effort required to converse in English, with others on board who are not native English speakers, is often too great to discuss anything other than the minimum necessary to perform their job: just to give or understand instructions.
>
> This effort required to converse, while natural, does explain a reluctance on the part of the three bridge watchkeeping officers to ask for clarification on the matter of using the main engine controls on the bridge. During interview, each officer expressed a different reason for why he would not be inclined to use the main engine controls on the bridge to slow the engine speed at sea. ...
>
> The lookout on the bridge of *Hyundai Dominion* at the time of the collision was Turkish. His knowledge of English was poor, ... The chief officer, also on the bridge at that time, was Yugoslavian, but his standard of English was good. Thus, these two men had no common language in which they could discuss any complex matter. The lookout also performed the role of watchman and carried out fire rounds. Had he found anything untoward during these rounds, it is uncertain how he could have effectively explained the situation to the chief officer by telephone or portable radio. He would be forced to return to the bridge and explain matters using sign language and his very limited English. [580]

There also is the tendency of a group to communicate in its native language when confronted by an atypical situation, thereby breaching the communication loop with a potentially helpful outsider. This commonly occurs between a crew and pilot, as was demonstrated in, among others, the *Bright Field* and *APL Sydney* situations. Another perspective is shown from the 1999 MARCOM Project report: "If there are also problems of communication contributing to a lack of mutual confidence, suspicions and misunderstandings, then the opportunities for human errors leading to dangers to the ship, people on board and the environment, are greatly increased."[581]

Of course, communication in the wider sense includes more than verbalization, as "body language" can convey significant information with the possibility of misunderstanding every bit as serious as with verbal communication. For example, in a passage taken from a collection of legally oriented short stories:

> Dr. Veraswami was waving his head vigorously from side to side as I spoke. This, I had earlier discovered, was a frequent Indian gesture easily mistaken for dissent, but having the larger meaning of a qualified assent – in effect, you are nearly right but not quite.[582]

Culture also may affect an individual's reception of technology, reflecting observation that "[t]echnology is not a good traveler unless it is culturally calibrated."[583]

Also, a particularly great challenge in dealing with multiculturalism is awareness and acceptance of the level of insecurity or sensitivity that people may have of themselves. This aspect is likely to be especially relevant to issues of monitoring and challenging. A striking example is the respective views held by NTSB and the Egyptian authorities relating to the 1999 crash of EgyptAir Flight 990. The flight data and cockpit voice recorders indicated that when the captain was out of the cockpit, the co-pilot disengaged the autopilot and calmly pushed the aircraft into a steep dive, and then fought the captain for control when the captain returned to the cockpit. The Egyptian investigators professed outrage that the crash and fatalities could be considered intentional, and deemed a causal finding of an intentional act to be a cultural slight. They developed numerous counter theories, all of which were disproved by NTSB and the aircraft's manufacturer.[584]

The "power" and influence of culture within an organization and within the shipboard way of doing things often goes unrecognized. Culture is so ingrained that little if any thought is given to the challenges presented. As a result, the issue is less whether mono-culture or multi-culture crews are safer but whether shore side and shipboard managers are appropriately aware of the differences and challenges presented and, if aware, know what should and is being done to address those challenges. Addressing the many issues brought forward by multiculturism requires the initial recognition that foremost among managerial misunderstandings across all multi-cultural domains is the overwhelming misunderstanding of cultural differences and their effect in the workplace.[585] This effect is exacerbated in the unique shipboard environment and wider maritime domain, so not all land oriented strategies for dealing with multi-cultural challenges are feasible from the beginning or have proven successful.

The first step is to assess the circumstances. Management must meet subordinates on the cultural ground of the subordinates.[586] The situation must be addressed early on and acceptable norms set; the obstacles to effective teamwork arising from cultural differences may be "subtle and difficult to recognize until significant damage already has been done."[587] Where workable, adaptation is often the best approach. The team members are willing to acknowledge and state their cultural differences and themselves accept responsibility for figuring out how to live harmoniously with those differences; sometimes, a facilitator will be needed to guide and moderate the interchange. This type of interchange is perhaps overly optimistic when dealing on board with ships' personnel but is achievable if wisely implemented. Neither structured nor managerial intervention lends itself to the ship board environment and, of course, making wholesale changes is unlikely to be economically viable.[588] While the return of investment in hiring truly competent and managerially sophisticated masters and chief engineers has never been greater, the need is particularly acute where multicultural crews and shoreside management are involved.

Traditional bridge resource management should be viewed with wariness when considering multiculturism because the BRM concept is "western" in its premise of "aggressively" effective monitoring and challenge. Without officers understanding "power distance" and being sensitive to cultural differences, and showing willingness to adapt to effective team performance, whatever BRM training has been received will fall short of the need. Management should not presume that BRM certification suffices to establish existence of team effectiveness within the multicultural crew complement, or as well as with pilots and shoreside authority.

13

Organizational Management
of Maritime Risk

At the end, risk taking is the cause of almost all accidents. But it is not always easy to find those who took the risks; too often they are confused with those who ran the risks. — W. Wagenaar and G. Keren[589]

The best that organizations can hope for is to manage error effectively, decreasing the probability of errors and minimizing their consequences. — R. Helmreich, "Error Management As Organizational Strategy"[590]

If you think you are spending too much on safety, try having an accident in your business ... — Sir Stelios Haji-Iaonnou, Ninth Cadwallader Annual Memorial Lecture[591]

Theories abound addressing and informing managers of theoretical aspirant organizational perfection, though only a relatively small proportion of the literature concerns itself with wholly maritime organizations. Interest in such organizational theories is warranted. Re-analysis of Marine Transportation Research Board figures from as long ago as 1976 has "suggested that for 86 percent of the events analyzed, the 'responsibility appeared to be at least partially organizational in nature'." [592] What clearly emerges as concerns maritime safety enhancement, whatever theory may be attractive, is that senior management must demonstrably "buy in" if positive safety advance is to be gained.

The maritime industry is a particularly "open" system in the sense that every shipping company, whether owner, operator or managing operator, functions of necessity within an environment larger than itself. Each organization functions within the global maritime environment, one that includes challenges imposed by the sea itself as well as industry standards set by external regulators operating within a national or international "government." The total environment figuratively resembles the layers of an onion.

Outer-most is a governing layer, whose major concerns involve responsiveness to the concerns of society while also promoting economic growth. Next within is a regulatory layer, concerned with setting and enforcing industry standards. The organizational layer confronts the protection (safety) versus profit choice, determined to be the main driver initially at the senior management level, where decision must be made as to how limited resources are to be allocated consistent with the industry standard set by the regulators. To be sure, the regulators should understand the industry and not function merely as pawns of politicians and the media. Also, the regulators should thoroughly understand the regulations they promulgate. Too often in the maritime domain a request to a regulator for an explanation is met with little more than verbatim recitation of the regulation verbiage. What deck officer has not suffered through a Coast Guard inspection administered by an inspector who has little more than basic book knowledge of the regulations? Decisions of an organization's upper management are presumed consistent with all applicable regulatory requirements and reflect primary concerns of the organization. Finally, the cumulative production from these various layers filters through the safety climate of the mariners tasked with accomplishing the job of getting ships safely from point A to point B but also maintaining the organization's profitability.

Avoiding esoteric organizational theorizing, there are several commonly accepted theories addressing organizational safety factors. *Normal Accident Theory* (NAT) pessimistically considers that localized failures spread to affect the larger systemic organization in a manner that is inevitable – a sort of contamination theory. A *High Reliability Organization* (HRO) is more optimistic in accepting long periods of consistent safety as an achievable goal. NAT and HRO take an organizational view toward safety. A third theory considers safety less as a goal than as a system property "controlled" by safety constraints related to the functioning and behavior of system components, including the human element - all styled *Systems-Theoretic Accident Modeling and Processes* (STAMP).

The commercial, and to a lesser extent the military, maritime domains do not fit wholly within any of these theories. NAT tends to flow upstream from the operator, but increasingly the downstream effect of organizational culture is being acknowledged. Shipping also lacks the high level of complexity – though, complexity is increasing – and tight coupling – witness the gap between shore management and the vessels and personnel being managed – that largely feature in NAT analysis, though NAT advocate Charles Perrow does not ignore maritime casualties.[593]

HROs are characterized by proactively searching out failure and shortcomings for remediation, avoiding over simplification, recognizing the importance of communication, having a wariness of success, deferring to experience, and being committed to a safety culture. While these attributes broadly are encouraged by the ISM code, the shipping community, conservative by history and nature, cannot be said to have adopted these attributes wholeheartedly.

STAMP contends that accidents result from inadequate enforcement of constraints upon behavior within component systems of the organization as a whole. But too meddlesome control can impede or inhibit the many situation specific needs for response grounded in seamanship and maritime expertise. And, a culture of "silos," where distributed decision making prevails without coordination, such as occurred within the separate commands directing USS *Cole*, will run interference with necessary internal communication and sensitivity to the often "conflicting" goals of, on the one hand, the people behind the desks and, on the other hand, the people on the bridge or in the engine room.

But, while the pieces may not fit exactly, much of benefit to the maritime industry can be drawn from organizational analysis – whether NAT, HRO or STAMP.

Considering the wide variety and internationality of maritime ownership and management organizations, relatively little is known of their functioning and performance. Nor is there enough known about metrics that would enable the overall effectiveness of the organization to be determined. In the best of all possible worlds, there would be a set of proactive "leading" indicators predictive of the future so that appropriate intervention could be effected to prevent a casualty. Leading indicators are "conditions, events or measures that precede an undesirable event and that have some value in predicting the arrival of the [adverse] event, whether it is an accident, incident, near miss, or undesirable safety state."[594] Included would be near miss reports, hazard identification and analysis, and "lessons learned." For this to occur, there should be agreement as to what constitutes organizational behavior, then decision upon what "behaviors" are leading indicators of proficiency as well as of deficient professional behavior and, lastly, a methodology to measure accurately these indicators.

Positive effort is being made in this direction. Successful implementation of a leading indicators strategy involves, first, identifying significant safety factors, such as have been identified through HFACS, modified to be consistent with the maritime environment and, second, identify suitable metrics or leading indicators that correlate well with those safety factors.[595] These have been found to include basic factors in three safety areas capable of being improved:

1. organizational safety culture: hiring quality personnel, providing orientation toward safety, actively promoting safety, and creating a formal "learning from events" protocol;
2. shipboard safety "culture" [climate]: responsibility, communication, risk identification, prioritization, and feedback; and
3. the individual's safety culture: empowerment, responsibility, incident reporting, and feedback.

The underlying premise is that enhanced safety awareness in these three respective domains can be linked causally with the listed safety factors. The leading indicators strategy goes further, to draw upon core attributes of organizations that have proven themselves over time to operate at a highly reliable level – as high reliability organizations (HROs). Operations falling within this designation include aircraft carrier deck operations, air traffic control, and some nuclear power plants, to name a few.

From such HROs, an overlay of four distinguishing qualities has been identified as appropriate to include with the previously identified basic causes/explanatory factors. These are:

1. prioritization of safety and reliability as organizational and operational goals – equivalent to previously discussed safety culture;
2. redundancy in personnel and technology – while redundancy in personnel is not the same as redundancy in technology, redundant personnel allow dialogue as well as monitoring and challenging to eliminate "one person error";
3. chronic uneasiness – a regular and consistent ferreting out of safety relevant operational imperfections and RRPP deficiencies; and,
4. interpersonal trust – reflected in, for example, the free flow of information and effective BRM.

More broadly, and drawing from the various organizational theories, as well as in large part a summation of much of what has been discussed in preceding chapters, the most effective risk management derives from assessing that organization's resilience to opportunities for error to occur as well as to the consequences of error, and then addressing those areas in which resilience is low. An added challenge to maritime domain shore side management is the often substantial geographical and experiential distance between management and the vessels and personnel managed. Notwithstanding differing conceptual theories and other challenges, effective risk management can be related to several broad leading safety indicators.

Mindfulness of Risk

Mindfulness of risk encompasses the awareness and commitment of top level management to safety, awareness and "chronic unease" over the fact that error is unavoidable, that "zero tolerance" as a goal is unrealistic as well as more likely than not to create dangerous conditions than to inspire safe behavior, and that complacency and "surprise" are to be avoided.

Commitment of top level management manifests itself most strongly in the development of a strong safety culture and being receptive to unfiltered adverse reports For heads of large organizations to receive "unsanitized" information from people unless those people report directly is "notoriously difficult."[596] This hurdle ideally is surmounted through introduction of the ISM designated person. Top and senior level management can be seen as mindful and committed to safety not only through allocation of financial resources to benefit safety issues but also through their active and personal participation in senior officer safety seminars. Officers brought in from their vessels cannot fail but to be directly impressed by the company president or chief executive officer who spends a day attending a safety seminar, actively participates, and is available for discussion. Also, management is chargeable with knowing the truth regarding the company's safety culture: is there a safety culture in fact or merely verbiage. Testimony following a fatal air crash in Greece revealed how there can be real difference of safety culture and opinion in the highest reaches of the company:

CEO: ... had never been informed that the company had any problems that may be degrading safety ... Safety always was number one priority... [and] meetings were held regularly.

COO: ... there appeared to be a culture of fear where people were encouraged to stretch the rules to the limits.[597]

There needs to be awareness that honest "zero error" is not an attainable goal, that efforts expecting zero error are doomed to failure and, worse, are likely to have counter-productive consequences.[598] Risk assessment and response come from one of two streams: risk management and rule compliance. Risk management as envisioned by ISM tends toward risk "as low as reasonably practical," an explicit recognition that absolute safety is not feasibly attainable. Similarly, rule compliance does not guarantee absolute safety. Management should realize that the "best that organizations can hope for is to manage error effectively, decreasing the probability of errors and minimizing their consequences."[599]

Due to the overwhelming press of regulations, many managers defer to stressing shipboard adherence to existing regulations. Instead, the burden must be upon owners and operators to be self-regulating and perform self-critical auditing of what really is going on in the fleet. This obligation places a premium upon having one or more "designated persons" and reiterates the relevancy of Lord Donaldson's previously quoted "blind eye" statement.[600] Similarly addressing management's burden of inquiry and knowledge is Winston Churchill's response upon learning in December of 1941 that Singapore, rather than being impregnable, was highly vulnerable to seizure over land through Malaya: "I ought to have known. My advisors ought to have known and I ought to have been told, and I ought to have asked."[601] To be avoided is a Pearl Harbor type "organizational surprise," which can be described as:

> likely to be a complicated, diffuse, bureaucratic thing. It includes neglect of responsibility but also responsibility so poorly defined or so ambiguously delegated that action gets lost. It includes gaps in [knowledge] but also [knowledge] that, like a string of pearls too precious to wear, is too sensitive to give to those who need it. It includes the alarm that fails to work, but also the alarm that has gone off so often it has been disconnected. It includes the unalert watchman, but also the one who knows he'll be chewed out

by his superior if he gets higher authority out of bed. It includes the contingencies that occur to no one, but also those that everyone assumes someone else is taking care of. It includes straightforward procrastination, but also decisions protracted by internal disagreement. It includes in addition, the inability of individual human beings to rise to the occasion until they are sure it *is* the occasion – which is usually too late. (Unlike movies, real life provides no musical background to tip us off to the climax.)[602]

As dangerous as surprise is complacency:

Complacency is a natural human behaviour in response to repeated exposure to situations in which no adverse consequences are experienced. This inevitably results in people feeling comfortable, and induces an attitude of 'it won't happen to me.' In turn, this leads to shortcuts and risks being taken and procedures being ignored. ... Combating complacency is a significant managerial challenge ..., for which there is no simple solution. Therefore, it would probably be beneficial to ... safety for ... owners and operators to share their experiences and understanding of complacency, as well as measures which have been found to be successful in preventing its occurrence.[603]

Over reliance upon sophisticated systems such as eNav and automation to conduct the navigation of the vessel can reinforce a tendency toward complacency. Emphasis upon professionalism can counter a drift toward complacency. And, though not to be encouraged, nothing reverses complacency as well as a major "close call." The matter was directly, if not eloquently, put in an anonymous "The Stupid Shall Be Punished" blog following the collision between the nuclear submarine USS *Hartford* and surface vessel USS *New Orleans*, where complacency was rampant in *Hartford*:

I've gotta believe that they'd have been a lot less complacency amongst the *Hartford* group if someone, somewhere, sometime had been in seriously deep kim chi before.[604]

Handling of Error

Given the prevalence of error, as much as possible should be learned from the errors committed. "At sea the importance of experiencing failure is second only to avoiding failure in the first place."[605] Only by dissecting the mistake and all issues relevant to the mistake will the organization have benefitted from and positively accepted the errors that are inevitable in any human endeavor. Increasingly there is recognition that safety is enhanced in a "just culture" environment. From the disclosure aspect of a just culture, the organization is put into a position of learning both of and from error. NTSB member Robert Sumwalt commented that "[t]hose of us with a safety focus, ..., realize that a punitive culture cannot co-exist within an effective safety culture."[606]

Knowledge is a precious commodity and knowledge of how mistakes occur and can be avoided is squandered if the people making the mistakes are shunted aside. While great strength of character would be necessary, what better way to transfer acquired knowledge than for the person who made the mistake to discuss the error, the bounded reality/mental model of the situation, contributing factors and how the error may be avoided in the future, and then address relevant questions? Such a discussion carries far more weight and instructive value than scanning a dry investigation report. The alternative is the likelihood of the error being repeated by someone else. As "anonymous" from The Stupid Shall Be Punished blogged, "Not that you want to encourage this sort of direct experience, but firing everyone in sight doesn't likely to help [sic] much in terms of honing future instincts by way of scar tissue and muscle memory." Certainly not every error should go unsanctioned. Nor is every error deserving of punishment. Sound management distinguishes between the two by achieving a balance between safety and accountability.

A blame culture carries many liabilities. Attention is mis-directed away from determination of true root causes and toward the operator, a direction strongly criticized by a 2006 *Fairplay* Editorial: "Shipping needs to tackle the blame culture by understanding that there's more to a bad decision than an incompetent officer."[607] A blame culture runs counter to a guiding principle of the ISM Code.[608] A blame culture accentuates the negative over the positive and impedes voluntary incident reporting – which has proven in other safety critical domains particularly effective in reducing error. A blame culture encourages second guessing.[609] Draconian application of a punitive blame culture may deprive society of subsequent valued services.[610] But, most significantly, a punitive or blame culture allows an organization to "deny responsibility for a disaster and to convince both [it]self and others that one does not need to change at all. Its fundamental function is to maintain the status quo indefinitely."[611] Such self-delusion makes the mistake of denying the inevitability of human error and sets the stage for further casualties.

Contrasted to the punitive or blame culture,[612] a "just" culture offers organizational and individual learning opportunities from mistakes.

Allocation of Financial Resources between Production and Profit

A primary challenge to financial investment in safety (as distinct from development of a philosophical safety culture) is that *protection* often is perceived as being at odds with *production/profit*. Production, in the sense of investing in those components of the business that generate profit, receives primacy as well because production generates the income necessary to pay for protection.

In another of the many ironies of maritime safety, investment in safety often is justified as a means to increase profit, such as by equipping vessels with more modern navigational equipment so those vessels "can" go faster in restricted visibility. As explained by the risk homeostasis theory, such thinking marginalizes the safety otherwise gained.

A related challenge is the absence of empirical data sufficient to "prove" that organizational profit can be derived from enhanced safety. This absence cogently was commented upon in the 2007 *Report of the BP U.S. Refineries Independent Safety Review Panel:*

> ...how should management measure the benefits of expenditures intended to improve process safety performance, such as expenditures for training or additional testing of equipment? The costs, in terms of present dollars to be spent, can be determined or estimated with relative certainty; the benefits, in terms of incremental reduction of process risk (i.e. incremental reduction of likelihood of occurrence of a process incident), perhaps occurring over an indeterminate period, can often be very difficult to estimate. The benefit of some of these types of expenditures may not be known or realized for many years.[613]

In fact, studies show that short term assessment, say over one year or so, looking at lost time injuries or the non-occurrence of a significant accident that are the commonly applied metrics, generally reveal little or anything about the true state of site or operation specific process safety, or about the potential for a serious accident for several reasons. For instance, a static condition of no accidents may be a random coincidence, with latent deficiencies in place for years before the consequential accident occurs. Also, the metrics required to measure process safety performance and capabilities differ from metrics used to assess performance in other areas, and are difficult to create. Safety suffers because only "what gets measured gets managed."[614] There is recognition that

> [i]n industrial organizations, there are two distinct types of safety: individual safety and process safety. A ... ship ... can excel at one while simultaneously failing at the other. Logging few worker injuries, while commendable, has little bearing on whether a major disaster is brewing.[615]

The dichotomy between logging few incidents and process safety is illustrated by the *Deepwater Horizon* tragedy. In 2011, Transocean, Ltd., owner of the vessel, had its "best year in safety performance" based upon the "total rate of incidents and their severity" despite the tragedy in the Gulf, and various company executives "received two-thirds of their target safety bonus."[616] The Coast Guard investigation report notes that

> [t]horoughout the joint investigation, Transocean consistently maintained that *Deepwater Horizon* was a safe vessel. It pointed to the facts that *Deepwater Horizon* possessed all required valid statutory safety certificates, and that the company was awarded a "Safety Award for Excellence" by the [involved United States regulatory agency] in 2008. Moreover, on the day of casualty, several BP and Transocean senior executives were onboard to congratulate the crew on their outstanding safety and performance records. However, Transocean's view of the effectiveness of its company and *Deepwater Horizon*'s safety management system (SMS) is not supported by the evidence of numerous instances on *Deepwater Horizon* and

other Transocean vessels of deficiencies in safety-related systems, inoperable or poorly maintained equipment with the potential to impact safety, and lack of proper personnel training on issues relating to safety.[617]

However, general theoretical models do demonstrate organizational benefits of safety expenditures in the maritime domain. In one study, where all managerial and organizational factors were rated "adequate," there was a theoretical 93.1% reduction from powered/drift groundings where such factors were inadequate, and a 99.55% reduction where those factors were rated "excellent."[618] A three year study in detail of at least one thousand vessels and nine ship owners showed that the "top 25% are 7 times better then [sic] the 25% worse [sic] in terms of accident statistics and 3 times better than the average."[619] Persuasive as these figures are, they may lose some effect when the randomness of casualties is considered.[620] With such randomness apparently in mind, in a letter of sympathy shortly after the 1964 collision between the aircraft carrier HMAS *Melbourne* and HMAS *Voyager* in which *Voyager* sank, Second Sea Lord Admiral Sir Royston Wright wrote:

> Collisions at sea can seldom be completely explained; with all the care and attention that we give to the training of our officers, they usually seem to be "impossible." Yet with relentless regularity they crop up in the best trained Fleets. The fact is that ours is a dangerous calling and every now and again Fate extracts a penalty.[621]

Of course, wholly absent from these studies is reference to the positive effects of a safe operation upon ship board morale and freedom from port control detention.

Other concerns of varying significance are relevant to the protection-profit schism. Certainly, logic suggests that ethical ship owners and operators will invest reasonably to protect their assets, human and inanimate. Public relations will play a role, greatest when passenger[622] or oil tankers are concerned but unfortunately descending toward third world crewed bulk carriers.

Receptivity of Information and Exercise of Two-way Communication

A critical feature of organizational culture is how information is accepted and responded to, especially adverse information. One authority[6023]classifies organizations as having "pathological," "bureaucratic," or "generative" behavioral patterns. A pathological organization discourages information flow and penalizes, at least implicitly, people who raise safety related issues. Studies of adverse events show that middle and junior levels of management frequently find difficult their passing bad news up the chain of command.[624] Also, absent direct communication between the communicator and top management, the information tends to become filtered and "sanitized" to be more palatable. The "designated person" has been inserted by the IMS Code to counter this impediment; much of the success of this insertion depends upon the character of the designated person. A bureaucratic organization is generally effective in handling information regarding routine challenges, albeit superficially. Consequently, latent factors of the type previously discussed are likely to continue unresolved. On the other hand, a generative organization encourages information flow and rewards behaviors that nurture active inquiry to find, report and resolve issues at their root. Where news is valued and the communicator is protected, there is real likelihood that information will flow upward in time for proper action to be taken.

Note must be taken of a demeaning attitude that may exist between shipboard personnel, the source of most of the adverse safety information, and shore side management. For example, one master was quoted as hesitating to discuss his profession with "lesser beings" (non-mariners) because they "always screw it up."[625] Interviews conducted in the course of researching this book confirm that this is not an atypical attitude. This attitude is exacerbated where no, or inadequate, response is forthcoming from management to information coming from shipboard personnel, particularly if that information initially had been solicited by shore side management. Downstream flow of information is equal in importance to upstream flow.

A related issue is how any response from management may be subject to varying interpretations:

"When convenient"–what is the perimeter of "convenience;" when funds are allocated and what is the priority assigned?

"At earliest opportunity"- but we haven't prioritized or sufficiently planned ahead to give you a date.

"We have reminded the Master" – has a written record been made so this information will be readily available on board in its original wording and for the Master's successor?

"The parts have been delivered on board" – are the parts identified so as to ensure that they are the proper parts. Will the ship reply that the parts have been installed and are working properly?

As major oil companies have become more safety conscious, a proper response to questions arising during the vetting of vessels being offered for charter has taken on increased importance:

> Issue: "The vessel does not have on board a vapor release plan."
>
> Response: "Recognizing that the Master was not aware of where the vessel vapor release plan is located in our SMS manual, we immediately advised the Master by email dated December 10, 2010 of the plan's specific location within our SMS manual – section 5.6.17 of our SMS "procedures" manual. We sent our marine superintendent on board on the following day and he confirmed his review with the Master and all deck and engineering officers of the organization and substance of our SMS manuals. Additionally, we have requested input from our vessels regarding the functionality and usability of our manuals and will address these responses in order to make our manuals more user friendly."

Organizations need to be mindful of any *culture of denial*, which leads to complacency and overconfidence. Such a culture fends off, trivializes and embarrasses dissenting opinions or adverse information. Where a culture of denial exists, risk assessment is unrealistic and warnings are dismissed without full investigation. There is descent from failing to recognize a risk, to failing to properly address the risk once recognized, to finally justifying and treating the risk as acceptable. Managers convince themselves that at any one point in time a little further operation with a degraded safety margin will not increase risk – largely because nothing bad had happened at an already degraded safety level. The relation of a communicative culture of denial to normalization of deviance is obvious.

Operating Within a Regulatory Framework

A further challenge is that vessel owners and operators function within a complex national and international regulatory framework.[626]

The nature of regulation is to be reactive, so many latent error inducing factors will, unless identified through the occurrence and investigation of a casualty, remain unregulated. There is basis for strong argument that regulation substantially lags behind the operational environment. And, once regulation comes into being is not to say that the regulation is adequate, appropriate or wholly effective.

The tribulations of the car carrier *Cougar Ace* while complying with a ballast water exchange regulation suggest an insufficiently considered and implemented regulation. A requirement that ballast water be exchanged at sea was considered necessary by lawmakers and regulators to minimize introduction into local waters of foreign invasive marine organisms. Maritime interests replied that the process could impose an added risk upon the ship, her personnel and goods on board. Such caution was generally disregarded by proponents of the regulation as an industry excuse to avoid regulation as well as the expense and inconvenience of compliance.

In July of 2006 the auto carrier *Cougar Ace*, en route to North America West Coast ports with more than 4,700 Mazda automobiles on board, was engaging in ballast water exchange at sea when she suddenly took an 80 degree list to port. The vessel's operator issued a statement: "[T]he probable cause of the listing has been identified as instability which occurred during the ballast water adjustment process. [Company] officials believe the listing was caused by discharging too much sea water from ballast tanks located in the bottom of the vessel. In the process of the adjustment work, the vessel rolled on the swell of the sea and suddenly listed."[627] Likely accurate, but the statement is not particularly informative.

This incident raises issues regarding the practicality of the regulation as well as whether the shipboard personnel were appropriately trained and had on board information sufficient to safely implement the regulation. Telling was one blogger's responsive comment: "it's a big wide world out there and some things that you will see in ships you haven't met yet will surprise you[,]"[628] corroborative of the fact that not every regulation suffices in itself.

The Maritime and Port Authority of Singapore, who investigated this incident involving the Singapore flagged *Cougar Ace*, concluded:

> 7. The investigation revealed the following inadequacies in the ship's ballast water exchange (BWE) operations:
>
> .1 there was improper planning and execution of BWE operations, leading to insufficient weights being present in the water ballast tanks below the ship's waterline;
>
> .2. the officer-in-charge of the BWE operations failed to ensure that the ship's stability was to be maintained throughout the operations; and
>
> .3 the shipboard procedures concerning BWE operations did not have sufficient safety guidelines or procedures specific to the *Cougar Ace* on the safe operations of the BWE operations in accordance with the recommendations of IMO. Considering the potential consequences of vessel capsizing, such instructions should be such as to be clearly understood and complied with by the Master, Chief Officer and persons involved in the BWE operations.

Safety Management System

The Safety Management System envisioned by the ISM, being a "paper" exposition of the company safety culture, is simply hazard management through a system of hazard identification and prioritization, evaluation, reduction or elimination, and control by analytic, design and management procedures. The concept may be referred to as "organizational common sense" but there is no SMS common to all organizations.[606] While ideally a safety system is implemented at the design stage and onset of the involved system, obviously this is not possible when the system to be managed already is up and running – such as a fleet in being. The concept of a safety "system" as a discipline includes:

1. Building safety in as the system evolves,
2. Safety is not compartmentalized,
3. Hazards are viewed as including more than failures,
4. Analysis is emphasized over successful experience, and
5. Recognition that trade-offs are necessary and conflicts exist such that safety issues may constrain other worthy objectives.[630]

Highly complex system failure situations are roughly congruent with failures within the less complex maritime situations, and suggest adaptable approaches that will enhance maritime operational safety:

1. Pursue "second" stories to determine the true cause or causes of incidents and accidents. The "first" story will generally focus upon operator error and the immediate fact of the event. The first story usually comes through the people most directly involved, who generally are people from the ship. Management should not expect to obtain objective and complete reports from ships' personnel for a variety of reasons, including a different language (first language as

well as professional terminology and knowledge), different culture (native as well as professional), no strong sense of loyalty to or from management (shipboard loyalty generally runs to shipmates and the ship), absence of or halfhearted response to prior vessel feedback, fear that employment will be jeopardized or terminated, to name but a few.

2. Escape hindsight bias. Knowledge of the outcome biases objective investigation of underlying conditions and the operator's bounded rationality as well as acceptance of too simplistic an explanation.

3. Understand the task as performed at the "sharp end" of the system. Safety advance depends upon understanding how people at the sharp end accept or adapt safety RRPP with their performance to accomplish tasks from their perspective of priorities.

4. Search for systemic vulnerabilities. Safety only rarely is found in a single person, device or department but rather is an emergent property of systems and not of their components. As an aspect of the safety culture of the organization and through information elicited through the designated person, analysis is made of how the system in question supports or fails to support detection and recovery from incipient failures.

5. Study how practice creates safety. This relates to how the people throughout the organization "cope" and accomplish their tasks in the face of challenges and tradeoffs.

6. Search for underlying patterns. Here the search is beneath the surface of the job to find how information and performance is coordinated to handle evolving situations and cope with the complexities of the work domain.

7. Examine how economic, organizational and technological change will produce new vulnerabilities and paths to failure. Recognition and consideration must be given to the reality that as circumstances change so also will vulnerabilities to unsafe operations change. This recognizes the homeostasis of risk theory.

8. Use new technology to support and enhance human expertise. Here is recognized that human expertise is to be given primacy over technology.

9. Tame complexity through new forms of feedback. Here is recognized the value of incident reporting.[631]

Because shore side management's perception of risk generally determines the nature and extent of systematic risk control measures, an overly compartmentalized shoreside operation runs the danger of seeing risk only one dimensionally or departmentally. This inherent danger can be avoided through a "deconstructive" approach to risk evaluation where, through input from various sections, risk data is subjected to multiple interpretations. From such pluralistic consideration and evaluation there is greater likelihood for identification of all risks that could cause some aspect of systemic failure. A wide variety of prospective risk is likely to be foreseen, and trapping and/or ameliorating defenses can be implemented. Too often, people, exercising a form of "silo mentality," in which " people retreat to their own organizational or occupational niches and deny [implicitly, at least] any broader responsibilities. ... Such a culture obviously compromises the goals of the larger organization or system."[632] The unfortunate result can be that the organization begins to work against itself.

Often, differences over types and degrees of risk versus the resources to be allocated to particular safety issues between departments or sections within departments are brought together only after an accident. A somewhat amusing example of this too common reality is the two exchanges between an airline's Flight Department and its Safety Management Department recently:

Exchange one: "Do you think we should put 'PARKING BRAKE OFF' on the Before Landing Checklist?"
"Nah, it's got to be released to make the take-off and surely a pilot wouldn't set it while airborne!"

Figure 6. Parking brake set before landing 1. *Courtesy www.dauntless-soft.com.*

Figure 7. Parking brake set before landing 2. *Courtesy www.dauntless-soft.com.*

Exchange several days later: "Do you think we should put 'PARKING BRAKE OFF' on the Before Landing Checklist?" "Good idea." [633]

Rules, Regulations, Policies and Procedures

The pervasiveness of RRPP presents operational as well as legal challenges. Unfortunately, in relation to the ubiquity of RRPP there is little written to give guidance as to how RRPP effectively can be managed, how to decide how much more or less is appropriate, how to decide the content and scope of those RRPP that are required by regulation or by circumstance, and how passive are the operators expected to be, because by their nature the RRPP influence an individual's freedom of choice. Here the skill, insight and effectiveness of the Designated Person are crucial. He or she while on board should inquire aggressively and ensure that the responses accurately portray just how the RRPP are received on board and within the vessel's safety climate:

do the mariners fully understand the RRPP and their purpose,

are the RRPP necessary,

are there better alternatives,

are the RRPP easily understood,

are the RRPP contradictory to stated goals,

are the RRPP compatible with the dynamic shipboard environment,

are there situations in which the RRPP cannot or ought not apply and, if so, why not,

are there situations that encourage violation,

which of the RRPP make your job more difficult, and how,

is there acknowledgement that there are situations in which no RRPP is likely to apply and in such circumstances, are responses discussed, and

is input from the mariners solicited and objectively considered?

Especially important are the questions: are you able to comply with the assets available? And, if so, *how* will you comply? A potentially instructive means to evaluate the functionality of the RRPP is objectively to consider the effect if *all* the RRPP were adhered to without deviation. This, of course, is what happens in labor disputes when employees "work to rule."

Heavy reliance upon prescriptive RRPP as a means of managing risk has been found counterproductive as discouraging employees from taking responsibility for safety, serving as a means of allocating blame and generating a sense of disempowerment that can create a sense of fatalism about accidents.[634]

Where RRPP are necessary, management should be aware that:

> Procedures ... are, however, also one of the least effective forms of safety assurance. Procedural documents do not usually make interesting reading, individuals may not read them properly or they overlook or forget provisions.[635]

A wise approach is to modify the safety culture in such a way that RRPP are expressed less as rules and the like that must be followed because someone in a higher position says so but rather because the value of the RRPP lies in them as safety defenses in place to protect people from harm. Similarly, there should not be ambiguity and the fears of employees regarding their employment security should be taken into account. This point was commented upon in the *Patriot* report, which considered the manner and style of communicating information by the company:

> Despite ... general guidance [in written safety procedure manuals and reference to master's prerogatives], the terms of the charter agreements and masters' [and chief engineers'] perceptions of the criteria used by the company to evaluate their job performance can motivate [them] to take undue risks in order to stay on schedule.[636]

The company should provide explicit guidance permitting deviation or delay in the interest of safety, and assurance that reasonable decisions taken in the interest of safety will have no adverse employment repercussions.

Likewise, manuals provided for shipboard use should be reviewed for clarity.

One recent study examined ship total losses from 1996 through 2005 and determined that 48.3% of those losses was attributed to foundering.[637] A collateral finding was that in many of those foundering situations, the stability books available "are written by designers for the authorities with the purpose of obtaining certificates."[638] As such, these stability books were of little, if any, real use to the ships' officers in a crisis. Better needs be done.[639]

The comments of the designated person should be given attention and consideration. Matters raised by the designated person but not appropriately addressed by management may be the Achilles heel of any defense to a lawsuit arising out of those matters.

Similar concern should be paid to the functionality of safety management systems. Another Achilles heel may be revealed where there is a gap between the onboard audit trail and the reality of tasks that cannot be accomplished within the standard set by the safety management system. A common example may be the inability of a container vessel's cargo officer to comply with the SMS, as well as with the practices of good seamanship. For instance, the January 2006 loss, due to a collapsed container stow, of containers overboard from the westbound *P & O Nedlloyd Genoa* in heavy seas. The vessel was on a scheduled 22 day North Atlantic rotation between Northern European and North Atlantic American ports. "Berth slots" were pre-booked at various ports of call, requiring guaranteed arrivals so as to avoid delay and consequential financial penalties. The vessel's maximum operational speed was 23.5 knots. Ship data from October and November in the year before showed a round trip required an average service speed of 17.8 knots. The westbound North Atlantic crossing was planned for 17.8 knots and the eastbound crossing at 18.2 knots. Additionally, the on deck container stow included heavy containers over stowed light containers and maximum permissible weights were exceeded. The

MAIB investigation report commented:

> Instructions contained in safety management systems are
> often well considered and intentioned, but full compliance
> with such instructions can sometimes be difficult for staff to
> achieve in practice. The discrepancies found in *P & O Nedlloyd
> Genoa's* lashing arrangements and the stow plan, suggest that
> while the onboard paper audit trail was being completed, in
> reality, the cargo officer might have been unable to fulfill his
> duties to the standard required by the SMS.

Reference was also made to the fact that

> [o]nce cargo operations were underway, there was little realistic
> chance of the chief officer imposing his own requirements[,]
> despite the fact that the shore side developed stow "plan was
> flawed, but allowed to proceed."[640]

The designated person should be a conduit through
whom to determine the effectiveness, or inadequacies, of
the shipboard paper records. Many problems are likely
hidden where the paper work is not checked against "how
things are really done." A "checklist" audit is problematic
as limiting "the flexibility of the audit, and knowledge
about the items on the checklist became so widespread
as to make it ineffective."[641]

A worst case scenario is presented by the explosion
and loss, with 21 fatalities, of the chemical tanker *Bow
Mariner.* With irony that has proven to be no stranger to
maritime casualties, only several years before that vessel's
loss, the vessel's operator had been praised by Frank J.
Iarossi, then American Bureau of Shipping Chairman,
for being one of the earliest major ship operators to
have implemented and become certified under each of
what Mr. Iarossi considered the four cornerstones of the
maritime safety culture. The circumstances surrounding

the vessel's loss have previously been discussed. Reference is made here because multiple irregularities were found in the records of training and drills as maintained in *Bow Mariner's* Minutes of Safety Committee Meetings that were regularly submitted to the operator:

> Many of the entries related to inspections were identical from month to month, including typographical errors, indicating portions of the Minutes were simply copied from month to month. The Minutes were sent to [operator's] officials ashore monthly, where they were reviewed. No single person was assigned to review the Minutes, and under the existing review procedure a different person might review the Minutes from month to month. As a result, it is likely each month's report was reviewed in a vacuum, without comparison to previous reports. It is unlikely this procedure would detect the problems noted in the Minutes reviewed for this investigation.[642]

The circumstances of *Bow Mariner's* Minutes tends to give credence to the comment of one Captain: "The paperwork is more important than the deed." [643] Because the "presence of company or external audits on board a vessel will often ensure that ship's staff are careful to simply be seen to comply with laid-down procedures and working routines … [,] … [there is belief that] the routine examination of [vessel data recorded] data would provide ships' managers with an incontrovertible assessment on the standards of watch keeping displayed by ships' staff under 'normal' operating conditions."[644] And, more than the absence of negative reports is required, a point brutally demonstrated from the capsizing of *Herald of Free Enterprise,* discussed in the following chapter.

14

Organizational Failure
and the Ro-Ro Ferry
Herald of Free Enterprise
– A Case Study

There is, perhaps, no maritime endeavor more prosaic than that of a ferry. Four minutes after passing through the jetties, the Herald rolled over and sank with the loss of 188 lives. – Daniel S. Parrott [645]

... by the autumn of 1986 the shore staff of the Company were well aware of the possibility that one of their ships would sail with her stern or bow doors open. — Barry Sheen, *Herald of Free Enterprise Report*[646]

The 1987 disaster involving the British ro-ro passenger and freight ferry *Herald of Free Enterprise* is particularly relevant to the management of maritime error because organizational knowledge of deficiencies in procedures and equipment existed at so high a managerial level well before the casualty. These deficiencies went insufficiently addressed as a result of systematic organizational failure, as well as a lagging shore side safety culture and shipboard climate. The *Herald* disaster resulted in the death of at least 150 passengers and 38 crew, the highest peacetime loss of life from any commercial British vessel since the loss of *Titanic* in 1912.[647] This high loss of life resulting from a casualty to a vessel registered under a historically respected maritime nation resulted in an industry-changing comprehensive investigation and follow up. A formal Court inquiry under British Lord Justice Sir Barry Sheen was initiated within 60 days of the casualty and the investigatory report was published by Her Majesty's Stationery Office (the "Sheen Report").[648] The Sheen Report is the foundation for much *Herald* commentary, and this Chapter draws heavily from the Report.

The *Herald* casualty draws together much that has been discussed of human error and organizational management theory in the maritime industry. Among the many noteworthy aspects of this casualty is the fact that – as with many maritime casualties – the ship was owned and operated by a reputable and prestigious company, Townsend Car Ferries Limited, a subsidiary of the legacy Peninsular and Oriental Steam Navigation Company – P&O (the "Company").

While certainly there were faults and omissions at the "sharp end" among *Herald's* officers and crew, there was found that from "top to bottom the body corporate was infected with the disease of sloppiness."[649] Among the characteristics of senior management were found "staggering complacency," "abject abdication of responsibility," "a vacuum at the centre," a "lamentable lack of directions ... and sense of responsibility," all "symptomatic of the malaise which infected the Company ... ."[650]

March 6, 1987

The ferry passage from Zeebrügge, Belgium, to Dover, England, for *Herald* was conservatively a four hour and thirty minute passage. On board the *Herald* were 459 passengers, a crew of 80 and 131 motor vehicles. *Herald* left Zeebrügge under the command of Captain David Lewry, five minutes "behind schedule," at 1805 Greenwich Mean Time (GMT). Captain Lewry was an experienced Master; he had served at sea for over 30 years, held a Foreign Going Master's Certificate for over 20 years, and had been in command of a ship for 10 years, five of which were in *Herald*.

Herald was a powerful triple screw vessel designed for rapid acceleration. At 1824 GMT, as *Herald* cleared the harbor breakwater, Captain Lewry increased power and *Herald* surged ahead from 14 to 18 knots. At 1828, just over one kilometer outside Zeebrügge harbor, *Herald* capsized onto her port side, fortuitously coming to rest on a sand bank, with her starboard side exposed. Rescue divers gathered within an hour of the capsizing. Rescue efforts continued for approximately eight hours, with the heroic efforts of many saving the lives of 351 passengers and crew. Despite these efforts, at least 188 lives were lost.

The immediate cause of loss quickly was attributed to the "G" deck bow doors being left open. *Herald* had eight decks, the uppermost being "A" deck and the lowest "H" deck; "G" deck was the primary and lower vehicle carrying deck, a through deck with a single weathertight door at the stern and double weathertight doors at the bow. The assistant bosun, whose duties included securing the bow doors, had failed to do so; he was asleep in his quarters. He had failed to hear or respond to the call to stations given over the vessel's address system. His absence and failure to close the bow doors had gone unnoticed, and *Herald* departed the port with her bow doors open to the sea. With speed increased to 18 knots, the bow wave grew sufficiently high to enter through the unsecured bow doors and rapidly flood the exposed and undivided "G" deck. So much sea water entered "G" deck that the entering water's free surface effect quickly destabilized the vessel. *Herald* returned from an initial 30 degree lurch to port, but within seconds again listed to port, was unable to recover, and capsized to port.

Figure 8. *Herald of Free Enterprise* showing clamshell bow doors and "G" deck level. *Courtesy www. maritimephotographic.co.uk.*

"E" Deck

Clamshell
Doors

"G" Deck

Contributing to the loss was a culmination of operational deficiencies which, though previously recognized, were allowed to go uncorrected because of organizational failures – shipboard and shoreside.

Ballasting Practice in Zeebrügge

Herald was a ro-ro passenger and vehicle ferry built in 1980 by Schichau Unterweser AG, Bremerhaven. The vessel was 7,951.44 gross registered tons with a length overall of 131.9 meters. She was one of three similar "Spirit Class" ships operated by the Company and originally designed for the comparatively short passage between Dover, England to Calais, France. The Spirit Class vessels featured two vehicles decks: the main vehicle deck ("G" deck) and an upper vehicle deck ("E" deck). At Dover and Calais, vehicles could be driven onto or from "E" and "G" decks simultaneously using double-deck shoreside linkspans at those ports. The linkspan at Zeebrügge, however, was designed for only single deck ferries and not for Spirit Class vessels such as *Herald*. As a result, the vehicle ramp at Zeebrügge could not be sufficiently raised to meet "E" deck during high water spring tides. *Herald* was to be modified to accommodate Zeebrügge during her refit later in the year.

Until the prospective refit, the operational remedy to the Zeebrügge limitation was to flood *Herald's* forward ballast tanks sufficiently to lower the bow, and thereby alter the vessel's trim, so "E" deck would become level with the ramp. But the ballast tanks were designed for stability, not for rapid trim adjustment, so upwards of two hours were required to flood or empty the forward tanks. Accordingly, the general practice was to begin flooding two hours prior to arrival at Zeebrügge and to begin deballasting 20 minutes prior to departing. This resulted in the practice of *Herald* sailing trimmed by her bow.

A Spirit Class vessel chief engineer had brought the matter to the attention of Company management in a February 1984 memorandum. Problems cited as associated with sailing trimmed by the bow included bad steerage, high fuel consumption and added stress upon the bow doors. The proposed solution was installation of a high capacity pump which would significantly reduce ballasting time. Shoreside management failed to recognize the issue as a safety matter and was of the opinion the chief engineer was "grossly exaggerating" the issue. Installation of a high capacity pump at a cost of £ 25,000 was dismissed as cost prohibitive.

Captain Lewry and his crew did exhibit risk awareness when sailing trimmed by the bow. The master and his deck officers testified that when entering or leaving Zeebrügge with the vessel trimmed by the bow, care was taken to limit speed to avoid any bow wave coming over *Herald's* bow spade. The Second Officer testified he would watch the spade and if water came to its lip he would inform the Master, and speed would be decreased, reducing the height of the bow wave. Speed would be restricted until the forward ballast tanks were pumped empty and proper trim restored. On the evening of March 6, Captain Lewry was likely focused upon "making up" time lost because of the departure delayed by five minutes, and accelerated speed prematurely and without consideration of the bow trim. With the vessel exceeding 18 knots, *Herald's* bow wave was well over the level of "G" deck's "lip" and, with the bow doors open, would flow into "G" deck. The bow wave was not being monitored the night of the casualty, indicating a failure in bridge resource management, which would be expected to coordinate attention toward important matters. While Captain Lewry's practice was to limit speed when departing Zeebrügge until achieving a safe trim, the company's established procedures failed to address the issue of trim; nor did Captain Lewry or any other Spirit Class master supplement the company standing orders to reflect any cautionary practice regarding speed when in the Zeebrügge service and trimmed by the head. Subsequent study indicated the bow wave would likely have remained below the open "G" deck at 16 knots, but at greater speeds the height of the bow wave quickly grew to a threatening and ultimately fatal level relative to water entering "G" deck.[651]

Sailing in excess of 16 knots in shallow water with commensurate "squat" effect,[652] exacerbated by the vessel being trimmed by the bow, reduced freeboard forward and resulted in a bow wave sufficiently high to enter and rapidly flood *Herald's* open "G" deck. While the chief engineer's memorandum did not envision the precise casualty scenario of flooding through unsecured bow doors and capsizing, investigative hearings revealed Company management's failure to exercise any meaningful consideration or foresight relevant to this situation presented by Spirit class vessels servicing a port they were not designed to serve.

Vessel Design Vulnerability

Upon visiting the site immediately after the casualty, British Prime Minister Margaret Thatcher commented "it is the fundamental design of the ferry that I understand is the problem."[653] Ro-ro ferries have indeed been recognized by the International Maritime Organization as being "exceptionally vulnerable to human error."[654] Even before the *Herald* casualty, statistics clearly demonstrated the ro-ro class of vessel to be less stable and hence less forgiving in conditions adversely affecting stability then conventional vessels of other design.[655]

A fundamental advantage of the ro-ro design is the ability to drive vehicles onto the vessel at one end and off at the other end. Like most traditional ro-ro ferries, *Herald's* "G" car deck was a continuous deck uninterrupted by bulkheads or any other separation. The design was intended to facilitate rapid and efficient vehicle loading and discharge. An obvious but unintended consequence of the design is susceptibility to uncontrolled flooding of such a space lacking compartmentalization and resulting free surface effect which likely would compromise the vessel's stability. Foundering would be a foreseeable and substantial risk. Stability is further compromised by typically high superstructures and often improperly stowed and/or secured vehicles. Additionally, the lower (or single) vehicle deck is generally located near the waterline for ease of loading and unloading. The vehicle deck is therefore easily threatened by heavy weather or through a defective trim or a sudden list, however caused (human error, allision, collision, cargo shift). The low-lying and continuous car deck is the greatest commercial strength of the ro-ro ferry design but also the greatest safety vulnerability. For that reason, design and security of stern and particularly bow doors on ro-ro vessels was a recognized priority long before the *Herald* casualty. These doors are the only defense to flooding of the vulnerable car deck; deck scuppers are generally intended to only drain minor water quantities – from washing decks, leaking pipes or fire fighting – and are not designed to remedy catastrophic water ingress. Appreciation of the "G" deck vulnerability was certainly not foreign to operators of Spirit class vessels. In October 1984, the master of another Spirit class vessel sent a circular to all deck officers, bosuns and assistant bosuns describing sailing with open doors as a "dangerous situation" and asking that door security be given "utmost attention."[656] That vessel had sailed from Dover with her bow and stern doors left open because the assistant bosun had fallen asleep and so failed to close the doors, an incident striking in its similarity to *Herald's* immediate cause of loss.

Traditional ro-ro ferries typically featured a single bow visor door, commonly when open had been visible from the bridge because of the vizor's upward articulation within line of sight from the bridge. Modern shipbuilding, however, with the Spirit class had "advanced" to clamshell-style bow doors, which open laterally side-to-side. Clamshell doors are considered stronger and less susceptible to failure because the vessel structure absorbs sea loads against closed doors rather than against the locking mechanisms and hinges as with a closed vizor door.[657] Spirit class vessels featured the stronger clamshell door design, but as is typical of that design, the status of the doors — whether open or closed — was not visible from the bridge. Nor did these vessels have any indicator light or mimic panel on the bridge to monitor or confirm door position or security. Between June 1985 and October 1986, three masters of Spirit class vessels requested the addition of a visual indicator on the bridge in a manner that called for "a considered reply." Shoreside management refused these requests, responding that such technology would be unnecessary redundancy of crew responsibility to secure the doors. Astonishingly, this sensible requested safeguard was mocked by management, whose internal memoranda included: "Do they need an indicator to tell them whether the deck storekeeper is awake and sober? My goodness!!" and "Nice but don't we already pay someone!" and "assume the guy who shuts the doors tells the bridge if there is a problem."[658] The Sheen Report noted "these replies display an absence of any proper sense of responsibility."[659] Also absent was the necessary quality of respectfully receiving, considering and responding to constructive reports and recommendations from subordinates. The Report further commented that shoreside management was "not qualified to deal with many nautical matters and were unwilling to listen to their Masters, who were well qualified."[660]

Herald's design vulnerabilities were factors increasing both the likelihood of and the serious consequences from human error. Following the *Herald's* capsize, the media dubbed her doors the "doors of death." The sense of the original suggestions was demonstrated by the fact that within only a matter of days after the disaster, indicator lights were installed in the remaining Spirit class vessels. Closed circuit cameras are an additional safeguard now employed on similar vessels.

Shipboard Failure
To Adhere To Procedure

The assistant bosun admitted that his duties included closing the bow doors at the time of *Herald's* departure from Zeebrügge. He had opened the bow doors upon arrival at Zeebrügge and after completing other duties went to his cabin at 1630, where he fell asleep. He failed to awaken at 1757, the time of the "Harbor Stations" loudspeaker call which ordinarily would summon him to "G" deck to close the doors. He did not awaken until the casualty.

With that said, a "ship's standing orders document issued by Company management in July 1984 stated: '2. The officer loading the main vehicle deck, G deck, to ensure that the water tight and bow/stern doors are secured when leaving port.'"[661] The Chief Officer relieved the Second Officer on "G" deck approximately 15 minutes prior to *Herald's* Zeebrügge departure. Under these circumstances, the Chief Officer's duty as the loading officer under the general instruction was to ensure proper closure of the bow doors. The Chief

Officer left "G" deck for his "harbor station" on the bridge after vehicle loading was completed, but before the bow doors were closed.

In practice, the general instruction "had been regularly flouted" as having been liberally interpreted to allow sufficient compliance by the loading officer merely seeing that the assistant bosun was at the controls and ready to close the doors. This practice, of course, fell short of "ensuring" that the doors were secured when the vessel left port. Though the Sheen Report concluded the Chief Officer was alone on "G" deck when he left to go to the bridge, he testified he left only after ensuring "there was a man standing by to close the bow doors, I do not remember who he was."[662] Regardless, as noted by the Sheen Report, "That is not the meaning of the instruction. ... [if the general instruction] had been enforced this disaster would not have occurred."[663] The Chief Officer's perception of a low level of risk apparent in his decision to leave "G" deck without personally ensuring door security demonstrated "confirmation" bias, having a strong foundation in his past experience of the doors having been properly closed and faith in his crew. The loose interpretation of the general instruction followed on *Herald* was a "short cut" – a routine violation – which arguably was "justified" by there being only two mates, with the Chief Officer having to be on the bridge to assist the Master on departure and lack of reprimand or even adverse reaction from the other ship officers. Because the rule required the impossibility of the Chief Officer being in two places at once – ensuring securing of the bow doors *and* on the bridge – the rule routinely was violated.

The Sheen Report concluded that if the Chief Officer had remained on "G" deck another three minutes, the disaster would have been avoided.[664] His premature departure to the bridge can be attributed to stress resulting from management's imposed urgency to sail at the earliest moment. His disregard of the general instruction to ensure proper closure of the bow doors was found the most immediate fault leading to the disaster.

Disregard of a Prior Significant Incident and Deficient Orders

A hauntingly similar incident occurred almost four years earlier on another Spirit class vessel. In October of 1983, the assistant bosun in *Herald's* sister ship *Pride* slept through the "Harbor Stations" loudspeaker call, resulting in *Pride* departing Dover with open bow and stern doors. In total, before *Herald's* capsizing there were no less than five occasions when one of the Company's ships went to sea with bow or stern doors open. Addressing this situation, one of the masters wrote to management pointing out that:

> There is no indication on the bridge as to whether the most important watertight doors are closed or not. That is the bow or stern doors. With the very short distance between the berth and the open sea on both sides of the channel this can be a problem if the operator is delayed or having problems on closing the doors. Indicator lights on [the bridge] could enable the bridge team to monitor the situation in such circumstances.

The virtues of this comment are many. Not only was it prescient, but it sets forth a specific solution based upon special knowledge of the situation bolstered by the master's expert and practical nautical knowledge. Management's response in not only failing to consider the safety implications but also not taking the report, reasoning and recommendation seriously, reflects the tendency to downgrade near misses as "part of the job" and conclude "it didn't bite us then and it won't in the future."[665] While the July 1984 general instruction issued by the Company assigned responsibility for ensuring the security of bow doors – the ship's standing orders issued by the Company made no reference to opening and closing bow or stern doors. Despite the Company's reliance upon crew performance, managers failed to include in the Standing Orders any requirement that closure of the doors be reported to the bridge and recorded in the log book. Also troubling is that not all prior incidents of sailing with doors open were brought to the attention of other Spirit class masters. Captain Lewry testified he would have required affirmative confirmation of door closure before proceeding to sea if he had been aware of the prior incidents. The veracity of Lewry's testimony is not known, though the fact is troubling that none of those Masters who were aware of the prior incidents changed their orders or procedures. This, however, does not negate the opportunity for management and conscientious shipboard personnel to learn and draw appropriate conclusions from reported and disseminated prior similar incidents.

Herald's standing orders were further deficient in failing to address any particulars of the Dover-Zeebrügge run, despite it being the route assigned *Herald*. The Zeebrügge run differed significantly from the Calais run. On the Dover-Calais schedule, for which the three Spirit class vessels were built, the deck officer complement was a Master, two Chief Officers and a Second Officer. The Zeebrügge run was substantially longer, allowing the officers more rest hours. Accordingly, the Company reduced the Zeebrügge complement by one deck officer. However, because the standing orders contemplated three deck officers, the Chief Officer effectively was required to be in two places at once - ensuring security of the bow doors and reporting to the bridge upon call to "harbor stations." Accordingly, the "harbor stations" call on the Zeebrügge run should have been contingent upon prior deck officer confirmation of bow door security. Another particularity of Zeebrügge was the linkspan designed for single deck ferries, which was accommodated by ballasting and deballasting to achieve proper trim.

The Sheen Report observes that, because of the uniqueness of the Zeebrügge service, "with proper thought the duties of the deck officers at Zeebrügge would have been organized differently from their duties at Calais."[666] The complement of one less officer on the Zeebrügge run itself merited adjustment in the standing orders. A further subject of a vessel or Spirit-class specific standing order for Zeebrügge service would have been to restrict speed when trimmed by the bow until the vessel reached deeper water, the bow tanks were pumped empty and proper trim was restored. Had proper procedure been formalized and memorialized by standing order, there would have been greatly enhanced likelihood of Captain Lewry conforming.

The need for formalized standing orders was all the greater because of the shipboard personnel turnover rate. This issue was twice brought to the attention of Company management by *Herald's* Senior Master, Captain Kirby, who stated most recently in a memorandum less than two months before the casualty:

> *Herald* badly needs a permanent complement of good deck officers … . During the period from 1st September 1986 to 28th January 1987 a total of 36 deck officers have been attached to the ship. … To make matters worse the vessel has had an unprecedented seven changes in sailing schedule. The result has been a serious loss in continuity. Shipboard maintenance, safety gear checks, crew training and the overall smooth running of the vessel have all suffered.[667]

Captain Lewry joined *Herald* in 1980 as one of five masters. Standing orders are not suggested as an adequate alternative to personnel continuity, which has inherent benefits. However, formal orders can articulate risks perhaps not immediately appreciated by personnel not yet familiar with the particularities of a specific vessel or route. In the case of *Herald*, revolving door assignment of masters, officers, and crew was only one more compelling reason to remedy the deficient standing orders.

Especially troubling was the Company's standing order 01.09, "Ready for Sea":

> Heads of Departments are to report to the Master immediately they are aware of any deficiency which is likely to cause their departments to be unready for sea in any respect at the due sailing time.
>
> In the absence of any such report the Master will assume, at the due sailing time, that the vessel is ready for sea in all respects.[668]

This order was "unsatisfactory in many respects." It accepts that negative reporting by silence equates with positive transmission of critical information. "Reporting" by silence does not equate with positive transmission of important information. The result is uncertainty and ambiguity: is everything OK *or* is everything *not* OK but for a multitude of possible reasons, no report of any deficiency is made. In fact, the Sheen Report makes clear that regularly there were conditions that made the vessel "unready for sea" — excessive number of persons on board, draft not read, insufficient officers to confirm that the bow doors are secured, etc. Yet, the wording of the order permitted — in fact directed — the Master to *assume* the vessel "ready for sea," i.e. seaworthy, in all respects in the absence of any adverse report.

No competent mariner should ever *assume* anything regarding the voyage or its preparation.

Shoreside Safety Culture?

In July 1986, the British Department of Transport had issued a Notice entitled "Good Ship Management," [recommending]

> that every company operating ships should designate a person ashore with responsibility for monitoring the technical and safety aspects of the operation of its ships and for providing appropriate shore based back-up. ...Stress is placed upon the importance of providing the Master with clear instructions to him and his officers. The instructions should include adequate Standing Orders. There should be close co-operation and regular and effective communication in both directions between ship and shore.[669]

Herald's management was aware of the Notice but took no action on it, believing themselves in compliance.[670] Ironically, in a meeting of senior Masters with management only a few months before the Notice issued, a topic raised for discussion was recognition of the Chief Officer as Head of Department and the roles of the Maintenance Master and Chief Officer. The position advocated on behalf of management – by the same executive who claimed compliance with the quoted Notice – was that "it was more preferable not to define the roles but to allow them to evolve."[671] The obvious lack of effective communication between ship and shore was evidenced by four specific issues raised by Masters: (1) complaints of taking passengers beyond certified capacity; (2) request for bridge means to indicate the closed or open position of the bow and stern doors; (3) lack of means enabling accurate ascertainment of the vessel's draft; and, (4) request for a high capacity ballast pump to better manage ballasting and deballasting at Zeebrügge. While not all issues bore causative relation to *Herald*'s capsize, all four accurately identified existing risk issues and presented legitimate concerns. Yet these issues, considered and submitted by vessel masters, "fell on deaf ears ashore."[672] Formal meetings between Spirit class senior Masters and management were intermittent; once two and a half years lapsed over which there were no such meetings. Management "not qualified to deal with many nautical matters"[673] nor receptive to shipboard input from vessel Masters was fatal. Rather than directly and timely addressing these legitimate concerns, management temporized and marginalized them by saying "we shall fully discuss" such matters.[674]

Additionally, in an example of disconnected "silo-like" thinking, there was disassociation of vessel-related concerns to technical, rather than marine, personnel for action.[675] Similarly, the *Herald* casualty may be offered as an example of faulty "bottom-up decentralized decision-making," where individuals and groups making issue specific decisions – here, vessel design, harbor design, cargo management, passenger count, trip scheduling, and vessel operations – were unaware of, or failed to take into account, the impact of their issue-specific decisions upon the thinking of other decision-makers within the company as well as upon the overall operation. This style of decentralized decision-making may be referred to as "silo mentality," "in which people retreat [in]to their own organizational or occupational niches and deny [implicitly at least] any broader responsibilities. ... Such a culture obviously compromises the goals of the larger organizational system."[676] In a complex system, each decision may be "correct" within the limited context in which the decision is made, but may lead to an accident if the individual decisions and organizational behaviors interact dysfunctionally. This suggests that in a complex system, safety should be seen as a property of the system as a whole, and not merely of the components.[677]

And, there was a fatal lack of assigned responsibility ashore[678] or – as concerns specifically *who* was to open and close the doors and ensure the doors were, in fact, open or closed – on board. This brings to mind Admiral Hyman G. Rickover's recognition that "[u]nless you can point the finger at the man who is responsible when something goes wrong, then you have never had anyone really responsible."[679]

Given previous reports of open door sailings, the decision to forgo installation of a bow door indicator light or mimic panel on the bridge and the neglect to revise standing orders revealed a total failure in organizational learning. Management's creation of a "sense of urgency to sail at the earliest possible moment" further escalated operating risk. In 1986 Company management endorsed a policy of early sailings from Zeebrügge to reduce the lateness of following departures from Dover. An internal memorandum from the operations manager at Zeebrügge stated:

> every effort has to be made to sail the ship 15 minutes earlier ... put pressure on the first officer if you don't think he is moving fast enough ... Let's put the record straight, sailing late out of Zeebrügge isn't on. It's 15 minutes early for us.[680]

This expectation that sailings be early could not be fulfilled the evening of 6 March 1987, given the high volume of vehicles to be handled. *Herald*'s scheduled departure time that night was 1800 GMT. Captain Lewry and his deck officers likely perceived the actual departure time of 1805 GMT as being 20 minutes late. Among results of management's induced "sense of urgency" were the Chief Officer's rush to the bridge before ensuring bow door closure as well as Captain Lewry's premature speed increase, before proper bow trim could be gained.

Management also reverted to remediation by reactive discipline rather than by proactive safety awareness. In partial response to further urging that an indicator light be installed on the bridge, management stated that "if the bow or stern doors are left open, then the person responsible for closing them should be disciplined."[681] This reactive "remedy" of discipline overlooks the fact that organizationally there was no one person assigned responsibility for actually opening and closing the doors and, also, "discipline" would not redress the problem if water entered through the open doors and as a result the vessel sinks – as in fact happened.

In the battle "protection vs. profit," the Company had acted to advance profit over protection:

> The shore-based managers had made their shareholders very happy in the preceding months by winning the stiff commercial competition for cross-Channel passengers; but in so doing they had fatally eroded the slim safety margins on these already capsize-prone ro-ro ferries.[682]

The Duty to Think and Challenge

The Sheen Report expresses that the masters of the Spirit class ro-ros "failed to apply their minds to [the order adopted by Senior Captain Kirby: '2. The officer loading the main vehicle deck, "G" Deck, to ensure that the water tight and bow/stern doors are secured when leaving port.'] and to take steps to have [it] changed."[683] Captain Kirby had interpreted and applied this order to be sufficiently complied with *if* the involved officer saw someone in position to close the doors, and the other masters, including Captain Lewry, followed Captain Kirby's interpretation.

The wording of the Report – "failed to apply their minds" – goes beyond merely condemning the subordinate masters' acceptance of Captain Kirby's interpretation. An intellectual responsibility is imposed.[684] There is an affirmative duty to question and seek clarification or modification. That duty is imposed upon *anyone* in a position to knowledgeably assess whether the order is appropriate in all respects within the circumstances within which the rule is to be applied. This presses people to step up to the knowledge-based performance level rather than to behave at the more comfortable skill or rule-based performance levels. Certainly Captain Lewry and his Chief Officer should have appreciated the significance of the Chief Officer in practice having to be in two places at once. The Captain saw the Chief Officer arrive on the bridge. The Chief Officer did not report that the bow doors were closed and the Captain did not ask, nor could the status of the bow doors be seen visually from the bridge. As a result of the negative reporting structure, *Herald* sailed on an assumption. They also should have recognized the danger of having no one person explicitly "responsible" - in writing - for in fact closing the doors. The bosun and assistant bosun further are obliged to speak up as experienced mariners charged with operation of the doors and vehicle deck safety. The "buck" stops everywhere and "chronic uneasiness" is introduced. An on board safety climate is encouraged.

Shipboard Safety Climate

There is no evidence that a safety *climate* existed on board *Herald*. Matters of safety often were addressed in terms of public relations and career,[685] rather than emphasizing safety concerns. The bosun, probably the last person to leave "G" deck, "took a narrow view of his duties and it is most unfortunate that that was his attitude."[686] The bosun had testified "It has never been part of my duties to close the doors or make sure anybody is there to close the doors."[687] Comment already has been made of the captains' acquiescence to negative reporting and failure "to apply their minds" to ambiguous orders as well as to unsafe practices and to the risks of continuing the practice of sailing though not in all respects ready to go to sea.

Casualty Aftermath

Incredibly, no then existing regulation or statute was violated by a ro-ro vessel going to sea with its bow doors open.[688] Ro-ros initially had been small and not particularly risk prone. However, larger ro-ros became more vulnerable, with large open spaces near the waterline that easily could flood if penetrated as the result of a collision or, as demonstrated by the *Herald* accident, if fundamental practices of maintaining hull integrity were violated. The design infringed upon basic naval architectural principles. But, the regulations failed to keep up with the ongoing developments. Unfortunately, "[v]ery few people paid any heed – why should they, if the statutory regulations did not demand any precautions?"[689]

Captain Lewry's certificate was suspended for one year and the certificate of the Chief Officer for two years. Manslaughter charges were brought against the Company, certain executives, as well as Captain Lewry, the Chief Officer and the assistant bosun. The criminal case was based upon the "obvious" risk the ferry would sail with open doors, thereby causing capsize and human casualty.[690] After 27 days of trial testimony, the presiding judge ruled there was insufficient evidence to convict the Company or five of seven individuals being tried – including Lewry – because "it was not obvious to any of these people until it happened to them."[691] The criminal case collapsed after the prosecution dropped the charges against the remaining two individuals, the First Officer and assistant bosun. In a public statement, Captain Lewry's defense attorney maintained that his client had relied upon established procedures for ensuring that the ship's bow doors were closed, procedures that had proved safe on 60,000 Channel crossings.[692]

Just as the loss of *Titanic* led to SOLAS, the *Herald* casualty gave rise to more expansive maritime safety legislation. The Sheen Report cast light on management and procedural deficiencies in the maritime industry and thereby generated pressure for the IMO to adopt operational guidelines. The IMO made significant strides with each passing biennial session. In November 1987, the Assembly adopted resolution A.596(15), entitled "Safety of Passenger Ro-Ro Ferries." The resolution made reference to the *Herald* casualty, noting "that a great majority of maritime accidents are due to human error and fallibility and that safety of ships will be greatly enhanced by the establishment of improved operating practices." In October 1989, the Assembly adopted resolution A.647(16) which applied to all ships and set forth the first IMO "Guidelines on Management for the Safe Operation of Ships and for Pollution Prevention." The stated purpose of the Guidelines was "to provide those responsible for the operation of ships with the framework for the proper development, implementation and assessment of safety and pollution prevention management in accordance with good practice." Revised guidelines were adopted by the Assembly in November 1991 through Resolution A.680(17) and again in November 1993 when the

Assembly adopted Resolution A.741(18), the annex of which contains the now familiar ISM Code.

Under the "old style" assessment of error, at "first sight the faults which led to this disaster were the aforesaid errors of omission on the part of the Master, the Chief Officer and the assistant bosun, and also the failure by [the Senior coordinating Master] to issue and enforce clear orders[,]" – errors at the "sharp end."[693] However, the investigating body elected to follow the error upstream and came "inexorably to the conclusion that the underlying or cardinal faults lay higher up in the Company."[694] From this disclosure of so great a lack of accountability on the part of shore side management the idea of having a Designated Person subsequently was pressed by the United Kingdom IMO delegation, lest lessons learned from the *Herald* casualty as relating to shore side management be forgotten.[695]

The ISM Code, initially promulgated as a voluntary recommendation, was incorporated into SOLAS with mandatory application to signatory nations becoming effective beginning in July 1998. By 2002, the ISM Code was mandatory for most commercial vessel types.

While the *Herald* casualty opened the opportunity for some mechanical remediation – such as installation of door indicator lights on the bridge – the more complex issues of organizational factors and human error were brought to the forefront as the casualty's primary lessons. With human error continuing as the dominant factor in the majority of maritime accidents, *Herald's* legacy remains a relevant study for the maritime industry.

15

Lessons Learned?

The time for taking all measures for a ship's safety is while still able to do so. Nothing is more dangerous than for a seaman to be grudging in taking precautions lest they turn out to have been unnecessary. Safety at sea, for a thousand years, has depended on exactly the opposite philosophy. — Admiral Chester W. Nimitz, Fleet Letter

The sea demands definite qualities in the seafarer – certain attitudes of mind and character. Humility, prudence, and a recognition that there is no end to learning and to the acquisition of experience. — Alasdair Garrett[696]

It should not be necessary for each generation to rediscover principles of process safety which the generation before discovered. We must learn from the experience of others rather than learn the hard way. — Jesse C. Ducommun, Safety Pioneer[697]

Society's system for managing risks to life and limb is deeply flawed ... whereas people generally overestimate the likelihood of low probability events ... they underestimate higher risk levels ... . — Viscusi, V. and Zeckhauser, R. "Risk within Reason"[698]

Lawyers also are now advising their clients about risk management, which, on the face of it seems hardly to be in

their best interests, as the more risk management is seriously implemented by companies, the less accidents will occur and, hence less work might be the result for lawyers. —Aleka Mandaraka-Sheppard, *Modern Maritime Law, at 1017*

... tell me, wasn't that the best time, that time when we were young at sea; ... . — Joseph Conrad, *Youth*[699]

The research for and writing of this book has coincided with several significant events relevant to maritime transportation safety.

On the one hand, as concerns the April 20, 2010 MODU [mobile off-shore drilling unit] *Deepwater Horizon*[700] vessel explosion, the January, 2011 *Report to the President by the National Commission on the BP* Deepwater Horizon *Oil Spill and Offshore Drilling* declares that

> [t]he blowout was not the product of a series of aberrational decisions made by rogue industry or governmental officials that could not have been anticipated ... [but] the clear root cause ... was a failure of industry management ... [and] ... many of the decisions that [were made and] that increased the risk ... clearly saved those companies significant time (and money).[701]

On the other hand, the Australian Transport Safety Bureau issued a preliminary report concerning the November 4, 2010 in-flight uncontained engine failure on a Qantas A380 aircraft with 469 persons on board, and successful landing of the severely damaged aircraft without any fatalities. A turbine disc in Number 2 (one of four engines) engine explosively degraded, with sections of the disc penetrating the aircraft and resulting in aircraft structure and systems failures. The affected engine was shut down and the many multiple systems failure/warning messages displaying on the electronic centralized aircraft monitor were dealt with. Basic airmanship was required to return the aircraft safely to Singapore. The preliminary report highlights the benefits of having a knowledgeable, competent and disciplined flight-crew working efficiently as a team in a wholly novel knowledge-based performance level situation.[702] This event to a "fly by wire" aircraft accentuates current concern that there is excessive reliance upon automation, deemed more reliable than humans, to the detriment of developing and maintaining traditional skills.[703]

These two events bookend the realm of safety concerns – at the worst, the specter of management appearing to "talk the talk but failing to do the walk"[704] and, at the best, the accomplishment of a crew executing principles congruent with effective bridge resource management.

As the preceding discussion has shown, many approaches exist relevant to maritime risk assessment and safety. As to which approach(es) may be appropriate, a major issue arises from the generally accepted fact that human error is a contributing "cause" in approximately 80% of maritime casualties. But there is a difference of opinion over the meaning of "cause" – whether the immediate event is the cause or, to ascertain a meaningful "cause" for purposes of remediation, must one move upstream from the event and, if so, how far. The growing view is that the 80% apportionment must include managerial "human error," but such acknowledgement does not suggest how far into management the "error" should be explored.[705] This issue will receive greater attention in view of the increasing tendency to criminalize managerial behavior, especially if death or pollution is a consequence of the casualty.

Another issue looks to from where the emphasis

Maritime Error Management

upon behavior should come. James Reason, already frequently cited, takes the position that the responsibility must come upstream and away from the actor, upon the argument that "[w]orkplaces and organizations are easier to manage than the minds of individual workers."[706] This approach includes the fact that though the inevitability of error cannot be removed as an embedded attribute of the human condition, the conditions under which persons make decisions and perform their tasks can be altered relatively easily. Another authority relates somewhat differently to the same 80% error data: "Hence, any attempts to reduce accidents at sea should concentrate on eliminating errors on board ships, since this is where the problem is greatest and where the biggest improvements should be made."[707] These views are not inconsistent. Appropriate measures taken upstream should have positive effects on board.

Among various suggestions addressing maritime risk and safety as a whole, some approaches will work in certain situations and others better in other situations, in keeping with the ISM philosophy that each company should determine and implement what works best within that company's particular context. As has been seen, the variety of theories and experiences is so great as to bring to mind the 19th century poem "Six Blind Men and the Elephant," where each of six blind men, all sharing the goal of describing an elephant and each feeling a different part of the elephant, offers a description wholly at odds with the others' respective descriptions:

> And so these men of Indostan
> Disputed loud and long,
> Each in his own opinion
> Exceeding stiff and strong,

Though each was partly in the right
And all were in the wrong![708]

However, and contrary to the quoted stanza, there is more right than wrong in the various perceptions and responses to maritime risk that have been discussed and for all the variety, certain truths do stand out:
- human error is ubiquitous, but organizations that invest in safety have a statistically greater likelihood of avoiding the risks addressed;
- the law of unanticipated consequences compels that RRPP be carefully considered for collateral effects;
- RRPP must be reviewed for their appropriateness in operation;
- RRPP must be adequately resourced;
- RRPP will not cover all situations, leaving the gap vulnerable to the training, education, initiative and attitude of the mariner actor;
- incident reporting and responsible response to the incidents reported pays safety dividends — the safety dividends are so significant as to warrant additional comment as one theorist holds that for every one significant accident there are about 29 lesser significant accidents, about 330 near misses and thousands of unsafe situations;[709]
- as safety is enhanced, so the willingness to accept greater risk increases;
- the safety culture will be accepted or not through the safety climate unique to each respective vessel;
- technology and automation must be subservient to the skills and initiative of the human navigator; and,
- intervention anywhere along the error chain can avoid an accident.

Another truth is the inter-relatedness of the majority of the factors that relate to maritime risk. For example, addressing bridge resource management effectively requires addressing also multicultural – national or hierarchical, or both – issues, monitoring and challenging, situational awareness, the three skill-, rule-, and knowledge-based performance levels, and RRPP. And a successful safety culture depends upon its acceptance or rejection within the shipboard safety climate, which implicates RRPP and multicultural issues, and so on.

This phenomenon of inter-relatedness strongly suggests that remediation or intervention to prevent the occurrence of any one adverse factor has the potential of affecting in a positive manner other factors in a ripple effect. The significance of this conclusion is highlighted when one considers that shipping is a relatively "simple" system, with comparatively rudimentary safety measures. In consequence, a combination of only 2 or 3 unsafe factors may be needed, or be sufficient, to bring about a serious maritime accident. On the other hand, in more complex systems, such as oil and gas exploration and production, more than 50% of the major accidents have required more than 7 interlinked unsafe acts.[710] This means that there may be fewer opportunities to intervene to prevent a significant maritime casualty, so full advantage should be taken of those opportunities that do present, or that can be created. The suggested effectiveness of intervention is confirmed by a 2010 study that found that an airline pilot may commit an *average* of 7.49 errors per hour.[711] Despite this fact, the commercial airline industry has developed an impressive safety record, demonstrating that the defense of monitoring and challenging error when error occurs can be as effective in avoiding adverse consequences as can be avoiding error in the first place.[712]

And, overall, there is ample evidence that a well structured, implemented and accepted safety program will pay safety dividends. Statistics provided in Chapter

Thirteen demonstrate, by way of theoretical models, the direct relation between managerial and organizational safety factors and vessel safety. Further evidence comes from the record of the United States Navy SUBSAFE program[713] within the United States nuclear submarine fleet, introduced in 1963 following the loss of USS *Thresher.* Since SUBSAFE took effect, no SUBSAFE certified submarine has been lost.[714]The narrow focus of SUBSAFE is to provide maximum reasonable assurance of: 1. watertight integrity of the submarine's hull, and 2. operability and integrity of critical systems related to control and recovery from any hazard that poses a risk of flooding of the boat.

Crucially important to the success of SUBSAFE, and what renders SUBSAFE particularly relevant to the commercial shipping industry - is the absolute independence of the safety and quality assurance authority that ensures that the purpose of SUBSAFE is not subverted by expediency or other considerations. Here, the parallel with the ISM Designated Person is inescapable. Also, SUBSAFE is permeated with "chronic uneasiness" lest – by way of normalization of deviance - there be any drift away from program fundamentals.

The management of assets, equally true within the commercial maritime industry as elsewhere, in a manner most likely to achieve safety resilience requires three qualities:

Diagnosis – the ability to find and recognize cues indicative of operational drift toward deviance from safe practices. This involves mindfulness of actual operational practices, which encompasses gathering and understanding relevant information and anticipating how the involved activity or system will develop.

Decision making – after recognizing the drift toward unsafe practice, the ability to choose an appropriate response successfully to redress the diagnosed drift; and

Assertiveness – sufficient to persuade relevant managerial
and operational personnel, including more senior
personnel, that the determined appropriate response
must be taken and that necessary resources will
be allocated or sacrifices made to implement that
response.[715]

Another conclusion to be drawn is that the maritime
industry is a "people" industry. People commit errors
but people are also the means to prevent those errors
from becoming accidents, and so people are the key
to safety. Also, people in the maritime industry do not
begin their days intending to have an accident.[716] From
this, the conclusion becomes self-evident that the most
effective means to manage maritime risk is through
people, and the most effective means of reaching people
in a meaningful way affecting their propensity to err
is through education that explains in a context rich
environment the limitations and motivations acting upon
human cognitive faculties, and why human behavior is as
it is. This conclusion is in line with the broad principle
that a primal human driving force is self interest,
including self interest in not wishing to be a participant
in an accident. And, there is an added benefit: If we get
this right, we have the opportunity to secure not only a
greater level of safety and accident prevention but, at
the same time, deliver substantial operating efficiencies
with consequent commercial benefits.[717]

So, how do we "get this right?" Following a sixty
million dollar hull damage incident, a senior manager
within the involved company commented that "Sixty
million dollars can buy a hell of a lot of training."[718]
Of course, presumably less than sixty million dollars
would be so invested, but the issue becomes "what sort
of training?" There are many physical assets directed
toward training in which investment could be and has
been made, but in spite of "the continuous application

of rules designed to prevent accidents at sea and the technological and education advances, the frequency of casualties does not show a downward trend, as expected."[719]If this statement is correct – and if it is not correct, it is not too far wrong – something obviously is missing from the presently applied training. After all, mariners already are receiving mega-bursts of technical training and certification.

The missing piece stands out to be education - education upstream and downstream explaining and discussing those factors that do bear upon how mariners do perform in reality and can better carry out their tasks and responsibilities. There is great truth in the comment from Admiral Gehman, expressed in the context of the USS *Cole* inquiry: "You train for certainty, you educate for uncertainty[,]"[720] the latter addressing knowledge-based performance level events. But the "training" and "education" referred to by Admiral Gehman cannot be considered complete without the actor having some understanding of the psychological and contextual factors that influence his or her decision-making capability and execution of the decisions made.

This desirable education can best come from dissection within a just culture of past events, especially if participants are willing to openly and candidly discuss how the event came into being and their thinking process, together with objective consideration of how the event related to broader operational and organizational issues and practices. Reports of investigations cannot be relied upon for full disclosure of all relevant factors.[721]

Properly handled, such as with one or more persons within the very top level of company management attending and offering comment, this type of discussion within senior officer seminars can overcome the resistant mind-set of "That was foolish – I am not foolish – I won't ever be in that position."

Lest these approaches be criticized as too "soft and fuzzy" for the seafaring community, consider the warning from Admiral Nimitz is his previously cited Fleet Letter: "There are certain psychological factors which have fully as much to do with safety at sea as any of the more strictly technical ones." Consider also the leadership style adopted by Bernhard Rogge, commanding officer of the German surface raider *Atlantis*, which during World War II successfully stayed at sea for more than 500 days:

> ... we tried to talk the man's own language, to stimulate his thinking processes, to keep his interest in the ship awake and to strengthen it. In this way, the ship, as I had wished it, became, in the best sense of the word, his home.[722]

But there is also a vexing question of just how much written instruction must or should be given competent senior ship's officers. Lawyers defending shipping owning and operating interests hope to see all operational aspects covered in excruciating written detail and this appears to be the direction being taken by post-ISM investigation reports. Safety Management Systems are criticized, for example, for failing to include written directive that crew members not go onto the weather deck in heavy weather, for failing to include a specific off-track limitation distance, or for failing to indicate the minimum level of bridge manning during pilotage periods. Yet, there surely must be legitimate concern that the initiative of senior officers is likely to be hobbled and overall professionalism diminished if they gain the impression that all they need consider will be written in the ship's SMS. Safety at sea compels otherwise:

> ... navigation ... is left neither to Judges nor the Elder Brethren of Trinity House nor those who, in the garb of experts , from the security of a swivel chair now lay out the

course with great conviction. … It is the Master, then, who must make these decisions and who, clothed with great responsibility, enjoys the greatest and widest of good faith latitude in professional judgment. … Safe navigation denies the proposition that the judgment and sound discretion of a captain of a vessel must be confined in a mental strait-jacket.[723]

Authoritative comment has been made that people generally avoid initiating activity at the knowledge-based level of performance. Won't excessively detailed SMSs discourage treading into the knowledge-based realm and undermine the willingness and enthusiasm of ship's officers to educate themselves regarding subjects and issues likely to be encountered as one progresses beyond every day routine? Admiral Nelson prevailed upon the exhortation that "England expects that every man will do his duty." Do today's professional mariners no longer understand their duty as professionals nor have the knowledge to perform that duty?

Finally, other than perhaps an improved understanding of *why* people have committed errors of commission or omission, there are unlikely to be significant new "lessons learned" in the realm of maritime casualties. Already the fundamental lessons are known – certainly more than enough to reduce accidents if these lessons would be applied. These lessons have been taught, if yet to be applied, at tremendous cost in lives lost and property destroyed. The need and desirability of applying lessons already learned is in line with the observation that "the most egregious aspect of the organizational accident is the failure of management to recognize the signs of an impending disaster."[724]

Endnotes

Chapter 1. Past and Present in Maritime Safety

1. http://www.encyclopedia-titanica.org/print/titanic-captain-smith-a-captain's-career.html. Accessed March 9, 2010.

2. Donaldson, 1998 Donald O'May Lecture.

3. T. Soma, safety consultant for Maritime Solutions Nordie, quoted in "Chances of ship casualty double." The statistical frequency for navigational accidents – collisions, groundings and allisions - for large vessels (excluding passenger vessels) for the period 1993-2003 was 0.751% while for the period 2004-2007 was almost doubled, to 1.432%. Soma, "Are the accidental losses increasing [?]", 2. This despite Mark Twain's suggestion that: "The dangers and uncertainties which made sea life romantic have disappeared and carried the poetic element along with them." "About All Kinds of Ships." A 2006 study drawing from Port State Control data found that over the period 1999-2004, 4.9% of PSC eligible vessels that were inspected suffered a casualty within six months of inspection. This suggested two concerns: 1. improvement is needed of corrective action enforcement, and 2. there must be better safety management. A further concern was that about 32% of the PSC related casualties initiated in engine room related areas though only 9% of the detentions relate to those areas. Though inspected vessels generally have been at anchor or alongside and so "cold iron," this aberration indicates that PSC inspection of engine room related spaces has tended to miss engine room area deficiencies. Jalonen, "Safety Performance Indicators," 43.

4. MacDonald, *Curse of the Narrows*.

5. In terms of casualties, Texas City was the "worst industrial catastrophe" in United States history. Stephens, *Texas City Disaster*, xi.

6. Hooke, *Modern Shipping Disasters*, 411-12.

7. USCG, *Deepwater Horizon*, iii.

8. In a January 28, 2010 press release, Peter McIntosh, International Union of Marine Insurance's ocean hull committee chairman, explained that claims costs on partial losses are reaching the level of a total constructive loss or the agreed insured value more quickly than previously. Losses are increasingly expensive."... the average cost of fire and explosion claims seems to be soaring to ... more than double the level of earlier years with navigational claims arising from collisions, grounding and contact damage also moving up." Mulrenan, *Tradewinds*, 24.

9. Macalister, "Owners continue to sideline safety," 2.

10. Grabowski, "Accident Precursors," 285.

11. Ellis, "Safety and Perception of Risk," 2.

12. Psaraftis, Human Element.

13. Wagenaar, "Risk taking and accident causation," 279.

14. Chelminski, *Superwreck: Amoco Cadiz*, 35.

15. Kendra, "Looking Out the Window," 8.

16. Conrad, *Mirror of the Sea*, 129.

17. Szymanski, "Risk Management," 618.

18. Baker, C. and McCaffarty, D., ABS Review. Data developed by the Washington State Department of Ecology agree that human error, individual or organizational, has been a contributor in about 80% of maritime casualties where the casualty has been formally investigated. In contrast, where the incident was self-reported or not formally investigated, there was a marked increase in the probability that the cause is ascribed to equipment or external factors, likely due to the descriptive nature of the reporting. Washington State, Investigation of Marine Incidents.

19. Schulz, "Being Wrong," 30.

20. Zero tolerance as an error eliminating strategy is unrealistic because the nature of humans is to err. "Error results from physiological and psychological limitations of humans." Helmreich, "On Error Management," 781. "The best organizations can hope for is to manage error effectively, decreasing the probability of errors and minimizing their consequences." Helmreich, "Error Management as Organizational Strategy," 1.

21. As Joseph Conrad observed: "As long as men will travel upon the water, the sea-gods will take their toll. They will catch good

seamen napping, or confuse their judgment by arts well known to those who go to sea, or overcome them by the sheer brutality of elemental forces." "Protection of Ocean Liners," 251.

22. He added: "The fact is that ours is a dangerous calling and every now and again Fate extracts a penalty." Second Sea Lord, writing an unsolicited letter of sympathy shortly after the February 1964 collision between aircraft carrier HMAS *Melbourne* and destroyer HMAS *Voyager*, which sank with 82 fatalities. Quoted in Frame, *Where Fate Calls*, 356.

23 Barnett, "Searching for the Root Causes," 137.

24. Rowley, "Development of Guidance," 24.

25. Dekker, *Just Culture*, 131.

26. Szwed, "Development of a Safety Management Assessment System."

27. Reason, *Human Error*, 17.

28. Wagenaar, "Industrial Safety."

29. Soma, "Safety Excellence," 1. The 7.49 average of errors per hour comes from a 2010 study. Dismukes, "Checklists and monitoring," 10.

30. Ellis, "Safety and Perceptions of Risk," 105.

31. Pekcan, "Encouraging Attitude, Behavior and Cognitive Change."

32. This evasion was demonstrated in the comment of one U.S. fleet manager: "I do see … that a lot of companies are fiercely protective of their safety records and image and tend to look at a product [that addresses corrective measures] as some acknowledgement of a weak or failed system." Confidential email communication to the author.

33. DNV, Technical Report, 5.

34. Ibid., 25 percent of all ships, 1.

35. Pilots have commented to the author upon the increasing departure of ships' masters from the bridge to "finish paperwork" required by voyage end.

36. Wagenaar, "Accidents at Sea," 597.

37. Norton, "Unintended Consequences," 3.

38. Bastiat, "What is Seen." In 1936 the American sociologist Robert K. Merton identified five sources of unanticipated consequences: lack of all relevant knowledge, error, "imperious immediacy of interest," basic values, and "self-defeating prediction,"

by which public prediction brings about changes that adversely affect fulfillment of the prediction (the flip-side being a "self-fulfilling prophecy"). Merton, Robert K. "The Unanticipated Consequences," 894-904.

39. Guttridge, *Mutiny*, 5.

40. "The sea is, and always has been, a dangerous place. It holds dangers for ship owners, ship's crews, cargo owners and all who have an interest in enjoying a pollution free marine and coastal environment." Donaldson, "A Rocky Road," 3.

41. Dismukes e-mail. Granted, there are differences between maritime and aviation operations, but there are sufficient similarities to warrant borrowing where appropriate. Viewed objectively, the maritime industry appears some 20 years or more behind other safety-critical domains as concerns human factor issues. Perhaps this lag is attributable to "a deep strand in our culture ... which sees things maritime, and those who have followed the sea, as alien, other, incomprehensible and divided from ordinary human life." Greenhill, *Steam, Politics & Patronage*, 7. Research in the aviation domain has shown two predominant human factor categories germane to operational safety: selection and training. Selection looks to personality, referring to those relatively enduring characteristics of the individual which are resistant to change. Training looks to those aspects of the individual which are malleable, sensitive to change, and related to performance. These qualities have been found common, subject to national and professional cultural influences, to safety-critical domains, including the maritime domain.

42. Wagenaar, "Accidents at Sea," 596. Put another way: "There is a tendency in our planning to confuse the unfamiliar with the improbable. The contingency we have not considered seriously looks strange; what looks strange is thought improbable; what is improbable need not be considered seriously." Schelling, *Pearl Harbor*, vii.

43. To Count Mocenigo, Corfu, c. 4 August 1804, quoted in Maffeo, *Seize, Burn, or Sink*, 450. For example, though these are unlikely what Admiral Nelson was referring to:

The *Seiryu* officers were at a loss to explain their colleague's action in turning to port, into a collision: "Their only commentary was that the watch officer must have been possessed by demons or evil spirits." *In re Seiriki Kisen Kaisha*, 919.

A research vessel grounded minutes after the "relatively confined wheelhouse" was evacuated and the vessel left on autopilot following an incident of serious flatulence. *Professional Mariner,* "Attack of flatulence."

The chief officer was alone on the bridge of a container vessel when he fell while getting out of the wheelhouse chair and was knocked unconscious after catching his trouser leg cuff on the chair's control lever. Neither he nor his condition was found until after the vessel ran aground.

Chapter 2. Maritime Business Afloat and Uniquely Error Inducing

44. Perrow, *Normal Accidents*, 172.

45. Hetherington, "Safety in Shipping," 402.

46. This is but a modern day carry-over of that "part of the seafarer culture to be able to handle anything." Lutzhoft, "Integration Work," 64.

47. Underlying evaluations offered and conclusions drawn in this book is the review and critical analysis of some 650+ articles, dissertations and papers, 50+ books, 150+ accident reports and numerous interviews and discussions with active mariners, as well as many years personal experience in the maritime industry, initially as a "deck boy" on a Norwegian freighter, service in various deck officer positions in United States break bulk and container vessels and, most recently, as a maritime defense attorney.

48. During oral argument in the United States Supreme Court of the *Exxon Valdez* case, one of the Justices commented that "ships are filled with accidents." *New York Times,* February 28, 2008, A19.

49. Interview with former master of *Jean Lykes*, June 15, 2010.

50. Ellis, "Safety and Perceptions," 97.

51. *Ocean Marine Limited*, 499.

52. *Crowley Marine Service, Inc. v. Maritrans, Inc.*, 1175.

53. Belcher, "A Sociological Interpretation," 218.

54. Woodman, *Voyage East*, 220.

55. Coghlin, "Tightening the screw," 318.

56. The recent *New York Times* article "Web of Shell Companies" mentioned one vessel, tauntingly named *Alias*.

57. Greenstreet, "Organisational Structures."

58. The belief that a certificate or license is sufficient to qualify a person to undertake the duties and responsibilities of the position, without ascertaining the holder's competency is a "flawed assumption." NTSB, *Empress of the North*, 58.

59. Conrad, *Mirror of the Sea*, 46.

60. MAIB, *Cepheus J* and *Ileksa*, 20.

61. HSBE Report, *Fairplay*, 24.

62. Slocum, *Sailing Alone*, 263. "Long intervals for gathering work experience between promotions [historically] has ensured the existence of sufficient experience among the higher ratings, officers and masters." Jalonen, "Safety Performance," 41.

63. This regrettable regression has been discussed by Captain Le Goubin, "Mentoring."

64. http://www.merchantnavyofficers.com/cunard3.html, accessed August 20, 2010.

65. TNO Dutch study "Fatigue in the Shipping Industry," 2005 and "Seafarer Fatigue," Cardiff, 2006, among others. Also: ATSB, *Shen Neng1*, 20-25. *Shen Neng 1*'s watch officer "had only had about 2 1/2 hours sleep in the preceding 38 1/2 hours before the grounding," at page 18.

66. Boniface, "Assessing the Risks," 168.

67. Brown, "Shiptalk Survey," 20.

68. Rawlins, *Last American Sailors*, xii.

69. ATSB, *Bunga Teratai Satu*, 22.

70. Interview with Masters, Mates & Pilots union official David Boatner, June 15, 2010.

71. 18 U.S.C. section 1115.

72. United States Court of Appeals decisions: *United States v. Jho; In re City of New York; United States v. Hanousek*

73. Boniface, "Assessing the Risks," 169.

74. Evitt, A., MAIB, 1

75. USCG, *Santa Clara I*, 15. In another situation, the captain of a cruise liner testified that there were a "lot of times" he delayed a ship in port because of bad weather, showing that the company "was willing to incur costs and delays in order to ensure passenger safety." *Desiderio v. Celebrity Cruise Lines, Inc.*

76. Jones, *Plimsoll Sensation*, 22-23, also quoting one ship owning captain as saying "I like my fellows to understand that they've got to keep my craft afloat, or sink with her."

77. Plimsoll was widely disparaged in his time for his advocacy of sailors' rights. Illustrative is this comment in a *Vanity Fair* of 1873:

[Plimsoll] tells of men who go to certain death rather than have their courage impugned, of men who freely share their meager crust with companions in poverty, and he claims sympathy and admiration for them although it is well-known that they are ill-washed, uncouth and rude of speech. Manifestly such a proceeding could only be the offspring of a distempered brain, and so it has gone forth that the sailors' champion is 'mad on this question.'

78. Upham, "The Load Line," 30.
79. Conrad, *Mirror of the Sea*, 135.
80. Slocum, *Sailing Alone*, 263.

Chapter 3. Evolution of Current Maritime Safety Philosophy

81. An in-depth discussion of the *Herald* casualty, because it so closely illustrates so many of the management issues at the heart of this book is at Chapter Fourteen.

82. This narrative is taken from the National Transportation Safety Board *Exxon Valdez* Accident Report and Cahill, *Disasters At Sea*, 214-221. Certain litigation arising from the grounding and damages suffered by the local community is discussed in Lebedoff, *Cleaning Up*, though the author frequently tortures maritime usage.

83. NTSB, *Exxon Valdez*, 112.
84. Ibid., 8.
85. Ibid.
86. Lebedoff, *Cleaning Up*, 14.
87. Cahill, *Disaster at Sea*, 219 and 215.
88. Oil Pollution Act 1990, 33 U.S.C. sections 2701-2761.
89. *SeaRiver Maritime Financial Holdings, Inc. v. Mineta.*

90. Though former United States Supreme Court Justice Oliver Wendell Holmes, in his seminal work *The Common Law*, at 26-27, observed that a "ship is the most living of inanimate things," in recognition that admiralty law treats ships as though "endowed with personality."

91. Veiga, "Safety Culture in Shipping," 22.

92. Iarossi, "Foundation of a Safety Culture." Mr. Iarossi had been the President of Exxon Shipping, and at the time of the cited

1998 speech was speaking as the Chairman of the American Bureau of Shipping, a major classification society.

93. Evans, "The Criminal Prosecution," 186-192. Granted, *in rem* "personification" of a vessel continues to serve a salutary purpose in admiralty law, but Congress' reversion to deodand in the situation of *Exxon Valdez* is more medieval than contemporary.

94. Spector, *On Course*, vi and 63. The President of the company is quoted at page vii as saying: "While pursuing Chevron's commercial objectives, our sailors have been true to the traditions of the sea. They have steadfastly protected it from pollution and fearlessly rescued its victims."

95. Beveridge, *1 Titanic, Design and Construction*, 553.

96. Green, *Building Titanic*, 38-39.

97. Ibid., 79.

98. This brief recap is taken from the Sheen Report. The circumstances of *Herald's* loss are discussed in depth in Chapter Fourteen.

99. Sheen Report, 14-15.

100. Taking, hopefully, a broad-minded and objective view, I have to wonder at the pre-eminence of rules, regulations, policies and procedures in United States maritime industry safety thinking. So many industry leaders and regulators have been and are graduates of maritime academies or colleges, where the number of demerits accrued or not accrued for violation of myriad "regs" heavily has influenced one's opportunity for appointment as a cadet officer, with attendant privileges – could this have inculcated a distorted subservience to rules, regulations, policies and procedures?

101. Upham, "The Load Line," 2.

102. Ramwell, *A Ship Too Far.*

103. See, for example, Edwards, *Return of the Coffin Ships.*

104. This encapsulation of the genesis of the ISM Code is drawn largely from Anderson, *ISM Code*, 13-19.

105. "The ISM Code," quoted in Anderson at 18. The ISM Code is a recognition of the legal proposition that an industry "in which safety is of the utmost importance ... must be accorded great leeway and discretion in determining the manner in which it may be operated most safely." *Murnane v. American Airlines, Inc.*, 101.

106. Some of the generic situations and misadventures the ISM Code is intended to eliminate are described in Cheek, *Legacies of Peril.*

107. Bailey, "Making Sense of Differences," 10.

108. Analysis of the legal status of the Designated Person and critique of all nuances of his or her responsibilities are beyond the scope of this book, but the interested reader is referred to Philip Anderson's *ISM Code* and his other writings.

109. *In re S.D.S. Lumber Co.*

110. Quoted in Anderson, *ISM Code*, 67.

111. IMO Assessment, 5.

112. Captain Nick Beer of the UK MAIB, quoted Gale, "Improving Navigation Safety," 4.

113. *IMO Study on the Impact of the ISM Code*, paras. 8.1 and 8.18.

114. Reason, *Human Error*, 197.

115. James Reason is a British professor of psychology who hypothesizes that most accidents can be traced to one or more of four levels of failure: organizational influences, unsafe supervision, preconditions for unsafe acts and the unsafe acts themselves. His thinking is in the forefront of evolving greater appreciation that often the seeds for error are planted well upstream of the actors on the bridge or in the engine room.

116. The origin of the SCM, though Reason did not so name it, lies in the biological metaphor of pathogens and the role of the body's anti-immune system in blocking those pathogens from causing disease. Reason, *Human Error*, 197-99.

117. An illustration would be a railway roadbed build adjacent to an area of beaver dams. Over the years, the beavers' digging away to build their homes over time had undermined the roadbed until some seventy five years later the weight of a passing train caused the roadbed to collapse and the train to derail.

118. Reason, *Managing the Risks*, 10-11. An example is the combination of factors in 1994 that led to the separation of the bow door of the ro-ro ferry *Estonia* and her foundering within less than an hour. Fatalities totaled 852.

119. Reason, *Managing the Risks*, 36.

120. Ibid., 11.

121. Ibid., 234.

122. Pomeroy, "Perception and Management," 7.

123. Having a maritime academy class study maritime casualty reports is a worthy idea. But, the value of the study is substantially

undermined where the findings of each report are deemed "gospel" and critical discussion of the conclusions and their bases is demeaned. This scenario is commented upon at http://adeeplife. blogspot.com/2010/04/casualty-analysis.htlm. Accessed July 23, 2010. Rather, greater value for the future watch officers would be gained by using the reports as jumping off points for discussion of the situations, how the situation developed and potentially available courses of action, and not as the final word.

124. Schager, "When Technology Leads," 68-69.

125. Report, 97 (emphasis added).

126. IMO, "Study on the Impact," 17.

127. Recognizing the importance of objectively addressing and answering the multi-level "why" question, the United States Air Force in its investigation of aviation accidents applies the "rule of five 'whys'." When looking at the cause of a mishap, the first "why" question is why a significant factor occurred. When the first level "why" is answered, the "why" for that why is asked and answered, and on up the chain of "whys." Lt. Col. Karen Heupel, head of the Human Factors Division of the Safety Center, is quoted, "If you don't get to five 'whys,' you're not looking closely enough." Goyer, "Safety Against the Odds," 56-57.

128. Well illustrated by the conclusions offering varying explanations of official investigations of the 1992 grounding of *Queen Elizabeth 2* off Cuttyhunk Island. The NSTB cited "squat" but ignored hydrographic issues. The United States Coast Guard emphasized uncharted rocks and the "short cut" urged by the pilot. An outside nautically experienced commentator cited a break down in BRM. Paul, *Seaways*, 29. Arguments presented in reports and, for that matter, court decisions, may be evaluated through a CAE (Cause, Analysis, Evidence) diagram, originating in root cause analysis techniques that delineate evidence and conclusions. The first step is separately to list each conclusion or recommendation drawn in the report, then search the report for and list every analytical thread that either supports or weakens each respective conclusion. This step may require considerable digging to ferret out all relevant analyses. Next, find and list every evidentiary finding, and its basis, that supports or weakens each evidentiary finding. Finally, construct a graph for each conclusion, based upon the aggregated supports (connected by solid lines) and weaknesses

(connected by dotted lines). CAE diagrams assist analysis of the consistency and logic of the arguments, and identifying areas of conflict, presented in the reports. Objectivity of the analysis is heightened by not paraphrasing the investigator's wording but instead quoting it verbatim. Johnson, "Using CAE Diagrams."

129. "Given an identical problem, an engineer will find an engineering solution, a programmer will find a programming solution, and a sociologist will find a societal solution." Dr, Dennis Mileti, Director, National Hazards Center.

130. ATSB, *Boeing 747-438, Bangkok, Thailand Report*.

131. Mattsson, *Out of the Fog*, 112. Critical of the Coast Guard and NTSB for similar reason is Leo Tasca's unpublished dissertation, *The Social Construction of Human Error*.

132. Reason, *Human Error*, 212-13.

133. In so doing, one hopes that the prevailing arguments will not be at the expense of safety. The facts of a case will lay the foundation for such arguments as may be made but attorneys may advocate and argue conclusions well beyond the facts. In one case, the sinking of a large freighter was attributed to the possibility of a telephone pole floating far out at sea where the sinking occurred, but the existence of such a telephone pole was never established. The risk manager reading the written opinion may read in ignorance of the one-sidedness of the prevailing argument. Reading a European maritime safety text, I found on an inserted CD an e-mail from a maritime attorney who referred to a paper that successfully had advocated a parametric rolling argument in a major case of numerous containers lost overboard. Included was the caveat "I do not recommend that the paper or its conclusions be used as they are as guidelines or recommendations for masters to navigate their vessels [because there are so many variables] to be confident that this paper alone provides sufficient practical information for [safe] ship operation." Diestel, H-H. *Compendium on Seamanship & Sea Accidents*. What was successful as advocacy would not necessarily have been successful in the crucible of the sea. See also: Levadou, "Operational Guidance."

134. Clarkson, *Blue Funnel Line*, 66. For his seamanship, notwithstanding storm damage sustained to the vessel, her Master was feted at a civic reception by the Lord Mayor of Liverpool but was required by his employer to forfeit the deposit all company

Masters were required to make to remind them that their vessels sailed without hull insurance. On a brighter note, the forfeit was returned upon the Master's retirement from the company.

135. Hughes, *In Hazard*, 224. The use of experts can have unexpected results. Some years ago I was prosecuting a claim on behalf of a hull insurer of a mega-yacht, whose inattentive and probably "influenced" one person watch "team" had allowed the yacht to maneuver erratically and eventually smash into the side of a large "stand-on" bulk carrier. The only available argument was that the watch officer on the bulk carrier should have appreciated the erratic maneuvers and, with the prevailing open sea room, altered course to clear. Counsel for the bulk carrier hired as his navigation expert, to assert that his client's vessel should not have changed course until "in extremis," the retired master of a large container ship in which, ironically, I had sailed as cadet. I remembered him but he had not remembered me. Among the issues was what distance constituted a safe "closest point of approach" (CPA) under the prevailing circumstances. On cross-examination, I succeeded in having him admit that his standing orders as a master had mandated a two-mile CPA in open waters, and that early action was to be taken to assure no closer CPA. The case resolved with the mega-yacht's insurer recovering 50% of the substantial damages suffered by the yacht. I then confided to the adverse expert our past connection. He acknowledged that he sailed with so many Merchant Marine Academy cadets that he remembered only the truly exemplary – good or bad. He graciously exempted me from the latter category.

136. *Otal Investments Ltd.*, 7. The law also recognizes the doctrine of supervening cause, an extraneous cause that "cuts" the error chain. *Exxon Co. U.S.A. v. Sofac, Inc.*, 517 U.S. 830 (1996).

137. *United States v. Hatfield*, 947.

Chapter 4. Safety Culture and Safety Climate

138. Together with the organizational safety culture there is a national culture, discussed in Chapter Twelve, and a culture of professionalism. "Effective efforts to achieve safety must recognize the importance of [these three] culture[s]. Organizations must have a full understanding of cultural influences on their operations if safety efforts are to succeed[,]" because each of these three cultures

influences critical operational behavior. Helmreich, "Building Safety on the Three Cultures of Aviation." An organizational culture has been defined as " ... a pattern of basic assumptions – invented, discovered, or developed by a given group as it learns to cope with its problems of external adaption and internal integration that has worked well enough to be considered valid and, therefore, to be taught to new members as the correct way to perceive, think, and feel in relation to those problems." Schein, *Organizational Culture and Leadership*, 385. This definition is particularly appropriate in relation to organizational response to the IMS Code mandate that a safety culture be established.

139. This definition is one of the earliest, and comes from the Advisory Committee on Safety in Nuclear Installations, HSE (1993), as quoted in Ellis, "Safety and Perception of Risk." Safety culture also may be defined as the "[s]hared values and beliefs that interact with an organization's structures and control systems to produce behavioral norms." *BP Review Panel*, 25 at footnote 18. More broadly, "culture" as such refers to a " ... persistent, patterned way of thinking about the central tasks of and human relationships within an organization." Nagl, *Learning to Eat Soup with a Knife*, 215.

140. Hermansson, *History of Stena Bulk*, 9. An in depth study of an organizational safety culture is sociologist Diane Vaughan's study of NASA and the Challenger space shuttle disaster of 1986 in *Challenger Launch Decision*.

141. The cumulative safety climate may be said to be the measure in practice of the organization's safety culture. Gadd, *Safety Culture: A Review of the Literature*.

142. "The single most important factor in creating a good process safety culture is trust. Employees and contractors must trust that they can report incidents, near misses, and other concerns – even when it reflects poorly on their own knowledge, skills, or conduct – without fear of punishment or [adverse] repercussion." *BP Review Panel*, 75.

143. Reed, *In Too Deep*, 141-43. Difficulties characteristic to altering a company's culture to bring about a true safety culture are described in particularly chapters seven and eight of *In Too Deep*.

144. Hughes, *In Hazard*, 151.

145. Ellis, "Safety and Perception of Risk," 105.

146. Meur, *Maritime Safety Culture*, 20 and 19. A major criticism of the ISM Code is the amount of paperwork the Code is perceived to require. One effect is that masters often will absent themselves from the bridge in pilotage waters to attend to paperwork, so degrading the bridge resource management in which the master is intended to be an active participant. Interview Penobscot Bay (Maine) pilot Captain "Skip" Strong.

147. Veiga, "Safety Culture in Shipping," 21.

148. "Safety isn't a formal destination – something we 'get' and hold on to forever – but is instead a never-ending pursuit." Gibb, "Classification of Air Force Aviation Accidents." And, Professor Reason has commented that "like a state of grace, a [true] safety culture is something that is striven for but rarely attained." *Managing the Risks*, 220.

149. Kaplan, *Conduct of Inquiry*, 28, referring to the *law of the instrument*: "Give a small boy a hammer, and he will find that everything he encounters needs pounding."

150. *BP Review Panel*, 434.

151. Part ii (1907).

152. MAIB, *CP Valour Grounding Report*.

153. This brings to mind Lecky's comment in *Wrinkles in Practical Navigation* that "Nothing could be more disturbing than running ashore, unless it be a doubt as to which continent that shore belongs."

154. Gilroy, *Black Atlantic*, 4. Admiral James Stavridis agrees, from his service as commanding officer of the destroyer USS *Berry*: " ... in the end, life on a ship is about devotion to work, conducted for the common good, with an agreed upon construct of rank, structure, order, and purpose." Stavridis, *Destroyer Captain*.

155. Gadd, *Safety Culture, 14*. The observation has been offered that the "immense variety of potentially hazardous situations requires that the governance of safe behavior is delivered at the level of the individual work group." Reason, *Human Contribution*, 67.

156. NTSB, *Concho Grounding Report*.

157. Gadd, *Safety Culture*, 13. About 50% of mariners admit to regularly breaching safety procedures. DNV, *Classification News* (October 2006), 4. Why this is likely so is discussed in Chapter Ten.

158. Ciavarelli, *Safety Climate and Risk Culture*, 7.

159. Joint Maritime Investigator, *Monarch of the Seas Grounding Report*, 49 (emphasis added). Independent investigation suggests that the events following the initial "raking" along the reef were not as calm and organized as the Report indicates.

160. Brown, "Tanker Environmental Risk," 4 and 8. And: "It is extraordinary how a new personality can change the psychological atmosphere of a ship." McFee, *In the First Watch*, 145.

161. NTSB. *Empress of the North Grounding Report*, 57.

162. URL:http://www.imo.org/HumanElement/mainframe.asp?topic_id=62.

163. Gray, *New Age Military Progressives*, 2-3.

164. Hunter, *A Society of Gentlemen*, ix.

165. Bailey, *Making Sense of Differences*.

166. Washington State, *Dona V*.

167. McCann, *Study of Irrational Decisions*.

168. Conrad, *Chance*, 3-4.

169. Burgess, *Fellowship of the Craft*, 152-155.

170. Chua-Eoan, Howard. "Disasters: Going, Going... ." Time, August 19, 1991 at www.time.com/time/printout/0,8816,973632,00html, accessed April 29, 2010. A defense is at http://answers.yahoo.com/question/index?qui=20061227070017AADqftI. Of course, Captain Avranas is not the first captain held to have abandoned his responsibilities. There was Captain Hugo de Chaumareys, whose "abandonment" of his post following the wreck of his command in 1816 inspired Gericault's painting *The Raft of the Medusa*. See Miles, *Wreck of the Medusa*. And Joseph Conrad, in *Lord Jim*, famously fictionalized the 1880 abandonment of the pilgrim ship *Jeddah* and 953 passengers by her European officers.

Chapter 5. Recognizing and Dealing with Maritime Risk

171. Merrick, "Prince William Sound Risk Assessment," 15.

172. Fuller, *Gnomologia: Adages and Proverbs*, #2353.

173. Gribben, *FitzRoy*, [1].

174. Letter to the fleet following substantial personnel and vessel losses suffered from a December, 1944 typhoon, quoted in Potter, *Nimitz*, 425.

175. National Research Council, *Minding the Helm*, 160.

176. Ibid.,166.

177. COLREGS Rule 2(a).

178. Byron, "The Captain," 45.

179. Baniela, "Risk Homeostasis Theory."

180. Amrozowicz, "Qualitative Risk."

181. Bichler-Robertson, *Maritime Commercial Passenger Ship Casualties*, 6-7.

182. Schager, "A Wise Captain," 3-5.

183. Merrick, "Speaking the Truth."

184. Ibid., 224-225.

185. Ibid., 225.

186. Ibid., 226.

187. Others include the Washington State Ferry system and expanding San Francisco Bay ferry service.

188. Merrick, "The Prince William Sound Risk Assessment."

189. Harrald, "Using system simulation."

190. Ibid.

191. Brown, "Assessing the Impact," 6-7.

192. Merrick, "Prince William Sound," 10.

193. Ibid.,13.

194. Transportation Research Board, *Risk of Vessel Accidents and Spills*, 29 – 50.

195. The United States court decision within which the "formula" first was articulated is *United States v. Carroll Towing Co.*

196. *In re City of New York.*

197. Posner, *Economics of Justice*, 5. There, Judge Posner acknowledges that "economists and economically minded lawyers have found that the law uncannily follows economics."

198. Harrald, "Using system simulation," 237.

199. Levee Investigation Team Report, 3.

200. Vistica, *Fall From Grace*, 207.

201. Morison, *Men, Machines, and Modern Times.*

202. Ibid.,114.

203. Ibid.,119.

204. A picture of *USS Wampanoag* can be found in volume 63 of the *Journal of Navigation* (2010) at page 730.

205. Frustration came as well from defective torpedoes, also eventually remedied.

206. DeRose, *Unrestricted Warfare*, 3-4.

207. Brown, "Truth or Consequences," 8.

208. Ghys, "An Investigation," 158.

209. Smith, "Extreme Waves and Ship Design."

210. *Suzuki & Co. Ltd. v. J. Beynon & Co. Ltd.*

211. A common stress point in the relation is likely to be limitation upon the manner in which the ship is to be utilized, arguably a further example of the risk homeostasis theory. The owner's right to use the ship for profit must be given full and fair effect, but that right ought not trespass into matters falling within the "specialized professional maritime expertise" of the master, whose appointment may be expected to have been in recognition of that expertise, when the safety of the ship, her personnel and cargo are involved. The master is the on-scene expert, who is responsible. See, for example, discussion in the decision *Whistler International Ltd. v. Kawasaki Kisen Kaisha Ltd. [The Hill Harmony]*.

212. Gatfield, "Are Current Risk Management Strategies," 2.

213. Bailey, "Perceptions of Risk."

214. This may translate into shore side management being particularly receptive to enhanced master-pilot "hand off" and bridge resource management education, whereas masters may be more resistant, feeling that "we know our business."

215. Coghlin, "Tightening the Screw," 316.

216. Cahill, *Disasters at Sea,"* 61.

217. Wagenaar, "Risk Taking Behavior," 279.

218. Morel, "Articulating the Difference," 13.

219. Pomeroy, "Perception and Management of Risk."

220. Admiral Horatio Nelson was leading the 1801 attack by sea against Copenhagen. After several hours of bombardment, the fleet commander Hyde Parker, some five miles away and with his view obscured by the smoke of battle, became concerned and hoisted flag signal No. 39: "Discontinue the action." Nelson, sure of success and not wishing to disengage, purportedly put a telescope to his blind eye and commented to his flag captain Sir Thomas Foley: "You know, Foley, I have only one eye – and I have a right to be blind sometimes ... ." Unfortunately for a good story, and not wishing to offend any British reader, for the sake of accuracy comment nonetheless must be made that the "blind eye" legend may be a myth, though certainly in the character of Nelson. Knight, *The Pursuit of Victory,"* 374.

221. TSB. *Great Century Grounding Report.*

222. *Papera Traders co. Ltd. v. Hyundai Merchant Marine Co., Ltd. [Eurasian Dream]*.
223. *T.J. Hooper.*
224. *Titania.*
225. *Davis v. Stena Line,* 27. The Court also commented regarding Stena's failure to carry out any appropriate risk assessment as to such an emergency: " ... given the wide-spread awareness of the problem and the likelihood of such an emergency occurring ... even if the ... shortcomings of Stena were representative of the standards of the industry at the time, that does not excuse them: ... ."

Chapter 6. Bridge T=Resource Management
226. Conrad, "Well Done," 183.
227. NTSB, *Orange Sun Allision Report,* 22.
228. NTSB, *Star Princess Grounding Report,* 22.
229. ATSB, *Hanjin Dampier Grounding Report.*
230. "Each [captain and engineer] must understand thoroughly the task of the other and interchange all the information necessary for working in complete unison." Frost, *On a Destroyer's Bridge,* 3.
231. In 1977, two 747 aircraft collided in heavy fog on a runway at Tenerife, killing 583 persons. The departing KLM aircraft, piloted by KLM's top 747 instructor, who also was pictured in KLM's print advertisements as the "face" of KLM, on its takeoff roll struck the taxiing PanAm 747. The two crews communicated with the airport tower on the same frequency, causing transmissions to be cut off. The KLM aircraft crew misunderstood one communication as authorizing its takeoff, and so began to roll. The KLM captain and co-pilot were concentrating upon the takeoff and failed to appreciate the significance of tower-PanAm communications relating to the PanAm aircraft exiting the runway, but the KLM flight engineer did. He asked his colleagues, "Did he not clear the runway - that Pan American?" He was answered "Yes." From subsequent investigation of the cockpit voice recorder, determination was made that the KLM co-pilot's concerns earlier had been brusquely rejected by the impatient captain. The co-pilot had only 95 hours in a 747 and was flying with the training captain who had cleared him for the 747, so likely would have been especially circumspect in his dealings with the captain. Job, *Air Disaster, Vol. 1,* 164-180.
232. Champlain, *Works of Samuel de Champlain Vol. VII,* 253 and 262-263. Champlain offered other pithy advice as to "what

is requisite in order to be a good and finished navigator," much of which remains valid for the mariner of almost 400 years later, including that he "should not allow himself to be overcome by wine; for when a captain or a seaman is a drunkard it is not very safe to entrust him with command or control, on account of the mischances that may result while he is sleeping like a pig, or has lost all sense and discretion and by reason of his drunkenness persists in insolence just when it is a matter of necessity to find some way of escape from the danger." Ibid. at 261-262. The early concept of BRM received a setback from the alleged act, discredited by many as myth, of Admiral Sir Cloudesley Shovell. Returning from an unsuccessful siege of Toulon with his 21 vessel fleet in 1707, he ordered to be hanged a seaman in his flagship who asserted by his reckoning that the fleet was in close proximity to the Scilly Islands. Exactly how the seaman arrived at his reckoning is not disclosed. In any event, the seaman was correct and the fleet navigators, who adjudged the fleet further to the west, were wrong. Many ships of the fleet were driven ashore and lost with great loss of life. http://www.hmssurprise. org/Resources/SIR_CLOUDESLEY_SHOVELL.html.

233. Barnett, "Recent Developments," 1.

234. MAIB, *Maersk Kendal Grounding Report,* 25.

235. Relations between pilots and mariners have not always been complimentary. In days gone past, if a pilot caused "merchants" loss through loss of or damage to the vessel by the pilot's ignorance, the pilot was called upon to satisfy the loss financially or, failing that, with his head – literally. Articles XXIII and XXIV of the maritime Code of circa 1266, the Rolls of Oleron, provided, respectively: "If a pilot undertakes the conduct of a vessel, to bring her to St. Malo, or any other port, and fail of his duty therein, so as the vessel miscarry by reason of his ignorance in what he undertook, and the merchants sustain damage thereby, he shall be obliged to make full satisfaction for the same, if he hath wherewithal; and if not, lose his head[,] And if the master, or any one of his mariners, or any one of the merchants, cut off his head, they shall not be bound to answer for it; but before they do it, they must be sure he had not herewith to make satisfaction."

However, in England a majority decision of the crew was sufficient to impose the ultimate punishment, without reference to whether the pilot had the option of making restitution. Harris,

Trinity House of Deptford, 102.

236. Hetherington, "Safety at Sea," 406.

237. Hanzu-Pazara, "Reducing of Maritime Accidents," 3-18.

238. Discussion with Los Angeles harbor pilot John Betz, August 30, 2007.

239. NTSB, *Orange Sun Allision Report,* 24.

240. MAIB, *Skagern - Samskib Courier Collision Report,* 43. The master, other than in the Panama Canal, remains in command while the pilot directs the vessel. "In order to avoid chaos in [emergency] situations, it is imperative that the vessel remain under the control of a single individual with complete and undisputed authority. The master of the vessel must assume authority in such a crisis and he has the responsibility to make the final decision as to what the proper course of action must be in view of all the factors concerned." *United States Steel Corporation v. Furhman,* at 1147.

241. ATSB, *Desh Rakshak Gounding Report,* 16.

242. MAIB, *Sea Express I- Alaska Rainbow Collision Report,* 36.

239. *Aleksandr Marinesko and Quint Star.*

244. NTSB, *Empress of the North Grounding Report,* 56. Interestingly, temporary assumption of "control," at least in the face of unexpected operational contingencies, by subordinate but more experienced personnel has been noted as an admirable characteristic of "high reliability organizations." Weick, *Managing the Unexpected,* 73. Among examples are flight operations on United States Navy aircraft carriers, with the comment   "[e]xpertise is not necessarily matched with hierarchical position, so organizations that live or die by their hierarchy are seldom in a position to know all they can about a problem [,]" 75.

245. NTSB, *Empress of the North Grounding Report,* 4.

246. A 2006 study of United States Air Force aircraft accidents occurring over the period 1992-2005 revealed that operational (flying) accidents most often were associated with judgment/decision making issues, implicating topics covered in aircraft crew resource management training. Gibb, "Classification of Air Force Accidents." This result is disturbing because of the emphasis given CRM over the study period. A similar concern exists in the commercial aviation sector.

247. Appropriately, Australian aviation pilots within this recalcitrant subset are referred to as "drongos." A "drongo" is

a "small bird that flies around and defecates on the heads of unsuspecting passers-by." Helmreich, "The Evolution of Crew Resource Management," 22, footnote 5.

248. Li, "Eastern Minds in Westernn Cockpits."

249. Hofstede, *Cultures and Organizations,*" 20.

250. Harrald, "Using system simulation," 239.

251. Amrozowicz, "Qualitative Risk," 39-40.

252. ATSB, *Atlantic Blue Grounding Report.*

253. International Convention for the Safety of Life at Sea, 1974, as amended.

254. *Atlantic Blue Report,* 11.

255. Ibid., 19.

256. Ibid., 21.

257. Ibid., 22.

258. Ibid., 26.

259. Ibid., 11, xi and 23.

260. Ibid., 10. At 0104, the third officer was handing the watch over to the second officer. Both officers had challenged the pilot's course change from 090 degrees to 105 degrees. The pilot had explained that the course of 105 degrees was per his passage plan.

261. Ibid., 26.

262. Ibid., 29.

263. Ibid., 32.

264. Ibid., 29.

Chapter 7. Nature of Error

265. Hanzu-Paraza, "Reducing of Maritime Accidents."

266. Tzannatos, "Human Element and Accidents," 121-22.

267. Study investigating 1970s tanker casualties, quoted in Barnett, "Human Error and Maritime Safety," 1.

268. This quotation is taken from an NTSB report of a tanker allision with a bridge span in Portland, Maine.

269. Nimitz Fleet letter from Potter, *Nimitz,* 425.

270. Gaouette, *Cruising For Trouble,* 163.

271. NTSB, *Crown Princess Heeling Incident Report.*

272. Grech, "Human Error in Maritime Operations," 1.

273. "Economy of operation is still something shipping managers expect of masters and is often a matter of continuous dispute between office and 'bridge.' " Harlaftis, *History of Greek-Owned Shipping,* 177.

274. Potter, *Nimitz*, 425. See also Helmreich, "Error results," 781.

275. McCallum, "Procedures for Investigating and reporting."

276. Wickens, *Engineering Psychology*, 366.

277. Perrow, *Normal Accidents*, 180-182.

278. Cowan, *Oil and Water*, 39-40. Given the ensuing pollution, the casualty failed to achieve the hope of the prayer attributed to Scilly Isles' chaplain Rev. John Troutbeck: "We pray thee, O Lord, not that wrecks should happen, but if wrecks do happen Thou wilt guide them into the Scilly Isles for the benefit of the poor inhabitants." Ibid., 42.

279. Wagenaar, "Accidents at Sea."

280. Rasmussen, "Human Errors," 316-18.

281. These performance levels are partially incorporated into a formula representing maritime competence, in which COMPETENCY = (KNOWLEDGE + SKILLS) x ATTITUDE. KNOWLEDGE represents the cognitive domain. SKILLS represents the psychomotor component. ATTITUDE represents the affective component. E-mail to author from Captain George Sandberg, USMMA, and Meurn, *Watchstanding Guide*, 158.

282. HEPs, PSFs and MOFs and their interrelations are discussed in Brown, "Assessing the Impact" and Amrozowicz, "The Quantitative Risk." Not surprisingly, the majority of relevant studies, of which these are but two, involve assessing the risk afloat of a major oil tanker stranding, because of the potential for environmental pollution resulting from such a stranding.

283. This process is applied by Brown to analyze factors contributing to hypothetical tanker power and drift groundings.

284. Brown, "Assessing the Impact," 6. Many of these factors are addressed within the ISM Code.

285. Ibid., 7.

286. Martins, "Human Error." 678-79.

287. Wiegmann, "Human Error Approach," 50. The four HFACS levels have been deconstructed into 321 types of human causal conditions. Leiden, "Context of Human Error."

288. October 15, 2003 the Staten Island (New York Harbor) ferry *Andrew J. Barberi* heavily struck its Staten Island berth, resulting in eleven fatalities and 70 injuries. The operator was found to have

been taking prescribed medications for multiple medical conditions. NTSB, *Barberi Allision Report*, 13-14.

289. MAIB, *Annabella Cargo Container Collapse Report*, 28.

290. Pate-Cornell, "Human and Management Factors."

291. Shapell, "Human Error and Commercial Aviation Accidents," 8. Causal overlap accounts for the allocations exceeding 100%.

292. Phimister, *Accident Precursor Analysis and Management*, 6.

293. Academians refer to this stage as "storage," but "storage" is too passive for my liking, so I prefer "advance," lest anyone develop the wrong impression that watch keeping is anything other than an active activity.

294. Boniface, "Assessing the Risks," 164-5.

295. Ibid.,162

296. Helmreich, "Culture, Threat, and Error." Three airlines participated, two U.S. carriers and one foreign carrier.

Chapter 8. Situational Awareness

297. Von Clausewitz, *On War*, 141.

298. Endsley, *Design and Evaluation*, 258.

299. Smith, "Situation(al) Awareness (SA)."

300. Ibid.

301. Job, *Air Disaster I*, 98-111.

302. Endsley, "Toward a Theory of Situational Awareness."

303. I was told by a retired APL master of his second officer who yelled from the ECDIS "We must come left, we are out of the channel!" when a look out the wheelhouse window would have shown the vessel squarely on the range.

304. MAIB, *Attilio Ievoli Grounding Report*.

305. NTSB, *Royal Majesty Grounding Report*.

306. Maritime Safety, *Aratere Near Grounding*.

307. Ibid., 36. Additionally, though the vessel was "an official paper based chart vessel" and there was posted on the electronic chart console a sign "WARNING The electronic charts displayed on this system do not replace official paper charts," no paper charts were used in the vessel's navigation, 22.

308. Comment by David Patraiko, FNI, at eNavigation 2010 Conference, Seattle, WA, November 16, 2010.

309. TSB, *Atlantic Huron – Griffon Contact Report*, 11.

310. Schager, "When Technology Leads Us Astray," 70.

311. TSB, *Atlantic Huron – Griffon Contact Report*, 12.

312. Endsley, "Situation Awareness and Human Error."

313. Fisher, "Criticality of data quality," 111.

314. *Eisenhower*'s commanding officer did not intend to embark a pilot until arriving at buoy 3. Some captains and officers of Norfolk based Naval vessels viewed taking a pilot seaward of buoy 3 "as a reflection that the vessels [sic] crew had less than a professional ship handling ability." NTSB, *Urduliz – Eisenhower Ramming Report*, 14.

315. Ibid., 17.

316. Ibid., 21.

317. Grech, "Human Error in Maritime Operations."

318. A 1987 study considered 100 Dutch maritime casualties from a spectrum broader than navigational incidents. The authors of this study broke behavior into five sequential decision phases. The causal factors related to SA were: receipt of information – 21%; detection of a problem – 27%; determining options – 15%; and, evaluating consequences/projection – 36%. At most, 1% of the accidents were attributable to explicitly deliberate risk taking behavior, the last of the five decision phases. Waagenaar, "Accidents at Sea."

319. Jones, "Investigation of Situation Errors."

320. Sneddon, "Safety and Situation Awareness in Offshore Crews."

321. Cited in Johnson, "Team-Based Operations," 9.

322. "Good SA should increase the probability of good decisions and performance, but does not guarantee [either]." Endsley, M. and Garland, D. eds. *SA Analysis and Measurement*," 367.

Chapter 9. Decision Making

323. Nicholls, *Seamanship and Nautical Knowledge*.

324. Dotterway, "Systemic Analysis of Complex Dynamic Systems."

325. Betts, "Anaysis, War, and Decision," 70.

326. Interview, Captain David Boatner, June 15, 2010.

327. " ... it must always be remembered that it is the risk of collision, not the collision itself, ..." that must be avoided. *Ocean SS Co. v. United States*, 784. This being so, the COLREGS are an

"accepted form of risk management." Allen, *Farwell*, 214. However, management is not synonymous with infallibility, leading one appellate court to nonetheless wonder "how two fully-equipped vessels several miles apart on a clear night somehow could manage to maneuver themselves into one another's sidequarters." *In re Potomac Transport*, 44.

328. James, "Timing of Collision Avoidance Maneuvers." "Judgment" may be defined as the ability to assess a situation accurately and objectively [free from biases and assumptions] and to prescribe an appropriate response, taking into account all material factors. If time permits, all steps leading to the conclusion should be carefully reviewed and the question asked – if any of the most critical bases are erroneous, how does that affect the ultimate decision? A study in the early 1980's using an admittedly small test group of 16 ship master's certificate candidates demonstrated that extroverts approach "other vessels more closely before taking action than did introverts" and "are more variable ... when they take action" and "tended to be more anxious." Hagart, "Personality Factors and Ship Handling Behaviour," 205 and 206.

329. A 2001 study of a 1994 NSTB analysis of 37 major aircraft accidents is instructive as to the influence of cognitive factors upon aviation decision errors, a presumption being that there is sufficient congruency in thinking processes between aviation pilots and maritime watch officers. One significant distinction, however, is that the high fatality rate in aviation accidents results in relatively infrequent actor explanation. More than half the errors were errors of omission, the failure to do something that should have been done, suggesting that the flight crew continued on in a normal manner despite one or more cues warning that a different response was called for. This is evidence of complacency, compatible with an unwillingness to invest more thought than absolutely necessary in a situation – a reluctance to engage in knowledge-based performance as has been commented upon previously. Such omissions also may be explained as the flight crew being seduced by a seemingly familiar scenario – a "wrong but strong" association. Slightly less than half the errors were of commission – taking actions out of the ordinary. This suggests a lack of knowledge or a different aspect of "wrong but strong," reversion to a strategy previously successful but inapplicable to the present situation. Of all errors, 22.8% were

monitoring and challenging errors, despite more than 20 years of crew resource management emphasis. This suggests that more than CRM/BRM "training" is necessary. Orasanu, "Cognitive and Contextual Factors" in E. Salas and G. Klein (eds.) *Applications of Naturalistic Decision Making*.

330. Here a problem may be encountered. Take two vessels approaching head to head, but displaced one mile to starboard – each to starboard of the other. In a "classic" 1977 study, two groups were presented with this situation and asked what they would do if commanding the two vessels. One group consisted of 10 randomly selected laymen, wholly unfamiliar with the COLREGS. Each layman group member maintained course, and the vessels passed safely port to port. The second group consisted of 10 master mariners. They found themselves in a quandary - is the situation such as to require a turn to starboard, crossing the bow of the other and decreasing the closest point of approach (CPA) or maintain course, perhaps altering to port to increase the CPA? Of the master mariners, half chose to go to starboard (the "Dance-of-Death," historically a major cause of collisions) and the other half maintained course. Devanney, *Tankship Tromedy*, 96-97. The clear implication is that at least in this situation (as well as others), the COLREGS introduce a dangerous ambiguity, compounding the difficulty inherent in decision making.

331. An interesting analysis of factors relevant to decisions made when USS *Vincennes* shot down an Iranian civilian jetliner is "*Vincennes* – A Case Study" by Lt.Col. (ret.) David Evans.

332. Zsambok, *Naturalistic Decision Making*, 5.

333. While the primary focus of this book is not on ship handling as such but rather upon cognitive factors to which any watch officer may be vulnerable, other aspects of the watch officer's responsibilities should not be overlooked. Among those factors, and certainly implicated in the *Ormiston – Searoad Mersey* incident, are the laws of physics relevant to passing ship interaction and bank and water depth effects. These laws are excellently explained in Edward T. Gates' book, *Maritime Accidents: What Went Wrong?* and, more broadly, I.C. Clark, *Ship Dynamics for Mariners*.

334. ATSB, *Ormiston–Searoad Mersey Near Collision Report*, 15.

335. MAIB, *Costa Atlantica – Grand Neptune Close Quarters Report*.

336. Klein, *Sources of Power*.

337. Too often there is an excess of information. The key to sound decision making is less the knowledge available from the *quantity* of information accessible but rather the understanding that can be developed from the *quality* of the information processed. Gladwell, *Blink,* 265.

338. Klein, *Sources of Power,* 65.

339. Rule 14 (a), International Regulations for Preventing Collisions at Sea and Inland Navigation Rules.

340. Perrow, *Normal Accidents,* 217-21. Of various commentators and researchers, sociologist Perrow is among the harshest when assessing the commercial maritime industry.

341. Klein, *Sources of Power,* 31.

342. Telephone interview.

343. Quoted in Puryear, Jr., *American Admiralship,* 78.

344. Klein, *Sources of Power,* 152.

345. Slocum, *Sailing Alone Around the World,* 263. Captain Slocum was an experienced "tall ship" mariner and master, and the first person recorded to have sailed alone around the world.

346. *N.Y. Times,* "Another Smooth Landing for a Hero." This comparison is intended in no way whatsoever to denigrate the competence or performance of the First Officer.

347. NTSB, *Loss of Thrust Both Engines US Airways Flight 1549 Report,* 2 and 5.

348. Wolgast, "Command Decision–making," 8. " ... being able to act intelligently and instinctively in the moment is possible only after a long and rigorous course of education and experience." Gladwell, *Blink,* 259.

349. An extensive list and description of cognitive biases capable of affecting decision making, behavior, beliefs and cognition generally can be found at http://en.Wikipedia.org/wiki/List_of_cognitive_biases.

350. Klein, *Sources of Power,* 274.

351. ATSB, *Pasha Bulker Grounding Report,* 27. Confirmation bias was addressed by Admiral Hyman Rickover: "It is a human condition to hope things will work out, despite evidence or doubt to the contrary. A successful manager must resist this temptation. This is particularly hard if one has invested much time and energy on a [plan or course of action] and thus has come to feel possessive about it. Although it is not easy to admit what a person once thought

correct now appears to be wrong, one must discipline himself to face the facts objectively and make the necessary changes – regardless of the consequences to himself. The man in charge must personally set the example in this respect. He must be able, in effect, to 'kill his own child' if necessary and must require his subordinates to do likewise." Rockwell, *The Rickover Effect,* 133.

352. Nimitz Fleet Letter. Written in 1945, Admiral Nimitz' admonition failed to anticipate subsequent advances in electronic navigation devices such as ARPA and ECDIS, which *do* include red lights and other visual and audible signals of warning. However, to prudent mariners, his cautionary tone rings true.

353. Wilde, *Target Risk 2.*

354. Ibid., 32.

355. Ibid., 34.

356. While in casual conversation a comment may kiddingly be made favoring high speed in fog so as to more quickly exit the restricted visibility, in a 1870 case such a contention successfully was argued in defense of a sailing vessel that, while running in fog with all sail set except studding sails, ran down an anchored fishing schooner. The case of the *Chancellor.* This information is cited merely for the sake of interest and *not* as legal suggestion or advice.

357. The benefit to safety and to risk evaluation of an appropriate incident reporting and dissemination protocol or "culture" has been so successfully demonstrated as to be beyond dispute. For example, in one year prior to introducing an incident reporting procedure, one major United States tanker fleet recorded only 47 near miss situations but suffered 33 recordable injuries, five lost time injuries and no fatalities. Four years after introducing an incident reporting protocol, there were 1132 reported near misses but only six recordable injuries and no lost time injuries or fatalities. Personal interview.

A major benefit from incident reporting is the enhanced accurate picture of safety that management derives from the nature and number of reported incidents. With an accident being the tip of a pattern of incidents, management is enabled through receipt and analysis of data showing accident precursors to focus in upon risk inducing circumstances and direct limited prevention oriented resources in a constructive direction. The importance of incident reporting as a significant factor in risk evaluation is illustrated by its inclusion in Professor Wilde's risk homeostasis model in box *e.* Without good information, including awareness of past "close calls," decisions too often are made on the basis of past successes and unrealistic risk assessment.

Underlying a successful incident reporting program is acceptance by management and staff of a "just" culture, in which a distinction exists between culpable and tolerable error as well as there being reciprocal trust that incidents objectively will be reported and management will respond by addressing error inducing conditions as well as that those persons committing the reported error(s) will be excused from other than willful violation of rules, regulations, policies and procedures, or repeated or gross error. The trust element is crucial to the success of an incident reporting program, which is bound to fail or be discontinued if the reporters come to believe they unfairly will be punished for the errors they report. Dekker, *Just Culture.*

Beyond the issue of trust, the program may be challenged by disagreement over what warrants reporting. At the most fundamental level, a reportable incident would be one where there would have been an accident but for some type of timely successful intervention. Ideally, a report would include a "stage setting" narrative of the underlying circumstances, with reference to all errors and omissions, including those of perception, that contributed to the coming into being of those circumstances, what risk was perceived as presented by those circumstances, what was done to remove the risk, and site oriented recommendations looking to remedying contributing causes. While respecting the privacy of involved persons, management should disseminate within the fleet the substance of these reports together with reference to what remedial action management has taken in response to the report or class of similar reports. Great care should be taken as to how management responds to incident reports. Without constructive response, shipboard personnel quickly will lose interest and cease participating, with management loosing invaluable safety related input. Of course, the reports of one company may be too few or sketchy to be helpful, so sharing of reports should be encouraged.

Unfortunately, the reported information could be used by unscrupulous persons to suggest a false facial impression of an unsafe operation. Also, the legal consequences, in terms of potentially admissible evidence, of an incident reporting system as well as self-critical analysis of incidents and safety meeting minutes should be considered. Weinstein, *Weinstein's Federal Evidence,* section 501.04[3].

Despite its unqualified success as a basis for setting up defenses to and traps of error, as well as eliminating precursors to accidents, incident reporting is antithetical to the popular albeit problematic "zero-tolerance zero-reported-incidents" school of thought.

358. Richter, *Selections from the Notebooks of Leonardo da Vinci,* 278.

359. Morel, "Articulating the Differences," 13.

360. Jones, *Sea Like a Mirror,* 9. Jones' book is an informative seafaring autobiography of a British master mariner pursuing and eventually attaining his goal – command of a ship.

361. Shalimar, *Down to the Sea,* 1.

362. A comment attributed to Admiral Arleigh H. Burke: "What's the difference between a good naval officer and a great one? Answer: about six seconds."

363. Transcript, ABC NEWS, NIGHTLINE, "The USS *Vincennes*: Public War, Secret War."

364. Telephone interview, Captain Prentice Strong.

365. Burger, "A Stranding in the Magellan Strait."

366. Sexton, "Error, stress, and teamwork in medicine and aviation."

367. McCann, "A Study of Irrational Decisions," 115. As concerns the capability, if not the propensity, of professionals to make irrational decisions, consider the characterization by the court at page 209 in the *Heranger* decision relative to the conning officer porting his helm in the Thames "as... so ill-advised, and such a breach of good seamanship, as almost to deserve the epithet 'suicidal' ... ."

368. Wagenaar, "Accidents at Sea," 595.

369. NSTB, *Cosco Busan Bridge Pier Allision Report,* 3 and 9-10.

370. This rescue was notable as well for resulting in an historically high salvage award. *Margate Shipping Company.* The tanker's master stated: "We didn't do it for money. We did it because we were the only ones around who could render assistance, ..." Strong, *In Peril,* xiii.

371. *In Peril,* 35.

372. Captain Strong: "At sea everyone is at risk at any given time; we simply take turns at being on the receiving end of trouble

and hope that others will be available to help." Ibid., 89.

373. Thus, the appellate court erred in saying in its opinion that Captain Strong "took his relatively unmaneuverable craft into perilous shoal waters in direct violation of standing orders." *Margate Shipping*, 981. Interview, Captain Strong.

374. *In Peril*, 88.

375. Opening the weather deck to access new lines stowed near the steering gear motors would run the risk of a sea breaking on board, flooding the space through the open hatch and disabling the steering gear and leaving the vessel without steering. Ibid., 90.

376. Ibid., 92-3.

377. Ibid., 103.

378. Ibid., 105.

379. Ibid., 106.

380. Ibid., 108.

381. Ibid., 108.

382. Ibid., 117.

383. Ibid., 120.

384. Ibid., 136.

385. *Margate Shipping*, 981 and 985.

386. In *Peril*, 146. Interviews with a number of masters confirms this opinion endorsing empathetic and knowledgable shoreside assistance as providing welcome stress relieving peace of mind. See also: Chelminski, *Super Wreck*, 53-62 and, as concerns post-casualty pre-established crisis management, Rynn, *Restoration* of Sea-Land Voyager, 244-45.

387. "Hazardous" and "safe" thoughts are variants upon efficiency – thoroughness trade-off (ETTO) "rules" expanded upon and discussed in Hollnagel, *The ETTO Principle*, 35-36. These ETTO "rules" are pervasive throughout individual and organizational tasking – for example, "It looks fine" = "so there is no need to do or check anything," meaning that an action or inspection may be skipped; "We always do it this way" = "so don't worry that the rules, regulations, policies and procedures say something else."

388. TAIC, *Jody F. Millennium Grounding*. See also TAIC, *Tai Ping Grounding*. Both reports discuss "hazardous" thoughts versus "safe" thoughts.

Chapter 10. Violation of Rules, Regulations, Policies and Procedures

389. Hopkins, "Risk Management and Rule Compliance," 6.

390. An extreme type of violation is the *deliberate violation*, beyond the scope of this discussion, where the violator intends an adverse outcome, such as sabotage or vandalism. However, in this context reference may be made to the court decision of the *Heranger*, previously cited. Similarly, the watch officer's behavior on a vessel that suddenly went to port and into collision by crossing the bow of an oncoming vessel was such that his colleagues testified in the resulting trial that he "must have been possessed by demons or evil spirits." *In re Seiriki Kisen Kaisha*, 919.

391. Reason, *Human Error*, 196.

392. Exemplified by the court decision of *The Lady Gwendolen*. Vessel logbooks for some seventy-five voyages, about half of which recorded excessive speed for the prevailing conditions, were submitted to shore side management. The company marine superintendent regularly received the logs. The ship owner was, as a result of failing to correct a notorious practice, denied limitation of liability.

393. *Hercules Carriers, Inc.*, 728 F.2d at 1572.

394. Martina, "Human Error Contribution," 680.

395. A Merchant Marine Academy classmate of the author defended his "pea soup" fog violation of the standing order to call the captain if in any doubt regarding the visibility by arguing, "I wasn't in any doubt. I couldn't see s**t!" Without agreeing with the classmate's rationale, his comment does illustrate that night and standing orders must be clear in phraseology and spirit, and the captain must enforce adherence to both: "The captain who has flawless night orders and standing orders and then runs aground could reasonably hope to be hanged with a better-quality rope – silk, perhaps – but the orders will do nothing to reduce the captain's full responsibility." Byron, "The Captain," 43.

A type of standing order helpful to a watch officer — particularly an embryonic watch officer — is illustrated by these partial standing orders drafted by Captain Robert Wiley, master of USNS *Guadalupe*:

Many years ago, I sailed with a ship's master who was …
hmmm … "challenging." His Standing Orders and Night
Orders were often ambiguous, conflicting, and many times
just about impossible to actually comply with. This captain

would often write down one thing and then tell you to do something entirely different. Any requests for clarification would be met by immediate rancor as well as accusations of refusing to comply with orders (with an implied threat). On several occasions I found myself in situations when I had to make the decision between complying with his orders (and place the ship in danger), or disobey the orders and keep the ship safe. Of course, this captain's motive was to protect himself in the event of an accident. He was not interested if his orders provided proper guidance. What he wanted was to shift any blame over to whoever was on watch at the time. Sailing with this guy was an eye opening experience for me (to say the least).

Let me irrefutably state here and now: At no time do I expect these Standing Orders (or my Night Orders) to conflict with what I expect of you in the performance of your duties or in the execution of our mission. In the event these Standing Orders (or Night Orders) cannot safely be complied with; or they conflict with other guidance; or perhaps just do not seem to make sense, you shall immediately notify me to seek resolution. You will never be taken to task for requesting clarification if you sense ambiguity. Furthermore, nothing in these orders should ever be construed as to obligate you to deliberately place this ship into danger.

A new graduate of another respected nautical academy came to grief when, rather than call the captain, his doubt regarding navigation of his vessel in restricted waters was resolved by him passing navigational authority to the unlicensed helmsman on his watch. NTSB, *Empress of the North Grounding Report.*

396. Interview with Captain Strong.

397. NTSB, *Crash of Pinnacle Airlines.*

398. Ibid., 45.

399. Ibid., 59.

400. The court in its decision allocating a salvage award, *Margate Shipping Co. v. M/V J.A.Orgeron,* commented at page 981 that the tanker's master "took his relatively unmaneuverable craft into perilous shoal waters in direct violation of [his company's] standing orders." In an interview with author, Captain Strong said that his actions did not violate explicit company orders, and that more

explicit orders were drafted in response to his actions; however, he acknowledged that his actions likely were contrary to the spirit of the company's orders.

401. Reason, *Managing the Risks*, 74.

402. Hanninen, *Negotiated Risks – the Estonia Accident*, 68.

403. Commissioner of Maritime Affairs, *Report*, 4.

404. "Below 40 degrees South [latitude]. there is no law, below 50 degrees, there is no God," an old seafarers' saying from the days of sailing ships rounding Cape Horn. *Explorer* was well below 50 degrees South altitude. Ibid. 10.

405. Ibid., 51-2. The vessel's voyage data recorder was not removed from the sinking ship, so its information was not preserved. Therefore, much of the factual narration is the subjective interpretation of crew and passenger observations.

406. Ibid., 41-2.

407. White, *Report*, 5. As well as being a passenger on the casualty voyage, Andy White was a Fellow of the Royal Institute of Naval Architects. He wrote at page 3, "I felt that the line between adventure and disaster was stretched paper thin."

408. Ibid., 68.

409. White, *Report*, 6.

410. Commissioner of Maritime Affairs, *Report*, 67-68.

411. White, *Report*, 7.

412. Technical aspects of this event are discussed in Job, *Air Disaster, Vol. 2*, 186-202.

413. Hayes, "Crash of United Flight 232," 10.

414. Habberley, "A Behavioural Study of the Collision Avoidance Task," 30. My own observation is that an approaching vessel at night should trigger something more than mere skill-based performance; at least a first appraisal based upon evaluation of the aspect presented by other vessel's navigation lights and initial relative bearing and whether that bearing remains constant.

415. Reason, *Human Error*, 85-86.

416. Habberley, "A Behavioural Study," 50.

417. Reason, *Human Error*, 86.

418. NTSB member R. Sumwalt in remarks to the Lawyer-Pilots Bar Association, "Professionalism," July 9, 2009.

419. Of the seven human actions that led directly to the Chernobyl catastrophe, five were deliberate violations of RRPP and

not slips, lapses or mistakes characteristic of error. Reason, "The Chernobyl Errors."

420. Allen, *Farwell's Rules,* 108-110.

421. Karwal, "Non-Adherence to Procedures." These categories are drawn from the aviation domain, so for present purposes have been modified to fit into the maritime domain, but without changing their essential character.

422. Karwal, "Non-Adherence to Procedures," 22-23.

423. NTSB, *Axel Spirit Ambrose Light Allision Report,* 27.

424. Verschuur, "Violations of Rules and Procedures."

425. Hudson, "Bending the Rules II."

426. While there is likely truth in the observation that "seafarers have an innate ability to understand and assess the risks that the job places before them and undertake intuitive risk analysis," Parker, *Managing Risks in Shipping,* chapt. 3, fn. 1, a study found that there is a 50-50 likelihood that a RRPP will be violated aboard ship. DNV, "Poor safety training," 4.

427. Hudson, "Bending the Rules," 18.

428. Huntzinger, *Motivating Factors and Perceptions of Risk,* 4.

429. Ibid.,148.

430. Chauvin, "Decision making."

431. Ibid., 264.

432. Ibid., 266-267.

433. Ibid., 268. Not surprisingly, cognitive demand on the stand-on vessel increases sharply when a collision threat arises from a rule violation by the give-way vessel. This reality is unlikely to be contested by any bridge watch officer who has been in that position.

434. Belcher, "A sociological interpretation," 217.

435. Ibid., 218.

436. MAIB, *CP Valour Grounding Report,* 28-29. Subsequently, the MAIB suggested that "[r]eluctance to follow procedures, and complacent attitudes, can be identified and addressed by monitoring the activities of ship staff during random audits of [vessel data recording] data." MAIB, *Maersk Kendal Grounding Report,* 33.

437. Given how much emphasis, implied if not explicit, is attached to meeting schedules despite reduced manning and limited shipboard resources, combined with management and regulators' seemingly mindless promulgation of RRPP as has

become endemic in the maritime industry (particularly after an incident or accident when new RRPP are likely to be a "knee jerk" reaction and more an impediment than asset to safety), a potentially lethal brew has been concocted for encouraging shipboard violations.

438. Mitchell, "Strategies to Reduce ... Procedural Non-Compliance."

439. Ibid., 61.

440. Bailey, "Perceptions of Risk."

441. ATSB, *Bunga Teratai Satu Grounding Report,* 22.

442. Hanninen, "Risk Regulation," 684.

443. Belcher, "Sociological interpretation of the COLREGS."

444. Mitchell, *"Strategies to Reduce,"* 61.

445. Reason, *Human Contribution,* 57.

446. Rochlin, "Self-Designing High-Reliability Organizations"

447. Hudson, *Bending the Rules,* 48.

448. The premise here is that no negative or amoral motivation, such as profit/production/schedule "at all costs," nor the deliberate sacrifice of safety nor permissive ethical climate, instigates the deviance, with "deviance" *not* used in its perjuritive sense.

449. An informative study of the nature and potential pervasiveness of normalization of deviance is Diane Vaughan's *The Challenger Launch Decision.*

450. "Practical drift is the slow steady uncoupling of practice from written procedure." Snook, *Friendly Fire,* 194.

451. MAIB, *P & O Nedlloyd Genoa Loss of Caro Containers Report,* 33 and 35.

452. Gehman, "Ethical Challenges for Organizations," 12-14.

453. Federal Bureau (Germany), *Pacific Challenger Grounding Report.*

454. Huntzinger, *Motivating factors and perceptions of risk,* 146.

455. Mitchell, "Strategies to reduce," 16 (emphasis added).

456. Chelminski, *Superwreck,* 62.

457. The greater the loose coupling between management policy statements and the understanding on the vessels of those policies, the greater is the ambiguity and likelihood for violation of those policies.

458. Chelminski, *Superwreck*, 61-62.

459. NTSB, *Patriot Near Grounding Report*.

460. A ship master's life is not easy in the commercial world. The dilemma or, if preferred, conflict between a master's concerns for his vessel and crew on the one hand and charter party obligations on the other hand was at issue in the House of Lords decision *Whistler International Ltd. v. Kawasaki Kisen Kaisha Ltd.* The charter's routing instructions prevailed. The master's decision to sail a rhumb line course from Vancouver to Japan on two (January/February and April/ May) voyages in preference to a shorter great circle was deemed unjustifiably cautious.

461. Washington: FAA Office of Aviation Medicine.

462. Patankar, *Root Cause Analysis*, 11 and 16.

463. DNV, "Poor safety training a hidden safety risk," 4.

464. "Many organizations attempt to take refuge in procedures … even if those procedures don't really capture all of the nuances and tricks of the trade [but instead support] accountability by letting managers more easily verify if procedures were followed [and] eliminate the need for judgment calls." Klein, *Power of Intuition*, 33 and 34.

465. Knudsen, "Paperwork at the Service of Safety?" 295 and 297.

466. An analogous concern was expressed by Paul Fussell in his comment about direct radio contact with senior military personnel having "profound and eminently 'modern' consequence on the self-respect and dignity of the high-ranking officer. Rapidity of communication tends to transform him from a self-reliant individual commander into a mere obeyer of orders received by radio."

467. Knudsen, "Paperwork," 297.

468. Morel, "Articulating the Difference," 14.

469. Schwartz, *Practical Wisdom*, 31.

470. Fischer, U. *Cultural Variability of Crew Discourse*, 2, citing a NTSB review of 37 serious accidents involving major United States air carriers between 1978 and 1990.

471. NTSB, *Star Princess Grounding Report*, 39 and 7.

472. USCG, *Montrose Grounding Report*, 10.

473. MAIB, *Maersk Kendal Grounding Report*, 32.

474. NTSB, *USS Greeneville - Ehime Maru Collision Report*, 17-25.

475. Fischer, *Cultural Variability*.

476. Other, less effective, strategies considered were commands

("Altitude! Altitude – watch the altitude!;" "Turn 40 degrees right!");
suggestions ("Let's ----."); queries ("Which heading should I take?;"
"Are you planning to ----?"); self-direction ("I am going to ----!; "My
plane!"); and, permission seeking ("You want me to ----?").

477. Orders invite neither debate nor delay, as is well known
and taught. When lecturing at the New York Maritime College, I
noticed engraved on the side of one building an exhortation from
Confederate States General "Stonewall" Jackson to like effect.

478. Gordon, *Rules of the Game*, 246.

479. Fischer, *Error-Challenging Strategies*, 1.

480. A vernacular translation in aviator speak was offered for
each of these four stages by Captain R. Besco:

PROBING: "Captain, aren't you painting yourself into a
corner, and aiming to shoot yourself in the foot."

ALERTING: "Captain, it is my function and responsibility
to protect your blind spots. I see you are about to walk off
a cliff."

CHALLENGING: "Captain, you are about to self destruct.
You have the equivalent of a very angry and armed bogey
in your six o'clock position. We are all about to get the civil
aviation equivalent of a 20 millimetre enema."

EMERGENCY: "Captain, you, your airplane and everyone
on board are about to be dead meat. I choose not to join
you. If you don't immediately cease and desist, I will take
the plane away from you. I owe it to myself, my family, our
passengers, and our company to restore an adequate margin
of safety." From Besco, *To Intervene or Not to Intervene?*

481. This culminating step has been described from the
wheelhouse as the fictional mine sweeper *Caine* battled a
typhoon:

"Captain, we'll have to use engines again, she's not
answering to the rudder ... . Sir, how about heading up into
the wind? She's going to keep broaching to with this stern
wind ---."

[Captain] Queeg pushed the handles of the telegraph. "Fleet
course is 180," he said.

"Sir, we have to maneuver for the safety of the ship ---."

"Sunshine knows the weather conditions. We've received no
orders to maneuver at discretion ---."

"We're not in trouble," said Queeg. "Come left to 180."

"Steady as you go!" [executive officer] Maryk said at the same instant. The helmsman [Stilwell] looked around from one officer to the other, his eyes popping in panic. "Do as I say!" shouted the executive officer. He turned to the OOD [officer of the deck]. "Willie, note the time." He strode to the captain's side and saluted. "Captain, I'm sorry, sir, you're a sick man. I am temporarily relieving you of this ship, under Article 184 of *Naval Regulations*."

"I don't know what you're talking about," said Queeg. "Left to 180, helmsman."

"Mr. Keith, *you're* the OOD here, what the hell should I do?" cried Stilwell ... .

"Commander Queeg, you aren't issuing orders on this bridge any more," said Maryk. "I have relieved you, sir. You're on the sick list. I'm taking the responsibility. I know I'll be court-martialed. I've got the conn ... ."

"Steady on 000, Stilwell," [Keith] said. "Mr. Maryk has the responsibility. Captain Queeg is sick." Wouk, *The Caine Mutiny*, 338-339. While USS *Caine* is fictional, the typhoon is not. Calhoun, *Typhoon: The Other Enemy*.

The shipboard climate, personality of the officers and immediate circumstances may dictate how an awkward situation is handled - short of taking the conn from a senior officer. I was told of one bridge team whose captain was habitually intoxicated whenever the vessel left port and, upon dropping the pilot, invariably gave irresponsible orders. Apparently this captain had either other redeeming qualities or impermissibly "forgiving" watch officers because, rather than relieving him, the watch officers "conspired" with the helmsman so that in those circumstances the helmsman verbally would "confirm" the captain's orders but comply only with the watch officers' orders.

Chapter 11. Technology and e-Navigation

482. Duckworth, *Destroyers on the Rocks*, 229, quoting from the Naval Court of Inquiry. The Court also was quoted at page 230: "No destroyer doctrine ever advocated the blind following of any leadership, ..."

483. Ibid., 231. Regarding the certainty of knowing or not

knowing a ship's position, a Lieutenant Barral wrote in *Digressions on the Navigation of Cape Horn*, 1857: "It is far better not to know where one is, and realize that one does not know, than to be certain one is in one place where one is not."

484. The IMO has used the term "e-nav," whereas eNavigation, or "eNav," has for a number of years been used by *Pacific Maritime Magazine* and is used herein with kind permission.

485. This discussion, though centered upon electronic navigation issues, is not intended to overlook that many shipboard operations beyond navigation are "automated," predominantly engine and cargo operations. Understanding and training in the proper use of these systems is of paramount importance. In 2005 *Savannah Express*, one of the world's largest container vessels, lost astern engine power entering port and as a result allided with a shore facility. The ship's engine was of a revolutionary design, with components that had been troublesome. Though the ship's engineers were experienced and properly certified, they were unable to diagnose or repair the problem. The MAIB commented upon the STCW training standards not having been updated to account for advances in modern engineering systems. Similarly, in 2008, about 50 nautical miles southeast of Boston, the liquefied natural gas carrier *Catalunya Spirit* experienced a five day blackout. The ship's crew lacked sufficient training to be able to re-start the failed system manually. The Coast Guard reportedly determined that the computerized "point and click" system "makes the crew so dependant on the computers that they became incapable of effectively using the manual controls on the system[.]" Yanchunas, "Crew of LNG tanker," 28.

486. Tsou, "Decision Support," 168. This point of view creates a self-fulfilling prophecy guaranteed to bolster confidence in automation. Because technological failures are easier to remedy than the shortcomings of human beings, the human factor component of maritime casualties is likely to *increase* as technological issues are resolved.

487. "Mariners are in a measured, evolutionary manner making way for the new, albeit remaining faithful and constant to the craft they know, and the skills that define them. ... Mariners often incorporate new tools in small steps. This approach allows them to test against their basic knowledge, ..." Lutzhoft, "Integration on the Ship's Bridge," 14 and 18.

488. To the amazement of some and as a "melancholy surprise" to others, the United States Naval Academy marked 1998 by terminating celestial navigation instruction. *N. Y. Times,* "Setting the Sextant Aside." This decision despite the authoritative "Bowditch" declaring that " ... the professional mariner must never forget that the safety of his ship and crew may depend on skills that differ little from those practiced generations ago. Proficiency in conventional piloting and celestial navigation remains essential." *American Practical Navigator,* 1.

489. "The relation between the technological resources involved in any activity and the influence of the physical environment upon that activity, [may] be described as being inversely proportional, ..." Morton, *Role of the Physical Environment,* 1.

49. "Yet, performance pressures on the overall system (greater efficiency or throughput) tend to push practitioners back to the edge of the performance envelope rather than taking the benefits of the changes in increased safety margin or lower workload. As a result, surprises occur in the form of accidents (fundamentally surprising new paths to failure) and in the form of negative side effects of the change unanticipated by designers – 'automation surprises'." Woods, "Anticipating the effects."

491. Rowley, *Development of Guidance,* 17.

492. Ibid., 20.

493. Kendra, *Looking Out the Window.*

494. *American Practical Navigator,* 1.

495. Grech, "Human Error in Maritime Operations."

496. Grech, *Human Factors in the Maritime Domain,* 125.

497. A graphic demonstration of this truism is the 2009 over-flight by about 150 miles of Flight 199, a passenger A320 operated by a major United States airline, past its intended destination of Minneapolis, MN. The two pilots contended that they had become distracted while checking schedules on their laptop computers. However, many aviation safety experts suggested that the greater likelihood was that they had fallen asleep during the cruise phase of the flight. The bad rap against automobile texting while driving is equally applicable, and no less dangerous, on the maritime highway. The containership *Berit* grounded after the watch officer missed a course alteration while texting on his mobile cell phone. MAIB, *Berit Grounding Report.*

498. Hadnett, "A Bridge Too Far?" 286.

499. Rowley, *Development of Guidance*, 26.

500. Kendra, *Looking Out the Window*, 172.

501. But remember, please, the law by which we live.
We are not built to comprehend a lie.
We can neither love nor pity nor forgive.
If you make a slip in handling us you die!
—Rudyard Kipling, "The Secret of the
Machines," 1911.

502. Lutzhoft, *"Technology is Great When it Work,"* 59.

503. Ibid.,59.

504. Hutchins, *Cognition in the Wild.* "Experience with engineered systems indicates that in the main … failures are firmly rooted in factors involving operating teams, the organizational factors that influence those operating teams, and the interactions between the operating teams and the other system elements." Hee, "Safety Management Assessment System (SMAS)." The human error factor can be great: In the northern Italian town of *Carpi*, a Swedish couple inquired of the local tourist office where they could find the famous Blue Grotto, believing themselves to be in *Capri*. They had misspelled the name Capri when entering their desired destination in their rental car's GPS so the satnav system had directed them 650 km out of their way to Carpi. Informed of their error, the couple returned to their car, reset the GPS and headed south. Accessed July 28, 2009 from http://news.bbc.co.uk/go/pr/fr/-/2/hi/europe/8173308.stm. And, incredibly, a merchant vessel departed Delaware Bay for South America but ran aground on Long Island. On departure, the gyro compass lost power and "spun ever more slowly until it was at least ninety degrees in error." No gyro error was determined when power was restored and the error remained, undetected. South had become east and north became west. McPhee, *Looking for a Ship*, 121. As a junior officer, I remember reading about this incident described on the backside of a Pilot Chart and thinking it too incredible to be true. In all instances, the identity of the ship involved has not been disclosed, to prevent embarrassment I presume.

505. Rowley, *Development of Guidance*, 20.

506. Lutzhoft, "Integration Work on the Ship's Bridge," 63. As *Bowditch* comments, "A navigator constantly evaluates the ship's position, anticipating dangerous situations well before they

arise, and always keeps 'ahead of the vessel'." *American Practical Navigator,* 1.

507. *Ballarat*'s commanding officer was named David. The comment of HAL 9000, the computer in the 1968 movie *2001: A Space Odyssey,* comes to mind: "Dave, I can see you're really upset about this." Particularly in the aviation domain there are instances of automated systems programmed and acting so as to override human intervention.

508. *Seaways,* "Aftermath of a Collision," 22. Also contributing to the officer's workload was intrusion of a seaman requiring an administrative logbook entry.

509. The mariner since the days of sail has already experienced at least one degree of separation from his or her "real" environment:

The watch keeping officer of a screw-driven vessel, standing serene on the eminence of his bridge, is too remote from the medium of his voyaging: he views the moving sea from too great a height, and it is seldom that he appreciates its life and power for, even if he catches some glimpse of its changing beauty in its incessant movement, he regards the deep ocean as a slave in his bondage. He cannot be blamed for such an attitude since that is the very heart of their relationship and one to which he has been trained since the day of his initiation. — Hurst, *Call of High Canvas,* 202.

510. NSTB, *Royal Majesty Grounding Report,* 45.

511. An informal consideration of tanker conditions and practices referred to "laments heard from numerous Masters" of watch officers' reluctance to look out the wheelhouse windows. Solly, *Nothing Over the Side,* 130. A significant response in aircraft is development and installation of Heads-Up Displays (HUDs). HUDs raise attention focus up from the instrument panel and allow attention to be given to the external environment.

512. Conrad, *The Mirror of the Sea,* 18.

513. McPhee, *Looking for a Ship,* 120. The latter admonition is represented as a quote from one of a ship's officers citing a posting at Maine Maritime Academy.

514. Kendra, *Looking Out the Window,* 139 and 160 (emphasis in original).

515. Schager, "When Technology Leads Us Astray," 69.

516. McCallum, *Procedures for Investigating and Reporting.*

517. *In re Waterstand Marine, Ltd.,* 1801.

518. NTSB, *Cosco Busan Bridge Pier Allision,* 4–9.

519. Federal Bureau (Germany), *LT Cortesia Grouding Report,* 50.

520. The tendency is that users are pushed ever closer to the edge of the operational envelope, rather than enhancing safer more conservative operations or reducing workload. This was the conclusion dawn from a study of the impact of new technology on the Desert Storm operation. Cordesman, *Lessons of Modern War Vol 4,* 25. While the military may be exceptional in the demands imposed upon its personnel, consideration of how technology has been applied in military operations and its effects upon personnel should not be disregarded for relevancy in the civilian world.

521. Kendra, *Looking Out the Window,* 92.

522. Sutton, "Helmsman as a Man-Machine Element."

523. Rowley, *Development of Guidance,* 20. Or, phrased differently, automation can exacerbate what automation is intended to ameliorate.

524. Squire, " Role of the Human Element," 13.

525. Hadnett, "A Bridge Too Far?" at 289.

526. Johannesen, *Behind Human Error,* 3.

527. Psaraftis, "Human Element as a Factor."

528. Schager, "When Technology Leads Us Astray," 67.

529. Though not without some embarrassing "glitches," the capability for technological accuracy is today an accepted given. This applies as well to the capability for navigational accuracy. Such accuracy, without careful monitoring, can have fatal consequences. In September of 2006 two aircraft, one a Legacy 600 private jet and the other a Boeing 737 passenger jet with 154 people on board, collided at 37,000 feet over the Amazon. Traveling in opposite directions, each on auto pilot, both aircraft remained at exactly their auto-pilot programmed 37,000 foot altitude along the perfect centerline of the assigned air corridor. Each plane flew as programmed. The problem: no one caught the fact that the Legacy was 1,000 feet off its assigned altitude. Langewiesche, "Devil at 37,000 feet."

530. An admonition I was introduced to when speaking at the United States Merchant Marine Academy.

531. Comment has been made that "masters and navigation officers on vessels engaged on repetitive runs, must be particularly

wary of carrying out actions that are simply 'rule-based'." Maritime Safety Authority of New Zealand. *Class A Accident Report ARATERE Near Grounding, Tory Channel, New Zealand,* at 52 (entering the Channel, the vessel on "automatic track keeping mode" (ANTS) failed to make a programmed course change, noticed by the bridge team with the master saying without apparent concern that he had seen cross track error of up to 85 meters with a flood current self-corrected, rule-based performance level: "if" the vessel gets off track, "then" the vessel's ANTS will (because it has previously) self-correct.

532. Billings, "Human-Centered Aviation Automation," 95.

533. "It does little good to remind human operators that automation is not always reliable or trustworthy when their own experience tells them it can be trusted to perform correctly over long periods of time." Ibid., 97.

534. Reliance placed in past GPS accuracy "leads to lack of activity that increases the risk of poor watch keeping habits." ATSB, *Bunga Teratai Satu Grounding Report,* 18.

535. There is the unfortunate view, probably now already fulfilled, that the "need for the highly trained professional [navigator] we now have, well versed in principles and skilled in the practice of his art, will diminish and in all probability he will eventually disappear as he has done in the air." Maybourn, "The Navigator – Man or Machine?" at 342.

536. Lutzhoft, "On Your Watch," 91.

537. Schager, "When technology Leads Us Astray," 70.

538. This casualty is particularly interesting when reading the NTSB report against the cited commentators.

Chapter 12. Multiculturalism

539. Today, the circumstances are not at all unusual for a vessel to be beneficially owned in nation A, registered in nation B, managed by a company based in nation C, with senior officers native to nation D, junior officers native to nation E and unlicensed crew native to nations F, G and H (add nations R, S, T, U, V, W, X, Y and Z if a passenger vessel), classed by a classification society of nation I, carrying cargo loaded in nations J, K and L for discharge in nation M, chartered to a company of nation N, insured through a Protection & Indemnity club registered in nation O, and taking on one or more pilots native, respectively, to each of the nations at

which the vessel makes intermediate port calls.

540. Despite the relative high degree of globalization within the maritime industry, there is strong suspicion that racism does exist to at least some degree. Anderson, *Cracking the Code,* 187.

541. For example: "Many Norwegians and other 'Dutchmen' were nattier workers, better fair-weather sailors, more sober and tractable men, especially on sailing-day, than the British. But when it came to a heavy gale in a short-handed ship, to imminent danger, to a time when a man with GUTS was needed, then the British Merchant Service Jack stepped forward. With a foul and unnecessary oath or two he rudely shouldered the foreigner into the background and took the brunt of the work and danger upon himself." Worsley, *First Voyage,* 83. Lest Frank Worsley be judged solely by this jingoistic comment, he should be recognized for his many nautical accomplishments. He had been master of Ernest Shackleton's Antarctic exploration vessel *Endurance* (1914-1916) and after *Endurance* became ice-bound, was navigator in *James Caird,* the 23'4" open boat in which he, Shackleton and several others successfully made an 800-mile voyage, one of the world's most famous small-boat journeys, through wintery seas to the island of South Georgia for help. See Thomson, *Shackleton's Captain.* Also: "As viewed from the wheelhouses of the American Merchant Marine, the butt of jokes – the oafs of the ocean – have long been the Greeks and the Haitians: unseaworthy-sailors-let-loose-in-unseaworthy-ships sort of thing, the worst on water, ship handlers of such negligible skill that one ought to cede them wider clearance than anyone else in the world with the exception of the United States Coast Guard." McPhee, *Looking For a Ship,* 68 (as McPhee is not himself a commercial mariner, I presume he "learned" these biases during his research). Additionally relevant to the prejudice shown against alleged nautical mavericks is the ditty familiar to many merchant mariners:

> Red over red, Captain dead,
> Red over green, sailing machine,
> Painted gray, stay away.

Of course, to acknowledge a prejudice held by some in the industry is not to advocate that the prejudice has any validity in fact.

542. United States Coast Guard, *Bow Mariner Explosion and Sinking Report.*

543. Ibid., 42.

544. Knudsen, "Paperwork," 300.

545. The term "culture" in the national sense is used to denote "patterned ways of thinking, feeling, and reacting, … ; the essential core of culture consists of traditional ideas and especially their attached values." Kluckholm, C., "The Study of Culture" in D. Lerner and H.D. Lasswell, H.D. editors, *Policy Sciences*, 86-101. G. Hofstede, *infra*, refers to culture as a collective programming of the mind that distinguishes the members of one group from another.

546. Hofstede, *Culture and Organizations*, 2.

547. Gutridge, *Mutiny*, 5. See also "The confinement of ship's frame, the forced continuous interaction of the members of a crew, the cramped living conditions, the ennui which often accompanies shipboard routine, are factors which often induce conditions which enflame those who possess short tempers and occasionally even those reputed for even-temperedness." *Waters v. Moore-McCormack Lines, Inc.*, 193.

548. Dr. Samuel Johnson, quoted in James Boswell's *Life of Johnson*.

549. Hofstede, *Culture and Organizations*, 20.

550. Ibid., 41.

551. Li, "Eastern Minds in Western Cockpits," 5.

552. ATSB, *APL Sydney Ruptured Pipeline Report*.

553. Here is an incident where more searching inquiry by the investigators could have developed considerable information expanding awareness of the power distance index (PDI) in the maritime environment.

554. Harris, "An Open Systems Approach," 9.

555. NTSB, *Cosco Busan Bridge Pier Allision Report*, 111.

556. Ibid., 67-68.

557. An example being Captain Holly Graf, while commanding officer USS *Cowpens*.

558. This was jotted down several years ago from a *Journal of Navigation* article, unfortunately without the author or article name having been noted.

559. TAIC, *Anatoki Collision*, 20-21.

560. MAIB, *Dole America Allision Report*, 14.

561. Ibid., 16. Of course, the single nationality bridge team is unlikely due to the economics involved, at least until personnel from

less expensive nations achieve commands. While this may alleviate one aspect of the PDI on board, ironically the PDI issue relative to shore centered authority may be exacerbated, as illustrated in the *APL Sydney* discussion.

562. Ibid., 20.
563. ATSB. *Bunga Teratai Satu Grounding Report,* 8 and 22.
564. Ibid., 23.
565. MAIB, *Grounding Report,* 19.
566. USCG, *Bow Mariner Explosion and Sinking Report*, 42-43.
567. T.S.B. Canada, "Safety Study," 7.
568. Strauch, "Can Cultural Differences Lead to Accidents," 251 and 255.
569. Cited in Hetherington, "Safety in Shipping," 409.
570. Strauch, "Can Cultural Differences Lead," 258.
571. Merritt, "Culture in the Cockpit," 292. Cf. Strauch, "Can Cultural Differences Lead to Accidents?"
572. NTSB, *Cosco Busan Bridge Pier Allision Report,* 111.
573. Ibid.
574. NTSB *Cosco Busan* Hearing Testimony at 519.
575. NTSB, *Cosco Busan Bridge Pier Allision Report,* 4.
576. MAIB, *Xuchanghai - Aberdeen Collision Report,* 16.
577. Ibid.
578. NTSB. *Bright Field – Riverwalk Allision Report,* 3 and 60.
579. Hellenic Republic, *Helios Airways Report,* 122.
580. MAIB. *Hyundai Dominion – Sky Hope Collision Report,* 32-33.
581. MARCOM Project Report, 379.
582. Morris, *Brothel Boy,* 16.
583. Kaplan, "Culture at Work," 609.
584. Another example: I was acting for a major P&I club on behalf of a Turkish ship owner on whose vessel a defective heavy hinged deck crane window had dropped upon a stevedore's head, severely injuring and disabling the stevedore. The matter was on the eve of trial, with there being a strong likelihood of a multi-million dollar jury verdict. With the assistance of a magistrate judge a "recommend" settlement in the sum of several hundred thousand dollars was negotiated, but the personal agreement of the ship owner was required. During several telephonic conversations, the owner expressed understandable outrage that an American injured

stevedore could receive several hundred thousand dollars when the United States had paid a substantially lesser sum to the family of a Turkish junior naval officer accidently killed by an American naval vessel during a NATO exercise. Clearly, the delicacy of national cultural issues cannot be over emphasized.

585. Hofstede, *Cultures and Organizations*, 368.

586. Ibid.

587. Brett, "Managing Multicultural Teams," 86.

588. Ibid.

Chapter 13. Organizational Management of Maritime Risk

589. Wagenaar, "Does the Expert Know?"

590. Helmreich, "Error Management as Organizational Strategy," 1.

591. Sir Stelios is a ship owner and founder of Easy Jet. One of his earliest experiences in the ship owning family business was investigating an accident to one of the company's vessels. The experience made a lasting impression.

592. Bichler-Robertson, *Maritime Commercial Passenger Ship Casualties*, 21.

593. Perrow, *Normal Accidents*, 170-231.

594. Grabowski, "Leading Indicators," 1020..

595. Ibid., 1023.

596. Hopkins, *Safety, Culture and Risk*, 90.

597. Hellenic Republic, *Helios Airways Report*, 75.

598. There is the tale relayed by a ship master sailing with a company that did expect "zero error" and "zero reportable accidents." One of the company's vessels was on target for "zero reportable accidents," but for one crew member. As a financial bonus was involved, the unlicensed crew took this goal seriously – zealously seriously. In order to dissuade the recalcitrant crew member from reporting an accident, he was held by his heels over the side of the vessel to achieve "attitude adjustment." While the accuracy of this tale is not vouched, it does illustrate how a "zero reports" program can become corrupted.

599. Helmreich, "Error Management as Organizational Strategy," 1.

600. Donaldson, "The ISM Code," 531.

601. Allinson, *Global Disasters*, 11.

602. Schelling, Foreword in Roberta Wohlstetter, *Pearl Harbor,* viii.

603. MAIB, *Isle of Arran Linkspan Contact Report,* 39-40.

604. http://bubbleheads.blogspot.com/2009/11/uss-hartford-jagman-released.html. Accessed February 24, 2010.

605. Konrad, "Today's Captain," 18.

606 .NTSB, *Colgan Air,* 186.

607. Editorial, "Lookout." *Fairplay* (September 14, 2006) at 1.

608. "[While the blame culture] might be acceptable for certain areas of modern life … it does not make for good ship operations – which is partly why the ISM Code was developed." MAIB Chief Inspector Stephen Meyer, quoted in ibid.

609. "I would not dream of blaming a seaman for doing or omitting to do anything a person sitting in a perfectly safe and unsinkable study may think of." Conrad, "Protection of Ocean Liners," 256-57.

610. Future World War II Fleet Admiral Chester W. Nimitz escaped with public reprimand following, as an ensign, his 1908 stranding of his torpedo boat destroyer command in the Philippines after committing nine errors in seamanship. Edwards, "Court-Martial of Chester W. Nimitz." And, early in his military career, as a lieutenant Colin Powell, subsequently Chairman of the Joint Chiefs of Staff and Secretary of State, lost his sidearm. Rather than subject Powell to the rigors of the military justice system, which likely would have resulted in a potential career ending black mark, his commanding officer, exercising what Powell later characterized as "humane leadership," chose a different means of teaching a lesson in responsibility. That officer, who had found Powell's sidearm, first told Powell that the weapon had been found in the possession of young children, who allegedly had discharged it without injuring anyone. This sobering but false revelation made a lasting impression upon Powell, who later described a fact learned that "nobody ever made it to the top by never getting into trouble." Powell, *My American Journey,* 45.

611. Mitroff, *We're So Big,* 44.

612. The Navy equivalent is recognized as "accountability," perhaps best set forth in the May 14, 1952 *Wall Street Journal* editorial written by World War II destroyer escort captain Vermont C. Royster and addressing the collision between USS *Wasp* and USS *Hobson*, reading in part: "On the sea there is a tradition older

than the traditions of the country itself and wiser in its age than this new custom [that men should no longer be held accountable for what they do as well as for what they intend]. It is the tradition that with responsibility goes authority and with them both goes accountability."

613. *BP Panel Report*, 90.

614. *BP Panel Report*, 69.

615. Reed, *In Too Deep*, 125.

616. Gilbert, "Transocean Cities," B1.

617. USCG, *Deepwater Horizon* report, 89.

618. Brown, "Assessing the Impact," 7.

619. Soma, "Safety as a Competitive Edge," 10.

620. And, "[a] report commissioned by the Netherlands government in 1999 calculated that a substandard operator enjoyed significant cost advantages, typically 14% over one who met minimum international standards and the advantage was much greater in the case of high standard operators … ." Donaldson, "A Rocky Road to Maritime Safety," 4.

621. Frame, *Where Fate Calls*, 356.

622. During a nationally televised collegiate football game on November 13, 2010, the commentators exchanged remarks regarding a recent small fire aboard a large cruise vessel that several days previously had been towed into San Diego from sea.

623. Westrum, "Organisational dynamics and safety," 75-80.

624. Johnson, *On the Over-Emphasis*, 3.

625. Kendra, *Looking Out the Window*, 105.

626. A comprehensive discussion of the overall environment within which transportation organizations must function and the competing forces that profoundly affect safe operation is Moshansky, Hon. V.P. "Commission of Inquiry into the Air Ontario Crash at Dryden, Ontario: Final Report." Ottawa, Ontario: Ministry of Supply and Services, Canada (1992).

627. *Bridge Log*.

628. http://globallast.imo.org/forum/display_topic_threads.asp?

629. *BP Panel Report*, 173.

630. Leveson, "White Paper on Approaches to Safety Engineering."

631. Woods, "Nine Steps to Move Forward from Error."

632. Hopkins, *Safety, Culture and Risk,* 41.

633. http://www.dauntless-soft.com/PRODUCTS/Freebies/USAirParkingBrake/.

634. Hopkins, *Safety, Culture and Risk,* 23-78.

635. ATSB, *Bunga Teratai Satu Grounding Report,* 22.

636. NTSB, *Patriot Near Grounding Report,* 19.

637. Karlsson, " Chain Breakers," 183.

638. Ibid., 187.

639. When I sailed with Sea-Land Service, Inc., each class of vessels had simply worded and clearly diagramed stability books readily available on board for use as necessary.

640. MAIB. *P & O Nedlloyd Genoa Report,* 5, 33 and 28. This situation was commented upon in a New York arbitration: "The safety of the vessel and its crew remains paramount so a delay of a few hours, if necessary to check the stevedores' preliminary stow plans, is a requirement that cannot be minimized or ignored." *Arbitration between Maersk Sealand and CSX Lines.*

641. TSB, *Queen of the North Sinking Report,* 32.

642. NTSB, *Bow Mariner Report,* at 41-2.

643. Kendra, *Looking Out the Window,* 181.

644. MAIB, *Cepheus J - Ileksa Collision Report,* 20.

Chapter 14. Organizational Failure and the Ro-Ro Ferry *Herald of Free Enterprise*

645. Parrott, *Bridge Resource Management,* ix.

646. Sheen Report, para. 18.8 (emphasis added).

647. *HMS Iolaire,* previously named *Amalthaea,* was a British Admiralty yacht whose sinking on 1 January 1919 in the Minch resulted in at least 205 deaths of the 280 aboard. At the time of the casualty, the vessel was transporting sailors who fought in the First World War from Kyle of Lochalsh to the island of Lewis, Scotland.

648. Sheen Report.

649. Sheen Report, para.14.1.

650. Ibid.14.2-.3.

651. "Seconds From Disaster; Zeebrügge Ferry Disaster," Episode no. 18, first broadcast 16 August 2005 by National Geographic.

652. Squat refers to an overall decrease in the static under keel clearance. A vessel pushes water forward as she moves through water. This volume of water must return aft down the sides and

under the bottom of the vessel. Streamlines of return flow are more rapid under the hull, causing a drop in pressure which results in the vessel dropping to sit deeper in the water. The precise squat effect can be mathematically calculated using known variables including vessel velocity, water depth, and vessel draft. Clark, *Ship Dynamics,* 184-87.

653. Bell, "An unstable enterprise," 13.

654. Ibid.

655. A study compiled by Det Norske Veritas, which examined 341 casualties over the period of 1965-1982, concluded that total losses as a result of a collision were much higher for ro-ros than for other ships and that both collisions and uncontrolled shifts of cargo comparatively more frequently led to serious consequences with ro-ros. The study was submitted to IMO by Norway in 1983. www. globalsecurity.org/military/systems/ship/ro-ro-safety.htm, accessed November 14, 2010. Many such losses, with substantial loss of life, are listed in an article by Hanninen, "Risk Regulation in the Baltic Sea Ferry Traffic," 691. As recently as November, 2006, the Swedish ro-ro vessel *Finnbirch* suffered a cargo shift in "hard" weather in the Baltic, capsized and sank with two fatalities. Clearly, ro-ro ferries have had considerable "killing potential."

656. Sheen Report, para. 18.3

657. The September 1994 sinking of the ro-ro ferry *Estonia* in the Baltic Sea, which claimed 852 lives, is a grim demonstration of visor door failure. For a comprehensive and technical discussion of clam and visor door designs, function and load stress capabilities *see* M. Samuelides, "Bow door slamming of Ro/Ro ferries."

658. Sheen Report, para. 18.5

659. Ibid.

660. Ibid., para. 21.1

661. Ibid., para. 13.2

662. Ibid., para. 10.8

663. Ibid., para. 10.4

664. Ibid., para. 11.1

665. See generally Parker, *Managing Risk in Shipping,* 12.

666. Sheen Report, para. 7.4

667. Ibid., para. 13.1

668. Ibid., para. 12.3

669. Ibid., para. 14.2

670. Ibid.

671. Ibid.

672. Ibid., para. 16.2

673. Ibid., para. 21.1

674. Ibid., para. 17.9

675. Ibid., paras.17.12 and 20.0

676. Hopkins, *Safety, Culture and Risk,* 41.

677. Leveson, *Engineering a Safer World,* 13.

678. Sheen Report, paras. 16.2 and 19.6

679. Quoted in Duncan, *Rickover and the Nuclear Navy.*

680. Sheen Report, para. 11.3

681. Ibid., para. 18.7

682. Reason, *Human Contribution,* 88.

683. Sheen Report, para. 13.2

684. Allison, "Saving human lives."

685. Sheen Report, paras. 17.3, .7, and .10.

686. Ibid., para. 10.2

687. Ibid.

688. Ibid., para. 22.1

689. Meek, *There Go the Ships,* 224.

690. Los Angeles Times, "Manslaughter Trial in '87 British Ferry Disaster Collapses," October 19, 1990.

691. Ibid. See also Reason, *Managing the Risks,* 231.

692. Ibid.

693. Sheen Report, para. 14.1

694. Ibid.

695. Anderson, *ISM Code,* 173-4.

Chapter 15. Lessons Learned?

696. Garrett, quoted in Barnett, *Navy Strategic Culture,* 136.

697. Quoted in *BP Panel Report,* xx,

698. Viscusi, "Risk within Reason" in T. Connolly et al. (eds.) *Judgment and Decision-making.*

699. Conrad, "Youth," 42.

700. *Deepwater Horizon* is deemed a maritime "vessel." *In re TRITON ASSET LEASING GMBH,* para. 6.

701. National Commission, *Deepwater Horizon,* 122 and 125.

702. ATSB, *Airbus A380 In-flight Uncontained Engine Failure Report.*

703. *Wall Street Journal,* "Qantas Drama Fuels Cockpit Lessons."

704. "BP's management talked about safety and monitored slips and falls, but it glossed over the importance of installing a safety culture – a system that would analyze how disparate events such as a bad decision could combine with others, such as underfunded maintenance, to spark castastrophe." Steffy, *Drowning in Oil*, 61.

705. The legal aspect of this issue is beyond the scope of this book.

706. Reason, *Managing the Risks*, 223.

707. Greck, "Human Error in Marine Operations," 1.

708. Saxe, "Six Blind Men and the Elephant," final stanza. After each of the blind men had felt a different part of the elephant, the king went to each blind man and asked:"Well, blind man, have you felt the elephant? Tell me, then, what sort of a thing is the elephant?" The king received six different descriptions of the one elephant.

709. This theory is referred to as "Heinrich's law." Inoue, "Innovative Probabilistic Prediction," 31. While there has been quibbling over the specifics of Heinrich's law, because it originated in the 1920s and lacks empirical support as well as fails to account for modern safety improvements, the general principle behind the law – actual significant accidents are but the tip of a safety pyramid – remains unassailable.

710. Sneddon, A, Hudson, P.T.W. et al. "A Comprehensive Model for Human Behaviour in Industrial Environments." (n.d.) www.abdn.ac.uk/iprc/Documents/pdf. Accessed November 17, 2010.

711. Dismukes, *Checklists and Monitoring*, 10. This report almost doubles the average number of aviation pilot errors cited by Soma, "Safety Excellence" (see chap. 1, n. 31). The constructive lesson to be learned from the success of monitoring and challenging is thereby emphasized.

712. Soma, ibid.

713. Leveson, *Engineering for Safety*, 371-77. With the success of SUBSAFE established, comparison to recent anomalies in United States naval shiphandling – *not* part of SUBSAFE – is interesting, especially given that shiphandling, "both art and science," is the "heart" of "naval culture." Faller, "Shiphandling Training?" at 104. In keeping with Commander Faller's observation are those of John Paul Jones, that a naval officer must be a "Seaman both

in Theory and Practice," and of Captain Thomas Thruxtun, that professional development of naval officers is crucial because "ships cannot maneuver [sic] themselves ... ." Leeman, *Long Road to Annapolis,* 15 and 3. Yet, currently at least one informed opinion is that "[m]ost U.S. Navy ship captains are 'sea buoy to sea buoy' operators, but they know little of accepted practice at sea, where merchant mariners have learned that a gray hull with a U.S. flag is a dangerous amateur bully that does not understand or follow accepted safe maritime practices." Landersman, "Where Have ...," 56. At the time of his writing, Captain Landersman's job teaching shiphandling in simulators may provide possible bias. However, certainly there have been sufficient recent naval vessel casualties sufficient to fall within the principle of Admiral David Beatty's "[t]here seems to be something wrong with our bloody ships today" 1916 comment at the Battle of Jutland, uttered when several British vessels exploded upon being struck by German shells. History of War website, 5. In March of 2009, while crossing the Strait of Hormuz at periscope depth, the submarine USS *Hartford* collided with USS *New Orleans.* Incredibly, in *Hartford,* "[m]ost [junior officers of the watch], most [junior officers of the deck], and most [officers of the deck] stated [that] a contact with a high bearing rate [of change] was a larger concern than a contact with a 0-degree per minute bearing rate[,]" and so *Hartford*'s "[w]atch team did not recognize *New Orleans'* 0-degree per minute bearing rate as a collision threat." United States Navy, *Command Investigation,* paras. 2 and 162. Compare: Rule 7(d) of the COLREGS: "In determining if risk of collision exists the following considerations shall be among those taken into account: (i) such risk shall be deemed to exist if the compass bearing of an approaching vessel does not appreciably change; ... [,]" and, from the Court decision *Ocean S.S. Co.* at page 784: "A constant bearing is a sure sign of danger, ...; a danger [of collision] which should put every mariner on guard." Similarly, basic organizational as well as "sharp end" errors and omissions contributed to the even more publicly embarrassing stranding of the cruiser *Port Royal* off the end of a runway at Honolulu's international airport. Perhaps, absent more appropriate training and operational awareness of casualty inducing factors, the Navy should consider reverting to the early naval practice of having qualified experienced merchant marine "sailing masters" drive the Navy's ships, and naval officers fight them.

714. USS *Scorpion* (SSN-589) was lost in 1968, but *Scorpion* was not SUBSAFE certified. Leveson, *Engineering for Safety,* 372.

715. Flin, "Erosion of Managerial Resilience," 227-229.

716. However, people – even senior people – in the maritime industry occasionally act in a manner that defies description. For example, in 2000 the entire bridge team of the passenger ferry *Express Samina* abandoned the bridge when the vessel was but three miles from entering a rock strewn port in order to watch part of a soccer game on the ship's television. The ferry struck rocks, sank, and 82 lives were lost. Edwards, *Beware the Grey Widow-Maker,* 386-393. Similarly foolishly irrational behavior, not limited to the sea, is recorded in *The Darwin Awards* series by Wendy Northcutt.

717. From keynote address by Secretary General Efthimios Mitropoulos of IMO, May 22, 2006 at quadrennial IATA Conference, Shanghai, PRC.

718. Comment to author, November 17, 2010.

719. Banicla, "Risk Homeostasis Theory," 607-608.

720. Gehman, "Lost Patrol," 35.

721. Factors not publicly disclosed but brought to my attention through the research for this book were, among others, the almost "catatonic" post- casualty state of the bridge personnel on a large passenger carrying vessel whose potential foundering was averted by the timely arrival and intervention of the vessel's subordinate damage control officer and, in another case, the negotiated cover-up of watch officer omissions.

722. Rogge, "Leadership on Board Raider *Atlantis,*" 50.

723. *United Geophysical,* at 819 (internal quotations omitted).

724. Ciavarelli, "Safety Climate and Risk Culture," 4.

Bibliography

18 U.S.C. section 1115.

2001: A Space Odyssey (film, 1968).

33 U.S.C. sections 2701-2761 (The Oil Pollution Act of 1990).

ABC News Nightline, "The USS *Vincennes*: Public War, Secret War," first broadcast July 1, 1992.

Admiralty and Maritime Law Guide, http://www.admiraltylawguide. com/documents/oleron.html. Accessed November 2, 2010.

Aleksandr Marinesko and Quint Star [1998] I Lloyd's Reports 265 (Q.B. 1997).

Allen, C. *Farwell's Rules of The Nautical Road.* Annapolis, MD: Naval Institute Press, 2005.

Allison, Robert E. *Global Disasters: Inquiries into Management Ethics.* New York: Prentice Hall, 1993.

———. "Saving human lives: lessons in management ethics." *Issues in Business Ethics* 21(2005): 198-222.

Amrozowicz, M. *The Qualitative Risk of Oil Tanker Groundings.* Thesis: Massachusetts Institute of Technology, 1996.

Anderson, Philip. *Cracking the Code: The Relevance of the ISM Code and Its Impact on Shipping Practices.* London: The Nautical Institute, 2003.

———. *ISM Code: A Practical Guide To The Legal And Insurance Implications.* London: LLP Reference Publishing, 1998.

Arbitration between Maersk Sealand (Charterer) and CSX Lines, LLC (Owner), Society of Maritime Arbitrators 3992 (2008).

Australian Transport Safety Bureau. *Boeing Co 747-438, VH-IJH, Bangkok, Thailand, 23 September 1999.* Report 199904538. April 2001.

———. *Independent Investigation into the Rupture of a Submarine Gas Pipeline by the Hong Kong Registered Container Ship APL Sydney in Port Phillip, Victoria 13 December 2008.* Report 260. April 2010.

———. *Independent Investigation into the Grounding of the Hong Kong Registered Products Tanker Atlantic Blue at Kirkcaldie Reef, Torres Strait, 7 February 2009.* Report MO - 2009 - 001. 2009.

———. *Independent Investigation into the Grounding of the Malaysian Flag Container Ship Bunga Teratai Satu, Sudbury Reef, Great Barrier Reef, 2 November 2000.* May 2001.

———. *Independent Investigation Into The Grounding of the Indian Registered Oil Tanker Desh Rakshak in the Entrance to Port Philip, Victoria, 4 January 2006.* Report 223. 2007.

———. *Independent Investigation into the Grounding of the Korean Flag Bulk Carrier Hanjin Dampier at Dampier, Western Australia, 25 August 2002.* Report 184. December 2003.

———. *Independent Investigation into the Near Collision between the Bulk Carrier Ormiston and the Roll On / Roll Off General Cargo Ship Searoad Mersey in Port Phillip, Victoria, 16 May 2007.* Report 242. 2008.

———. *Independent Investigation into the Grounding of the Panamanian Registered Bulk Carrier Pasha Bulker on Nobby's Beach, Newcastle, New South Wales, 8 June 2007.* Report 243. May 2008.

———. *Independent Investigation into the grounding of the Chinese bilk carrier Shen Neng 1 on Douglas Shoal, Queensland, 3 April, 2010.* Report MO-2010-003.2011.

———. *In-flight uncontained engine failure overhead Batam Island, Indonesia 4 November 2010 VH-OQA Airbus A380-842.* 2010.

Bailey, N. "Making Sense of Differences in Perceptions of Risk," SRIC Symposium, Cardiff University, July 8-9, 2009.

Bailey, N. and N. Ellis. "Perceptions of Risk in the Maritime Industry: Ship Casualty." Cardiff, UK: Seafarers International Research Centre, 2006.

Bailey, N., Ellis, N. and Sampson, H. "Safety and Perceptions of Risk: A Comparison Between Respondent Perceptions and Recorded Accident Data." Cardiff, UK: The Lloyd's Register Educational Trust Research Unit, 2010.

Bailley, T. "Managing Risk on Board Ship," in C. Parker *Managing Risks in Shipping: A Practical Guide.* (1999).

Baker, C.C. and D.B. McCafferty. "Accident Database Review of Human-Element Concerns: What Do the Results Mean for

Classification? Paper presented before Royal Institute of Naval Architects, Human Factors in Ship Design, Safety and Operation, 2005.

Baker, James and Frank I. "Skip" Bowman. *The Report of the BP U.S. Refineries Independent Safety Review Panel.* Houston, TX, 2007.

Baniela, Santiago and Rios, Juan. "The Risk Homeostasis Theory." *Journal of Navigation* 63(2010): 607-626.

Barnett, Michael. "Human Error and Maritime Safety: An Exploration of the Causes of Maritime Casualties." Ph.D. Dissertation, University of Wales College of Cardiff, 1989.

———. "Searching for Root Causes of Maritime Casualties – Individual Competence or Organisational Culture?" *WMU Journal of Maritime Affairs* 4(2005): 131-145.

Barnett, Michael and Claire Pekcan. "Recent Developments in Crew Resource Management (CRM) and Crisis Management Training." Southampton Engineering Maritime Research Centre, Southampton Institute, n.d.

Barnett, Roger W. *Navy Strategic Culture:Why the Navy Thinks Differently.* Annapolis, MD: Naval Institute Press, 2009.

Bastiat, Frederic. "What is Seen and What is Not Seen." http://www. econlib.org/library/Bastiat/basEss1.html. Accessed December 11, 2010.

BBC News, "Ship wrecked by 'trouser snag'." August 6, 2003.

Beatty, David. www.historyofwar.org/articles/people_beatty_david. html. Accessed December 21, 2010.

Becker, Jo. "Web Of Shell Companies Veils Trade By Iran's Ships." New York Times June 7, 2010. http://www.nytimes. com/2010/06/08/world/middleeast/08sanctions.html Accessed December 11, 2010.

Belcher, P. "A sociological interpretation of the COLREGS." *Journal of Navigation* 55 (2002): 213-224.

Bell, John. "An Unstable Enterprise." *New Scientist,* March 12, 1987: 13.

Besco, R. "To Intervene or Not to Intervene? The Co-Pilot's 'Catch-22'." Paper (n.d.)

Betts, Richard K., "Analysis, War, and Decision: Why Intelligence Failures Are Inevitable." *World Politics 31* (1978): 61-89.

Betz, John (Los Angeles Harbor Pilot), interview by author, August 30, 2007.

Beveridge, Bruce and Scott Andrews. *Titanic The Ship Magnificent: Volume One: Design and Construction*. Stroud: The History Press, 2009.

Bichler-Robertson, Gisela M. *Maritime Commercial Passenger Ship Casualties, 1950-1998: An Analysis of Negligent Corporate Risk-Taking and System Hazard*. Ph.D. Dissertation, Newark, NJ: The State University of New Jersey, 2000.

Bigano, Andrea and Sheehan, Paul. "Assessing the Risk of Oil Spills in the Mediterranean: The Case of the Route from the Black Sea to Italy." http://ssrn.com/abstract=886715. Accessed March 16, 2011.

Billings, C.E. "Human-Centered Aviation Automation: Principles and Guidelines." Moffett Field, CA: NASA (February 1996).

Boatner, Captain David, interview by author, June 15, 2010.

Boniface, D. and R. Bea, "Assessing the Risks of and Countermeasures for Human and Organizational Error." *SNAME Transactions*. 24 (1996): 157-77.

Book-Carter, N. and P. Leach, Greenstreet Berman, Ltd. *"Organizational Structures: The Influence Of Internal & External Structures On Safety Management Performance, A Review For The Maritime & Coastguard Agency Final Report."* C859 Issue 2. Maritime and Coastguard Agency (UK), May 2006.

Brett, J., Behfar, K. and M. Kern, "Managing Multicultural Teams." *Harvard Business Review* (November 2006): 84-91.

Bridge Log (September 13, 2006) http://www.Bridge-log.com/articles/cougar-ace-incident-illustrates-ballst-water-exchange. Accessed June 25, 2009.

Brown, Alan and Michael Amrozowicz. "Tanker Environmental Risk – Putting the Pieces Together." Joint SNAME/SNAJ Conference on Design and Methodologies for Collision and Grounding Protection of Ships, San Francisco, CA, 1996.

Brown, Alan. and B. Haugene, "Assessing the Impact of Management and Organizational Factors on the Risk of Tanker Grounding." Cambridge, MA: MIT 8th International Offshore and Polar Engineering Conference, May 1998.

Brown, Michael. "Truth or Consequences: Inquiries and Marine Disasters." London: Institute of Maritime Law – The Donald O'May Lecture in Maritime Law, 1993.

Brown, T and E. Brown. "Shiptalk Survey." Tyne and Wear: Shiptalk Limited, 2008.

Berger, W. and A.G. Corbet. "A Stranding in the Magellan Strait." *Journal of Navigation* 32 (1998): 325-33.

Burgess, C.F. *The Fellowship of the Craft: Conrad on Ships and Seamen and the Sea.* Port Washington, NY: Kennikat Press, 1976.

Byron, Cmdr. John L. "The Captain." *United States Naval Institute Proceedings,* September, 1982: 39-45.

Cahill, Richard. *Disasters at Sea: Titanic to Exxon Valdez.* London: Random Century, Ltd., 1990.

Calhoun, C. *Typhoon: The Other Enemy – The Third Fleet and the Pacific Storm of December 1944.* Annapolis, MD: Naval Institute Press, 1981.

Cambone, J. and F. Guarnieri. "Towards a new tool for measuring Safety Management Systems performance." Paper, n.d. www. resilience-engineering.org/REPapers/Cambon_Guarnieri_ Groeneweg.pdf. Accessed December 21, 2010.

CBS News. "Wayward Pilots: We were Working on Laptops," October 26, 2009. http://www.cbsnews.com/stories/2009/10/26/national/ main5422282.shtml. Accessed June 26, 2010.

Chancellor, 5 Fed. Cases 439 (S.D.N.Y. 1870).

Champlain, Samuel de. *The Works of Samuel de Champlain.* Vol. VII. Toronto: Champlain Society, 1922-1936.

Chauvel, Alain-Michel. *Managing Safety and Quality in Shipping: The key to success.* London: The Nautical Institute, 1997.

Chauvin, C. and Lardjane, S. "Decision making and strategies in an interaction situation: Collision avoidance at sea." Science Direct, Transportation Research Part F ll (2008): 259-269.

Cheek, P.M. *Legacies of Peril: A Merchant Navy Odyssey.* Lewes: The Book Guild Limited, 1986.

Chelminski, Rudolph. *Superwreck: Amoco Cadiz: The Shipwreck That Had To Happen.* New York: William Morrow and Company, Inc., 1987.

Chua-Eoan, Howard. "Disasters: Going, Going ... ." *Time,* August 19, 1991. http://www.time.com/time/printout/0,8816,973632,00html. Accessed April 29, 2010.

Ciavarelli, Anthony. "Safety Climate and Risk Culture: How Does Your Organization Measure Up?" Paper, Human Factors Associates, Inc., 2007. *In re City of New York,* 522 F.3d 279 (2d Cir. 2008).

Clark, I.C. *Ship Dynamics for Mariners*. London: The Nautical Institute, 2005.

Clarkson, John and B. Harvey. *Blue Funnel Line*. Preston, UK: Ships in Focus Publications, 1998.

Coghlin, Terence. "Tightening the Screw on Substandard Shipping." *Lloyd's Maritime and Commercial Law Quarterly*, Issue 3, August 2005: 316-326.

Commissioner of Maritime Affairs, Republic of Liberia. *Report of Investigation in the Matter of the Sinking of Passenger Vessel Explorer (O.N. 8495) 23 November 2007 in the Bransfield Strait near the South Shetland Islands*. Monrovia, Liberia: Bureau of Maritime Affairs. 2009.

Conrad, Joseph. *Chance*. Garden City, NY: Doubleday, Page & Company, 1926.

———. *The Mirror of the Sea: Memories and Impressions*. London: J.M. Dent and Sons, Ltd., 1906.

———. "Protection of Ocean Liners" *Notes on Life and Letters*. London: Doubleday Page & Co., 1925.

———. "Well Done" *Notes on Life and Letters*. London: Doubleday Page & Co., 1925.

———. *Youth: A Narrative*. Garden City, NY: Doubleday, Page & Company, 1926.

Cooke, F.S.A. *The Shipwreck of Sir Cloudesley Shovell, on the Scilly Islands in 1707*. Gloucester: John Bellows. http://www.hmssurprise.org/Resources/SIR_CLOUDESLEY_SHOVELL.html. Accessed July 19, 2008.

Cordesman, A.H. and A.R. Wagner. *The Lessons of Modern War: The Gulf War*. Boulder, CO: Westview Press, 2006.

Cowan, E. *Oil and Water: The Torrey Canyon Disaster*. Philadelphia, PA: J.B. Lippencott Company, 1968.

Crowley Marine Services, Inc. v. Maritrans, Inc., 530 F. 3d (9th Cir. 2008).

Davis v. Stena Line [2005] 2 Lloyd's Report 13 (Q.B.).

Deep Water Writing Of Life At Sea And On Shore, "Casualty Analysis," April 16, 2010. http://adeeplife.blogspot.com/2010/04/casualty-analysis.html. Accessed July 23, 2010.

Defense Mapping Agency. *The American Practical Navigator: An Epitome of Navigation*. Bethesda, MD: Defense Mapping Agency Hydrographic/Topographic Center, 1995.

Dekker, Sidney. *Drift into Failure: From Hunting Broken Components to Understanding Complex Systems*. Burlington, VT: Ashgate Publishing Company, 2011.

———. *Just Culture: Balancing Safety and Accountability*. Burlington, VT: Ashgate Publishing Company, 2007.

DeRose, James F. *Unrestricted Warfare: How a New Breed of Officers Lead the Submarine to Victory in World War II*. New York, New York: John Wiley & Sons, Inc., 2000.

Desiderio v. Celebrity Cruise Lines, Inc., 1999 American Maritime Cases 2723 (S.D.N.Y. 1999).

Devanney, J. *The Tankship Tromedy: The Impending Disasters In Tankers*. Tavernier, FL: The CTX Press, 2006.

Dewar, M. D. *Collision at Sea — How?* Gasgow: Brown, Son & Ferguson, Ltd. 1989.

———. "Uses and Abuses."

Diestel, Hans-Hermann. *Compendium on Seamanship & Sea Accidents: A practical guide to improve Seamanship and to prevent Sea Accidents*. Hamburg: Seehafen Verlag GmbH, 2005.

Dismukes, R. Key, email to author, June 14, 2010. and Ben Berman. "Checklists and Monitoring in the Cockpit: Why Crucial Defenses Sometimes Fail." Moffett Field, CA: NASA, 2010.

DNV. "Poor safety training a hidden safety risk." *DNV Classification News* (October 2006): 4.

Donaldson, Lord of Lymington. "A Rocky Road to Maritime Safety." Royal Nautical Lifeboat Institute/University of Southampton Annual Lecture (December 2001) http://www.eprints.soton. ac.uk. Accessed March 13, 2010.

———. "The ISM Code: the Road to Discovery." *Lloyd's Maritime and Commercial Law Quarterly*, 1998: 526-531.

Dotterway, K. "Systemic Analysis of Complex Dynamic Systems: The Case of the USS *Vincennes.*" Thesis. Monterey, CA: Naval Post Graduate School, 1992.

Duckworth, S. *Destroyers on the Rocks: Seven Ships Lost*. Fort Bragg, CA: Cypress House, 2005.

Duncan, Francis. *Rickover and the Nuclear Navy: The Discipline of Technology*. Annapolis, MD: Naval Institute Press, 1990.

Eaton, John. "A Captain's Career." *Encyclopedia Titanica*. http://www.encyclopedia-titanica.org/titanic-captain-smith-a-captains-career.html. Accessed March 9, 2010.

Editorial. "Lookout." *Fairplay* (September 14, 2006): 1.

Edwards, Bernard. *Beware the Grey Widow-Maker.* New York: Brick Tower Press, 2004.

Edwards, Bernard. *Return of the Coffin Ships: The Derbyshire Enigma.* New York: Brick Tower Press, 1998.

Edwards, Michael M. "The Court-Martial of Chester W. Nimitz." *Naval Institute Proceedings* (June 1994): 66-68.

Ellis, Nick. "Making Sense of Differences in Perception of Risk." Paper, Cardiff Symposium, 2009: 9-24.

———. "Safety and Perception of Risk," Fourth International Symposium, Seafarers International Research Centre, Cardiff University, 2006.

Endsley, M. *Design and Evaluation for Situational Awareness.* (1999).

Endsley, M. "Situation Awareness and Human Error: Designing to Support Human Performance." *Proceedings of the High Consequence Systems Security Conference*: Albuquerque, NM (1999).

Endsley, M. "Toward a Theory of Situational Awareness in Dynamic Systems." *Human Factors* 37(1995): 32-64.

Endsley, M. and Garland, D. eds. *SA Analysis And Measurement.* Mahwah, NJ: Lawrence Erlbaum Associates, 2000.

Ermann, M.D. and R.J. Lundman (eds.). *Corporate And Governmental Deviance: Problems Of Organizational Behavior In Contemporary Society,* New York: Oxford University Press, 2001.

Evans, David Lt. Col. *"Vincennes – A Case Study," United States Naval Institute Proceedings*, August, 1993: 49-56.

Exxon Shipping Company v. Baker, 554 U.S. 471 (2008).

Faller, Craig. "Shiphandling Training? Ask Your JOs." *Naval Institute Proceedings* (March 2003):104-05.

Federal Bureau of Maritime Casualty Investigation (Germany). *Grounding of the LT Cortesia on 2 January 2008 on the Varne Bank in the English Channel.* 01/08. 1 April 2009.

———. *Summary Investigation Report – Grounding of the M/V Pacific Challenger to the East of Oro Bay/Papua New Guinea on 9 April 2008.* Report 167/08. 2 February 2009.

Finkelstein, S., J. Whitehead and A. Campbell. *Think Again: Why Good Leaderss Make Bad Decisions and How to Keep It From Happening to You.* Boston, MA: Harvard Business Press, 2008.

Fisher, C. and B. Kingma. "Criticality of data quality as exemplified in two disasters." *Information & Management* 39 (2001): 109-16.

Fischer, U. *Cultural Variability of Crew Discourse: Final Report*. Atlanta, GA: Georgia Institute of Technology, n.d.

Fischer, U. and J. Orasanu. *Error-Challenging Strategies: Their Role in Preventing and Correcting Errors*. San Diego, CA: Proceedings of the International Ergonomics Association, August 2000.

Flin, Rhona. "Erosion of Managerial Resilience: From VASA to NASA" in Erik Hollnagel, David D. Woods and Nancy Leveson, eds. *Resilience Engineering: Concepts and Precepts*, 223-233. Burlington, VT: Ashgate Publishing Company, 2006.

Frame, Tom. *Where Fate Calls: The HMAS Voyager Tragedy*. Sydney, Australia: Hodder & Stoughton, 1992.

Frost, Holloway H. *On a Destroyer's Bridge*. Annapolis, MD: United States Naval Institute, 1930.

Fuller, Thomas. *Gnomologia: Adages and Proverbs*. 1732.

Gadd, S. and A.M. Collins. *Safety Culture: A Review of the Literature*. Sheffield: Health and Safety Laboratory, 2002.

Gale, Harry and David Patraiko. "Improving Navigation Safety." *Seaways* (July 2007): 4-8.

Gaouette, Mark. *Cruising For Trouble: Cruise Ships as Soft Targets*. Santa Barbara, CA: Praeger, 2010.

Gates, Edward T. *Maritime Accidents: What Went Wrong?* Houston, TX: Gulf Publishing Company, 1989.

Gatfield, D. "Are Current Risk Management Strategies Within the Commercial Shipping Industry Adequate?" Southampton: Warsash Maritime Centre, 1999.

Gehman, H. "Ethical Challenges for Organizations: Lessons Learned from the USS *Cole* and Challenger Tragedies." Speech, 2005. www.usna.edu/Ethics/Publications/GehmanPgl-28_Final.pdf. Accessed October 17, 2009.

———. "Lost Patrol: The Attack on the *Cole*." *Naval Institute Proceedings* (April 2001): 34-37.

Ghys, R. and N. Cormack. "An Investigation into the Loss of the Steel Bark *Admiral Karpfanger*." *Marine Technology* 40 (2004): 141-158.

Gibb, Randy and Wes Olson. "Classification of Air Force Accidents: Mishap Trends and Prevention." Tempe, AZ: Arizona State

University, Department of Industrial Engineering, 2006.

Gilbert, Daniel and Tennille Tracy. "Transocean Cites Safety in Bonuses." *Wall Street Journal* (April 2, 2011): B1-3.

Gilroy, Paul. *The Black Atlantic: Modernity and Double Consciousness.* Cambridge, MA: Harvard University Press, 1993.

Gladwell, Maxwell. *Blink: The Power Of Thinking Without Thinking.* New York: Little Brown and Company, 2005.

Gordon, A. *The Rules of the Game: Jutland and British Naval Command.* Annapolis, MD: Naval Institute Press, 1996.

Goyer, Robert. "Safety Against the Odds." *Flying* (May 2010): 50-58.

Grabowski, Martha. "Accident Precursors and Safety Nets: Initial Results from the Leading Indicators of Safety Project." *ABS Technical Papers 2007*: 285-93.

———. "Leading Indicators of Safety in Virtual Organizations." *Safety Science* 54 (2006): 1013-43.

Gray, David. *New Age Military Progressives: United States Army Officer Professionalism in the Information Age.* Carlisle Barracks, PA: United States Army War College, 2001.

Grech, Michelle and Tim Horberry. "Human error in maritime operations: Analysis of Accident reports using the Leximancer tool." Paper presented at the 46th Annual Meeting of the Human Factors and Ergonomics Society, Baltimore, MD, 2002.

Grech, M. and Tim Horberry. *Human factors in the Maritime Domain,* Boca Raton, FL: CCH Press, 2008.

Green, Rod. *Building the Titanic: The Creation of History's Most Famous Ocean Liner.* Pleasantville, NY: Readers Digest, 2005.

Greenhill, Basil and Ann Giffard. *Steam, Politics & Patronage: The Transformation Of The Royal Navy 1815-1854.* London: Conway Maritime Press, 1994.

Gribben, John and Mary Gribben. *FitzRoy: The Remarkable Story of Darwin's Captain and the Inventor of the Weather Forecast.* New Haven, CT: Yale University Press, 2004.

Gutridge, L. *Mutiny: A Study of Naval Insurrection.* Annapolis, MD: Naval Institute Press, 1992.

Habberley, J.S. and C.A. Shaddick. "A Behavioural Study of the Collision Avoidance Task in Bridge Watchkeeping." Marine Directorate, Department of Transportation, January 31, 1986.

Hadnett, E. "A Bridge Too Far?" *Journal of Navigation.* 61(2008): 283-289.

Hagart, J. and Crawshaw, C.M. "Personality Factors and Ship. Handling Behaviour." *Journal of Navigation.* 34 (1981): 202-06.

Hanninen, Hannu. *Negotiated Risks – the Estonia Accident and the Stream of Bow Visor Failures in the Baltic Ferry Traffic.* Helsinki: Helsinki School of Economics, 2007.

Hanninen, H. and Laurila, J. "Risk Regulation in the Baltic Sea Ferry Traffic: The Successive Failures in Bow Door Technology." *Science Technology Human Values* 33 (2008): 683-706.

Hanzu-Pazara, R. and others. "Reducing of Maritime Accidents Caused by Human Factors Using Simulators in Training Process." *Journal of Maritime Research,* V (2008): 3-18.

Harlaftis, Gelina. *A History of Greek-Owned Shipping.* London: Routledge, 1996.

Harrald, J.R. and T.A. Mazzuchi. "Using System Simulation to Model the Impact of Human Error in a Maritime System." *Safety Science* 30 (1998): 235-47.

Harris, D. and F. Morley. "An Open Systems Approach to Safety Culture: Actions, Influences and Concerns."

Harris, G. *The Trinity House of Deptford 1514-1660.* London: The Athlone Press, 1969.

Haynes, Al. "The Crash of United Flight 232." Speech, Edwards, CA: NASA, Dryden Flight Research Facility, 1991.

Hee, D.D. and B.D. Pickrell. "Safety Management Assessment System (SMAS): a process for identifying and evaluating human and organizational factors in marine system operations with field test results." *Reliability Engineering and System Safety.* 65 (1999).

Hellenic Republic Ministry of Transport & Communications - Air Accident Investigation & Aviation Safety Board. *Aircraft Accident Report Helios Airways Flight HCY522 Boeing 737-31S at Grammatiko, Hellas on 14 August 2005.*

Helmreich, Robert. "Building Safety on the Three Cultures of Aviation," Proceedings of the IATA Human Factors Seminar, Bangkok, Thailand, 1998.

———. "Culture, Threat, and Error: Assessing System Safety." Austin, TX: University of Texas at Austin, Human Factors Research Project 257, (circa 2000).

————. "Error Management as Organizational Strategy." Austin, Texas: University of Texas Aerospace Crew Research Project, 1998.

————. "On error management: lessons from aviation."*British Medical Journal* 320 (2000): 781-85.

Helmreich, Robert and Ashley Merritt. "The Evolution of Crew Resource Management Training in Commercial Aviation." *International Journal of Aviation Psychology* 9 (1998): 19-32.

Heranger [1938] 62 Lloyd's Rep. 204.

In re Hercules Carriers, Inc., 728 F.2d 1359 (11th Cir. 1984) (en banc), *cert. denied*, 469 U.S. 835 (1984).

Hermansson, R. *The History of Stena Bulk*. Goteborg, Sweden: Breakwater Publishing, 2007.

Hetherington, Catherine, Rhona Flin and Kathryn Mearns. "Safety in Shipping: The Human Element." *Journal of Safety Research* 37 (2006): 401-411.

Hockey, G.R.J., A. Healy, M. Crawshaw, D.G. Wastell and J. Sauer. "Cognitive demands of collision avoidance in simulated ship control." *Human Factors* 45 (2003): 252-264.

Hofstede, Geert and Geert Jan Hofstede. *Cultures and Organizations: Software of the Mind*. New York: McGraw-Hill, 2005 (2d ed.).

Hollnagel, Erik. *The ETTO Principle: Efficiency – Thoroughness Trade – Off*. Burlington, VT: Ashgate Publishing Company, 2009.

Holmes, Oliver Wendell. *The Common Law*. Cambridge, MA: Harvard University Press, 1963.

Hooke, N. *Modern Shipping Disasters 1963-1987*. London: Lloyd's of London Press, 1989.

Hopkins, Andrew. "Risk Management and Rule Compliance: Decision Making in Hazardous Industries." Paper, Australian National University, 2010.

———— *Safety, Culture and Risk: The Organisational Causes of Disasters*. Sydney, NSW, Australia: CCH Australia Limited, 2005.

Houtman, Irene and others. "Fatigue In The Shipping Industry." Netherlands Organization for Applied Scientific Research Academic Medical Centre ("TNO"), 2005. http://www.he-alert. org/documents/published/he00605.pdf. Accessed December 11, 2010.

Hudson, P. and others. "Bending the Rules II: Why do people break rules or fail to follow procedures? And what can you do about it?" Leiden: Universiteit Leiden, n.d.

Hughes, Richard. *In Hazard: Four Days of Terror at Sea.* Old Saybrook, CT: Capstan Press, 1998.

Hunter, Mark. *A Society of Gentlemen: Midshipmen At The United States Naval Academy.* Annapolis, MD: Naval Institute Press, 2010.

Huntzinger, David Lee. *The motivating factors and perceptions of risk associated with intentional rule breaking among aviators.* Ph.D. Thesis: The Union Institute, 1995.

Hurst, A.A. *The Call of High Canvas.* London: Cassell & Company Ltd., 1958.

Hutchins, Edward. *Cognition in the Wild.* Cambridge, MA: MIT Press, 1995.

IMO. "Study on the Impact of the ISM Code and its Effectiveness in the Enhancement of Safety of Life at Sea and Protection of the Marine Environment." 2005.

Inoue, K. and M. Kawase. "Innovative Probabilistic Prediction of Accident Occurrence." Paper, Gdynia, Poland: Transnav, 2007.

International Regulations for Preventing Collisions at Sea (1972 COLREGS), as amended.

Jalonen, R. and K. Salmi. "Safety Performance Indicators for Maritime Safety Management." Helsinki, Finland: Helsinki University of Technology, 2008.

James, M. "The Timing of Collision Avoidance Manoeuvers: Descriptive Mathematical Models." *Journal of Navigation.* 47 (1984): 259-72.

Job, Macarthur. *Air Disaster* Vol. 1. Fyshwick, Australia: Aerospace Publications Pty Ltd., 1994.

———. *Air Disaster* Vol. 2. Weston Creek, Australia: Aerospace Publications Pty Ltd., 1996.

Johannesen, L.J. and others. *Behind Human Error: Cognitive Systems, Computers And Hindsight.* Dayton, OH: CSERIAC, 2000.

Johnson, Chris W. and C.M. Holloway. "On the Over-Emphasis of Human 'Error' as a Cause of Aviation Accidents: 'Systemic Failures' and 'Human Error' in United States NTSB and Canadian TSB Aviation Reports 1996-2003." Paper, n.d.: 1-34.

Johnson, Chris. "Using CAE Diagrams To Visualize the Arguments in Accident Reports." University of Glasgow, 1999. http://www.dcs.

gla.ac.uk/~johnson/papers/cae_99/. Accessed March 1, 2007.

Jones, A. *Sea Like A Mirror – Reflections Of A Merchantman*. Caithness: Scotland, 2005.

Jones, D. and M. Endsley. "Investigation of Situation Errors." Columbus, OH: Eighth International Symposium on Aviation Psychology, 1995.

Jones, Nicolette. *The Plimsoll Sensation: The Great Campaign to Save Lives at Sea*. London: Little Brown Book Group, 2006.

Kaplan, Abraham. *The Conduct of Inquiry: Methodology of Behavioral Science*. San Francisco, CA: Chandler Publishing Co., 1964.

Kaplan, M. "The Culture at Work: Cultural Ergonomics." *Ergonomics* 38 (1995): 606-12.

Karlsson, U. and A. Ufvarson. "Chain Breakers – A Survey of Fatal Ship Accidents with Event-Chain Method." *Marine Technology*. 48 (2008): 182-190.

Karwal, Arun and R. Verkaik. "Non-Adherence to Procedures – Why does it happen?" crm.devel.com/resources/paper/Non%20Adherence%20to%20Procedures %20Karwal.pdf. Accessed January 10, 2010.

Kendra, J. *Looking Out the Window: Risk, Work, and Technological Change in U.S. Merchant Shipping*. Dissertation. New Brunswick, NJ: The State University of New Jersey, 2000.

Kern, Tony. *Darker Shades of Blue: The Rogue Pilot*. New York, NY: McGraw-Hill.

Kipling, Rudyard. "The Secret of the Machines," 1911.

Klein, G. *The Power Of Intuition*. New York, NY: Doubleday, 2004.

Klein, G. *Sources Of Power: How People Make Decision*. Cambridge, MA: MIT Press, 1998 (2d ed.)

Kluckholm, C. "The Study of Culture" in Lerner, D. and H.D. eds., *The Policy Sciences*. Palo Alto, CA: Stanford University Press, 1951.

Knight, Roger. *The Pursuit of Victory: The Life and Achievement of Horatio Nelson*. New York: Basic Books, 2005.

Knudsen, F. "Paperwork at the Service of Safety? Workers' reluctance against written procedures exemplified by the concept of 'seamanship'." *Safety Science*. 47 (2009): 295-303.

Konrad, John. "Today's Captain is Expected Not to Make Any Mistakes." *Sidelights* (Fall 2009): 18-19.

———— and Tom Shroder. *Fire on the Horizon: The Untold Story of the Gulf Oil Disaster.* New York, NY: Harper-Collins Publisher, 2011.

Kuo, Chengi. *Safety Management and its Maritime Application.* London: The Nautical Institute, 2007.

Lady Gwendolen [1965] 1 Lloyd's Rpt. 335 (C.A.).

Landersman, Stuart. "Where Have All the Shiphandlers Gone?" *Naval Institute Proceedings* (August 2006): 54-58.

Langewiesche, William. "The Devil at 37,000 feet." *Vanity Fair* (January 2009).

Le Goubin, Andre. "Mentoring and the Transfer of Experiential Knowledge in Today's Merchant Fleet." Weintrit (ed.) *Marine Navigation and Safety of Sea Transportation.* London: Taylor & Francis Group, 2009.

Lebedoff, David. *Cleaning Up: The Story Behind the Biggest Legal Bonanza of Our Time.* New York: The Free Press, 1997.

Leeman, William. *The Long Road to Annapolis – The Founding of the Naval Academy and the Emerging American Republic.* Chapel Hill, NC: University of North Carolina Press, 2010.

Leiden, K. and John Keller. "Context of Human Error in Commercial Aviation." Boulder, CO: Micro Analysis & Design, Inc., 2001.

Levadou. Marc and Guilhem Gaillarde. "Operational Guidance to Avoid Parametric Roll." http://www.marin-nl/upload-mm.e.1.f.1806711731-7999999096-dal0722.pdf. Accessed May 10, 2010.

Levee Investigation Team Report. http://www.ce.berkeley.edu/~neworleans/report/Draft/CH13.pdf. Accessed February 23, 2009.

Leveson, Nancy. *Engineering a Safer World.* Cambridge, MA: MIT Press, (in press).

Leveson, Nancy. "White Paper on Approaches to Safety Engineering." Paper adapted from Leveson, *Software.* Addison-Wesley, 1995.

Li, W-C. and D. Harris. "Eastern Minds in Western Cockpits: Meta-Analysis of Human Factors in Mishaps from Three Nations." *Aviation, Space, and Environmental Medicine* (2007).

Los Angeles Times, "Manslaughter Trial in '87 British Ferry

Disaster Collapses," October 19, 1990. http://articles.latimes.
com/1990-10-19/business/fi-2903_1_ferry-disaster. Accessed
November 27, 2010.

Louie, Vivianne and Toni Doolen. "A Study of Factors that Contribute
to Maritime Fatigue." *Marine Technology* 44 (2007): 82-92.

Lutzhoft, Margareta. *The Technology is Great When it Works: Maritime
Technology and Human Integration on the Ship's Bridge.* Linkoping
Studies in Science and Technology. Dissertation No. 907 (2004).

Lutzhoft, M. and S. Dekker, "On Your Watch – Automation on the
Bridge." *Journal of Navigation* 55 (2002): 83-96.

Lutzhoft, M. and J. Nyce, J., "Integration Work on the Ship's Bridge."
Journal of Maritime Research. V (2008): 59-74.

Macalister, Terry. "Owners Continue To Sideline Safety." *Tradewinds*,
May 1, 2009, 2.

MacDonald, Laura. *Curse Of The Narrows.* New York: Walker &
Company, 2004.

Maffeo, Steven. *Seize, Burn or Sink: The Thoughts And Word Of Admiral
Lord Horatio Nelson.* Lanham, MD: Scarecrow Press, Inc., 2007.

Mandaraka-Sheppard, Aleka. Modern Maritime Law: and Risk
Management. London: Routledge-Cavendish, 2007 (2nd ed.).

Margate Shipping Co. v. J.A. Orgeron, 143 F.3d 976 (5th Cir. 1998).

Marine Accident Investigation Branch (UK). *Report On The Investigation
Of The Collapse Of Cargo Containers On Annabella Baltic Sea 26
February 2007.* Report 21/2007. September 2007.

————. *Report on the Investigation of the Grounding of the Italian Registered
Chemical Tanker Attilio Ievoli on Lymington Banks in the West Solent,
South Coast of England, 3 June 2004.* Report No. 2/2005, February
2005.

————. *Report on the Investigation of the Grounding of Berit Trindelen
Bank, near Gedser, Denmark 5 January 2006.* Report No. 17/2006,
July 2006.

————. *Report On The Investigation Of A Close Quarter Situation Between
Costa Atlantica And Grand Neptune In The Dover Strait On 15 May
2008.* Report 20/2008, November, 2008.

————. *Report on the investigation of the collision between Cepheus J and
Ileksa in the Kattegat 22 November 200,* July 2005.

————. *Report on the Investigation of the Grounding of the Vessel CP Valour
in Baia de Praia do Norte, Faial, Azores on 9 December 2005.* Report
22/2006, August 2006.

———. *Report on the Investigation of the Collision of Dole America with the Nab Tower in the Eastern Approaches to The Solent on 7 November 1999.* Report 32/2000.

———. *Report on the Investigation of the Collision between Hyundai Dominion and Sky Hope in the East China Sea, 21 June 2004.* Report 17/2005, August 2005.

———. *Report on the Investigation of the Contact by Isle of Arran with the Linkspan at Kennacraig West Loch Tarbert, Kintyre 6 February 2010.* Report 13/2010, October 2010.

———. *Report on the Investigation of the Collision between Sea Express I and Alaska Rainbow on the River Mersey, 3 February 2007.* Report 22/2007, 2007.

———. *Report on the Investigation of the Collision between Skagern and Samskip Courier in the Humber Estuary, 7 June 2006.* Report 6/2007, April 2007.

———. *Report on the Investigation of the Investigation of the Grounding of Maersk Kendal on Monggok Sebarok Reef in the Singapore Strait on 16 September 2009.* Report 2/2010, March 2010.

———. *Report on the Investigation of the Loss of Cargo Containers Overboard from P&O Nedlloyd Genoa, North Atlantic Ocean on 27 January 2006.* Report 20/2006, August 2006.

———. *Report on the Investigation of the Collision between Xuchanghai and Aberdeen at Immingham Oil Terminal 12 December 2000.* Report 30/2001, August 2001.

Maritime & Coast Guard Agency (MCA). "Driving Safety Culture: Identification of Leadership Qualities for Effective Safety Management." Research Project 521 (October 2004).

Maritime Investigator of Norway and United States Coast Guard. *Report of Investigation into the Circumstances Surrounding the Grounding of the Monarch of the Seas on Proselyte Reef in Great Bay, Philipsburg, St. Maarten, Netherlands Antilles on December 15, 1998* (Joint Investigation). April 2003.

Maritime Safety Authority of New Zealand. *Aratere Near Grounding, Tory Channel,* Class A Accident Report, 2005.

Martins, Marcels Ramos and Marcos Coelho Maturana. "Human Error Contribution in Collision and Grounding of Oil Tankers. *Risk Analysis* 30 (2010): 674-698.

Mattsson, Algot. *Out of the Fog: The Sinking of Andrea Doria.* Centreville, MD: Cornell Maritime Press, 2003.

Maybourn, R. "The Navigator – Man or Machine?" *Journal of Navigation* 40 (1988): 334-43.

McCallum, M. and others, "Procedures for Investigating and Reporting Human Factors and Fatigue Contributions to Marine Casualties – Final Report." Groton, CT: Coast Guard Research & Development Center, 1996.

McCann, Captain Derek. *A Study of Irrational Decisions by Experienced Personnel While Working Under Time Constraints.* Dissertation, Liverpool: John Moores University, 2009.

McFee, William. *In the First Watch.* New York: Random House, 1946.

McPhee, J. *Looking for a Ship.* New York: The Noonday Press – Farrar Straus Giroux, 1990.

Meek, Marshall. *There Go the Ships.* London: The Memoir Club, 2003.

MerchantNavyOfficers.com. "The Cunard Steam-Ship Company Limited." http://www.merchantnavyofficers.com/cunard3.html. Accessed August 20, 2010.

Merrick, Jason and Rene van Dorp. "Speaking the Truth in Maritime Risk Assessment," *Risk Analysis* 26 (2006): 223-237.

Merritt, Ashleigh. "Culture in the Cockpit: Do Hofstede's Dimensions Replicate?" *Journal of Cross-Culture Psychology* 31 (2000): 283-301.

Merton, Robert K. "The Unanticipated Consequences of Purposive Social Action." *American Sociological Review* (December 1936): 894-904.

Meur, Chrystelle le. "Maritime Safety Culture." LLM Thesis: University of Northumbria School of Law, 2003.

Meurn, R. *Watchstanding Guide for the Merchant Officer.* Centreville, MD: Cornell Maritime Press, 2008.

Miles, Jonathan. *The Wreck of the Medusa: The Most Famous Sea Disaster of the Nineteenth Century.* New York: Atlantic Monthly Press, 2007.

Mitchell, E. *Strategies to Reduce Aviation Employee's Procedural Non-Compliance.* London: City University, 2005.

Mitroff, Ian and Thierry Pauchant. *We're So Big and Powerful Nothing Bad Can Happen to Us: An Investigation of America's Crisis Prone Corporations.* Secaucus, NJ: Birch Lane Press, 1990.

Mitropoulos, Efthimios, IMO Secretary General, keynote address at quadrennial IATA Conference, Shanghai, PRC, May 22, 2006.

Morel, Gael, Rene Amalberti and Christine Chauvin. "Articulating the Difference Between Safety and Resilience: The Decision-Making Process of Professional Sea-Fishing Skippers." *Human Factors* 50 (2008): 1-16.

Morison, Elting E. *Men, Machines, and Modern Times.* Cambridge, MA: M.I.T. Press, 1966.

Morris, N. *The Brothel Boy and Other Parables of the Law.* London: Oxford University Press, 1994.

Morton, J. *The Role of the Physical Environment in Ancient Greek Seafaring.* Leiden: Koninklijke Brill NV, 2001.

Moshansky, Hon. V.P. "Commission of Inquiry into the Air Ontario Crash at Dryden, Ontario: Final Report." Ottawa, Ontario: Ministry of Supply and Services, 1992.

Murnane v. American Airlines, Inc., 667 F.2d 98 (D.C. Cir. 1981).

Nagl, J. *Learning to Eat Soup with a Knife: Counterinsurgency Lessons.* Chicago: University of Chicago Press, 2005.

National Commission on the BP Deepwater Horizon Oil Spill and Offshore Drilling, *Deep Water: The Gulf Oil Disaster and the Future of Offshore Drilling.* Washington, DC, 2011.

National Research Council. *Minding the Helm: Marine Navigation and Piloting.* Washington, DC: National Academic Press, 1994.

National Transportation Safety Board. *Loss of Control on Approach Colgan Air, Inc. … Bombardier DHC-8-400, N200WQ Clarence Center, New York February 12, 2009.* AAR-10/01, 2010.

———. *Crash of Pinnacle Airlines Flight 3701 Bombardier CL-600-2B19, N8396A Jefferson City, Missouri October 14, 2004.* AAR-07/01, January 9, 2007.

———. *Loss of Thrust Both Engines after Encountering a Flock of Birds and Subsequent Ditching on the Hudson River US Airways Flight 1549 Airbus A320-214, N106 US Weehawken, New Jersey January 15, 2009.* AAR-10-03, May 4, 2010.

———. *Allision of Staten Island Ferry Andrew J. Barberi, St. George, Staten Island, New York, October 15, 2003.* MAR-05-01, 2005.

———. *Allision of Bahamas-Registered Tankship M/T Axel Spirit with Ambrose Light Entrance to New York Harbor November 3, 2007.* MAR-09-02, April 7, 2009.

——. *Allision of the Liberian Freighter Bright Field with the Poydras Street Wharf, Riverwalk Marketplace and New Orleans Hilton Hotel Ii New Orleans, Louisiana, December 14, 1996.* MAR-98-01, January 13, 1998.

——. *Grounding of the U.S. Tankship S.S. Concho at Constable Hook Reach of Kill Van Kull Upper New York, Harbor, January 19, 1981.* MAR-81-11, August 11, 1981.

——. *Allison Of Hong Kong-Registered Containership M/V Cosco Busan with the Delta Tower of the San Francisco-Oakland Bay Bridge, San Francisco, California, November 7, 2007.* MAR-09-01, February 18, 2009.

——. *Heeling Accident on M/V Crown Princess Atlantic Ocean off Port Canaveral, Florida July 18, 2006.* MAR-08-02, January 30, 2008.

——. *Grounding of U.S. Passenger Vessel Empress of the North, Intersection of Lynn Canal and Icy Strait Southeast Alaska, May 14, 2007.* MAR-08-02, November 4, 2008.

——. *Grounding of U.S. Tankership Exxon Valdez on Bligh Reef, Prince William Sound near Valdez, AK, March 24, 1989.* MAR-90-04, July 31, 1990.

——. *Collision between U.S. Navy Submarine USS Greeneville and Japanese Motor Vessel Ehime Maru Near Oahu, Hawaii, February 9, 2001.* MAB-05-01, September 29, 2005.

——. *Allision of the Liberian-Registered Fruit Juice Carrier M/V Orange Sun with U.S.-Registered Dredge New York Newark Bay, New Jersey, January 24, 2008.* MAR-09-03, December 2, 2009.

——. *Near Grounding of the Liberian Tank Ship Patriot, Bay off Campeche, Mexico, October 15, 1995.* MAR-97-01, April 8, 1997.

——. *Grounding of the Panamanian Passenger Ship Royal Majesty on Rose and Crown Shoal near Nantucket, Massachusetts, June 10, 1995.* MAR-97-01, April 2, 1997.

——. *Grounding of the Liberian passenger ship Star Princess on Poundstone Rock, Lynn Canal, Alaska, June 23, 1995.* MAR-97-02, June 20, 1997.

——. *Ramming of the Spanish Bulk Carrier Urduliz by the USS Dwight D. Eisenhower (CVN 69) Hampton Roads, Virginia August 29.* MAR-90-01, January 3, 1990.

New York Times, "Another Smooth Landing for a Hero," January 9, 2010: C-3.

New York Times, "Setting the Sextant Aside" (editorial), May 22, 1998.

Nicholls, *Seamanship and Nautical Knowledge.* Glasgow: Brown, Son & Ferguson Ltd. 1966.

Norske Veritas. Study submitted to the IMO by Norway in 1983. www.globalsecurity.org/military/systems/ship/ro-ro-safety.htm. Accessed November 14, 2010.

Ocean Marine Limited v. United States Lines Company, 300 F.3d 496 (2d Cir. 1962).

Ocean S.S. Co. of Savannah v. United States, 38 F.2d 782 (2d. Cir. 1930).

Orasanu, J., Martin, L. and J. Davidson. "Cognitive and Contextual Factors in Aviation Accidents: Decision Errors" in Salas, E. and G. Klein (eds.) *Applications of Naturalistic Decision Making.* Mahwah, NJ: Lawrence Erlbaum Associates, 2001.

In re Otal Investments Ltd., 2006 WL 14512 (S.D.N.Y.), aff'd in part, rev. in part *Otal Investments, Ltd. v. M.V. Clary,* 494 F.3d 40 (2d Cir. 2007).

In re Potomac Transport, Inc., 909 F.2d 42 (2d Cir. 1990).

Pantankar, Manoj. "A Comparative Review of Safety Cultures." St. Louis, MO: St. Louis University, 2005.

———. *Root Cause Analysis of Rule Violations by Aircraft Maintenance Technicians.* Washington, DC: FAA Office of Aviation Medicine, 2002.

Papera Traders co. Ltd. v. Hyundai Merchant Marine Co., Ltd. [Eurasian Dream] [2002] All ER 101.

Parker, Bruce. *The Power of the Sea: Tsunamis, Storm Surges, Rogue Waves, and Our Quest to Predict Disasters.* New York: Palgrave Macmillan, 2010.

Parker, C.J. *Managing Risk in Shipping.* London: The Nautical Institute, 1999.

Parrott, Daniel S. *Bridge Resource Management for Small Ships. The Watchkeeper's Manual for Limited-Tonage Vessels.* Camden, Maine: International Marine/McGraw Hill, 2011.

Pate-Cornell, M.E. and D. Murphy. "Human and Management Factors in Probabilistic Risk Analysis: The SAM Approach and Observations from Recent Applications." *Reliability Engineering and Systems Safety* 53 (1996): 115-126.

Patraiko, David. eNavigation 2010 Conference. Seattle, WA.

November 16, 2010.

Paul, G.A.S. "Correspondence." *Seaways* (February 2005): 29.

Pekcan, C. "Encouraging Attitude, Behaviour and Cognitive Change in Ship's Officers: As Simple as A B C?" 7th International Conference on Simulators, circa 2006.

Pekcan, C. and David Gatfield. "Content and Context: Understanding the Complexities of Human Behaviour in Ship Operation. Paper, n.d.

Perrow, C. *Normal Accidents: Living With Risk Technologies.* Princeton, NJ: Princeton University Press, 1999 (2d ed.).

Phimister, J.R. and V.M. Bier. *Accident Precursor Analysis and Management: Reducing Technological Risk Through Diligence.* Washington, DC: National Academic Press, 2003.

Pomeroy, V. "Perception and Management of Risk – Dependence on People and Systems." Paper, World Maritime Technology Conference, 2006.

Posner, Richard. *The Economics of Justice.* Chicago, IL: University of Chicago Press, 1981.

Potter, E.B. *Nimiz.* Annapolis, MD: Naval Institute Press, 1976.

Powell, Colin and Joseph Persico. *My American Journey.* New York: Random House, 1995.

Professional Mariner. "Attack of flatulence may have caused Florida grounding." 13 (June-July 1995): 56-7.

Psaraftis, H.N. and P. Caridis. "The Human Element as a Factor in Marine Accidents." (2000).

Puryear, Edgar F. Jr., *American Admiralship – The Moral Imperatives of Naval Command.* Annapolis, MD: Naval Institute Press, 2005.

Ramwell, D. and T. Madge. *A Ship Too Far: The Mystery of the Derbyshire.* London: Hodder & Stoughton, 1992.

Rasmussen, Jens. "Human Errors: A Taxonomy for Describing Human Malfunction in Industrial Installations." *Journal of Occupational Accidents,* 4 (1982): 311-33.

Rawlins, Michael. *The Last American Sailors: A Wild Ride In The Modern Merchant Marine.* Lincoln, NE: iUniverse, Inc., 2003.

Reason, James. "The Chernobyl Errors," *Bulletin of the British Psychological Society.*106 (1997): 321-31.

———. *Human Error.* Cambridge: Cambridge University Press, 1990.

————. *Managing the Risks of Organizational Accidents*. Burlington, VT: Ashgate Publishing Company, 1997.

————. *The Human Contribution: Unsafe Acts, Accidents and Heroic Recoveries*. Burlington, VT: Ashgate Publishing Company, 2008.

Reed, Stanley and Alison Fitzgerald. *In Too Deep: BP and the Drilling Race that Took It Down*. Hoboken, NJ: John Wiley & Sons, Inc. 2011.

Richter, I.A. *Selections from the Notebooks of Leonardo da Vinci*. London: Oxford University Press, 1952.

Rochlin, G. and others. "The Self-Designing High-Reliability Organization: Aircraft Carrier Flight Operations at Sea." *Naval War College Review* (Autumn 1987): 76-90.

Rockwell, Theodore. *The Rickover Effect: How One Man Made a Difference*. Lincoln, NB: iUniverse, 2002.

Rogge, Bernard. "Leadership on Board the Raider *Atlantis*." *Naval Institute Proceedings* (February 1962): 40-51.

Rowley, Ian. *Development of guidance for the mitigation of human error in automated shipborne maritime systems*. Gosport, United Kingdom: QinetiQ (MCA RP545), 2006.

Royster, Vermont C. "Editorial." *Wall Street Journal*, May 14, 1952.

Rynn, N. et al. "The Restoration of *Sea-Land Voyager*: Lessons Learned from a Flooded Engine Room." SNAME Transactions 104 (1996): 239-73.

In re S.D.S. Lumber Co., 567 F.Supp.2d 1302 (D.Or. 2008).

Samuelides, M. and D.P. Servis. "Bow door slamming of Ro/Ro ferries." *Marine Structures* 15 (2002): 285-307.

Sandberg, Captain George. United States Merchant Marine Academy, email to author, April 8, 2009.

Saxe, John Godfrey. "Six Blind Men and the Elephant."

Schager, Bengt. "A Wise Captain Knows His Own Mind." Paper. www. marine-profile.com/ bdh_filearea/pdf/a_wise_captain.pdf. Accessed December 21, 2010.

————. "Advantages of Psychological Assessment Prior to Employment and Promotion." Paper. www.marine-profile.com/bdh_filearea/ pdf/advantages.pdf. Accessed December 21, 2010.

————. *Human Error in the Maritime Industry: How to Understand, Detect and Cope*. Marine Profile Sweden AB, 2008.

————. "When Technology Leads Us Astray: A Broadened View of Human Error." *Journal of Navigation*. 61 (2008): 63-70.

Schein, E.H. *Organizational Culture and Leadership*. San Francisco,

CA: Jossey-Bass, 1985.

Schelling, Thomas C. "Foreword" in Roberta Wohlsetter, *Pearl Harbor.* Stanford, CA: Stanford University Press, 1992.

Schulz, Katherine. *Being Wrong: Adventures in the Margin of Error.* London: Portobello Books, 2010.

Schwartz, Barry and Kenneth Sharp, *Practical Wisdom: The Right Way to Do the Right Thing.* New York, NY: Riverhead Press, 2010.

SeaRiver Maritime Financial Holdings, Inc. v. Mineta, 309 F.3d 662 (9th Cir. 2002).

Seaways, "Aftermath of a Collision." (July 2000): 18. "Seconds From Disaster; Zeebrügge Ferry Disaster," Episode no. 18, first broadcast 16 August 2005 by National Geographic.

In re Seiriki Kisen Kaisha (Seiryu - Stena Freighter), 629 F. Supp. 1374, 1986 American Maritime Cases 913 (S.D.N.Y. 1986).

Sexton, J. Bryan and Eric J. Thomas. "Error, stress, and teamwork in medicine and Aviation: cross sectional surveys." *British Medical Journal* 320 (2000): 745-49.

Shalimar (Hendry, F.C.). *Down To the Sea.* Edinburgh: William Blackwood & Sons Ltd., 1937.

Shapell, D. and C. Detwiler. "Human Error and Commercial Aviation Accidents: A Comprehensive, Fine-Grained Analysis Using HFACS." *Human Factors* 49 (2007): 227-42.

Sheen, Barry. *Herald of Free Enterprise Report: Formal Investigation Report of Court No. 8074* [Sheen Report]. London: Her Majesty's Stationary Office, 1987.

Slocum, Joshua. *Sailing Alone Around the World.* London: Rupert Hart-Davis, The Mariner's Library, 1963.

Smith, Andy and Paul Allen. *Seafarer Fatigue: The Cardiff Research Programme.* Cardiff: Cardiff University, Centre for Occupational and Health Psychology, 2006.

Smith, Craig B. *Extreme Waves.* Washington, DC: Joseph Henry Press, 2006.

———. "Extreme Waves and Ship Design." 10th Intl. Symposium on Practical Design of Ships and Other Floating Structures. Houston, TX: (2007 PRADS) v. 2 pp. 1033-1040.

Smith, D. "Situation(al) Awareness (SA) in Effective Command and Control." (2003) www.smithrisca.Damon.co.uk/situational-awareness.html. Accessed April 2 2007.

Sneddon, A. and others. "Safety and Situation Awareness in

Offshore Crews." Richardson, TX: *Proceedings of the Seventh SPE International Conference on Health, Safety and Environment in Oil and Gas Exploration and Production*, 2004.

Sneddon, A. and P.T.W. Hudson. "A Comprehensive Model for Human Behaviour In Industrial Environments." Paper, n.d. www.adbn.ac.uk/iprc/Documents/pdf. Accessed December 21, 2010.

Snook, S. *Friendly Fire: The Accidental Shootdown Of U.S. Black Hawks Over Northern Iraq*. Princeton, New Jersey: Princeton University Press, 2000.

Solly, R. *Nothing Over the Side: Examining Safe Crude Oil Tankers*. Caithness, Scotland: Whittles Press, 2010.

Soma, Torkel. "Chances of ship casualty double." *Fairplay* (February 2008).

———. "Safety as a Competitive Edge." *American Club Currents* (June 2006).

Soma, Torkel and G. Fuglerud. "Safety Excellence – Safety that Lasts." Hovik, Norway. DNV Maritime Solutions (n.d.).

Spector, Robert. *On Course: Chevron's Century at Sea*. Woodinville, WA: Documentary Book Publishers Corporation, 1995.

Squire, D. "The Role of the Human Element in Navigation and Other Ship Systems." SOURCE

Stavridis, James. *Destroyer Captain: Lessons of a First Command*. Annapolis, MD: Naval Institute Press, 2008.

Steffy, Loren C. *Drowning in Oil: BP and the Relentless Pursuit of Profit*. New York, New York: McGraw Hill, 2010.

Stephens, H.W. *The Texas City Disaster 1947*. Austin, TX: University of Texas Press, 1997.

Strauch, Barry. "Can Cultural Differences Lead to Accidents? Team Cultural Differences and Their Effects on Sociotechnical System Operations." *Human Factors: The Journal of the Human Factors and Ergonomics Society* 52 (2010): 246-63.

Strong, Captain Prentice "Skip." Telephone interview June 4, 2010.

——— and Twain Braden. *In Peril: A Daring Decision, A Captain's Resolve, and the Salvage that Made History*. Guilford, CT: The Lyons Press, 2003.

Sutton, and Towill. "The Helmsman as a Man-Machine Element." *Journal of Navigation* 39 (1986).

Suzuki & Co. Ltd. v. J. Beynon & Co. Ltd., (1926) 42 TLR 269, 274.

Swedish Accident Investigation Board. *Loss of m/s Finnbirch between Olnd and Gotland, 1 November, 2006.* Report RS 2008:03e. 2007.

Szwed, P.S. and R.G. Bea. "Development of a Safety Management Assessment System for International Safety Management Code." Paper (n.d.).

Tasca, Leo. *The Social Construction of Human Error.* Dissertation, Stony Brook, NY: State University of New York, 1990.

The Plimsoll Club, http://www.plimsoll.com/history.html. Accessed July 29, 2010.

T.J. Hooper, 60 F.2d 737 (2d Cir. 1932).

Thomson, J. *Shackleton's Captain: A Biography of Frank Worsley.* Toronto: Mosaic Press, 1999.

Titania, 19 Fed. 101 (S.D.N.Y. 1883).

Trafford, Sean M. *Maritime Safety: The Human Factors.* Sussex, ENG: Book Guild Publishing, 2009.

Transport Accident Investigation Commission. *Marine Occurrence Report Bulk Log Carrier Jody F. Millenium, Grounding Gisborne 6 February 2002.* Report 02-201. Auckland: New Zealand, 2002.

———. *Marine Occurrence Report Coastal Bulk Carrier Anatoki and Bulk Carrier Lodestar Forest Collision Taurauga Harbour Roads 28 April 2008.* Report 08-202. Auckland: New Zealand, 2008.

———. *Marine Occurrence Report Bulk Carrier Tai Ping Grounding, Bluff Harbour 8 October 2002.* Report 02-206. Auckland: New Zealand, 2002.

———. *Marine Occurrence Report Passenger Ferry Aratere, Loss of Mode Awareness Leading to Near Grounding, Tory Channel.* Report 04-214. Auckland: New Zealand, 2004.

Transportation Research Board. *Risk of Vessel Accidents and Spills in the Aleutian Islands.* Washington, DC: Transportation Research Board, 2008.

Transportation Safety Board of Canada. "A Safety Study of the Operational Relationship Between Ship Masters/ Watchkeeping Officers and Marine Pilots." Report Number SM9501., n.d.

———. *Striking Bulk Self-Unloader Atlantic Huron and Canadian Coast Guard Ship Griffon, Pelee Passage, Lake Eire, 25 September 2000.* Report M00C0069.

————. *Grounding: The Bulk Carrier Great Century Off Batiscan, St. Lawrence River, Quebec, 26 February 2003.* Report M03L0026, December 15, 2004.

————. *Striking and Subsequent Sinking Passenger and Vehicle Ferry Queen of the North off Gil Island, Wright Sound, British Columbia 22 March 2006.* 2008.

In re Complaint and Petition of TRITON ASSET LEASING GMBH et al. United States District Court, Southern District of Texas, Houston Division, Docket No. 10CV01721, May 13, 2010.

Tsou, M. and others, "Decision Support from Genetic Algorithms for Ship Collision Avoidance, Route Planning and Alert." *Journal of Navigation* 63 (2010).

Twain, Mark. "About All Kinds of Ships." XVI Authorized Edition *The Complete Works of Mark Twain.* New York: Harper & Brothers, 1892.

Tzannatos, E., "Human Element and Accidents in Greek Shipping." *Journal of Navigation* 63 (2010): 119-24.

United Geophysical Co. v. Vela, 231 F.2d 816 (5th Cir. 1956).

United States v. Carroll Towing Co., 159 F.2d 169 (2d Circuit 1947).

United States v. Hanousek, 176 F.3d 1116 (9th Cir. 1999).

United States v. Hatfield, 591 F.3d 945 (7th Cir. 2010).

United States v. Jho, 534 F.3d 398 (5th Cir. 2008).

United States Coast Guard. *Report of Investigation into the Circumstances Surrounding the Explosion, Fire, Sinking and Loss of Eleven Crew Members Aboard the Mobile Offshore Drilling Unit Deepwater Horizon in the Gulf og Mexico April 20-22, 2010.* 2011.

United States Coast Guard. *Report of Investigation into the Circumstances Surrounding The Grounding of the M/V Montrose on February28, 2007.* 2007.

————. *M/V Santa Clara I – Board of Inquiry Concerning Loss of Hazardous Material in the Atlantic Ocean near the New Jersey Coast on 4 January 1992.* 1992.

United States Navy. *Command Investigation into the Facts and Circumstances Surrounding the Collision of USS Hartford (SSN 768) with USS New Orleans (LPD 18) in the Strait of Hormuz on or about 20 March 2009.*

United States Steel Corporation v. Furhman, 407 F.2d 1143 (6th Cir. 1969) *(Cedarville – Topdalsfjord collision).*

Upham, Neville. *The Load Line – A Hallmark of Safety.* Greenwich: National Maritime Museum, 1978.

USA Today, "3 airlines drop self-reporting safety program," December 5, 2008.

Vaughan, Diane. *The Challenger Launch Decision: Risky Technology, Culture and Deviance at NASA.* Chicago: University of Chicago Press, 1996.

Veiga, James L.. "Safety Culture in Shipping," *WMU Journal of Maritime Affairs,* 1 (2000): 17-31.

Verschuur, W. and P. Hudson. "Violations of Rules and Procedures: Results of item analyses and tests of the Behavioral Cause Model." Field Study NAM & SHELL Expo Aberdeen: Leiden University Rept. R-97/66. 1997.

Viscusi, V. and R. Zeckhauser. "Risk within Reason" in Connolly, T. and others (eds.) *Judgment and Decision-making.* Cambridge: Cambridge University Press, 2000.

Vistica, Gregory L. *Fall From Grace.* New York: Simon & Schuster, 1995.

Von Clausewitz, Karl. *On War.* London: Penguin Books Ltd., 1968.

Wagenaar, W. "Risk Taking and Accident Causation," in Yates, J.F. ed, *Risk-Taking Behavior.* New York: John Wiley & Sons, 1992.

Wagenaar, W. and J. Groeneweg. "Accidents at Sea: Multiple Causes and Impossible Consequences." *International Journal Man-Machine Studies,* 27 (1987): 587-98.

Wagenaar, W. and K. Keren, "Does the Expert Know? The Reliability of Predictions and Confidence Ratings of Experts" in E. Holland et al. (eds.) *Intelligent Decision Support in Process Environments.* Berlin: Springe-Verlag, 1986.

Wall Street Journal. "Qantas Drama Fuels Cockpit Lessons." December 4, 2010.

Washington State Office Of Marine Safety. *Prevention Bulletin 95-01: The Dona V.* Publication 00-08-010. March 2000. http://www.ecy.wa.gov/pubs/0008010.pdf. Accessed December 11, 2010.

Waters v. Moore-McCormack Lines, Inc., 309 F.2d 191 (2d Cir. 1962).

In re Waterstand Marine, Ltd., 1991 American Maritime Cases 1784 (E.D.Pa. 1988).

Weick, Karl and Kathleen Sutcliffe. *Managing the Unexpected: Resilient Performance in an Age of Uncertainty.* San Francisco, CA: Jossey-Bass, 2007 (2d ed.).

Weinstein, Jack. *Weinstein's Federal Evidence, "Self-Critical Analysis Privilege."* sec. 501.04[3].

Westrum, R. "Organisational dynamics and safety," in N. McDonald and N. Johnston *Applications of Psychology to the Aviation System* (Vol. 1). Burlington, VT: Ashgate Publishing Company, 1995.

Wickens, C. *Engineering Psychology and Human Performance.* New York, NY: Harper Collins, 1992.

Whistler International Ltd. v. Kawasaki Kisen Kaisha Ltd. [The Hill Harmony] [2001] Lloyd's Rep. 147, AC 638 (House of Lords).

White, Andy. "Report on the Sinking of MS Explorer." RINA Journal *The Naval Architect.* http://www.rina.org.uk/c2/uploads/report.%20on%20the%20sinking%20if%20MS%20Explorer_find.pdf. Accessed April 22, 2011.

Wiegmann, D. and S. Shapell. *A Human Error Approach to Aviation Accident Analysis: The Human Factors Analysis and Classification System.* Burlington, VT: Ashgate Publishing Limited, 2003.

Wilde, G.J.S. *Target Risk 2: A New Psychology of Safety and Health.* Toronto: PDE Publications, 2001 (2nd ed.).

Wolgast, K. "Command Decision-making: Experience Counts." Paper, 2005.

Woodman, Richard. *Voyage East: A Cargo Ship in the 1960s.* London: John Murray (Publishers) Ltd., 1988.

Woods, David and R.I. Cook. "Nine Steps to Move Forward from Error." *Cognition, Technology and Work.* 4 (2002):137-144.

———— and Sidney Dekker. "Anticipating the effects of technological change: a new era of dynamics for human factors." Draft article - *Theoretical Issues in Ergonomics*, (2001): 1-11.

————, Sidney Dekker, Richard Cook, Leila Johannesen and Nadine Sarter. *Behind Human Error.* Burlington, VT: Ashgate Publishing Company, 2010.

Worsley, Frank. *First Voyage in a Square-Rigged Ship.* London: Geoffrey Bles, 1938.

Wouk, Herman. *The Caine Mutiny.* New York, NY: Doubleday & Company, 1952.

Yanchunas, D. "Crew of LNG tanker that lost power lacked training in restarting engine manually." *Professional Mariner* (September 2010): 26-28.

Zsambok, C. and Klein, G. *Naturalistic Decision Making.* Mahwah, NJ: Lawrence Erlbaum Associates, 1997.

Index

About the Author

Geoff Gill began his maritime career when he signed on as a 15-year old *jungmann*/deckboy on the Norwegian freighter *Concordia Viking*. Graduation from the United States Merchant Marine Academy and service in deck officer positions in break bulk and container vessels in world-wide service followed, as well as Master of a sailing vessel carrying passengers for hire on the U.S. East Coast. Further formal education was pursued through the United States Naval War College and Fordham University School of Law.

Geoff has made a study, drawing heavily from studies in other safety-critical domains, of shipboard and organizational error as a factor in maritime casualties. Having addressed aspects of this issue at several maritime academies, before professional groups, and internationally with senior shipping company management, a number of his conclusions and recommendations have been incorporated into training received by maritime officers as well as into operational practices. He is a Member of The Nautical Institute and the forensics panel of the Society of Naval Architects and Marine Engineers.

He is a formally admitted attorney-at-law in California, Florida and New York. The majority of his legal work has included the investigation of maritime casualties and defense of involved interests. He has authored a multi-volume maritime law book and has attained Proctor status in the Maritime Law Association. He is "of Counsel" to the international transportation law firm of Countryman & McDaniel, Los Angeles, California.

Geoff continues to volunteer as crew and watch officer in the brigantines of the Los Angeles Maritime Institute, operated for the development of character and team building of area youth.

US $50.00

9 780870 336263

55000

ISBN: 978-0-87033-626-3